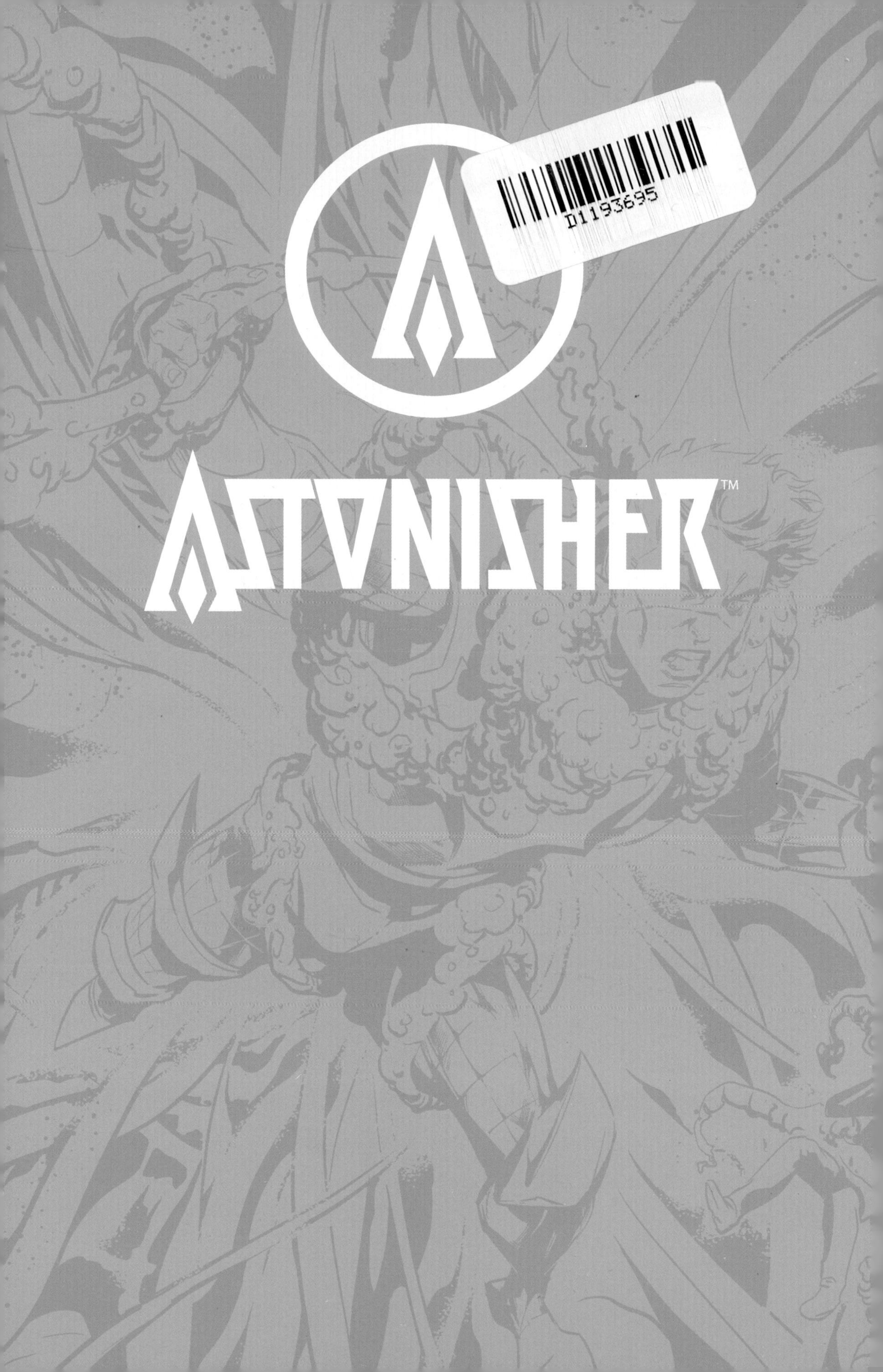

ASTONISHER™

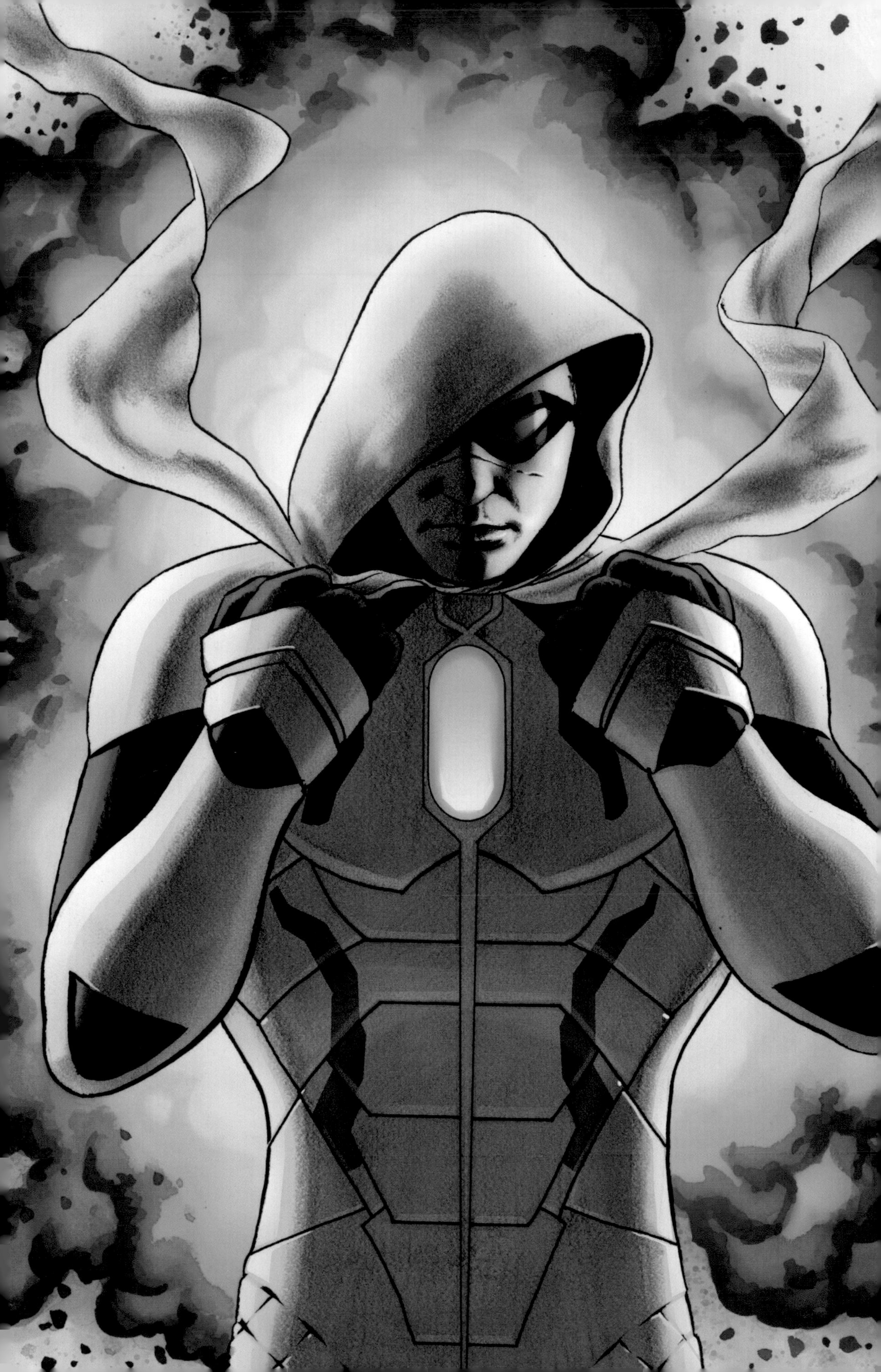

CATALYST PRIME

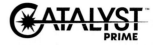

ASTONISHER™

THE ENEMY WITHIN

written by **ALEX DE CAMPI**
illustrated by **POP MHAN**
lettered by **AW'S TOM NAPOLITANO**
colored by **JESSICA KHOLINNE**

THE EVENT

written by **PRIEST** and
JOSEPH PHILLIP ILLIDGE
illustrated by **MARCO TURINI** and **WILL ROSADO**
lettered by **ANDWORLD DESIGN**
colored by **JESSICA KHOLINNE**

JOSEPH ILLIDGE • senior editor
DESIREE RODRIGUEZ • editorial assistant
cover by **POP MHAN** and **JESSICA KHOLINNE**

LION FORGE

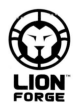

ISBN: 978-1-941302-63-7

Library of Congress Control Number: 2017958690

10 9 8 7 6 5 4 3 2 1

CHAPTER ONE

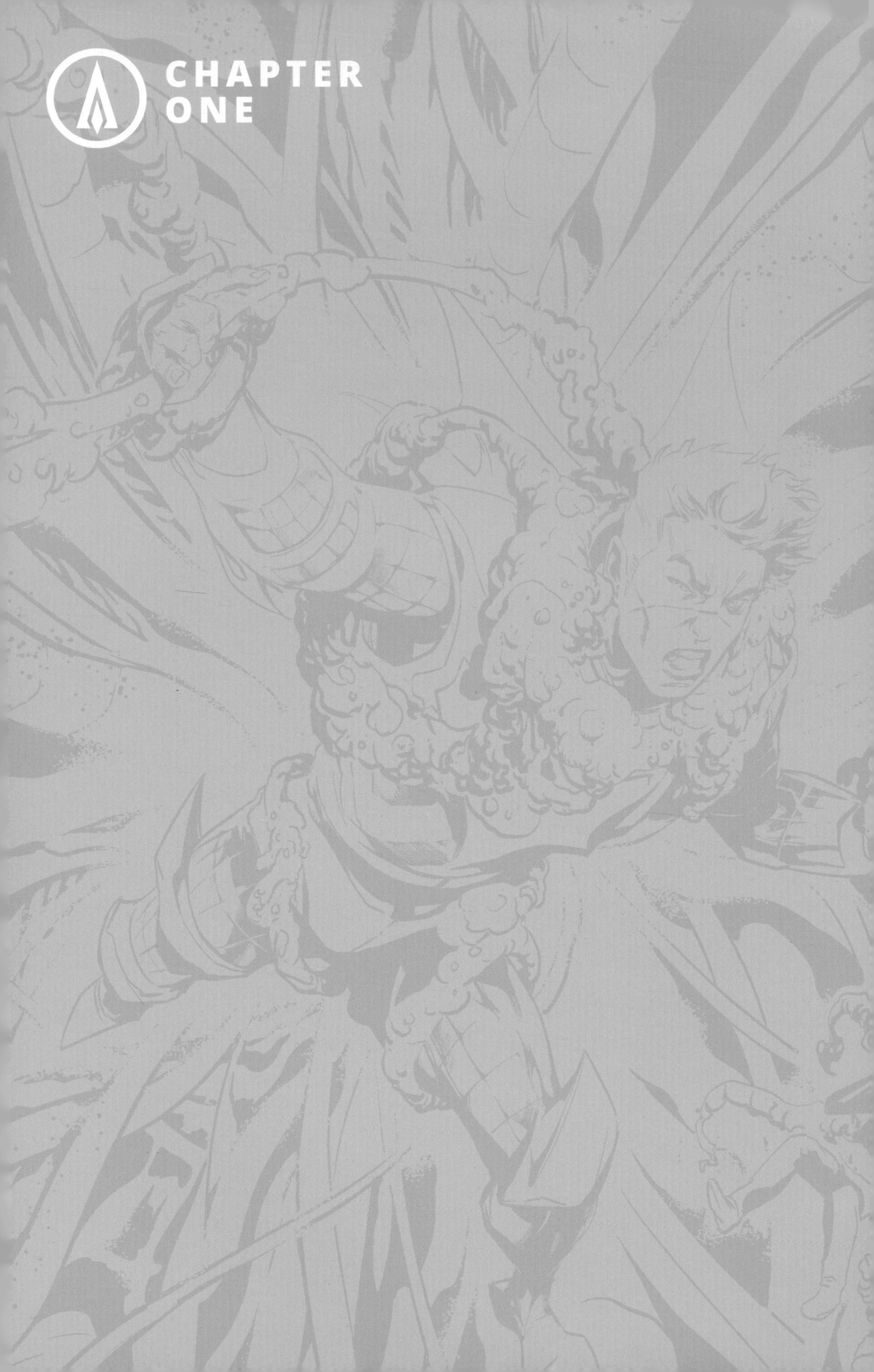

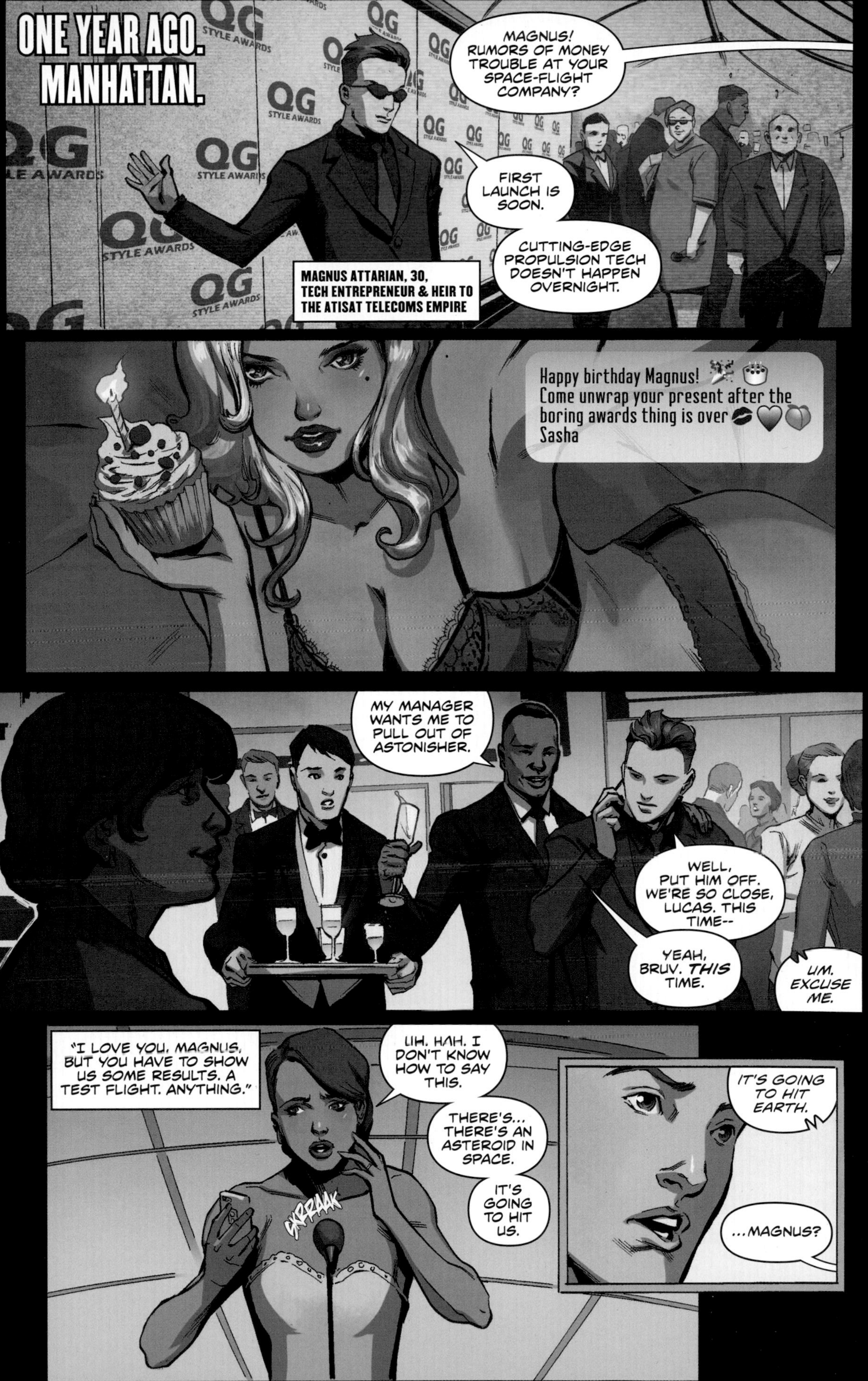
ONE YEAR AGO. MANHATTAN.
MAGNUS! RUMORS OF MONEY TROUBLE AT YOUR SPACE-FLIGHT COMPANY?
FIRST LAUNCH IS SOON.
CUTTING-EDGE PROPULSION TECH DOESN'T HAPPEN OVERNIGHT.
MAGNUS ATTARIAN, 30, TECH ENTREPRENEUR & HEIR TO THE ATISAT TELECOMS EMPIRE
Happy birthday Magnus! Come unwrap your present after the boring awards thing is over Sasha
MY MANAGER WANTS ME TO PULL OUT OF ASTONISHER.
WELL, PUT HIM OFF. WE'RE SO CLOSE, LUCAS. THIS TIME--
YEAH, BRUV. THIS TIME.
UM. EXCUSE ME.
"I LOVE YOU, MAGNUS, BUT YOU HAVE TO SHOW US SOME RESULTS. A TEST FLIGHT. ANYTHING."
UH. HAH. I DON'T KNOW HOW TO SAY THIS.
THERE'S... THERE'S AN ASTEROID IN SPACE.
IT'S GOING TO HIT US.
SKRAAK
IT'S GOING TO HIT EARTH.
...MAGNUS?

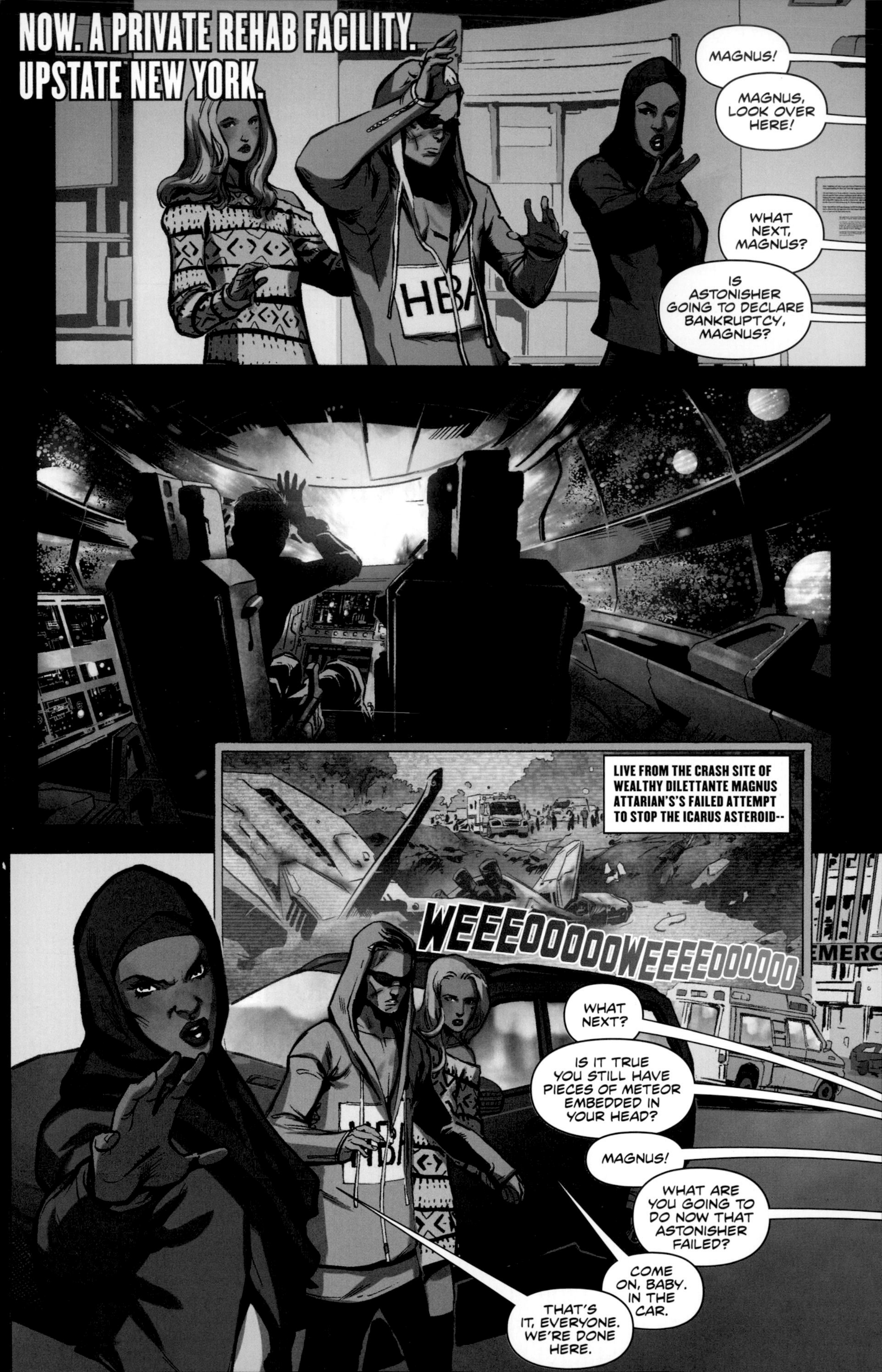
NOW. A PRIVATE REHAB FACILITY. UPSTATE NEW YORK.
MAGNUS!
MAGNUS, LOOK OVER HERE!
WHAT NEXT, MAGNUS?
IS ASTONISHER GOING TO DECLARE BANKRUPTCY, MAGNUS?
HBA
LIVE FROM THE CRASH SITE OF WEALTHY DILETTANTE MAGNUS ATTARIAN'S'S FAILED ATTEMPT TO STOP THE ICARUS ASTEROID--
WEEEOOOOOWEEEEOOOOOO
EMERG
WHAT NEXT?
IS IT TRUE YOU STILL HAVE PIECES OF METEOR EMBEDDED IN YOUR HEAD?
MAGNUS!
WHAT ARE YOU GOING TO DO NOW THAT ASTONISHER FAILED?
COME ON, BABY. IN THE CAR.
THAT'S IT, EVERYONE. WE'RE DONE HERE.

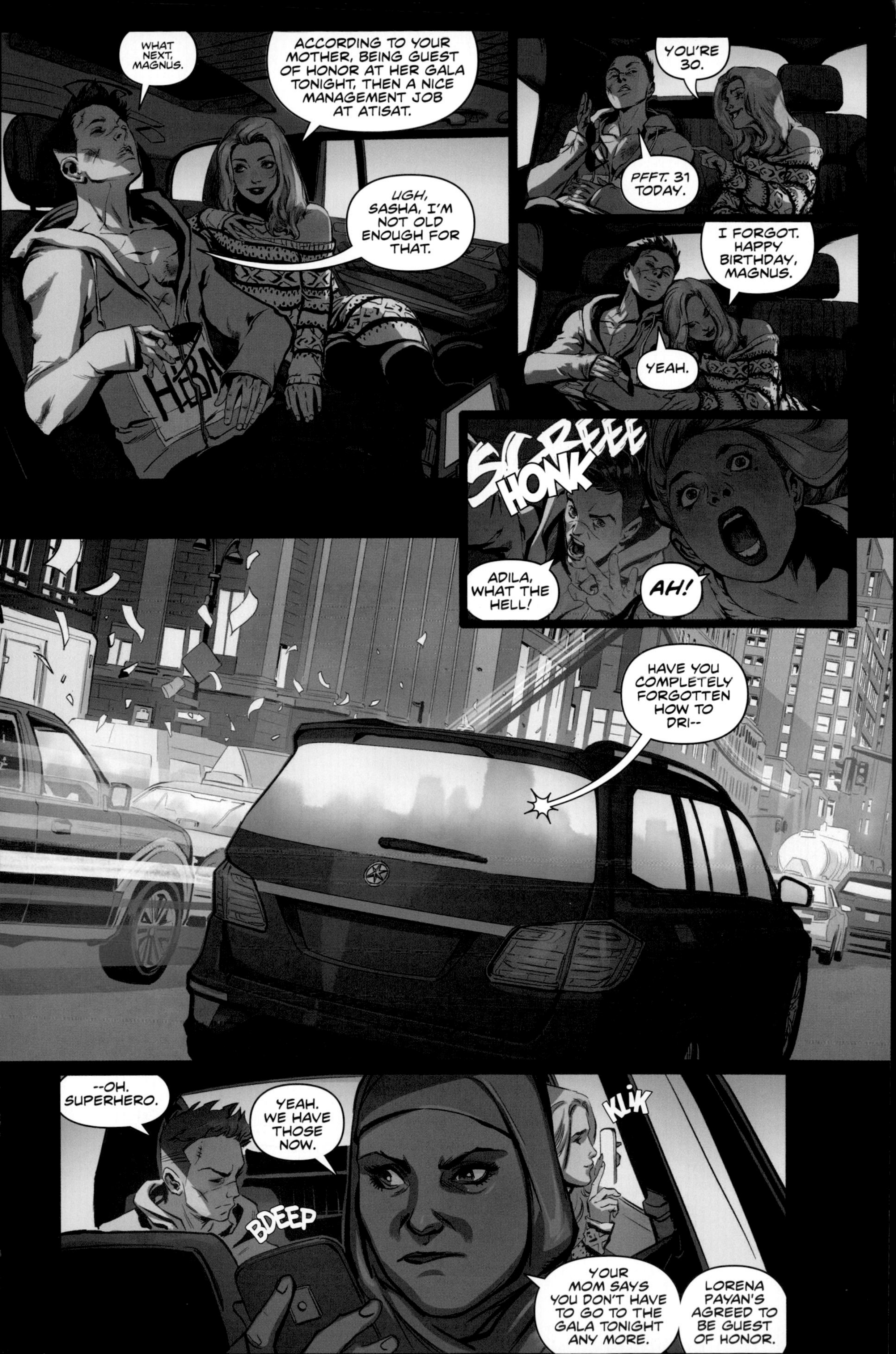
WHAT NEXT, MAGNUS.
ACCORDING TO YOUR MOTHER, BEING GUEST OF HONOR AT HER GALA TONIGHT, THEN A NICE MANAGEMENT JOB AT ATISAT.
UGH, SASHA, I'M NOT OLD ENOUGH FOR THAT.
HIBA
YOU'RE 30.
PFFT. 31 TODAY.
I FORGOT. HAPPY BIRTHDAY, MAGNUS.
YEAH.
SCREEEE
HONK
ADILA, WHAT THE HELL!
AH!
HAVE YOU COMPLETELY FORGOTTEN HOW TO DRI--
--OH. SUPERHERO.
YEAH. WE HAVE THOSE NOW.
KLIK
BDEEP
YOUR MOM SAYS YOU DON'T HAVE TO GO TO THE GALA TONIGHT ANY MORE.
LORENA PAYAN'S AGREED TO BE GUEST OF HONOR.

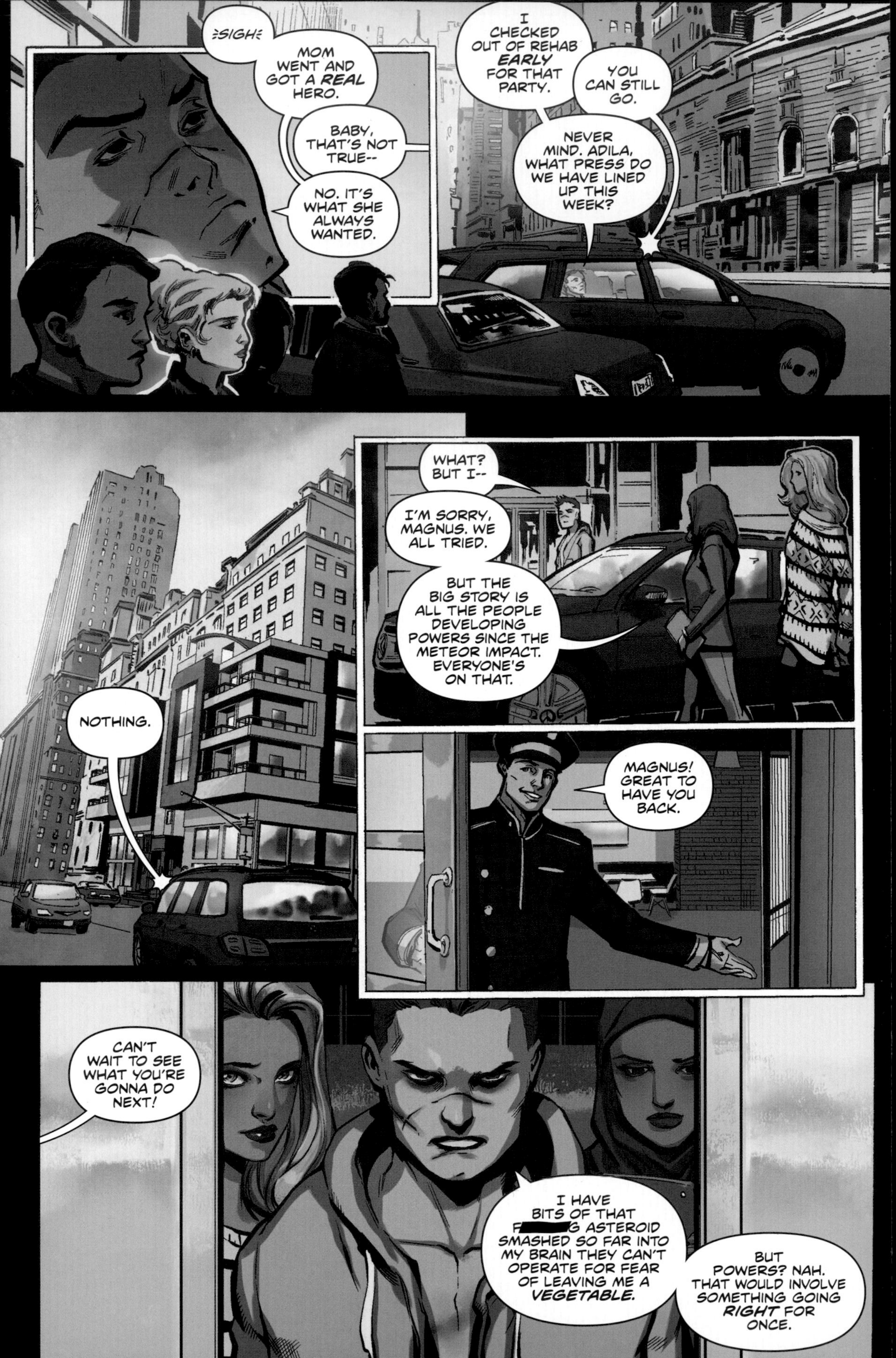

SIGH
MOM WENT AND GOT A *REAL* HERO.
BABY, THAT'S NOT TRUE--
NO. IT'S WHAT SHE ALWAYS WANTED.
I CHECKED OUT OF REHAB *EARLY* FOR THAT PARTY.
YOU CAN STILL GO.
NEVER MIND. ADILA, WHAT PRESS DO WE HAVE LINED UP THIS WEEK?
NOTHING.
WHAT? BUT I--
I'M SORRY, MAGNUS. WE ALL TRIED.
BUT THE BIG STORY IS ALL THE PEOPLE DEVELOPING POWERS SINCE THE METEOR IMPACT. EVERYONE'S ON THAT.
MAGNUS! GREAT TO HAVE YOU BACK.
CAN'T WAIT TO SEE WHAT YOU'RE GONNA DO NEXT!
I HAVE BITS OF THAT F[redacted]G ASTEROID SMASHED SO FAR INTO MY BRAIN THEY CAN'T OPERATE FOR FEAR OF LEAVING ME A *VEGETABLE*.
BUT POWERS? NAH. THAT WOULD INVOLVE SOMETHING GOING *RIGHT* FOR ONCE.

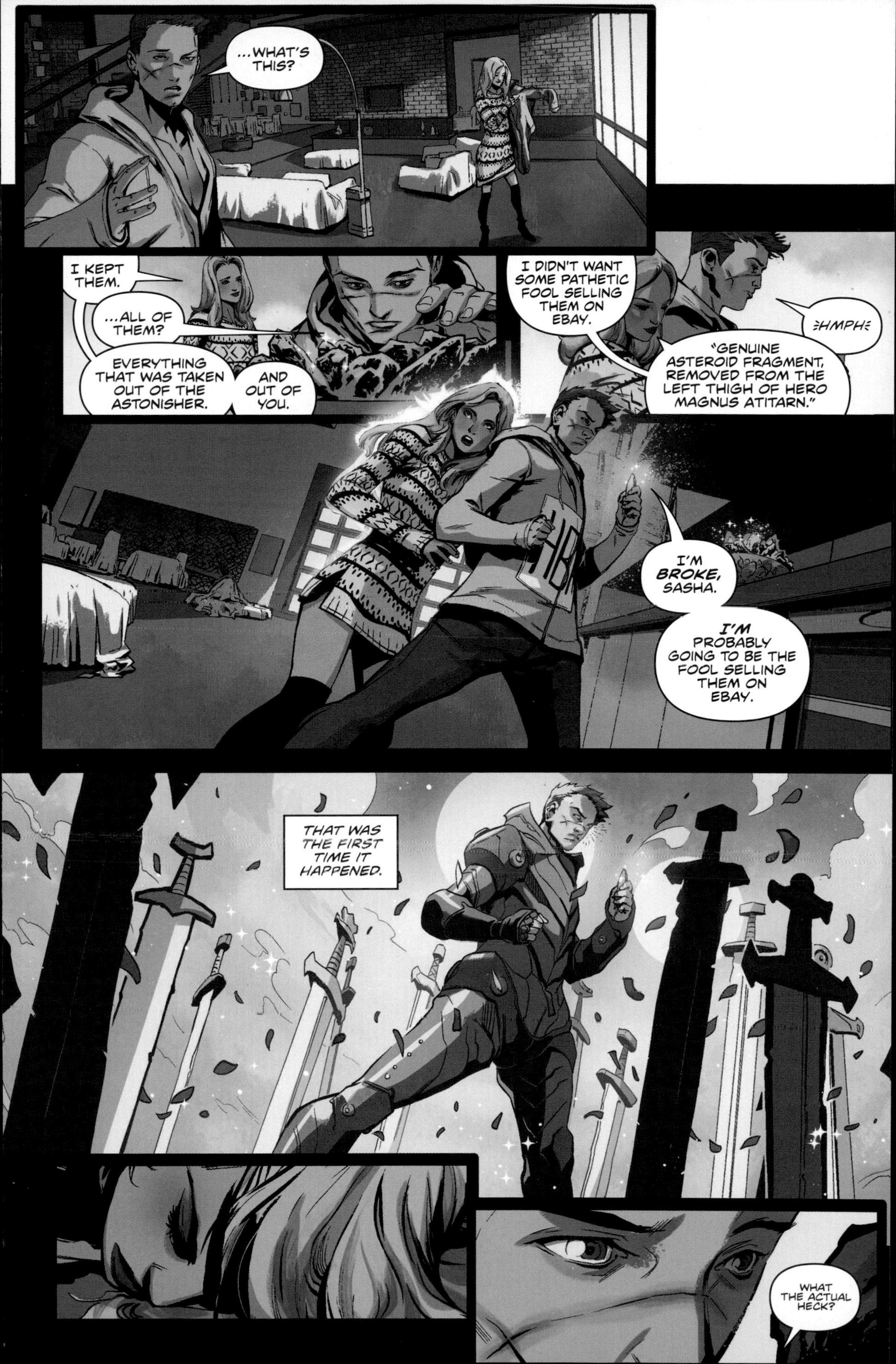
...WHAT'S THIS?
I KEPT THEM.
...ALL OF THEM?
EVERYTHING THAT WAS TAKEN OUT OF THE ASTONISHER.
AND OUT OF YOU.
I DIDN'T WANT SOME PATHETIC FOOL SELLING THEM ON EBAY.
HMPH
"GENUINE ASTEROID FRAGMENT, REMOVED FROM THE LEFT THIGH OF HERO MAGNUS ATITARN."
I'M BROKE, SASHA.
I'M PROBABLY GOING TO BE THE FOOL SELLING THEM ON EBAY.
THAT WAS THE FIRST TIME IT HAPPENED.
WHAT THE ACTUAL HECK?

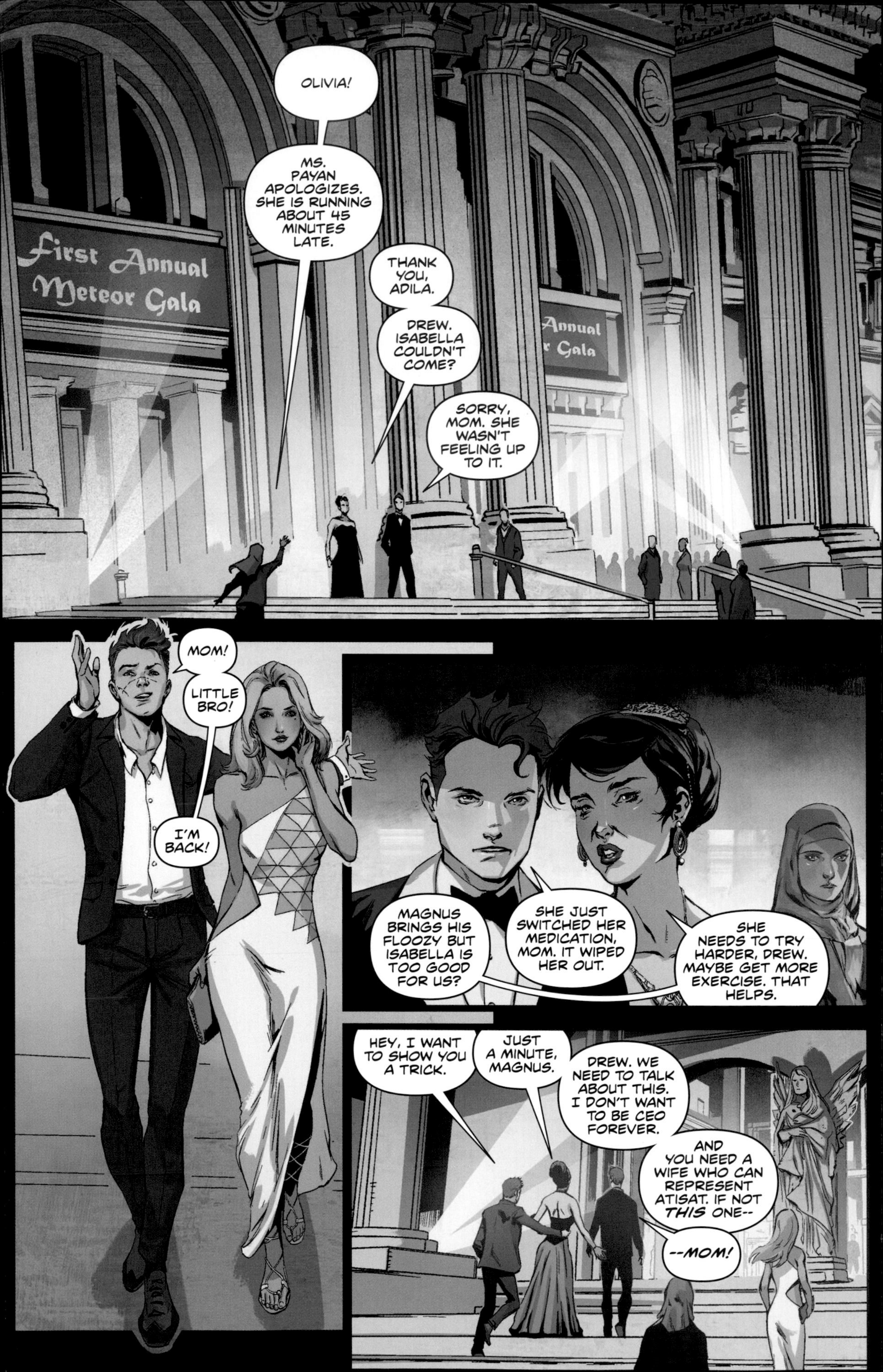
First Annual Meteor Gala
OLIVIA!
MS. PAYAN APOLOGIZES. SHE IS RUNNING ABOUT 45 MINUTES LATE.
THANK YOU, ADILA.
DREW. ISABELLA COULDN'T COME?
SORRY, MOM. SHE WASN'T FEELING UP TO IT.
MOM!
LITTLE BRO!
I'M BACK!
MAGNUS BRINGS HIS FLOOZY BUT ISABELLA IS TOO GOOD FOR US?
SHE JUST SWITCHED HER MEDICATION, MOM. IT WIPED HER OUT.
SHE NEEDS TO TRY HARDER, DREW. MAYBE GET MORE EXERCISE. THAT HELPS.
HEY, I WANT TO SHOW YOU A TRICK.
JUST A MINUTE, MAGNUS.
DREW. WE NEED TO TALK ABOUT THIS. I DON'T WANT TO BE CEO FOREVER.
AND YOU NEED A WIFE WHO CAN REPRESENT ATISAT. IF NOT *THIS* ONE--
--MOM!

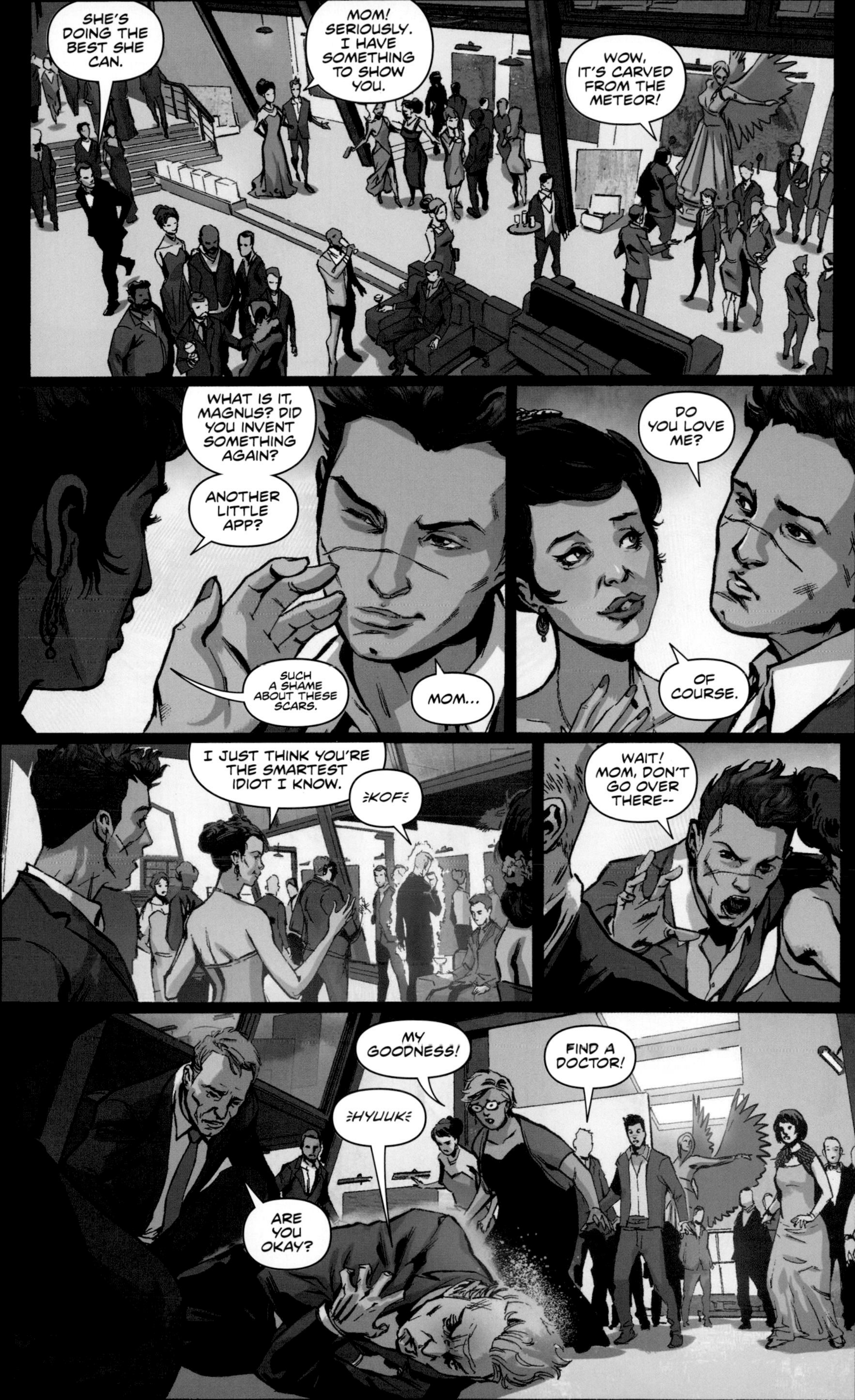
SHE'S DOING THE BEST SHE CAN.
MOM! SERIOUSLY. I HAVE SOMETHING TO SHOW YOU.
WOW, IT'S CARVED FROM THE METEOR!
WHAT IS IT, MAGNUS? DID YOU INVENT SOMETHING AGAIN?
ANOTHER LITTLE APP?
SUCH A SHAME ABOUT THESE SCARS.
MOM...
DO YOU LOVE ME?
OF COURSE.
I JUST THINK YOU'RE THE SMARTEST IDIOT I KNOW.
KOF
WAIT! MOM, DON'T GO OVER THERE--
MY GOODNESS!
FIND A DOCTOR!
HYUUK
ARE YOU OKAY?

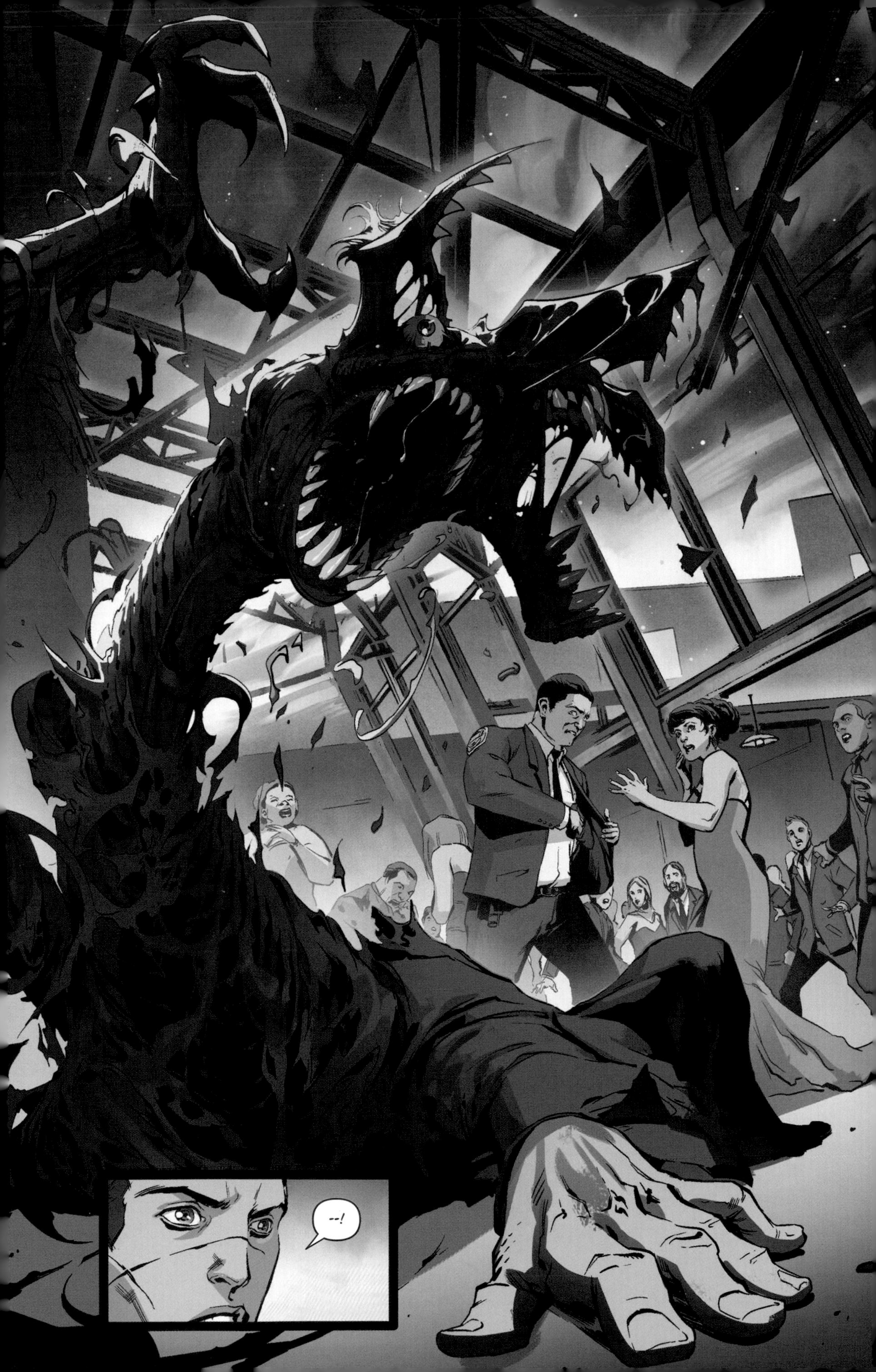
--!

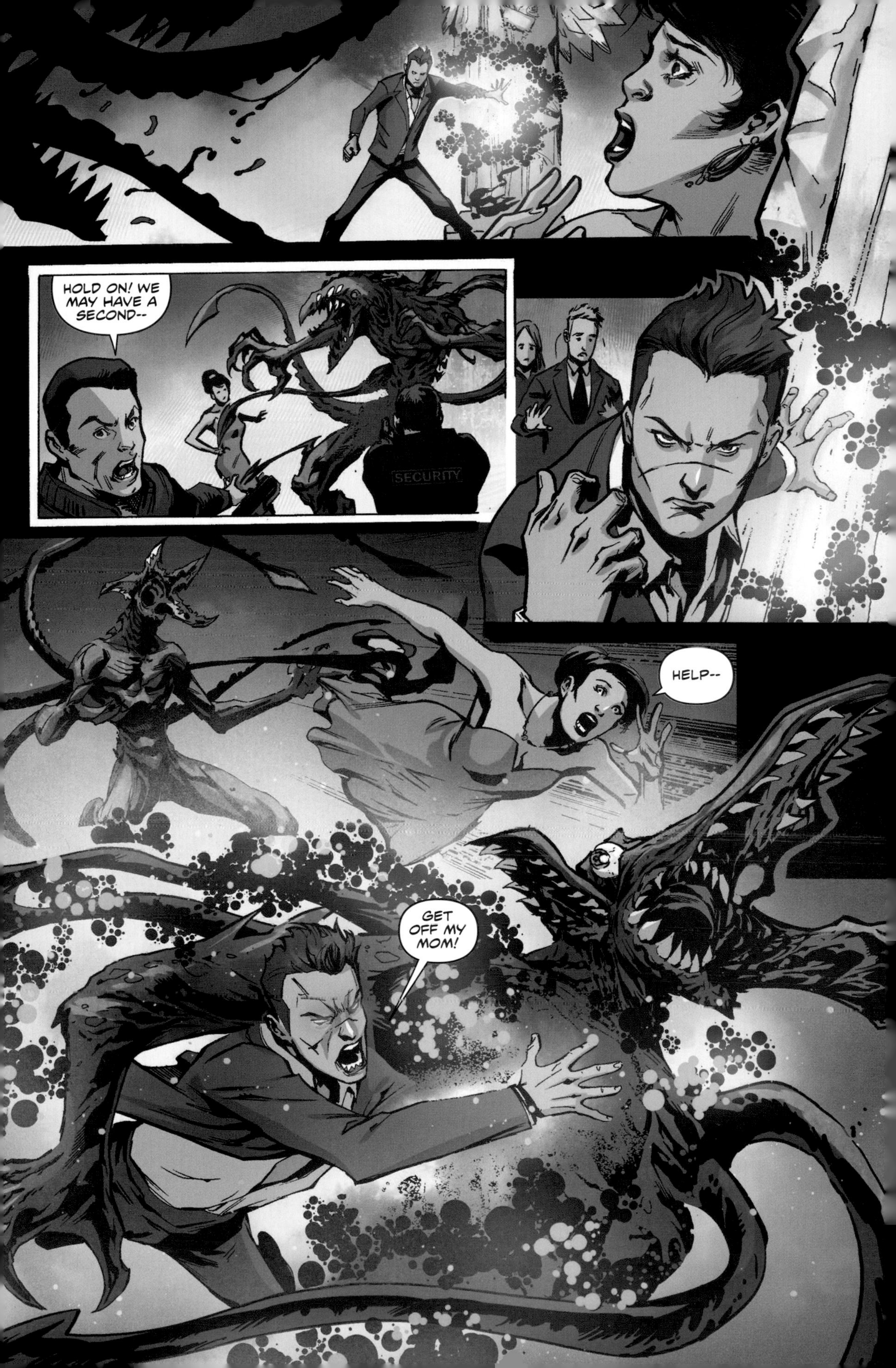
HOLD ON! WE MAY HAVE A SECOND--
SECURITY
HELP--
GET OFF MY MOM!

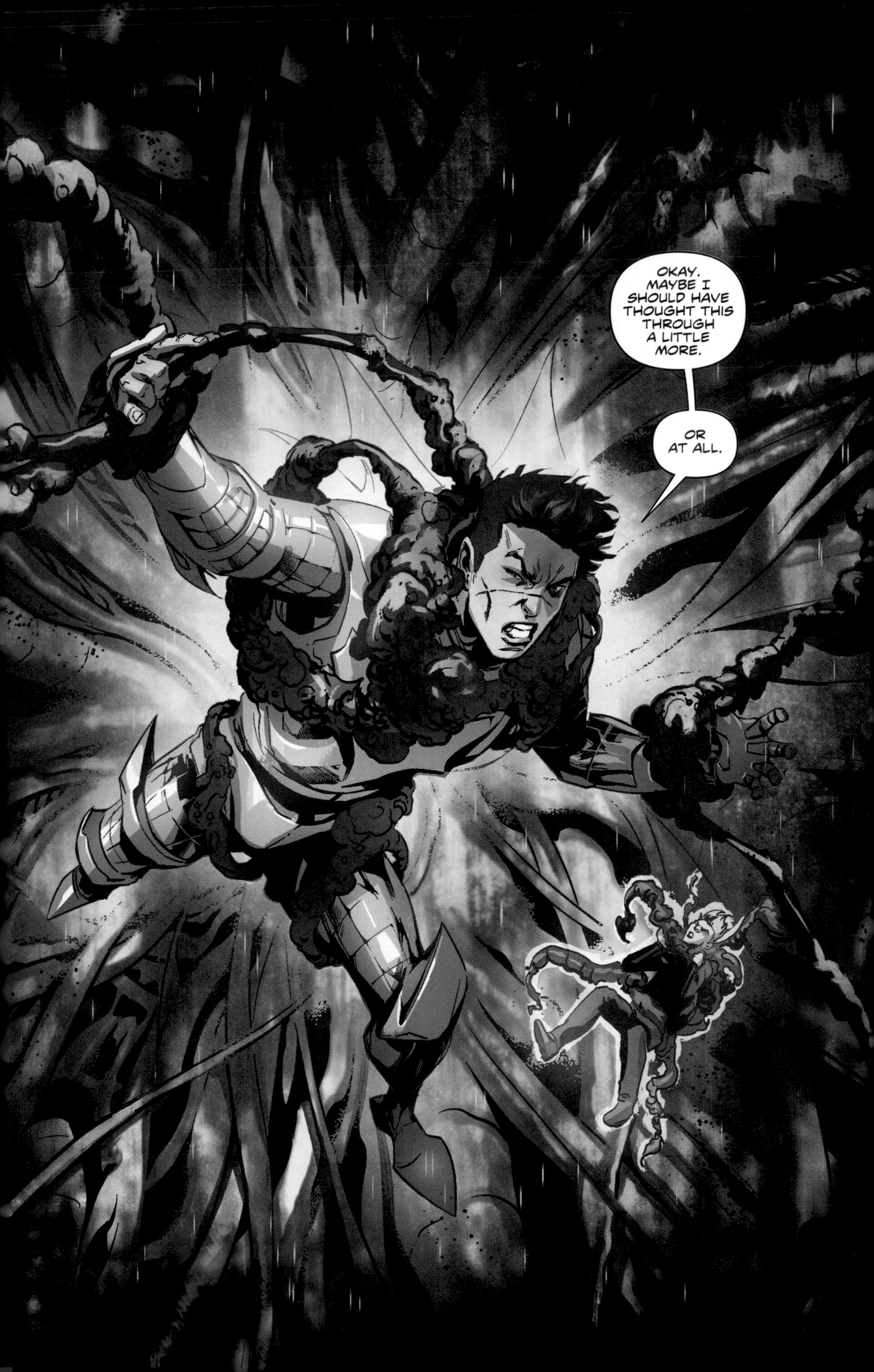
OKAY. MAYBE I SHOULD HAVE THOUGHT THIS THROUGH A LITTLE MORE.
OR AT ALL.

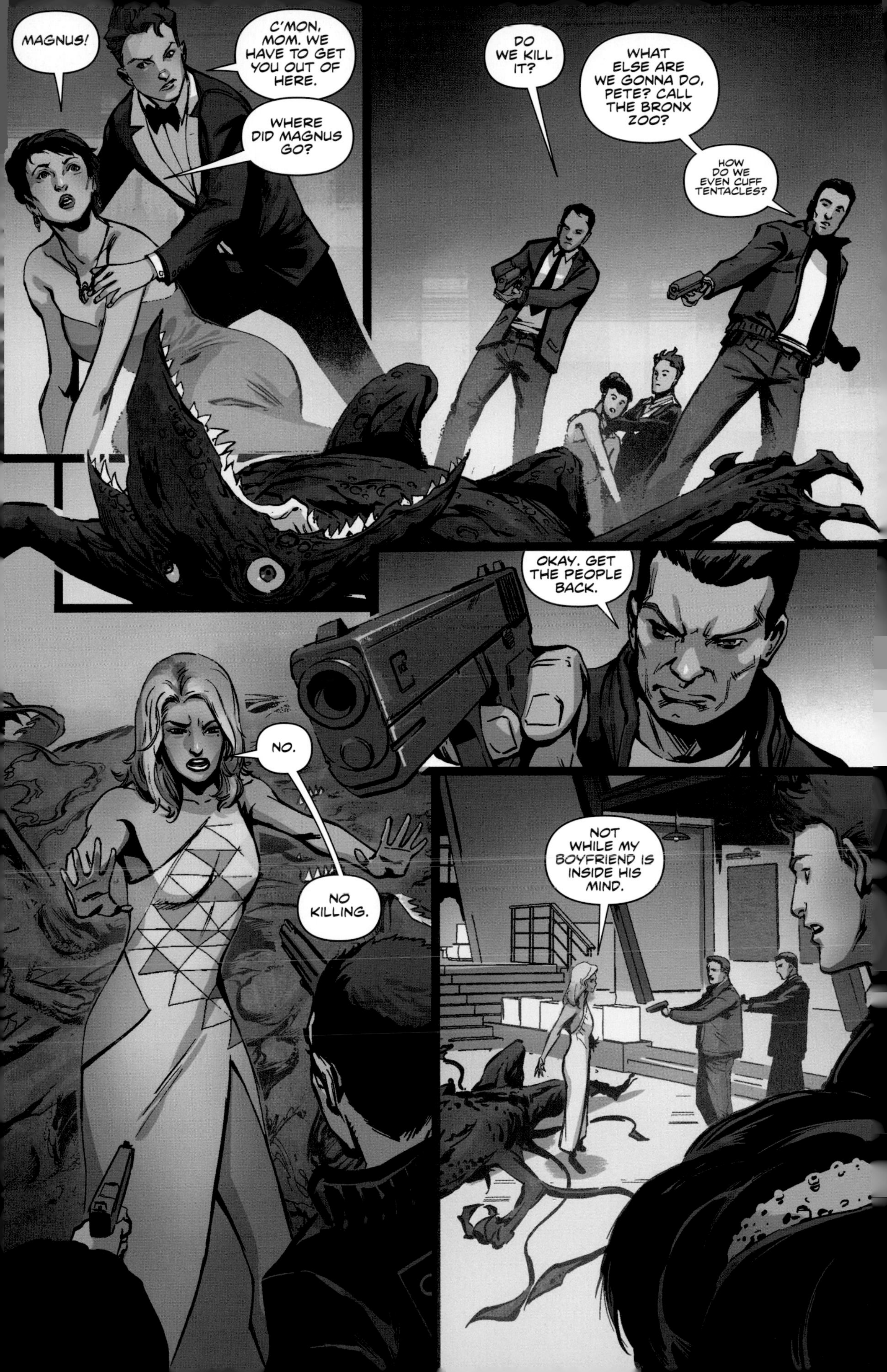
MAGNUS!
C'MON, MOM. WE HAVE TO GET YOU OUT OF HERE.
WHERE DID MAGNUS GO?
DO WE KILL IT?
WHAT ELSE ARE WE GONNA DO, PETE? CALL THE BRONX ZOO?
HOW DO WE EVEN CUFF TENTACLES?
OKAY. GET THE PEOPLE BACK.
NO.
NO KILLING.
NOT WHILE MY BOYFRIEND IS INSIDE HIS MIND.

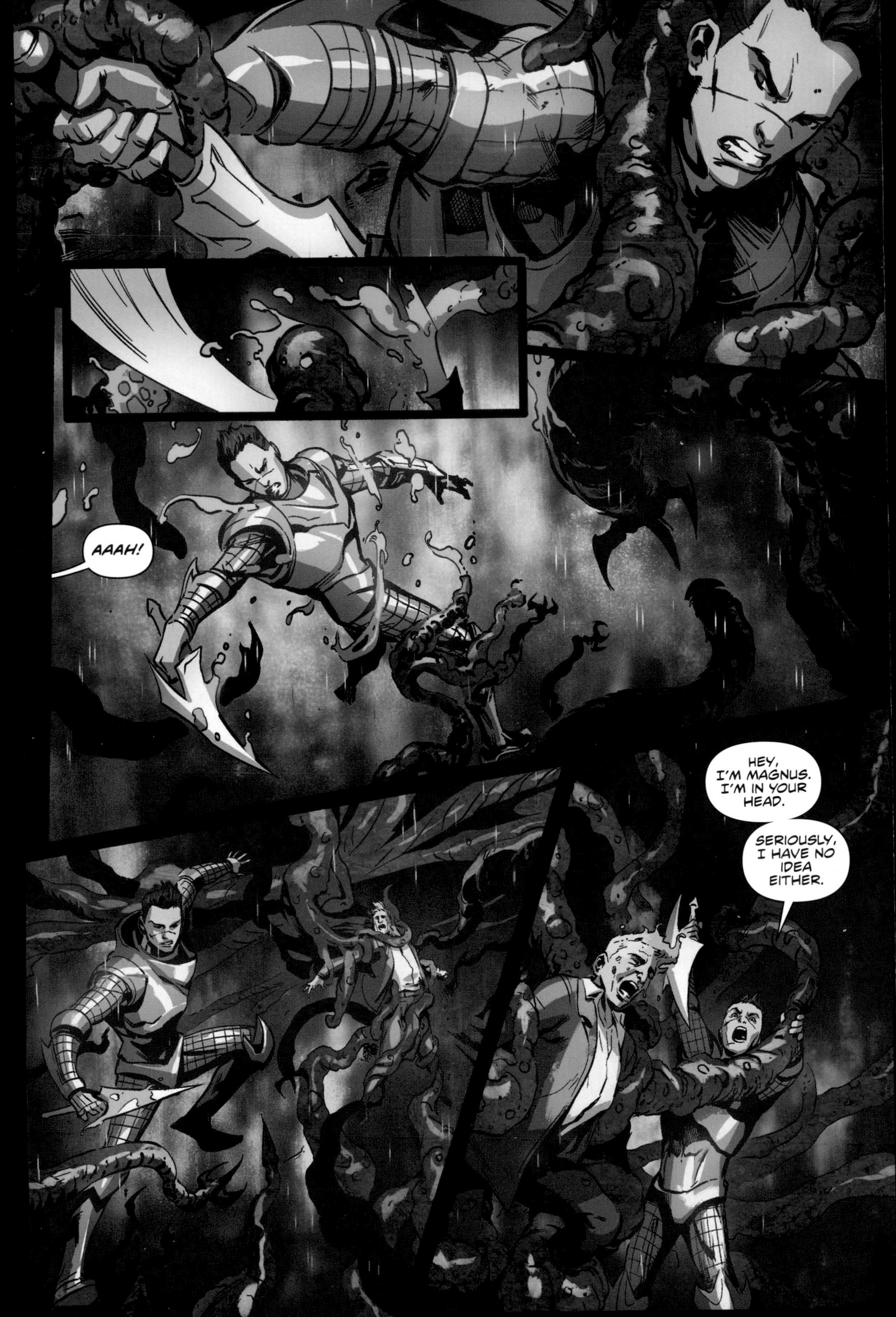
AAAH!
HEY, I'M MAGNUS. I'M IN YOUR HEAD.
SERIOUSLY, I HAVE NO IDEA EITHER.

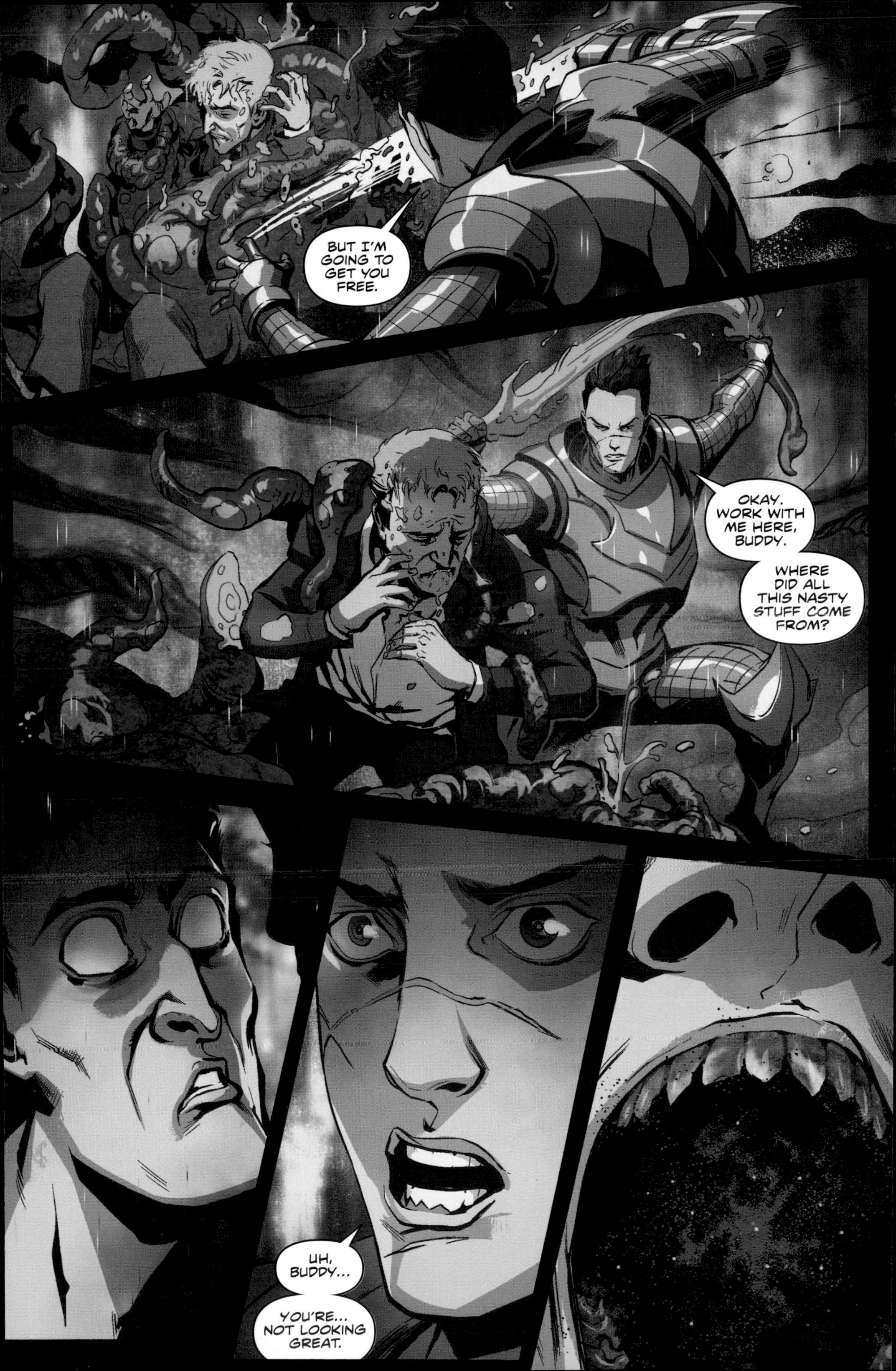
BUT I'M GOING TO GET YOU FREE.
OKAY. WORK WITH ME HERE, BUDDY.
WHERE DID ALL THIS NASTY STUFF COME FROM?
UH, BUDDY...
YOU'RE... NOT LOOKING GREAT.

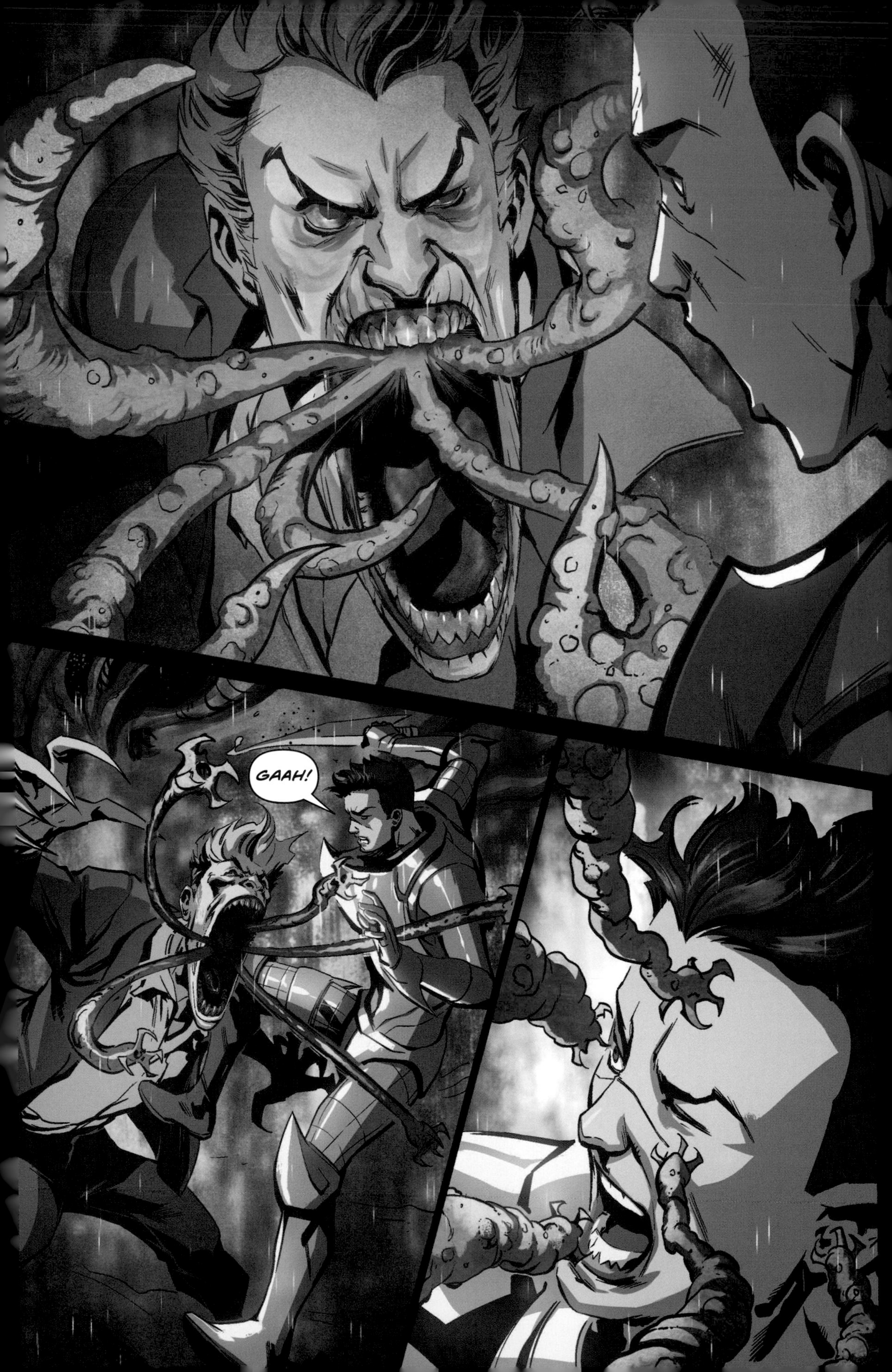
GAAH!

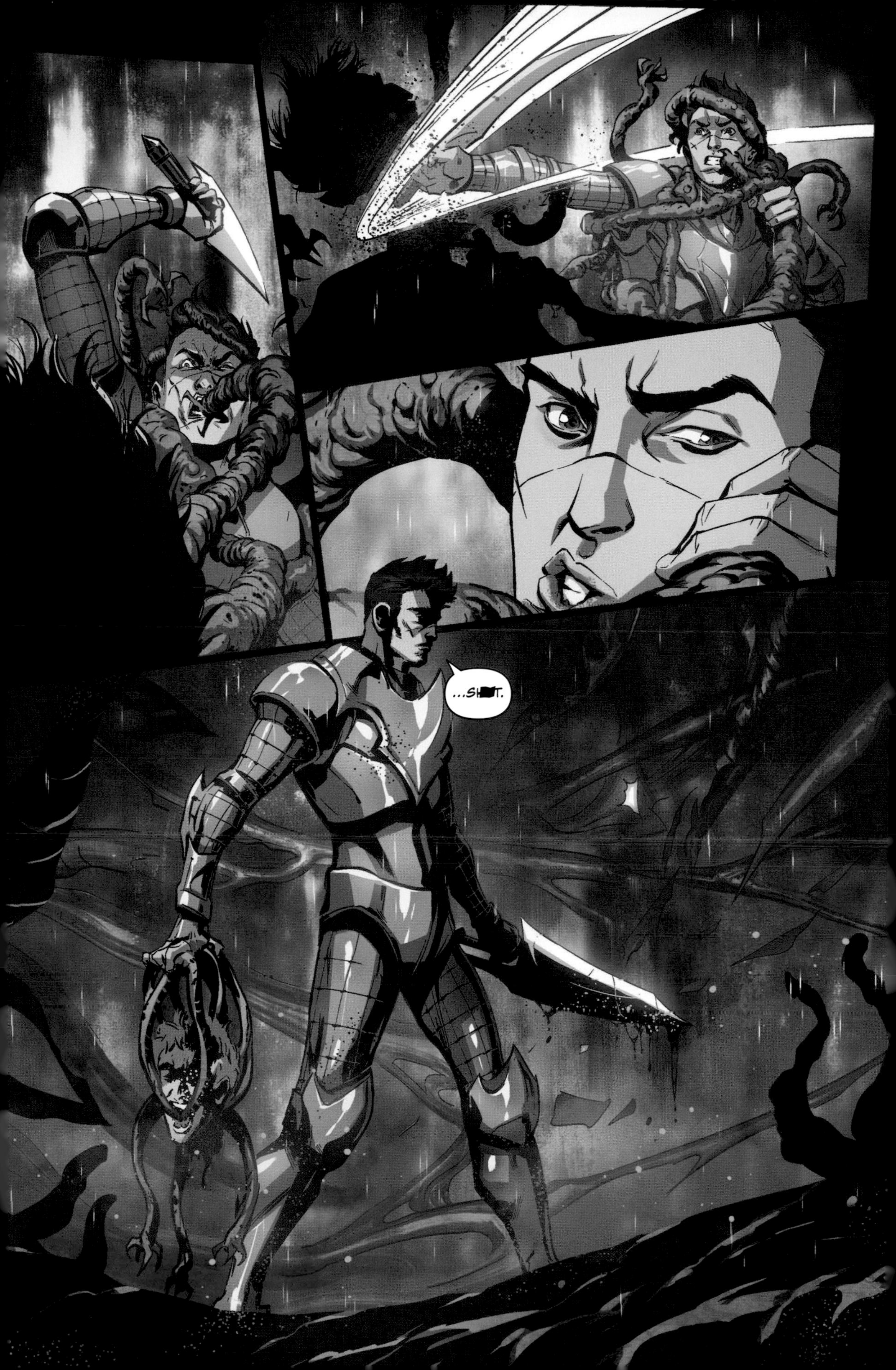
...SH[redacted]T.

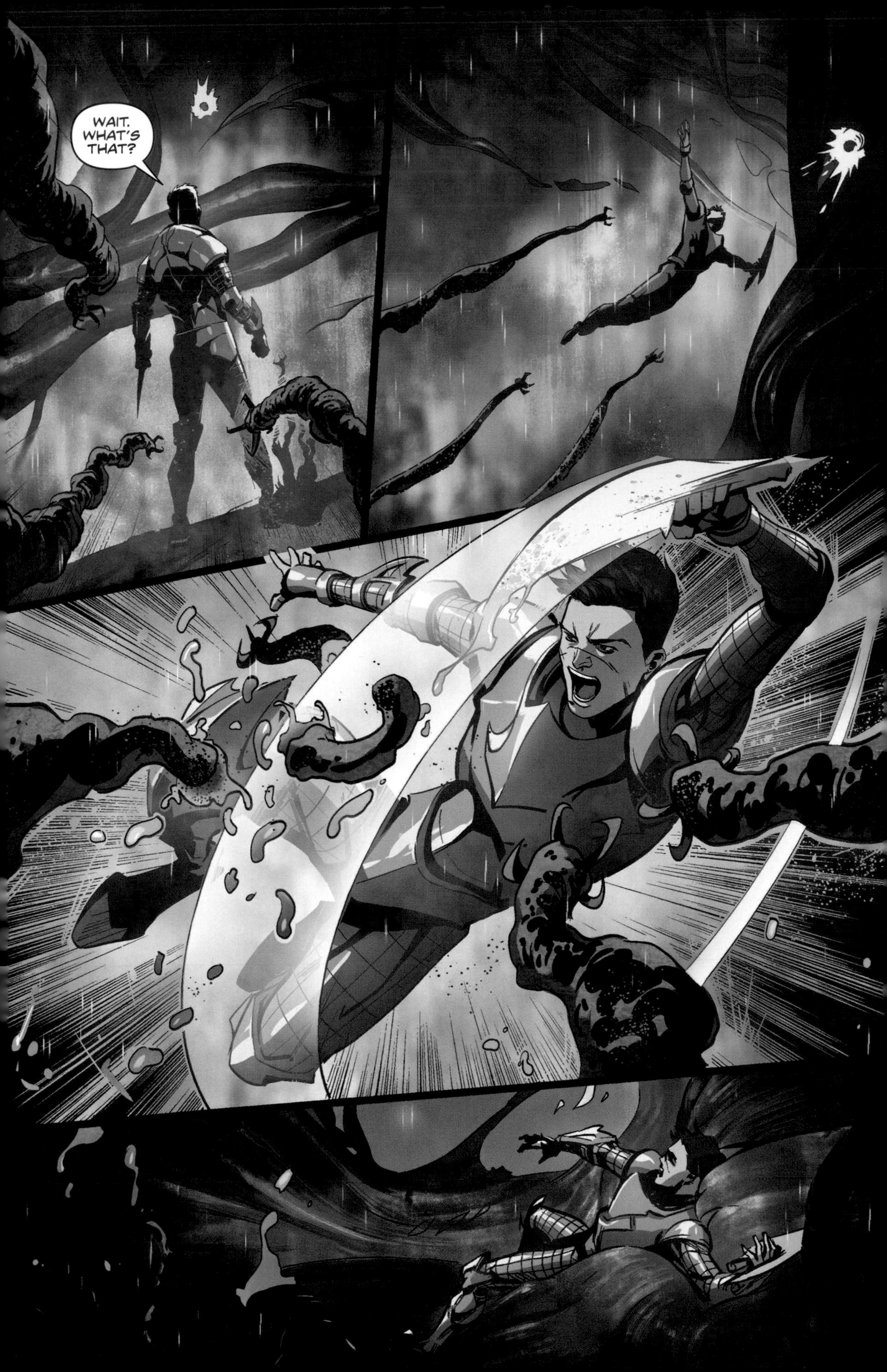
WAIT. WHAT'S THAT?

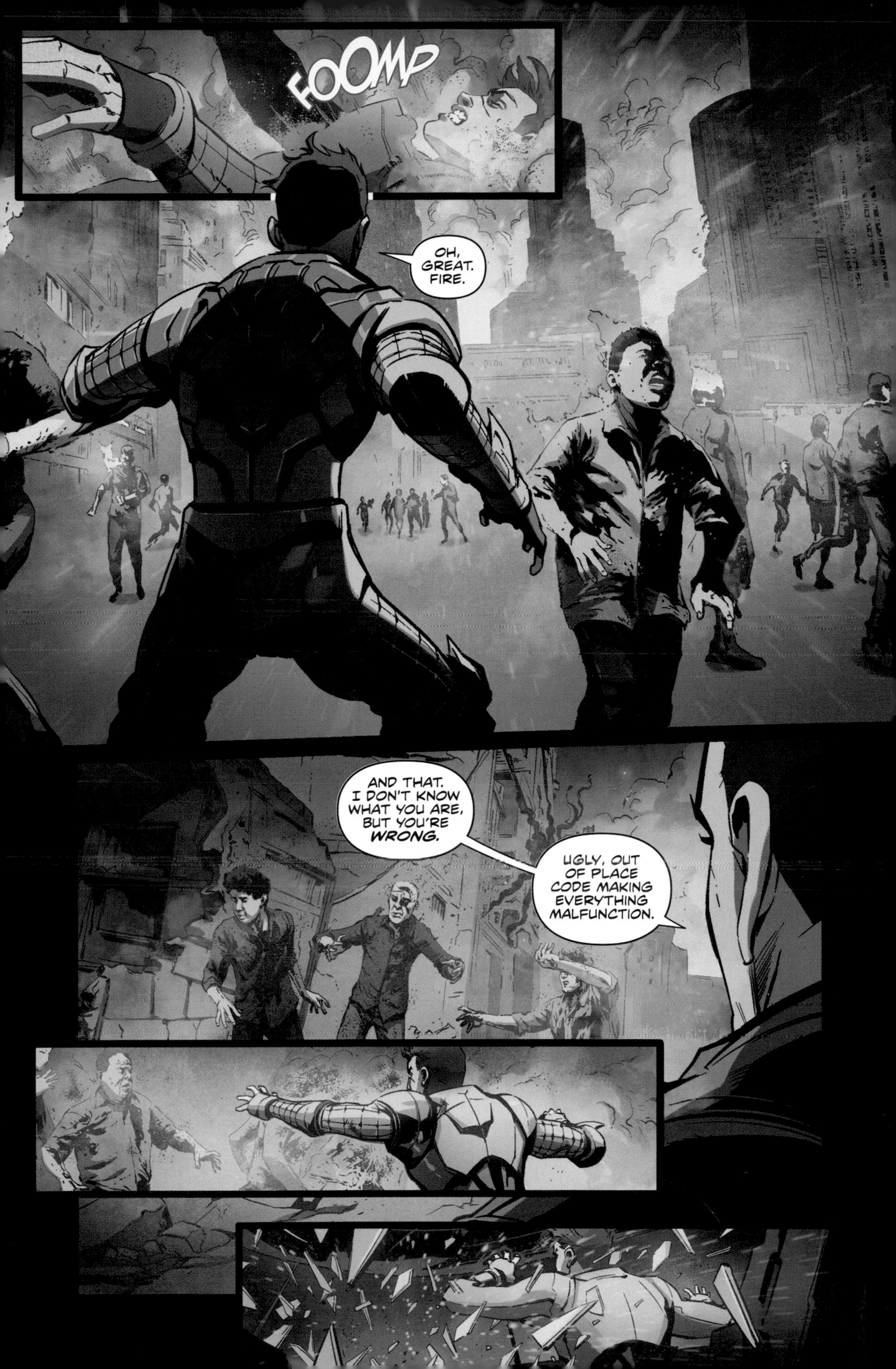
FOOMP
OH, GREAT. FIRE.
AND THAT. I DON'T KNOW WHAT YOU ARE, BUT YOU'RE WRONG.
UGLY, OUT OF PLACE CODE MAKING EVERYTHING MALFUNCTION.

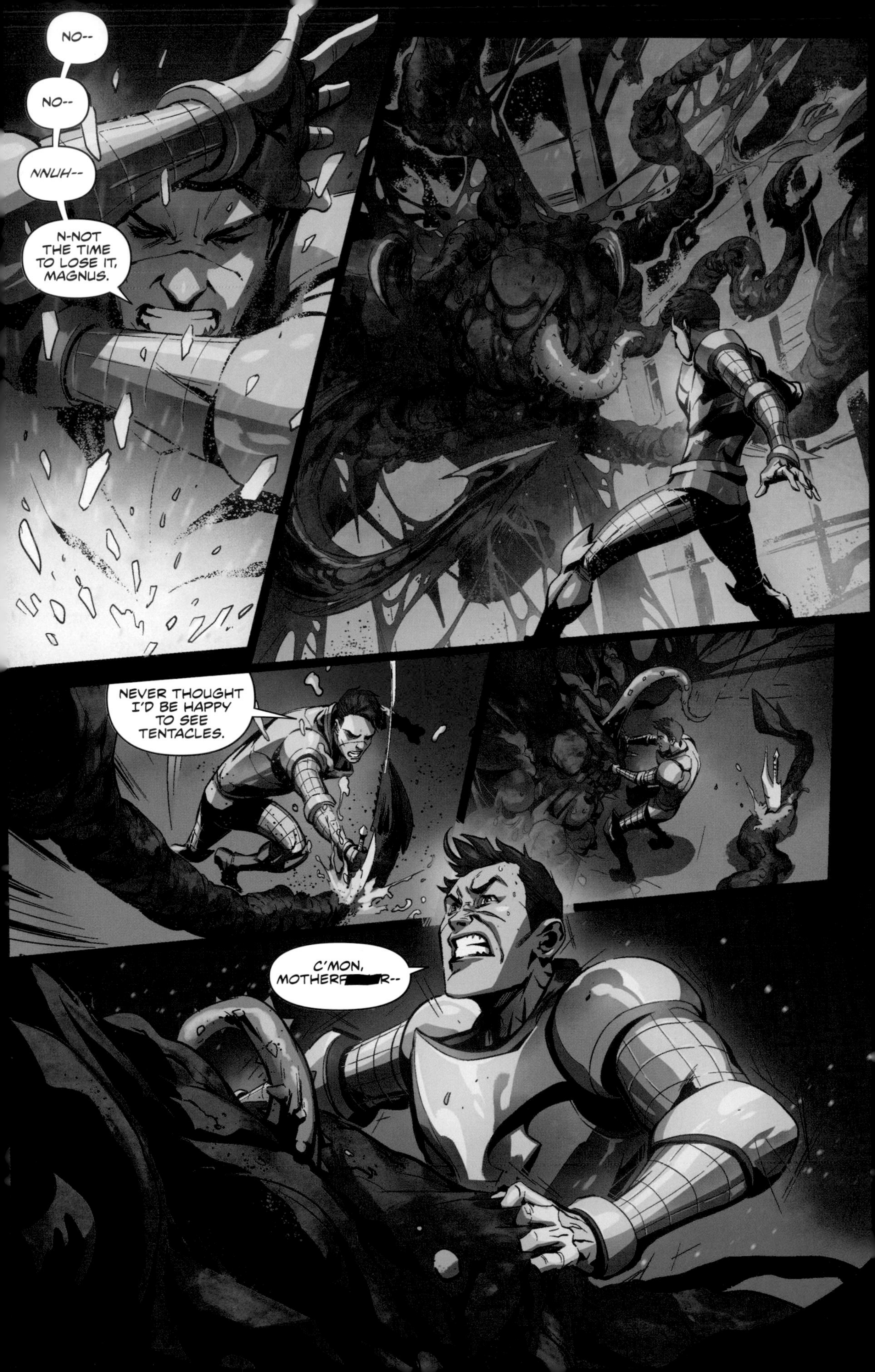
NO--
NO--
NNUH--
N-NOT THE TIME TO LOSE IT, MAGNUS.
NEVER THOUGHT I'D BE HAPPY TO SEE TENTACLES.
C'MON, MOTHERF[redacted]R--

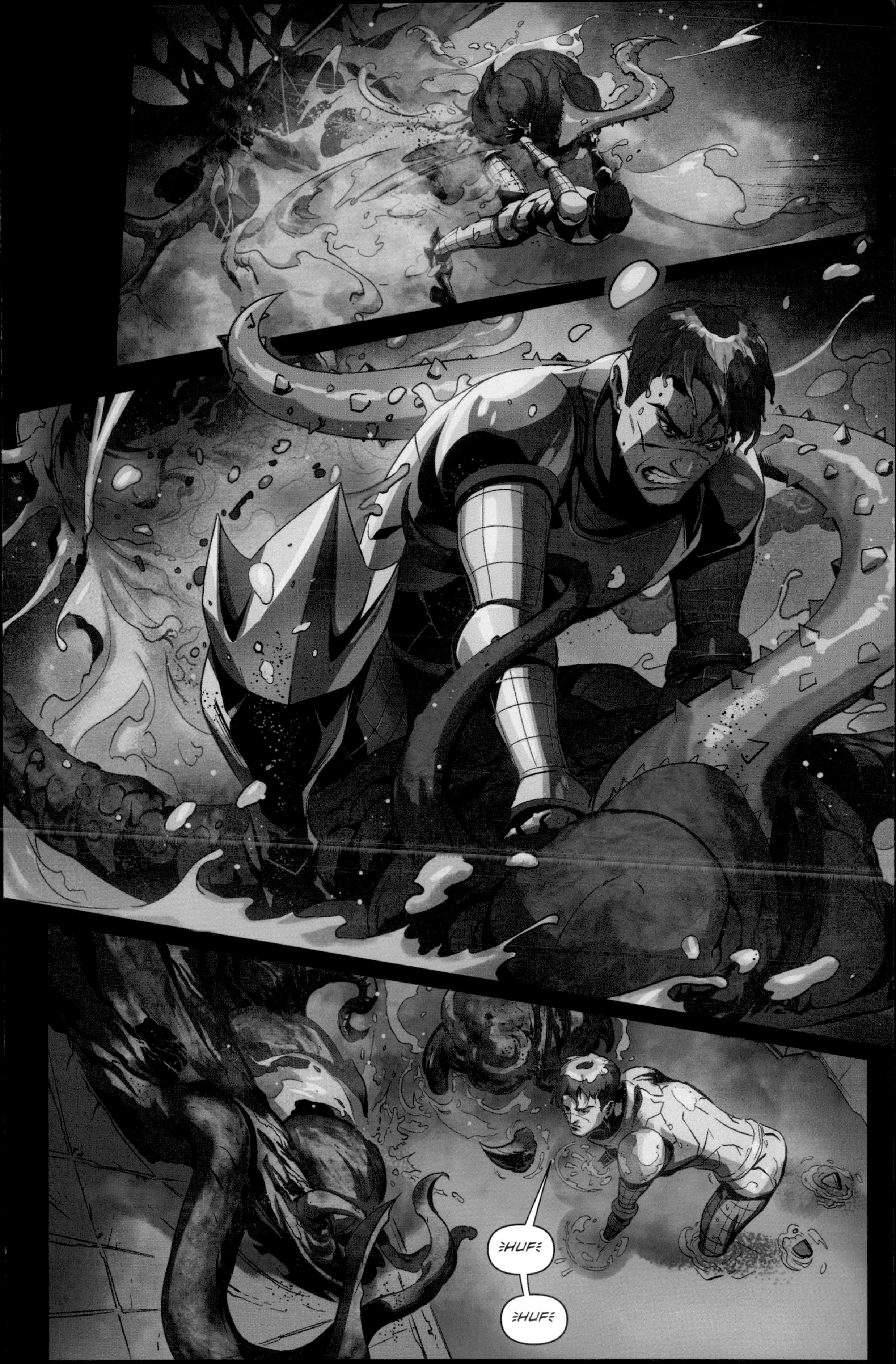
HUF
HUF

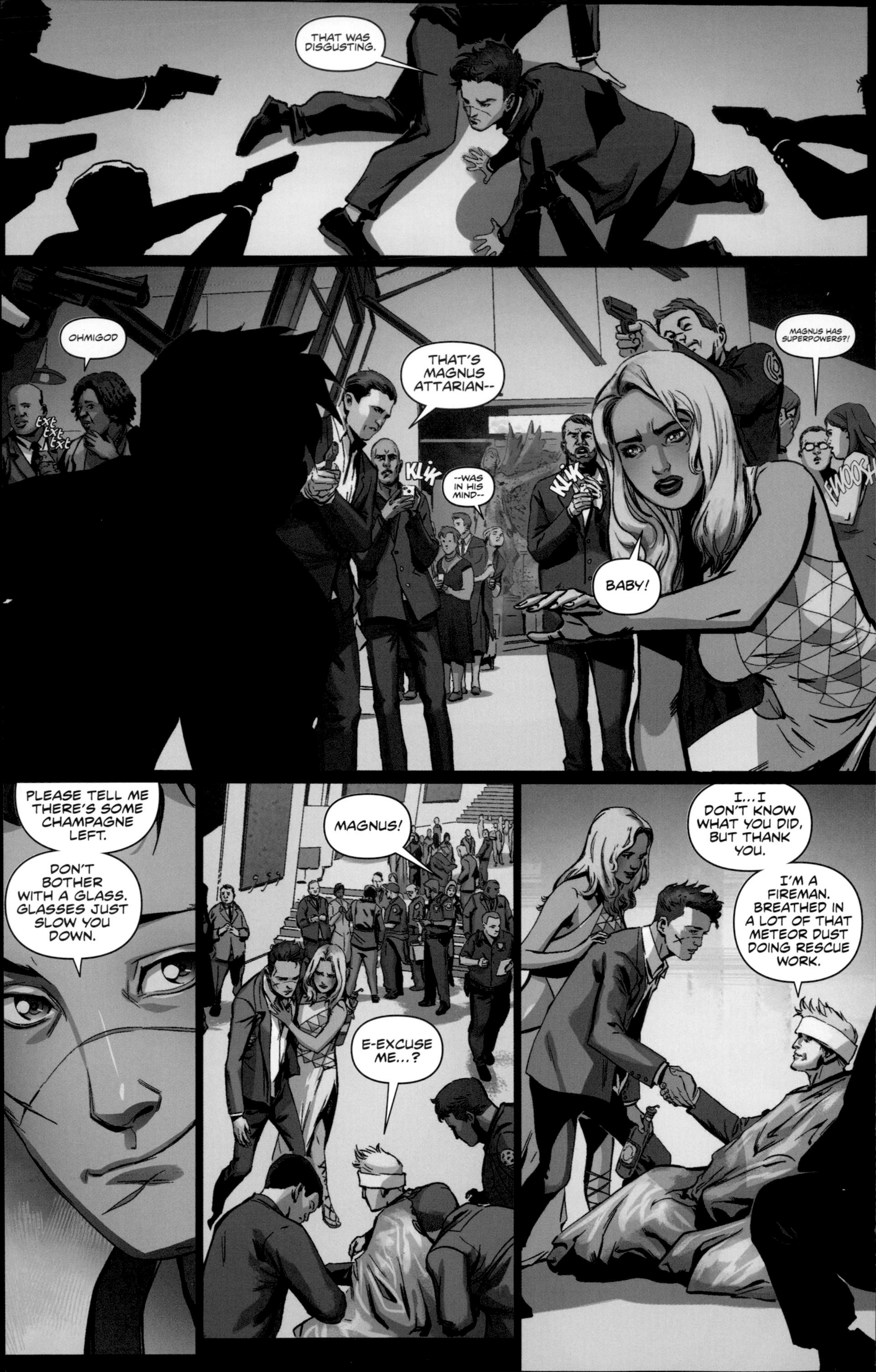
THAT WAS DISGUSTING.
OHMIGOD
txt txt txt
THAT'S MAGNUS ATTARIAN--
KLIK
--WAS IN HIS MIND--
KLIK
MAGNUS HAS SUPERPOWERS?!
FWOOSH
BABY!
PLEASE TELL ME THERE'S SOME CHAMPAGNE LEFT.
DON'T BOTHER WITH A GLASS. GLASSES JUST SLOW YOU DOWN.
MAGNUS!
E-EXCUSE ME...?
I...I DON'T KNOW WHAT YOU DID, BUT THANK YOU.
I'M A FIREMAN. BREATHED IN A LOT OF THAT METEOR DUST DOING RESCUE WORK.

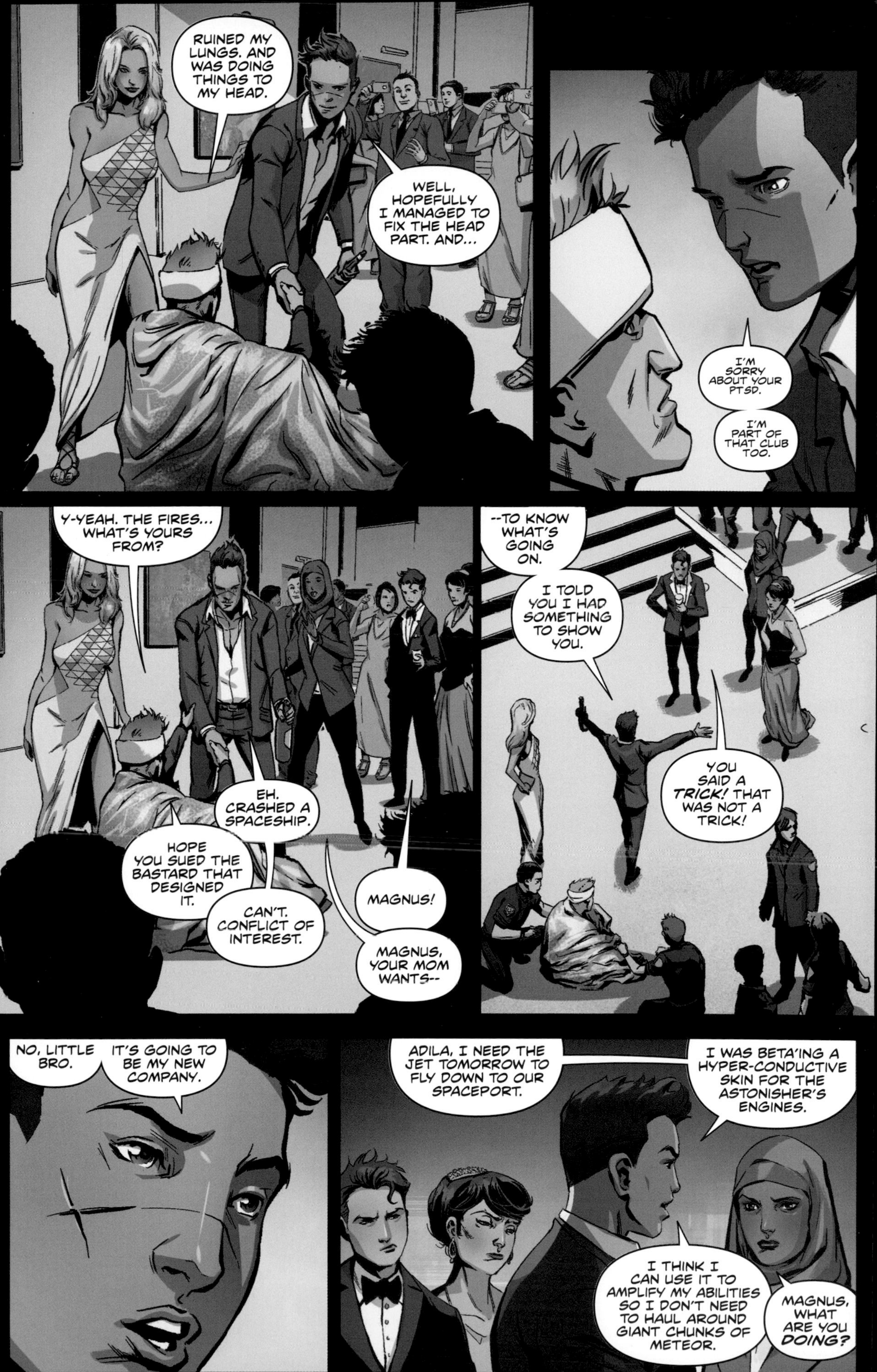
RUINED MY LUNGS. AND WAS DOING THINGS TO MY HEAD.
WELL, HOPEFULLY I MANAGED TO FIX THE HEAD PART. AND...
I'M SORRY ABOUT YOUR PTSD.
I'M PART OF THAT CLUB TOO.
Y-YEAH. THE FIRES... WHAT'S YOURS FROM?
EH. CRASHED A SPACESHIP.
HOPE YOU SUED THE BASTARD THAT DESIGNED IT.
CAN'T. CONFLICT OF INTEREST.
MAGNUS!
MAGNUS, YOUR MOM WANTS--
--TO KNOW WHAT'S GOING ON.
I TOLD YOU I HAD SOMETHING TO SHOW YOU.
YOU SAID A *TRICK!* THAT WAS NOT A TRICK!
NO, LITTLE BRO.
IT'S GOING TO BE MY NEW COMPANY.
ADILA, I NEED THE JET TOMORROW TO FLY DOWN TO OUR SPACEPORT.
I WAS BETA'ING A HYPER-CONDUCTIVE SKIN FOR THE ASTONISHER'S ENGINES.
I THINK I CAN USE IT TO AMPLIFY MY ABILITIES SO I DON'T NEED TO HAUL AROUND GIANT CHUNKS OF METEOR.
MAGNUS, WHAT ARE YOU *DOING?*

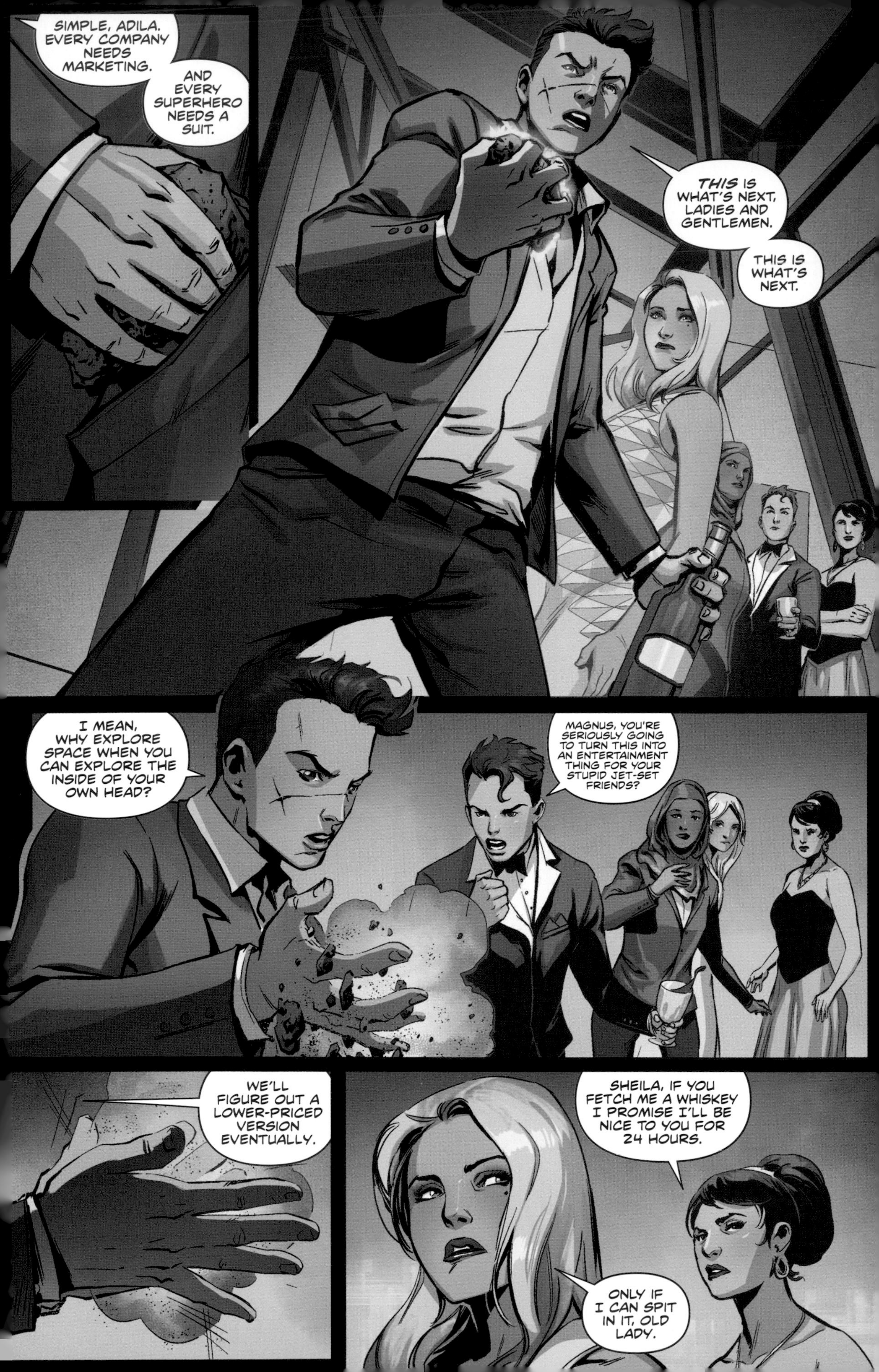
SIMPLE, ADILA. EVERY COMPANY NEEDS MARKETING.
AND EVERY SUPERHERO NEEDS A SUIT.
THIS IS WHAT'S NEXT, LADIES AND GENTLEMEN.
THIS IS WHAT'S NEXT.
I MEAN, WHY EXPLORE SPACE WHEN YOU CAN EXPLORE THE INSIDE OF YOUR OWN HEAD?
MAGNUS, YOU'RE SERIOUSLY GOING TO TURN THIS INTO AN ENTERTAINMENT THING FOR YOUR STUPID JET-SET FRIENDS?
WE'LL FIGURE OUT A LOWER-PRICED VERSION EVENTUALLY.
SHEILA, IF YOU FETCH ME A WHISKEY I PROMISE I'LL BE NICE TO YOU FOR 24 HOURS.
ONLY IF I CAN SPIT IN IT, OLD LADY.

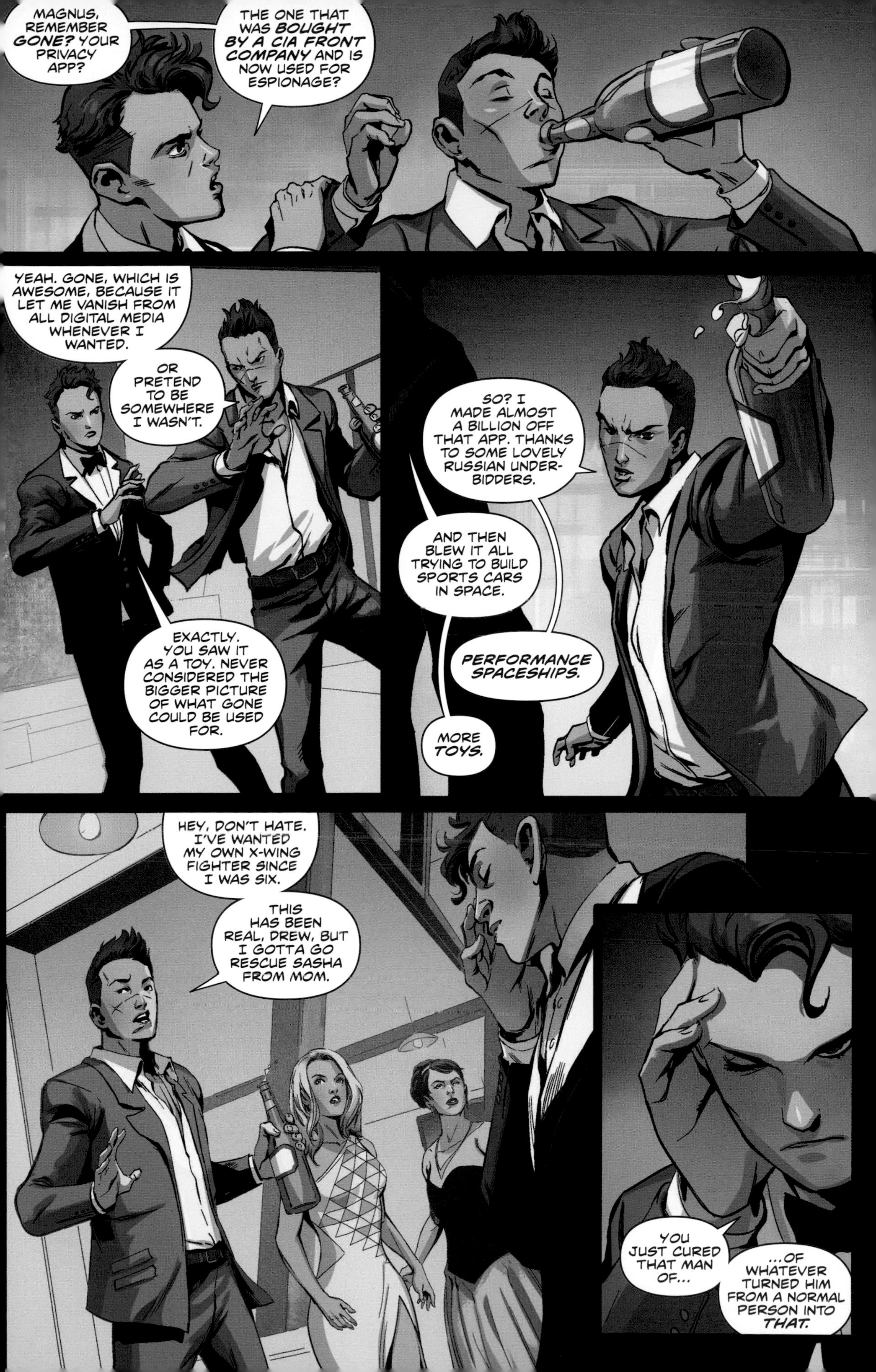
MAGNUS, REMEMBER GONE? YOUR PRIVACY APP?
THE ONE THAT WAS BOUGHT BY A CIA FRONT COMPANY AND IS NOW USED FOR ESPIONAGE?
YEAH. GONE, WHICH IS AWESOME, BECAUSE IT LET ME VANISH FROM ALL DIGITAL MEDIA WHENEVER I WANTED.
OR PRETEND TO BE SOMEWHERE I WASN'T.
EXACTLY. YOU SAW IT AS A TOY. NEVER CONSIDERED THE BIGGER PICTURE OF WHAT GONE COULD BE USED FOR.
SO? I MADE ALMOST A BILLION OFF THAT APP. THANKS TO SOME LOVELY RUSSIAN UNDER-BIDDERS.
AND THEN BLEW IT ALL TRYING TO BUILD SPORTS CARS IN SPACE.
PERFORMANCE SPACESHIPS.
MORE TOYS.
HEY, DON'T HATE. I'VE WANTED MY OWN X-WING FIGHTER SINCE I WAS SIX.
THIS HAS BEEN REAL, DREW, BUT I GOTTA GO RESCUE SASHA FROM MOM.
YOU JUST CURED THAT MAN OF...
...OF WHATEVER TURNED HIM FROM A NORMAL PERSON INTO THAT.

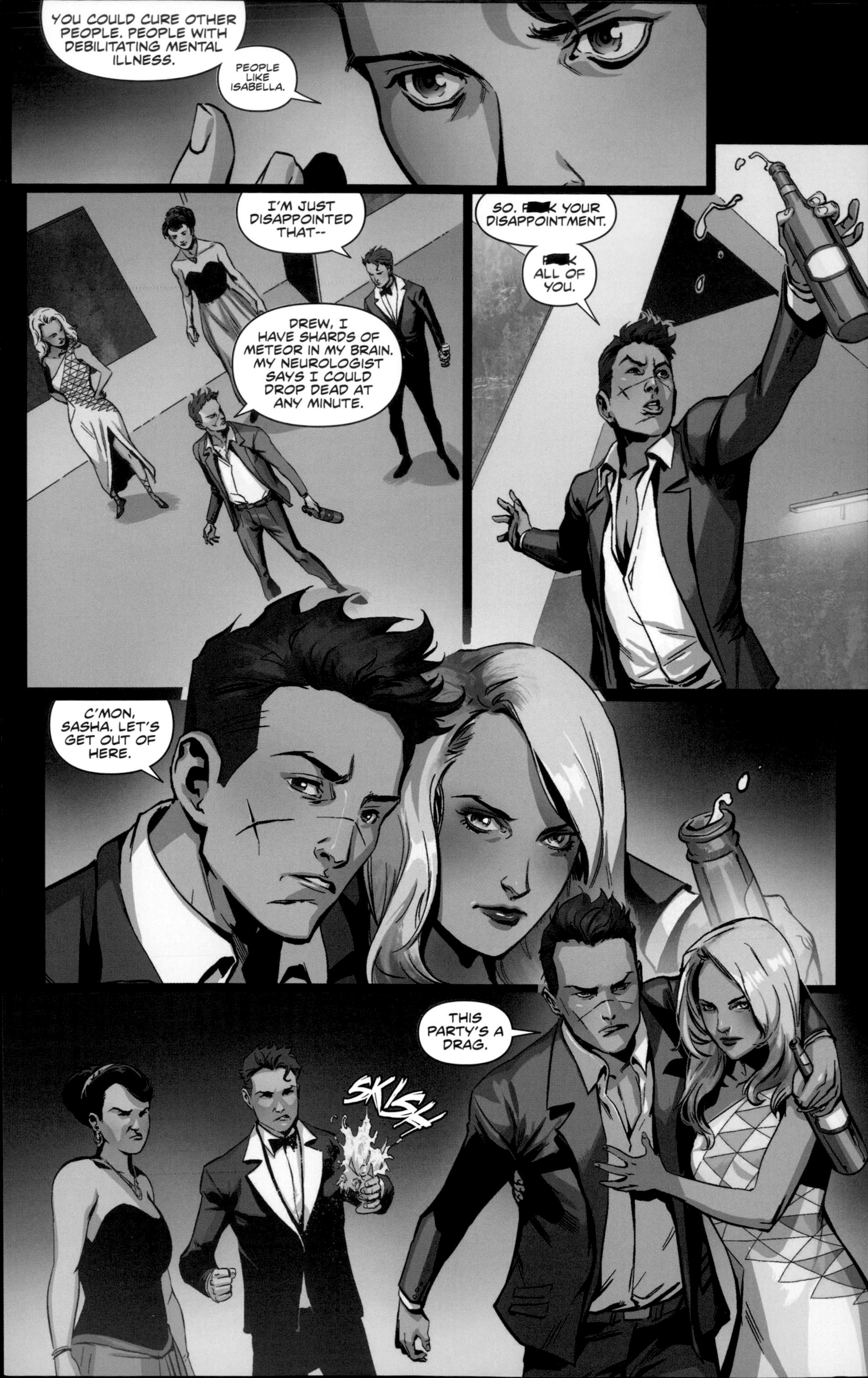
YOU COULD CURE OTHER PEOPLE. PEOPLE WITH DEBILITATING MENTAL ILLNESS.
PEOPLE LIKE ISABELLA.
I'M JUST DISAPPOINTED THAT--
DREW, I HAVE SHARDS OF METEOR IN MY BRAIN. MY NEUROLOGIST SAYS I COULD DROP DEAD AT ANY MINUTE.
SO. F[redacted]K YOUR DISAPPOINTMENT.
F[redacted]K ALL OF YOU.
C'MON, SASHA. LET'S GET OUT OF HERE.
THIS PARTY'S A DRAG.
SKISH

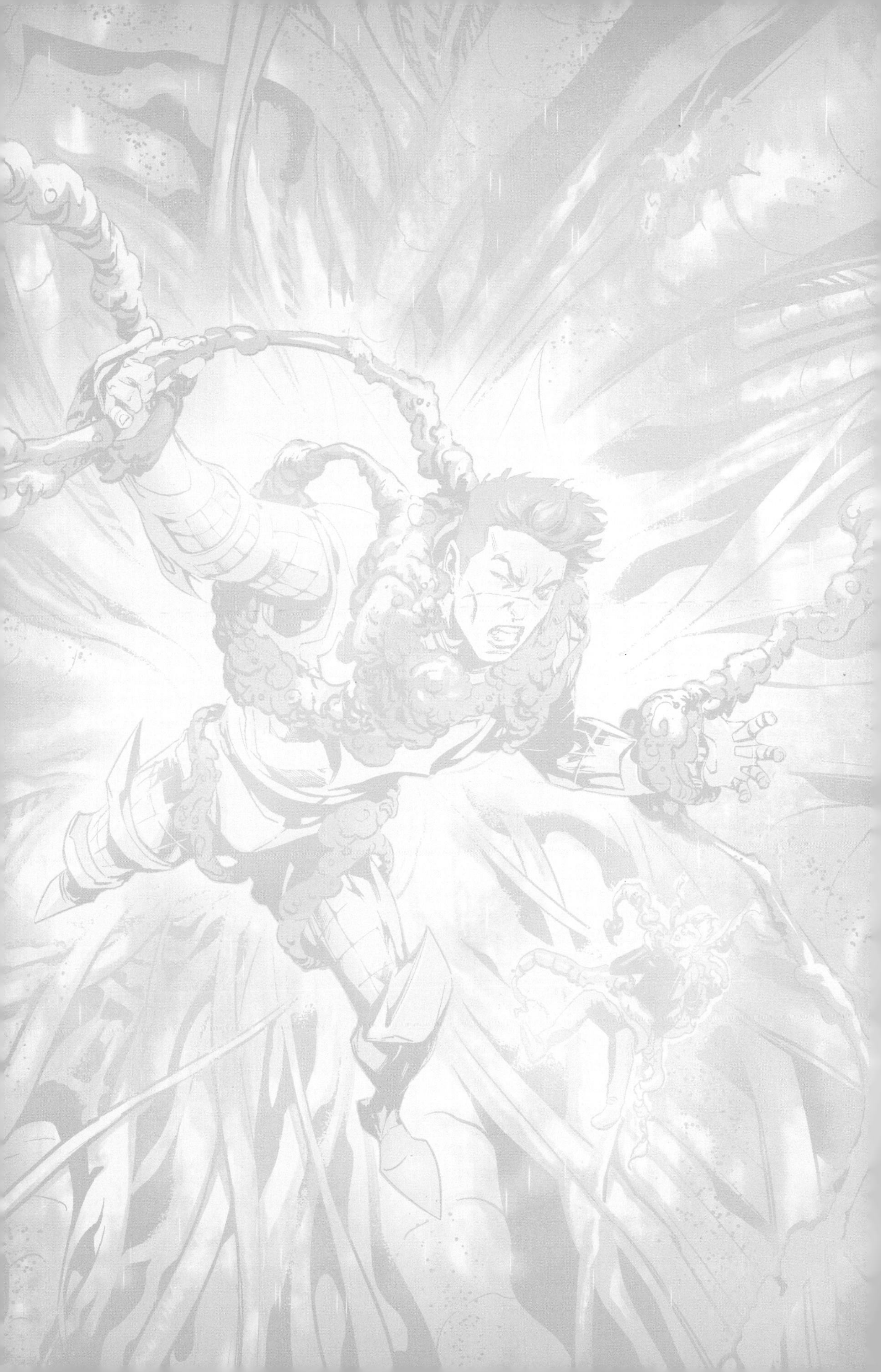

CHAPTER TWO

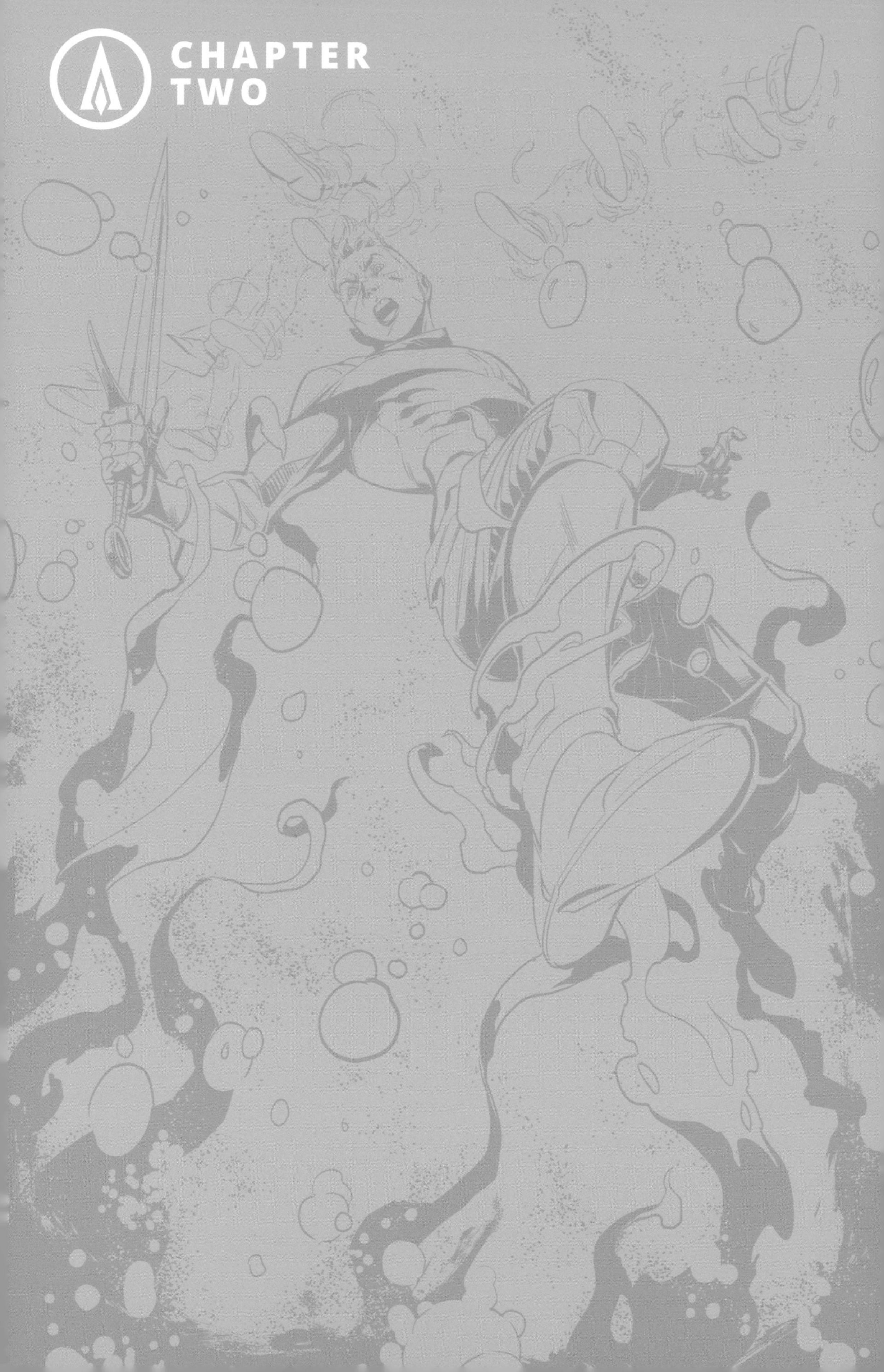

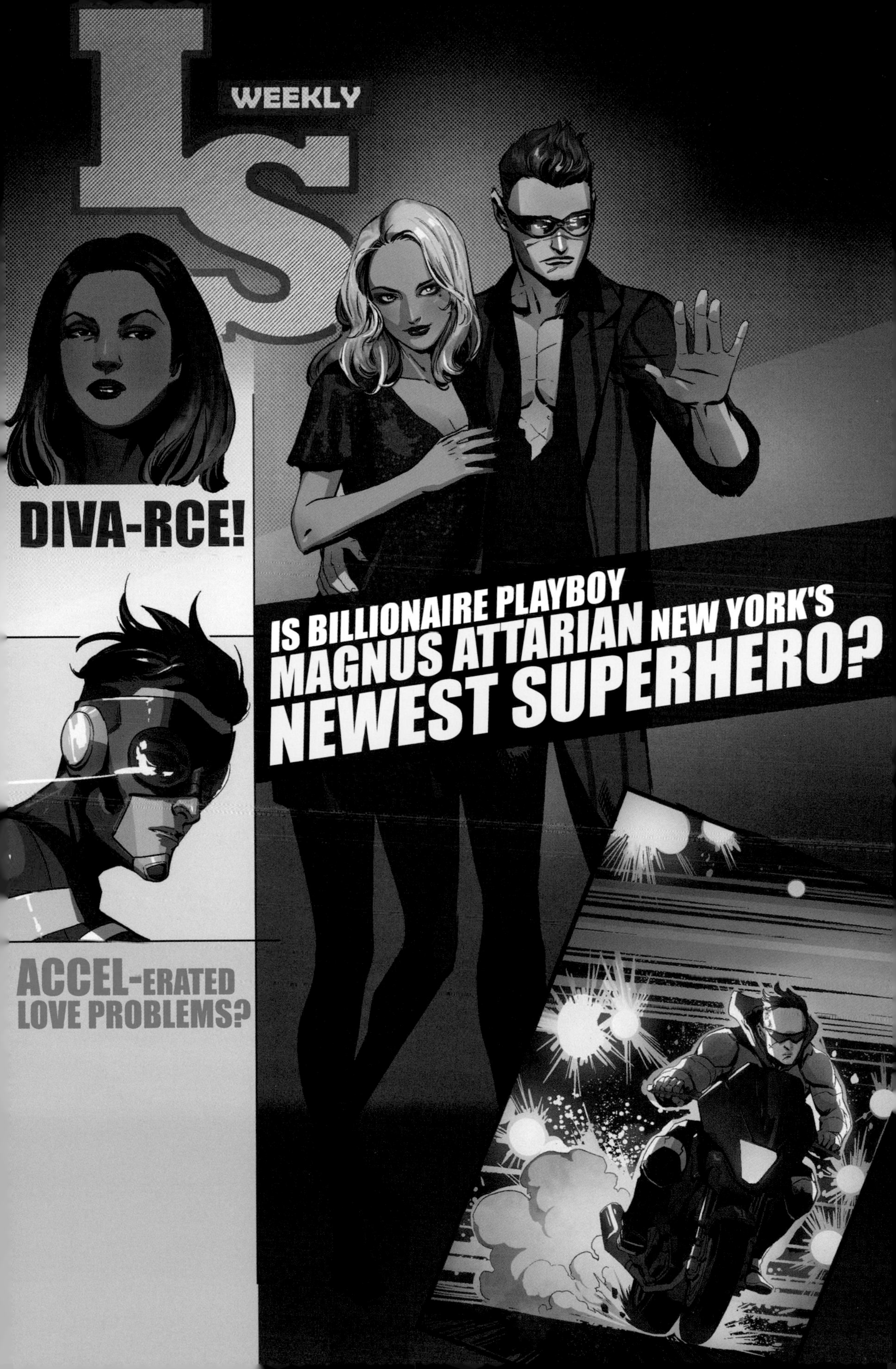

LS WEEKLY
DIVA-RCE!
IS BILLIONAIRE PLAYBOY MAGNUS ATTARIAN NEW YORK'S NEWEST SUPERHERO?
ACCEL-ERATED LOVE PROBLEMS?

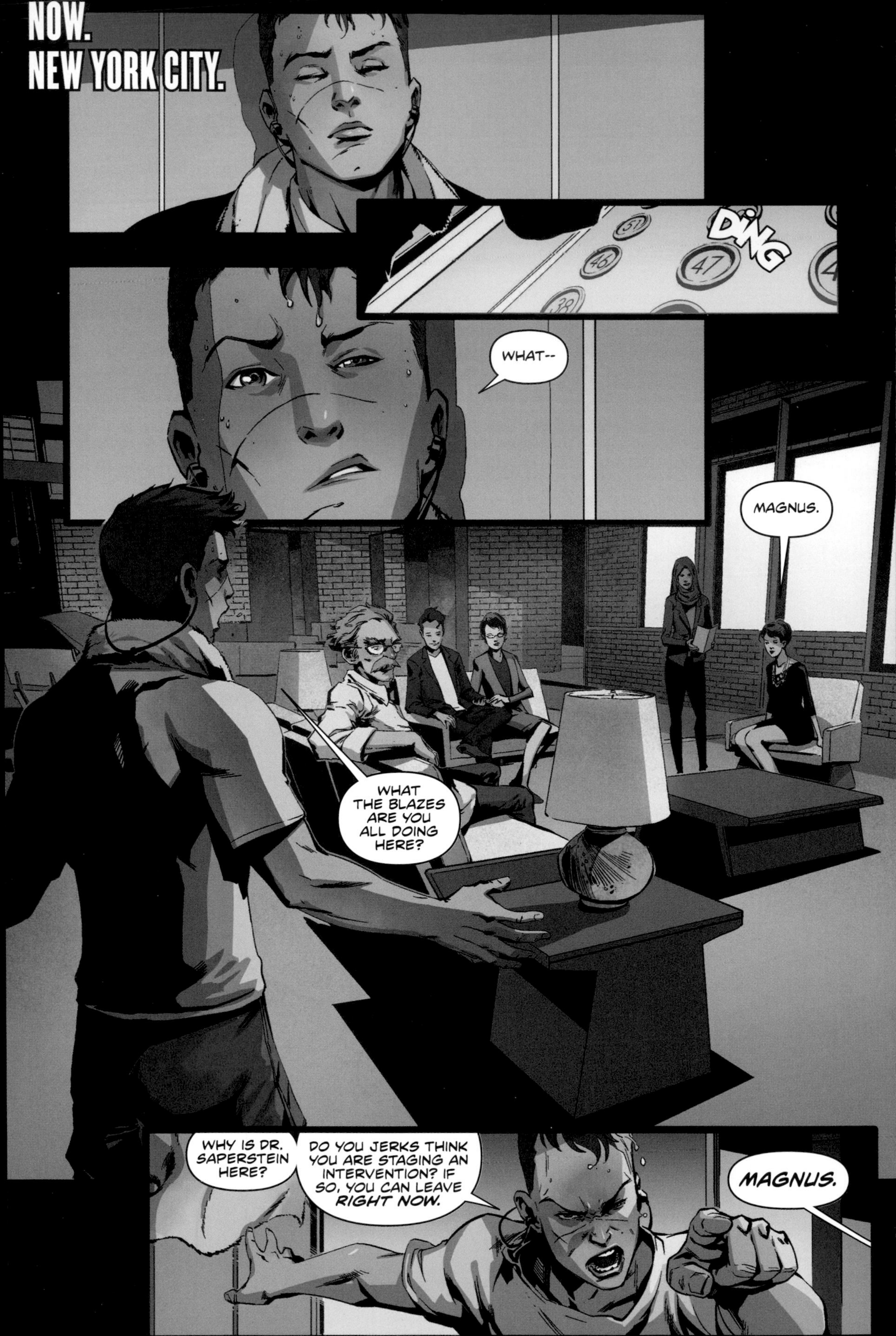
NOW.
NEW YORK CITY.
DING
WHAT--
MAGNUS.
WHAT THE BLAZES ARE YOU ALL DOING HERE?
WHY IS DR. SAPERSTEIN HERE?
DO YOU JERKS THINK YOU ARE STAGING AN INTERVENTION? IF SO, YOU CAN LEAVE *RIGHT NOW.*
MAGNUS.

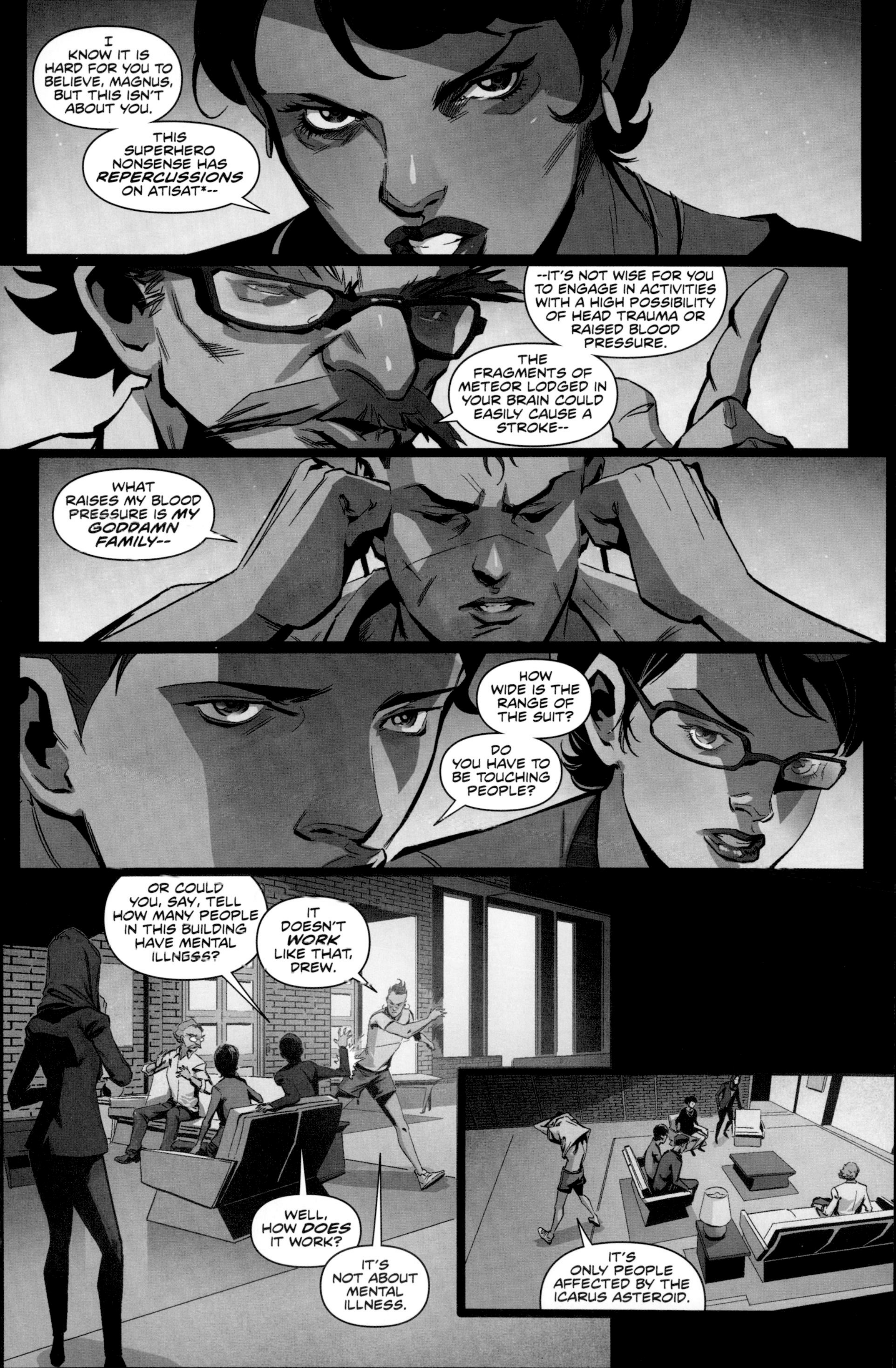
I KNOW IT IS HARD FOR YOU TO BELIEVE, MAGNUS, BUT THIS ISN'T ABOUT YOU.
THIS SUPERHERO NONSENSE HAS REPERCUSSIONS ON ATISAT*--
--IT'S NOT WISE FOR YOU TO ENGAGE IN ACTIVITIES WITH A HIGH POSSIBILITY OF HEAD TRAUMA OR RAISED BLOOD PRESSURE.
THE FRAGMENTS OF METEOR LODGED IN YOUR BRAIN COULD EASILY CAUSE A STROKE--
WHAT RAISES MY BLOOD PRESSURE IS MY GODDAMN FAMILY--
HOW WIDE IS THE RANGE OF THE SUIT?
DO YOU HAVE TO BE TOUCHING PEOPLE?
OR COULD YOU, SAY, TELL HOW MANY PEOPLE IN THIS BUILDING HAVE MENTAL ILLNESS?
IT DOESN'T WORK LIKE THAT, DREW.
WELL, HOW DOES IT WORK?
IT'S NOT ABOUT MENTAL ILLNESS.
IT'S ONLY PEOPLE AFFECTED BY THE ICARUS ASTEROID.

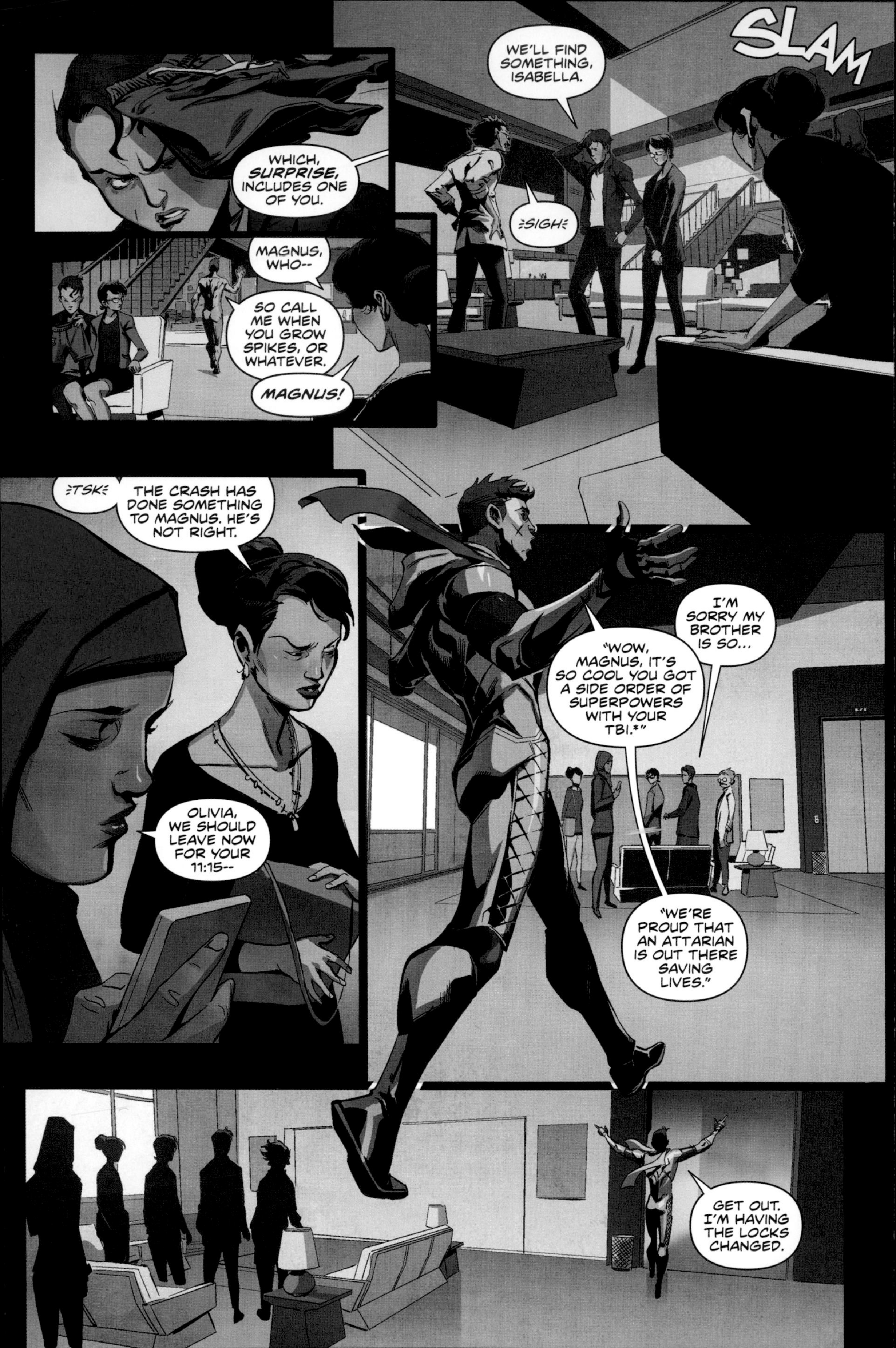
WHICH, SURPRISE, INCLUDES ONE OF YOU.
WE'LL FIND SOMETHING, ISABELLA.
SLAM
SIGH
MAGNUS, WHO--
SO CALL ME WHEN YOU GROW SPIKES, OR WHATEVER.
MAGNUS!
TSK
THE CRASH HAS DONE SOMETHING TO MAGNUS. HE'S NOT RIGHT.
OLIVIA, WE SHOULD LEAVE NOW FOR YOUR 11:15--
I'M SORRY MY BROTHER IS SO...
"WOW, MAGNUS, IT'S SO COOL YOU GOT A SIDE ORDER OF SUPERPOWERS WITH YOUR TBI.*"
"WE'RE PROUD THAT AN ATTARIAN IS OUT THERE SAVING LIVES."
GET OUT. I'M HAVING THE LOCKS CHANGED.

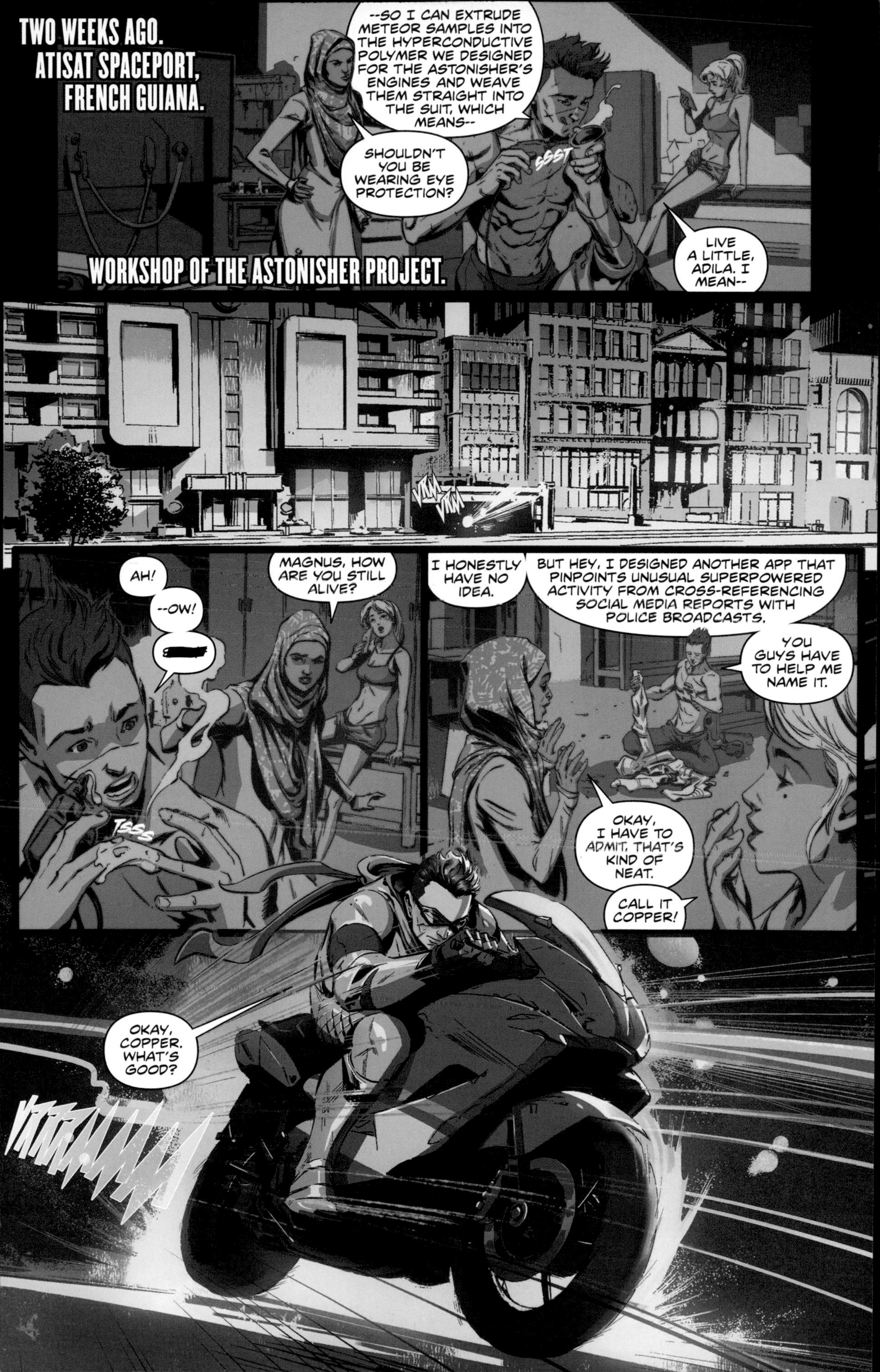
TWO WEEKS AGO. ATISAT SPACEPORT, FRENCH GUIANA.
--SO I CAN EXTRUDE METEOR SAMPLES INTO THE HYPERCONDUCTIVE POLYMER WE DESIGNED FOR THE ASTONISHER'S ENGINES AND WEAVE THEM STRAIGHT INTO THE SUIT, WHICH MEANS--
SHOULDN'T YOU BE WEARING EYE PROTECTION?
SSST
LIVE A LITTLE, ADILA. I MEAN--
WORKSHOP OF THE ASTONISHER PROJECT.
VRM VRM
AH!
--OW!
[redacted]
TSSS
MAGNUS, HOW ARE YOU STILL ALIVE?
I HONESTLY HAVE NO IDEA.
BUT HEY, I DESIGNED ANOTHER APP THAT PINPOINTS UNUSUAL SUPERPOWERED ACTIVITY FROM CROSS-REFERENCING SOCIAL MEDIA REPORTS WITH POLICE BROADCASTS.
YOU GUYS HAVE TO HELP ME NAME IT.
OKAY, I HAVE TO ADMIT, THAT'S KIND OF NEAT.
CALL IT COPPER!
OKAY, COPPER. WHAT'S GOOD?

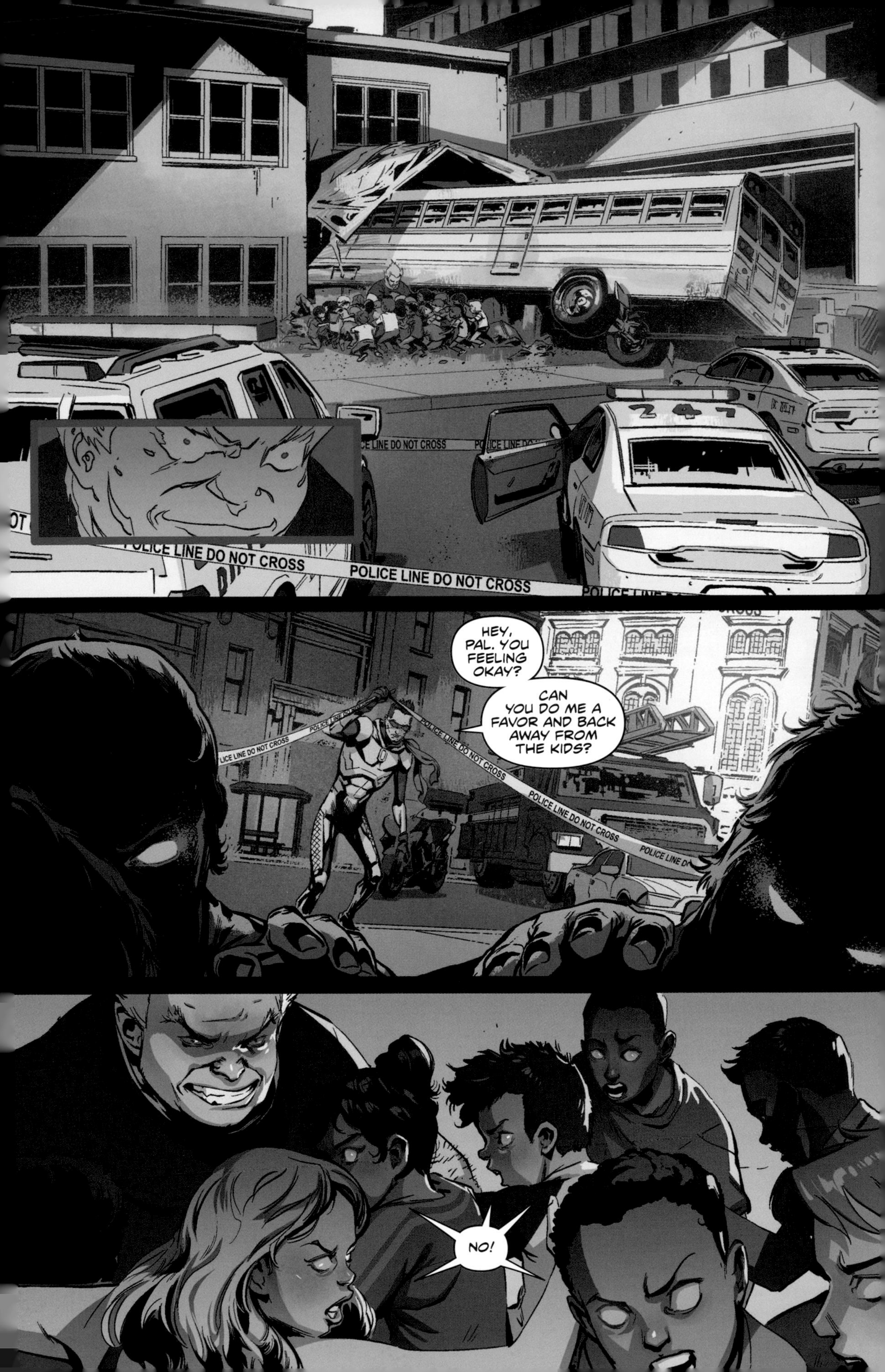
POLICE LINE DO NOT CROSS
POLICE LINE DO NOT CROSS
POLICE LINE DO NOT CROSS
HEY, PAL. YOU FEELING OKAY?
CAN YOU DO ME A FAVOR AND BACK AWAY FROM THE KIDS?
POLICE LINE DO NOT CROSS
POLICE LINE DO NOT CROSS
NO!

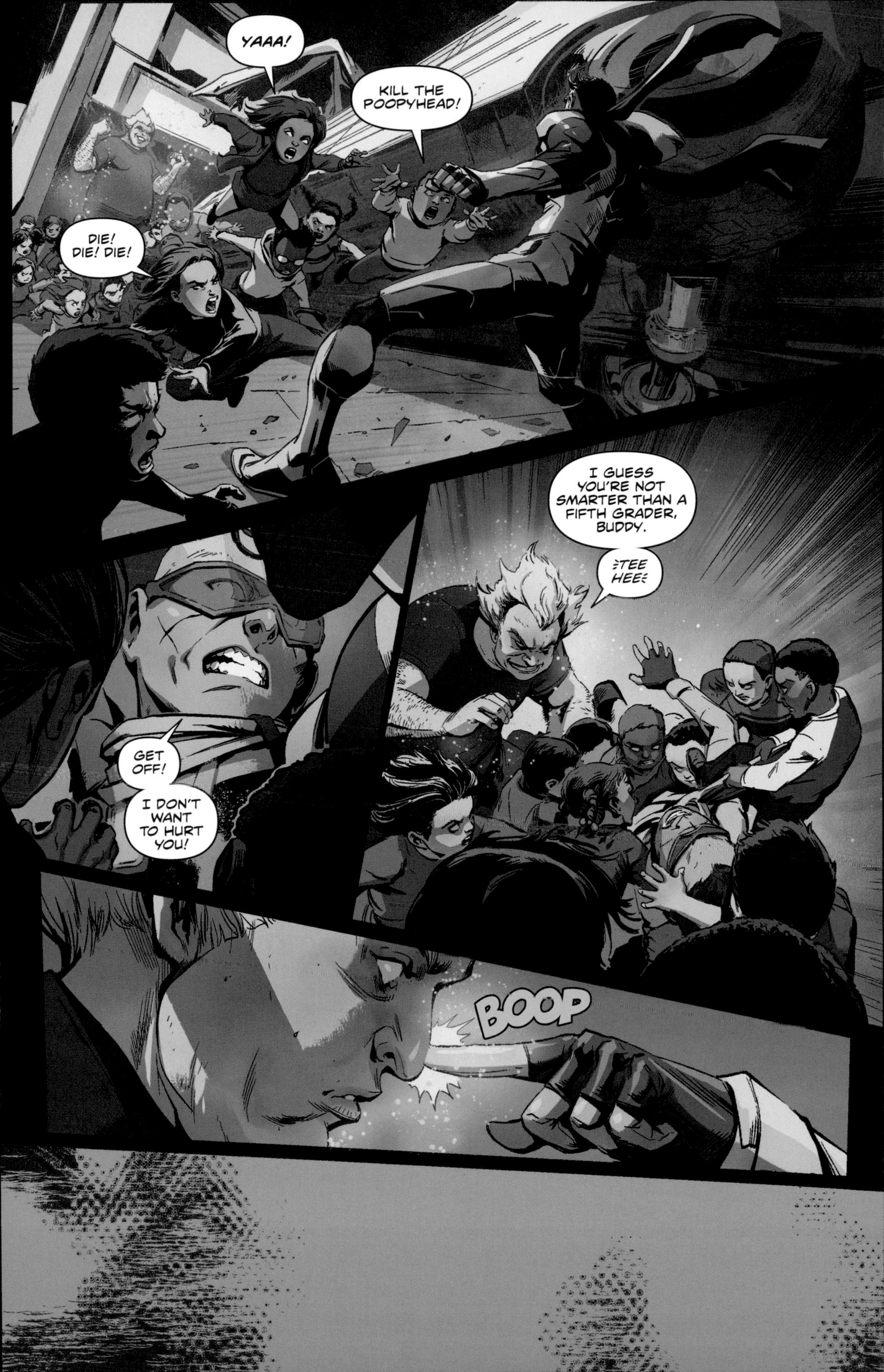
YAAA!
KILL THE POOPYHEAD!
DIE! DIE! DIE!
I GUESS YOU'RE NOT SMARTER THAN A FIFTH GRADER, BUDDY.
TEE HEE
GET OFF!
I DON'T WANT TO HURT YOU!
BOOP

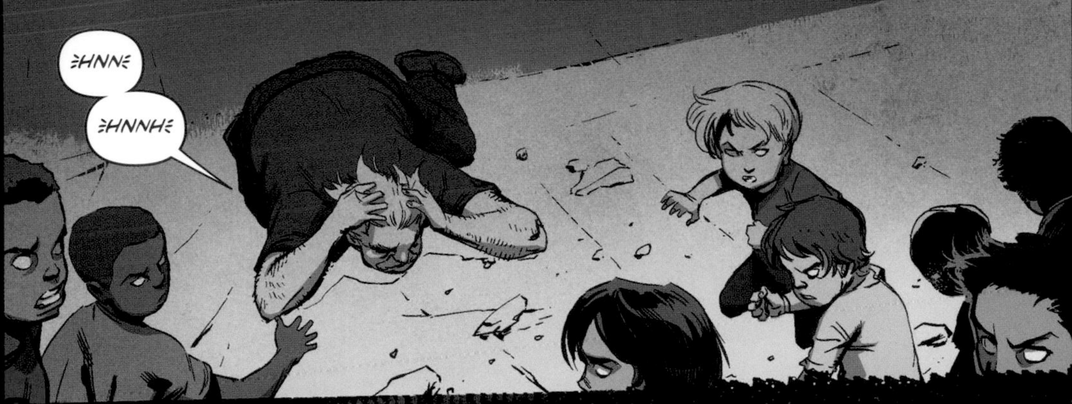
HNN
HNNH

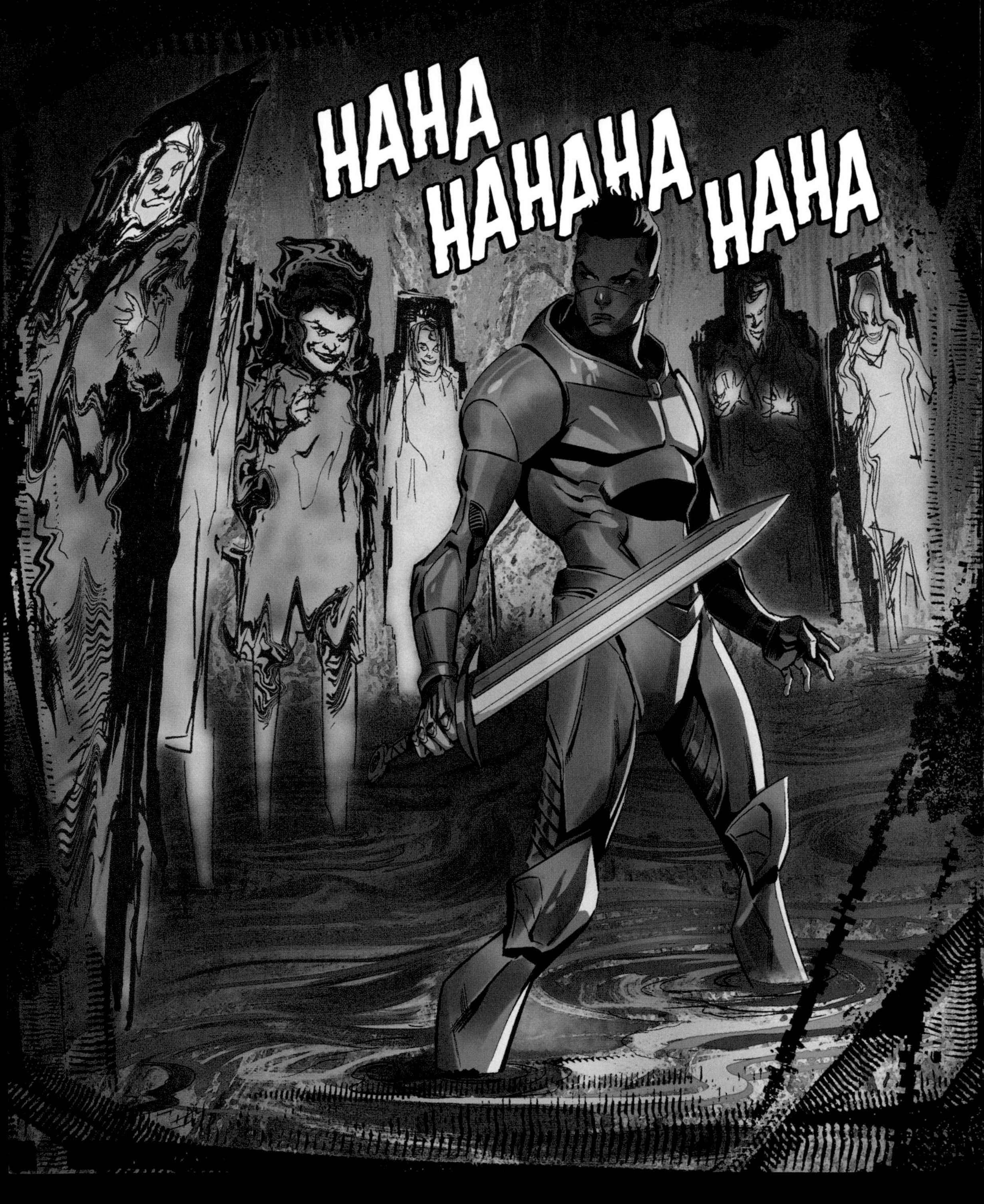
HAHA HAHAHA HAHA

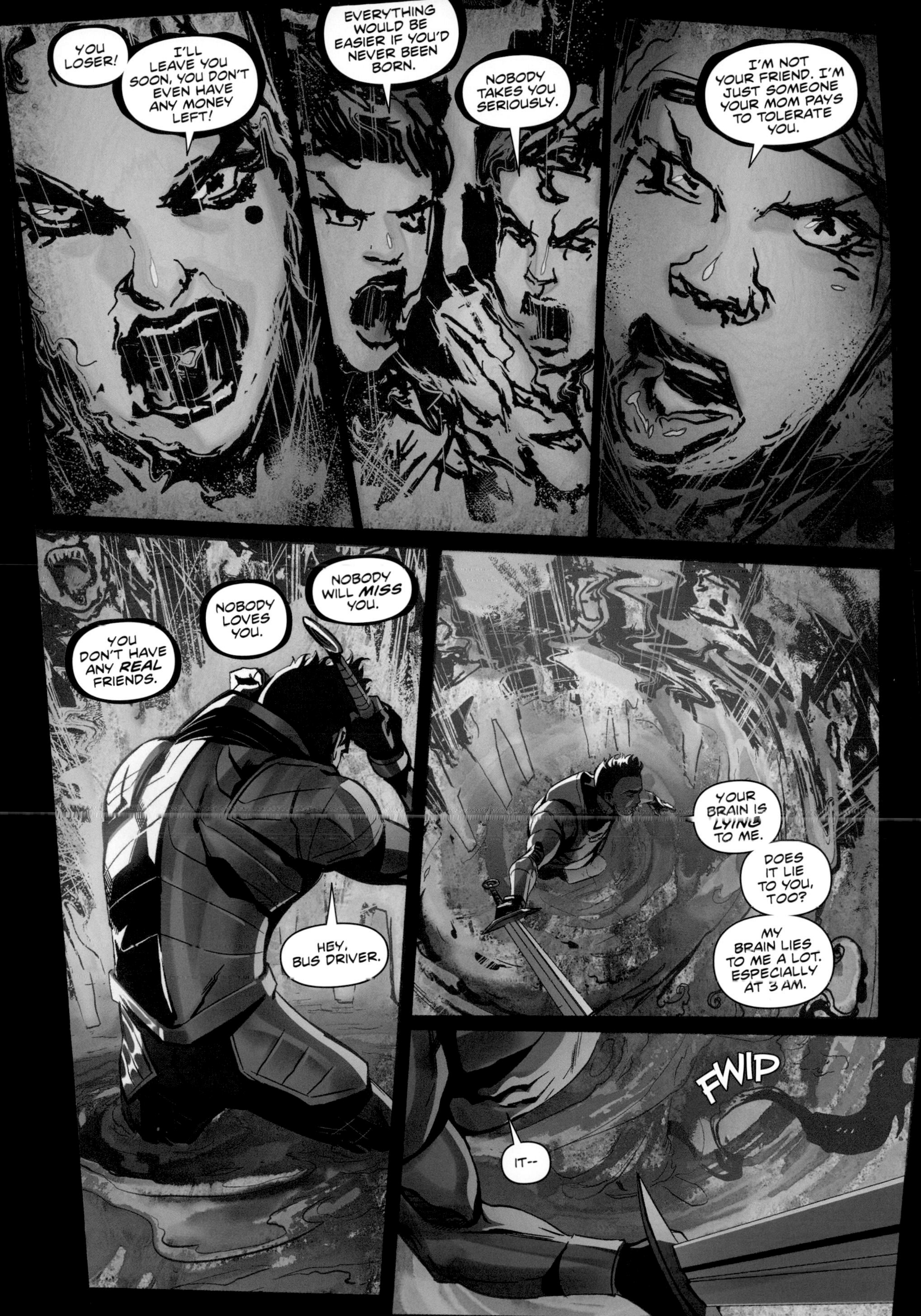

YOU LOSER!
I'LL LEAVE YOU SOON, YOU DON'T EVEN HAVE ANY MONEY LEFT!
EVERYTHING WOULD BE EASIER IF YOU'D NEVER BEEN BORN.
NOBODY TAKES YOU SERIOUSLY.
I'M NOT YOUR FRIEND. I'M JUST SOMEONE YOUR MOM PAYS TO TOLERATE YOU.
YOU DON'T HAVE ANY REAL FRIENDS.
NOBODY LOVES YOU.
NOBODY WILL MISS YOU.
HEY, BUS DRIVER.
YOUR BRAIN IS LYING TO ME.
DOES IT LIE TO YOU, TOO?
MY BRAIN LIES TO ME A LOT. ESPECIALLY AT 3 AM.
FWIP
IT--

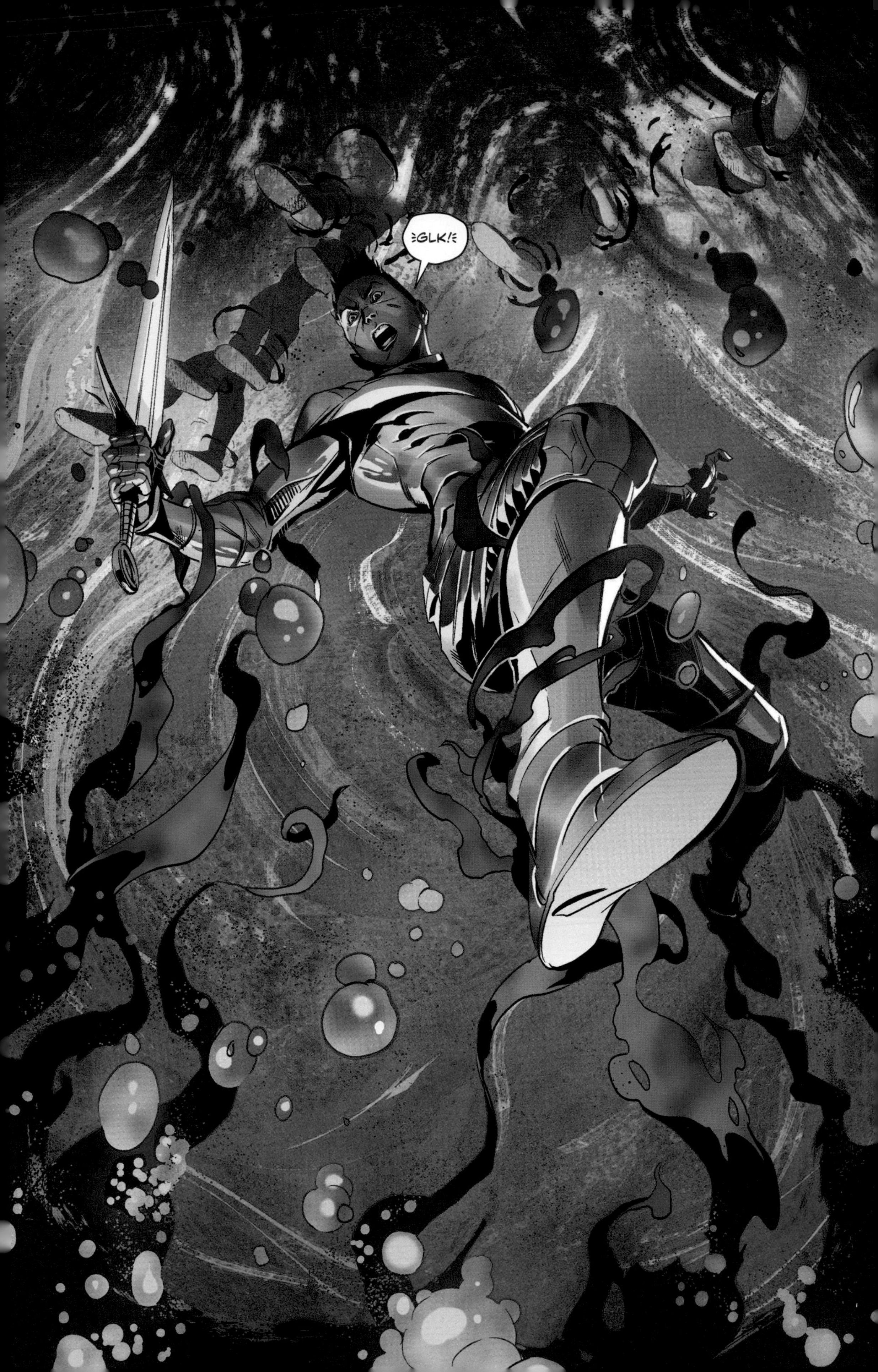
GLK!

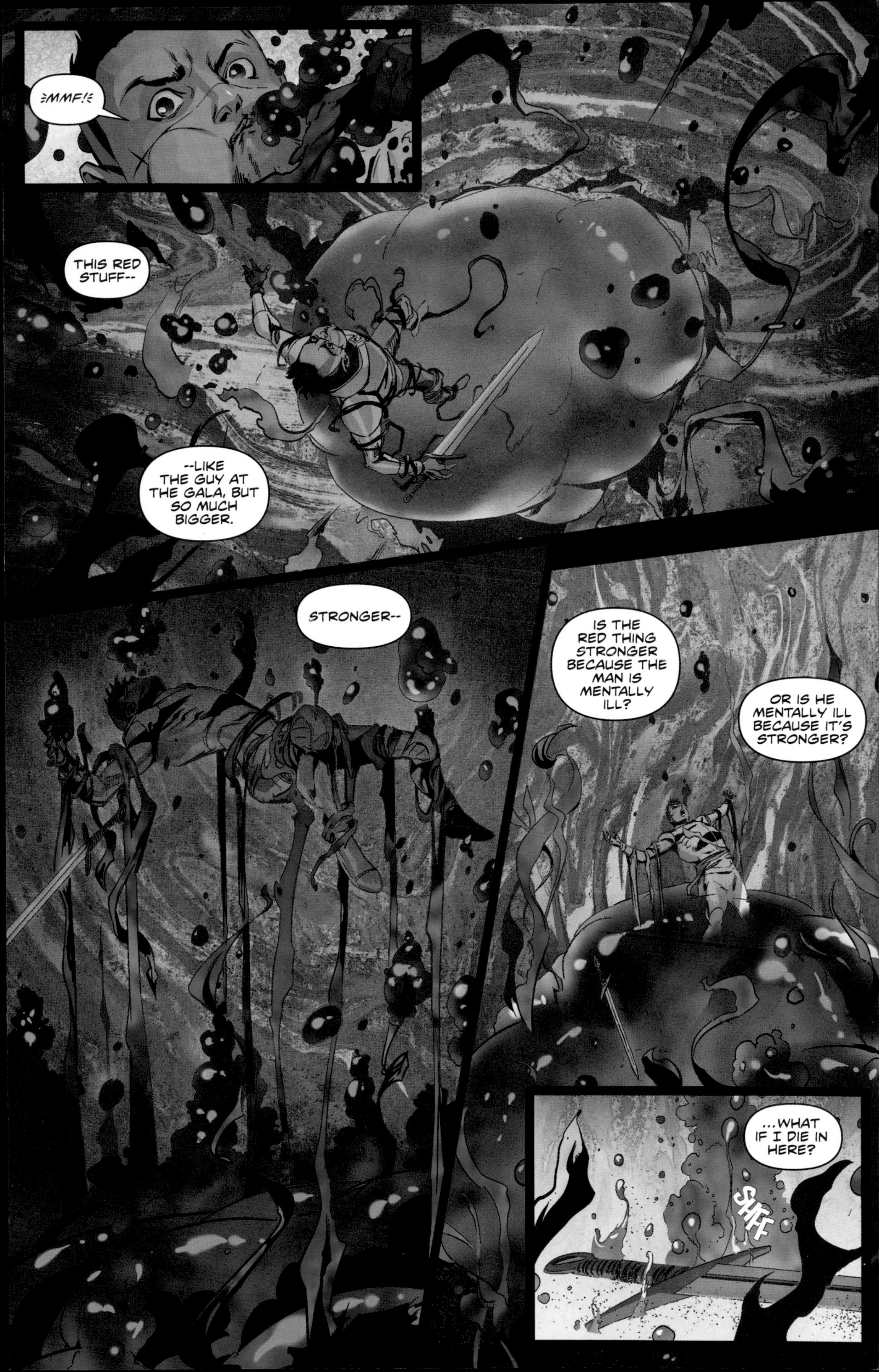
MMF!
THIS RED STUFF--
--LIKE THE GUY AT THE GALA, BUT SO MUCH BIGGER.
STRONGER--
IS THE RED THING STRONGER BECAUSE THE MAN IS MENTALLY ILL?
OR IS HE MENTALLY ILL BECAUSE IT'S STRONGER?
...WHAT IF I DIE IN HERE?
SHFF

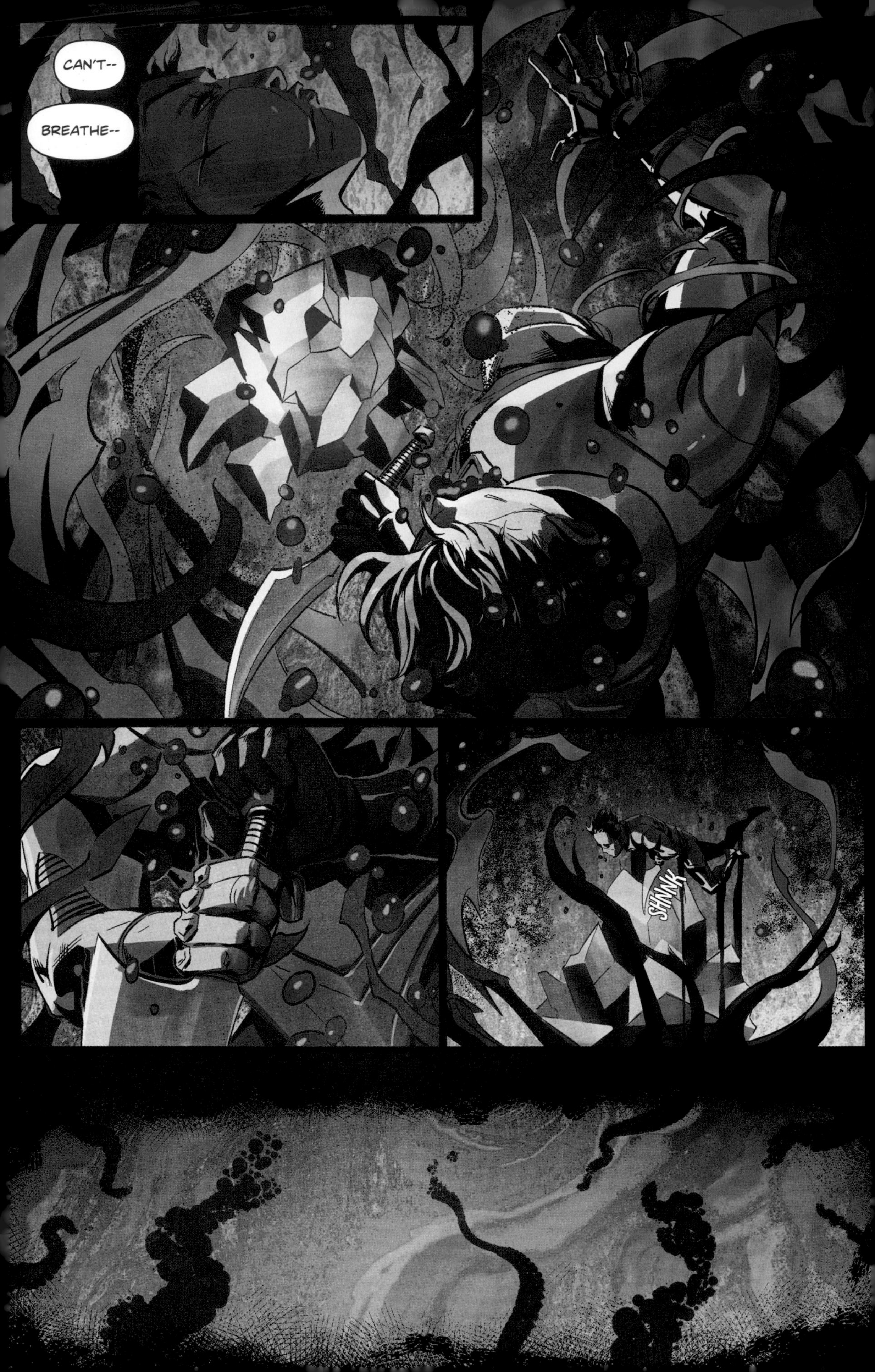

CAN'T--
BREATHE--
SHNNK

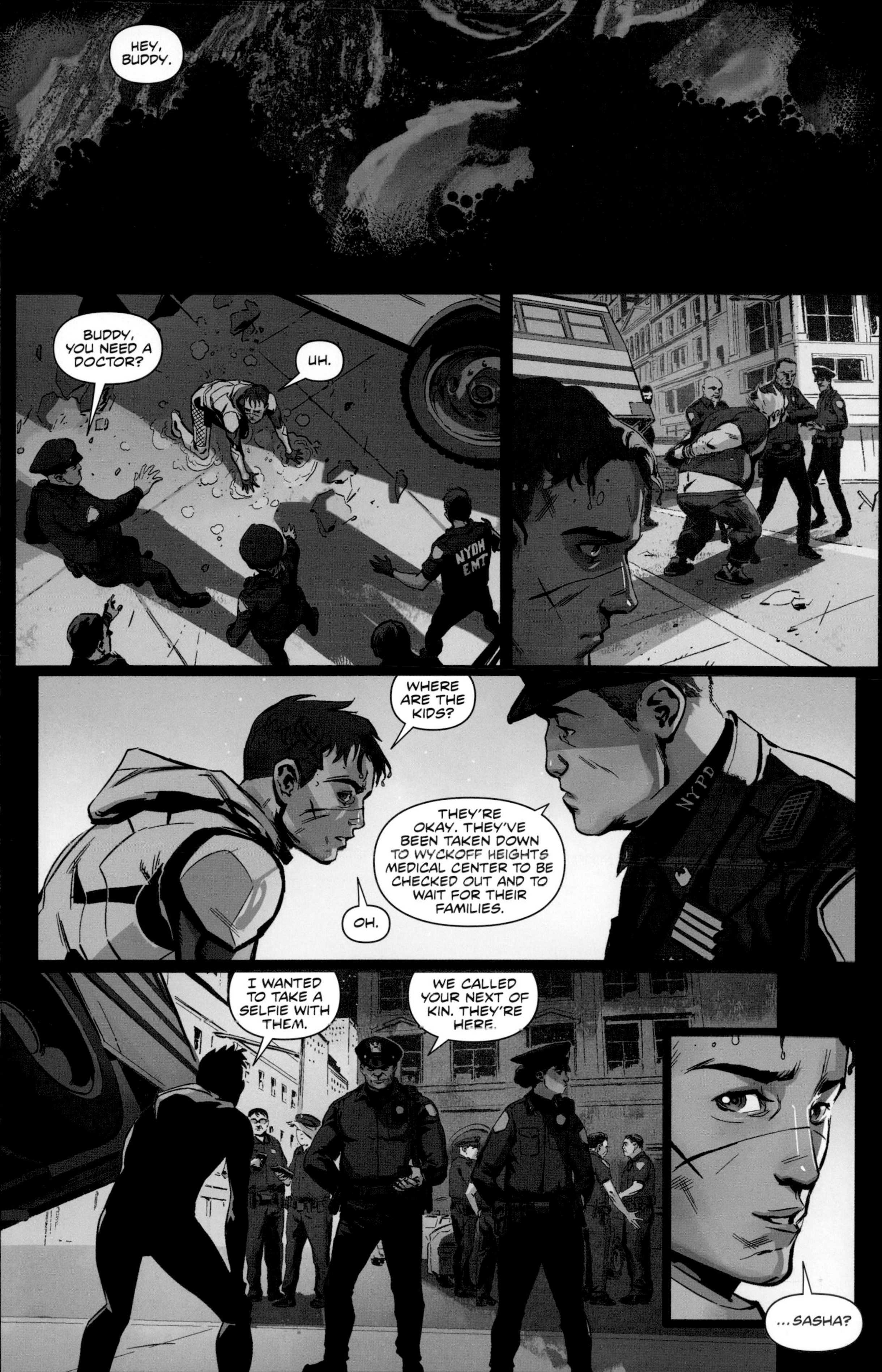
HEY, BUDDY.
BUDDY, YOU NEED A DOCTOR?
UH.
NYDH EMT
WHERE ARE THE KIDS?
NYPD
THEY'RE OKAY. THEY'VE BEEN TAKEN DOWN TO WYCKOFF HEIGHTS MEDICAL CENTER TO BE CHECKED OUT AND TO WAIT FOR THEIR FAMILIES.
OH.
I WANTED TO TAKE A SELFIE WITH THEM.
WE CALLED YOUR NEXT OF KIN. THEY'RE HERE.
...SASHA?

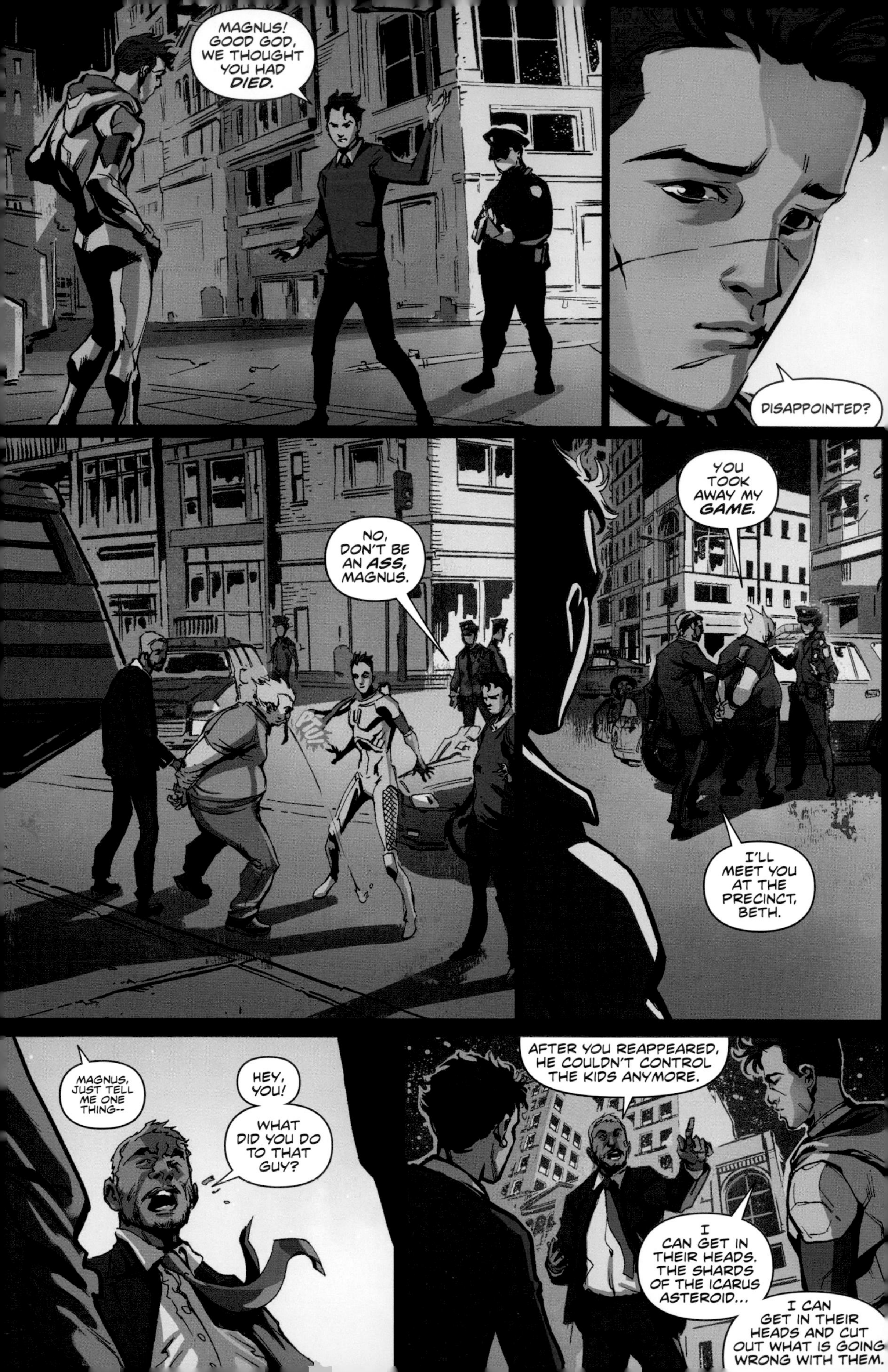
MAGNUS! GOOD GOD, WE THOUGHT YOU HAD *DIED.*
DISAPPOINTED?
NO, DON'T BE AN *ASS,* MAGNUS.
YOU TOOK AWAY MY *GAME.*
I'LL MEET YOU AT THE PRECINCT, BETH.
MAGNUS, JUST TELL ME ONE THING--
HEY, YOU!
WHAT DID YOU DO TO THAT GUY?
AFTER YOU REAPPEARED, HE COULDN'T CONTROL THE KIDS ANYMORE.
I CAN GET IN THEIR HEADS. THE SHARDS OF THE ICARUS ASTEROID...
I CAN GET IN THEIR HEADS AND CUT OUT WHAT IS GOING WRONG WITH THEM.

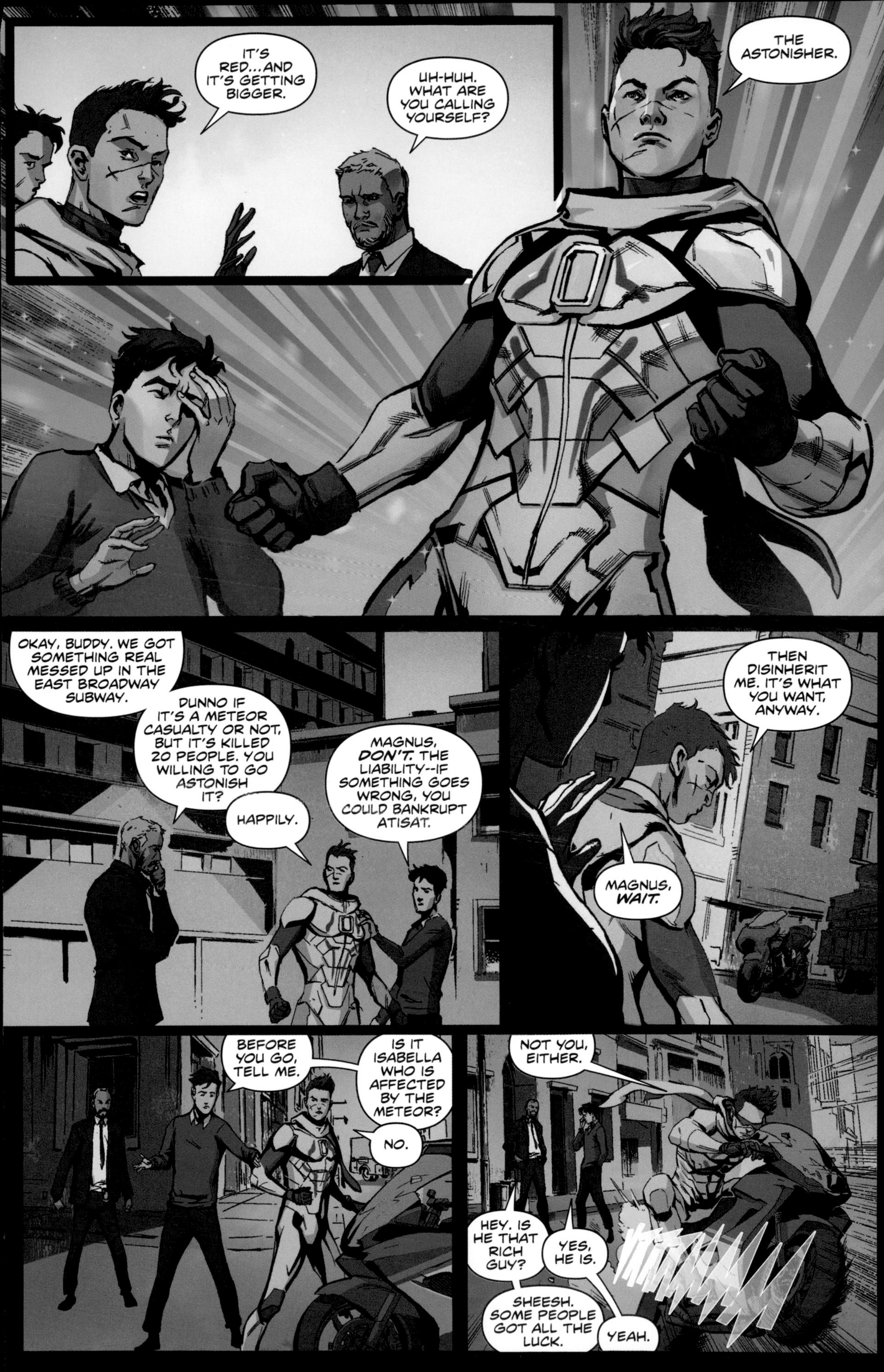
IT'S RED...AND IT'S GETTING BIGGER.
UH-HUH. WHAT ARE YOU CALLING YOURSELF?
THE ASTONISHER.
OKAY, BUDDY. WE GOT SOMETHING REAL MESSED UP IN THE EAST BROADWAY SUBWAY.
DUNNO IF IT'S A METEOR CASUALTY OR NOT, BUT IT'S KILLED 20 PEOPLE. YOU WILLING TO GO ASTONISH IT?
HAPPILY.
MAGNUS, DON'T. THE LIABILITY--IF SOMETHING GOES WRONG, YOU COULD BANKRUPT ATISAT.
THEN DISINHERIT ME. IT'S WHAT YOU WANT, ANYWAY.
MAGNUS, WAIT.
BEFORE YOU GO, TELL ME.
IS IT ISABELLA WHO IS AFFECTED BY THE METEOR?
NO.
NOT YOU, EITHER.
HEY. IS HE THAT RICH GUY?
YES, HE IS.
SHEESH. SOME PEOPLE GOT ALL THE LUCK.
YEAH.
VRRRAAAAAAM

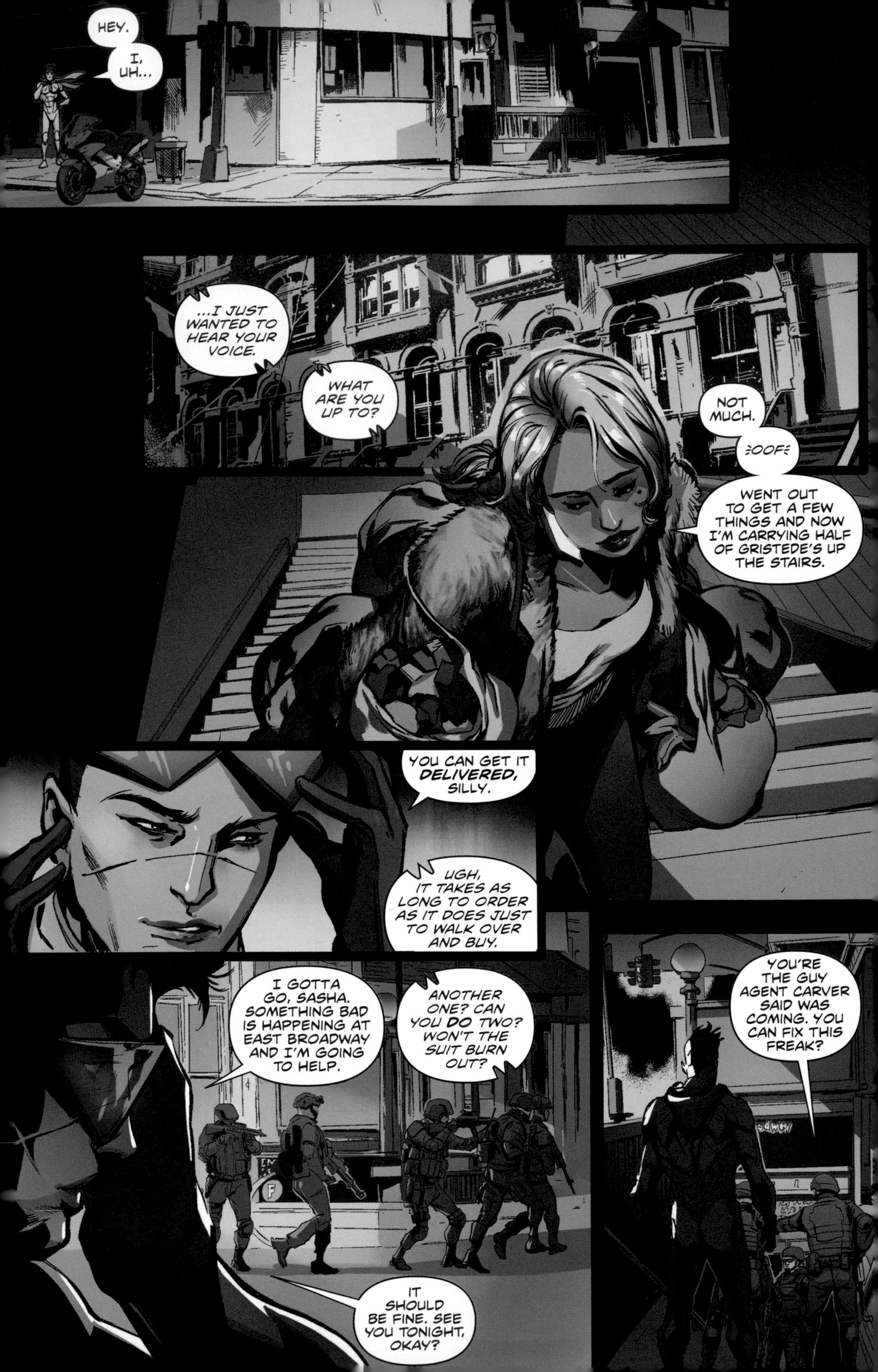
HEY.
I, UH...
...I JUST WANTED TO HEAR YOUR VOICE.
WHAT ARE YOU UP TO?
NOT MUCH.
OOF
WENT OUT TO GET A FEW THINGS AND NOW I'M CARRYING HALF OF GRISTEDE'S UP THE STAIRS.
YOU CAN GET IT DELIVERED, SILLY.
UGH, IT TAKES AS LONG TO ORDER AS IT DOES JUST TO WALK OVER AND BUY.
I GOTTA GO, SASHA. SOMETHING BAD IS HAPPENING AT EAST BROADWAY AND I'M GOING TO HELP.
ANOTHER ONE? CAN YOU DO TWO? WON'T THE SUIT BURN OUT?
IT SHOULD BE FINE. SEE YOU TONIGHT, OKAY?
YOU'RE THE GUY AGENT CARVER SAID WAS COMING. YOU CAN FIX THIS FREAK?

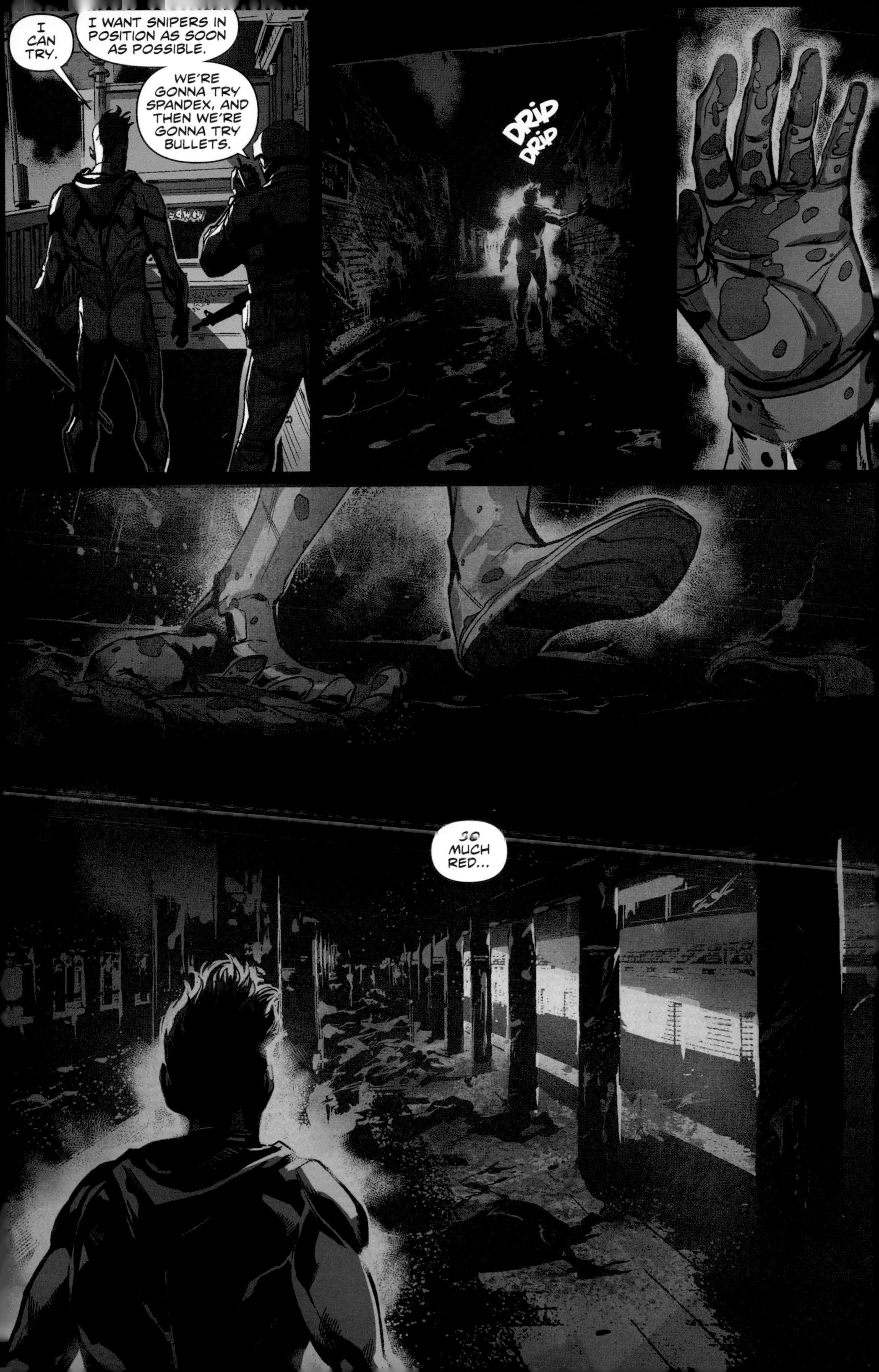
I WANT SNIPERS IN POSITION AS SOON AS POSSIBLE.
I CAN TRY.
WE'RE GONNA TRY SPANDEX, AND THEN WE'RE GONNA TRY BULLETS.
DRIP DRIP
SO MUCH RED...

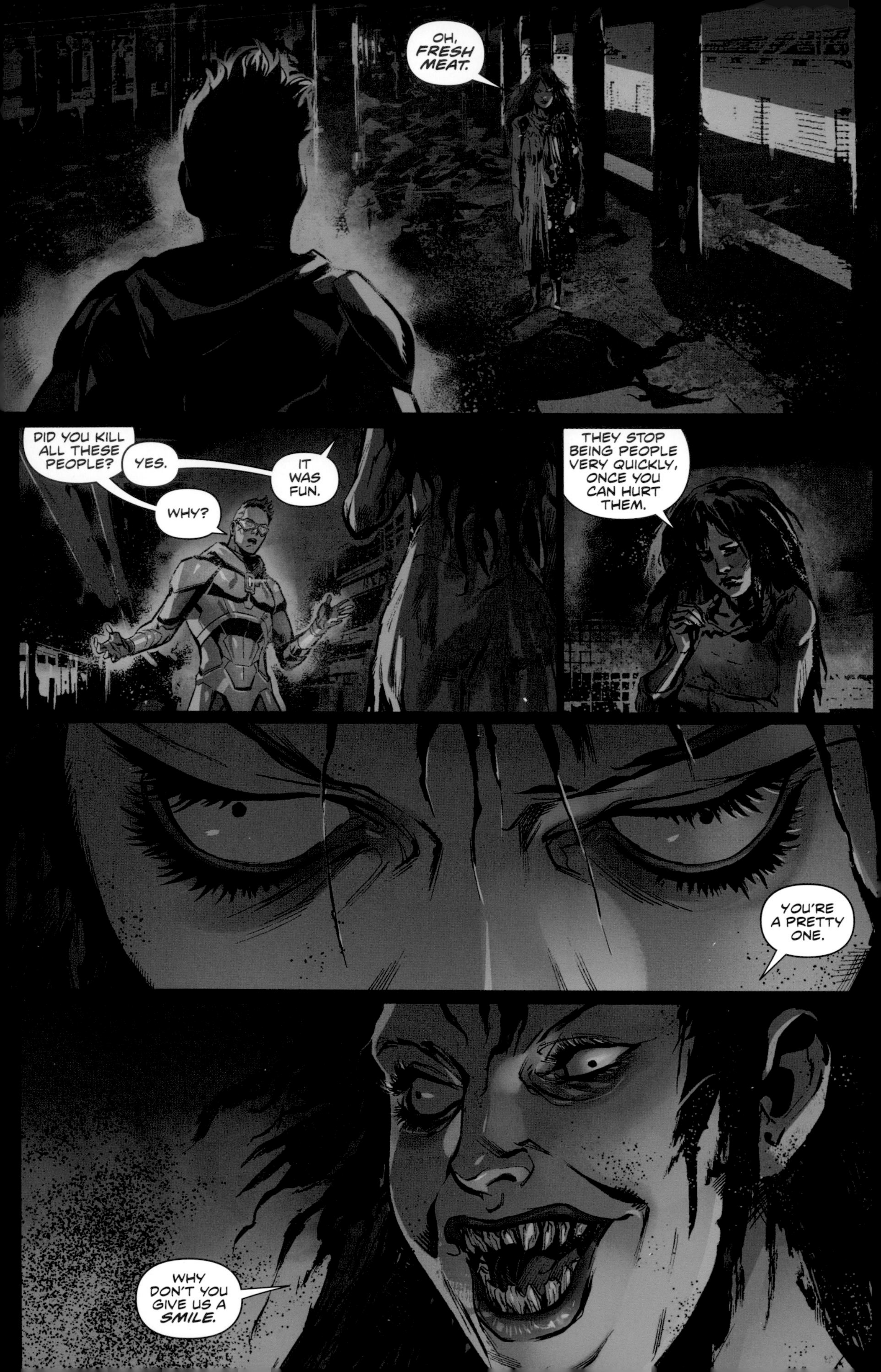
OH, FRESH MEAT.
DID YOU KILL ALL THESE PEOPLE?
YES.
IT WAS FUN.
WHY?
THEY STOP BEING PEOPLE VERY QUICKLY, ONCE YOU CAN HURT THEM.
YOU'RE A PRETTY ONE.
WHY DON'T YOU GIVE US A SMILE.

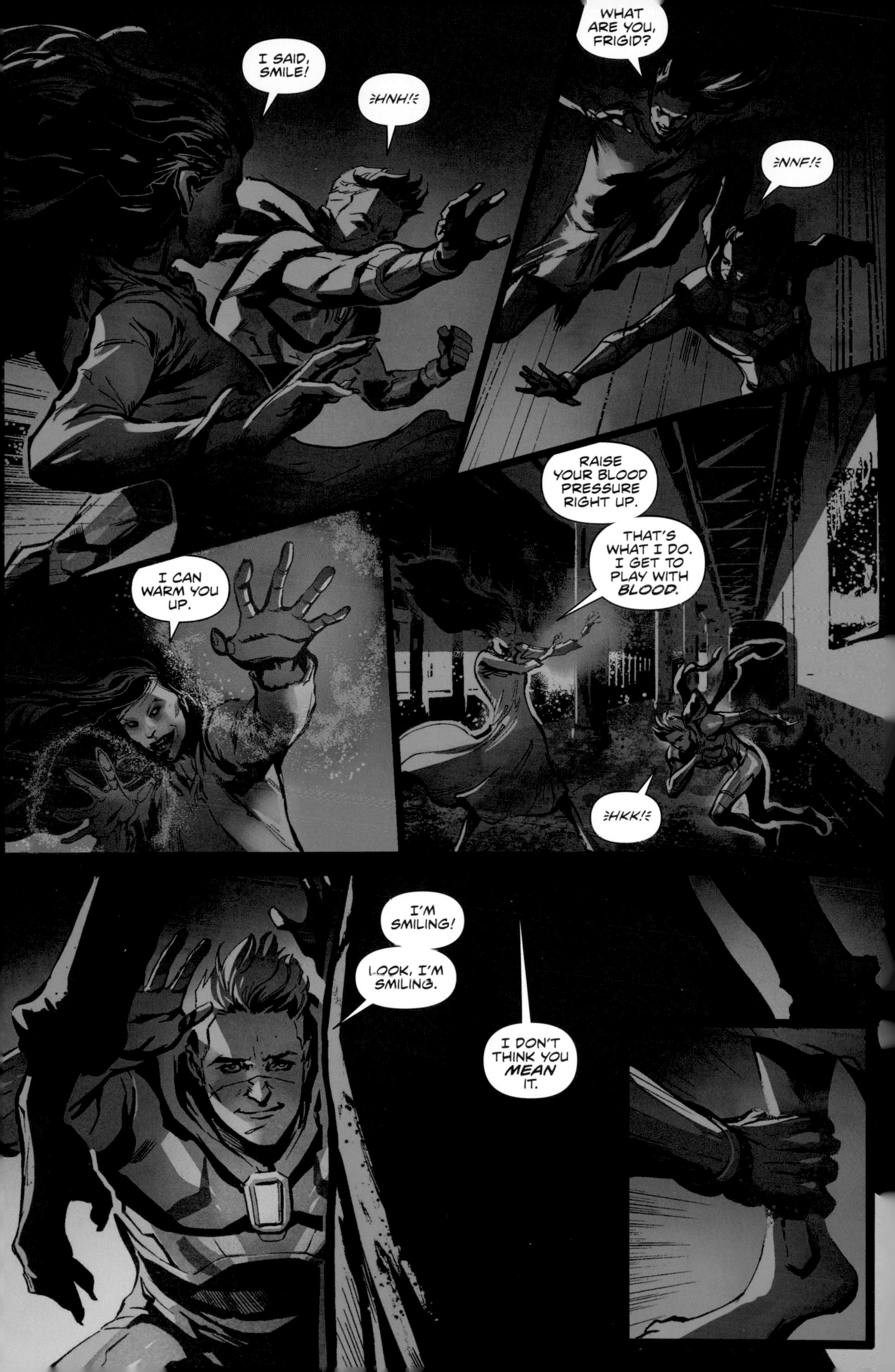
I SAID, SMILE!
HNH!
WHAT ARE YOU, FRIGID?
NNF!
RAISE YOUR BLOOD PRESSURE RIGHT UP.
I CAN WARM YOU UP.
THAT'S WHAT I DO. I GET TO PLAY WITH *BLOOD*.
HKK!
I'M SMILING!
LOOK, I'M SMILING.
I DON'T THINK YOU *MEAN* IT.

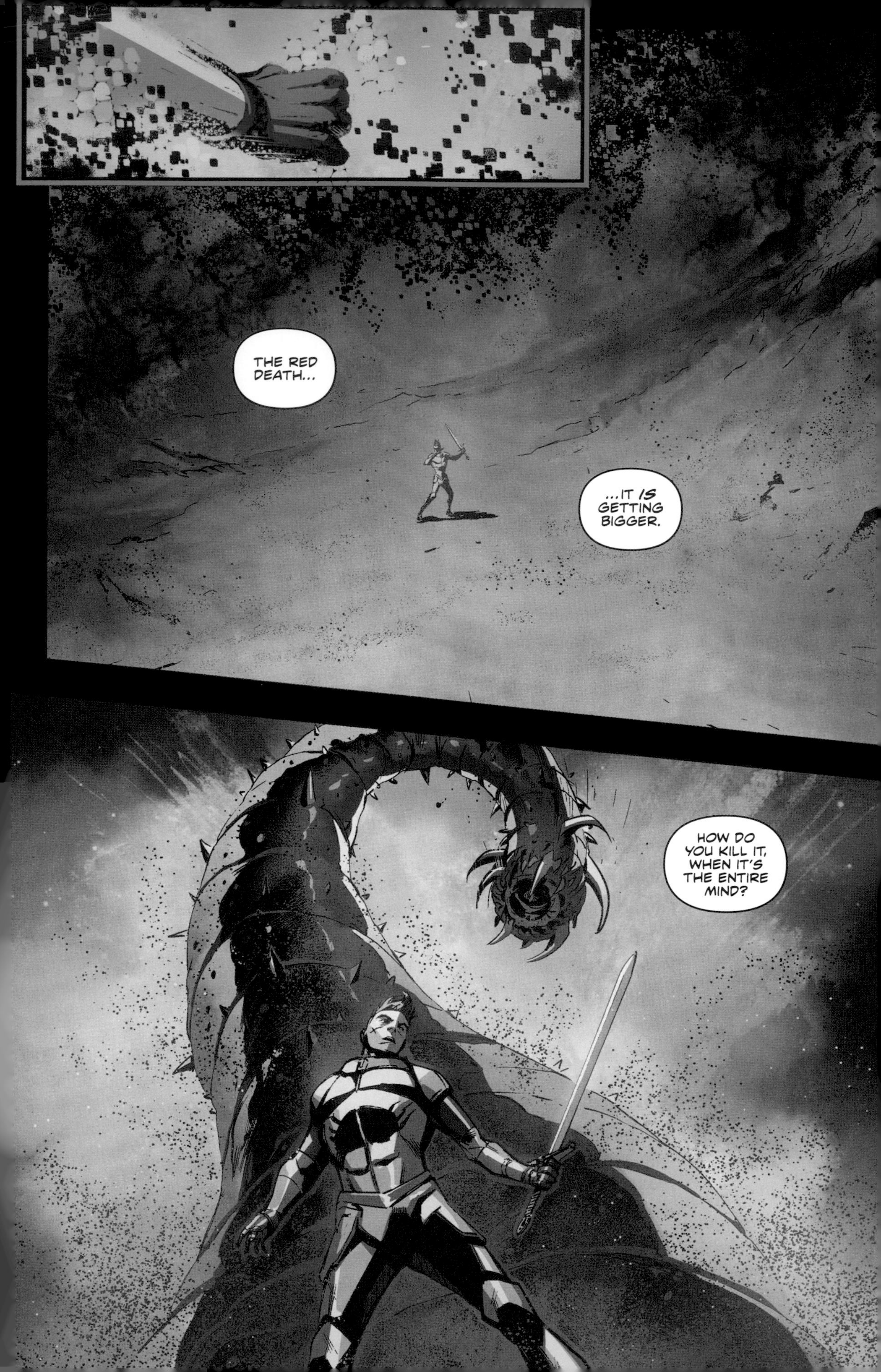
THE RED DEATH...
...IT IS GETTING BIGGER.
HOW DO YOU KILL IT, WHEN IT'S THE ENTIRE MIND?

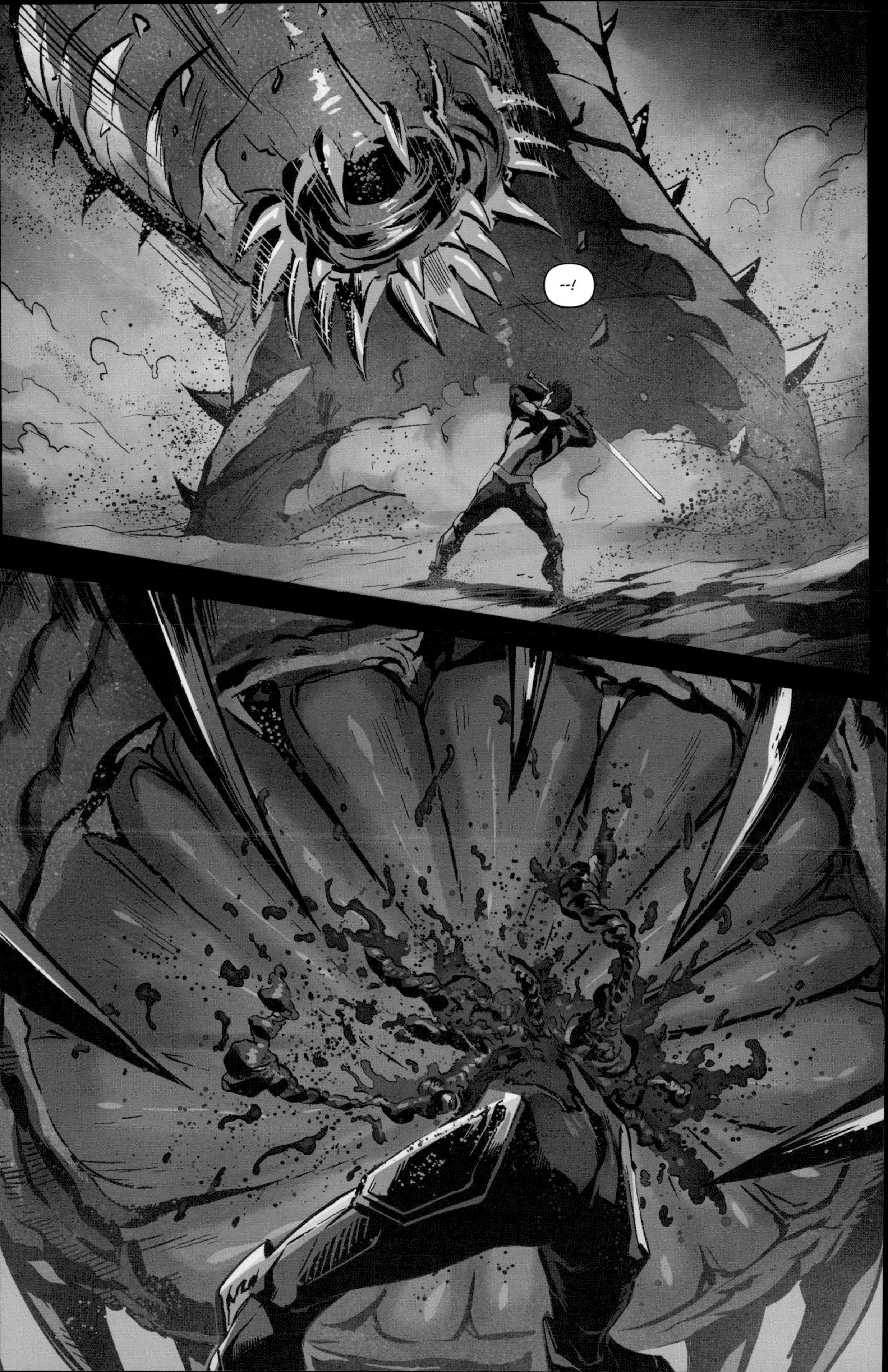
--!

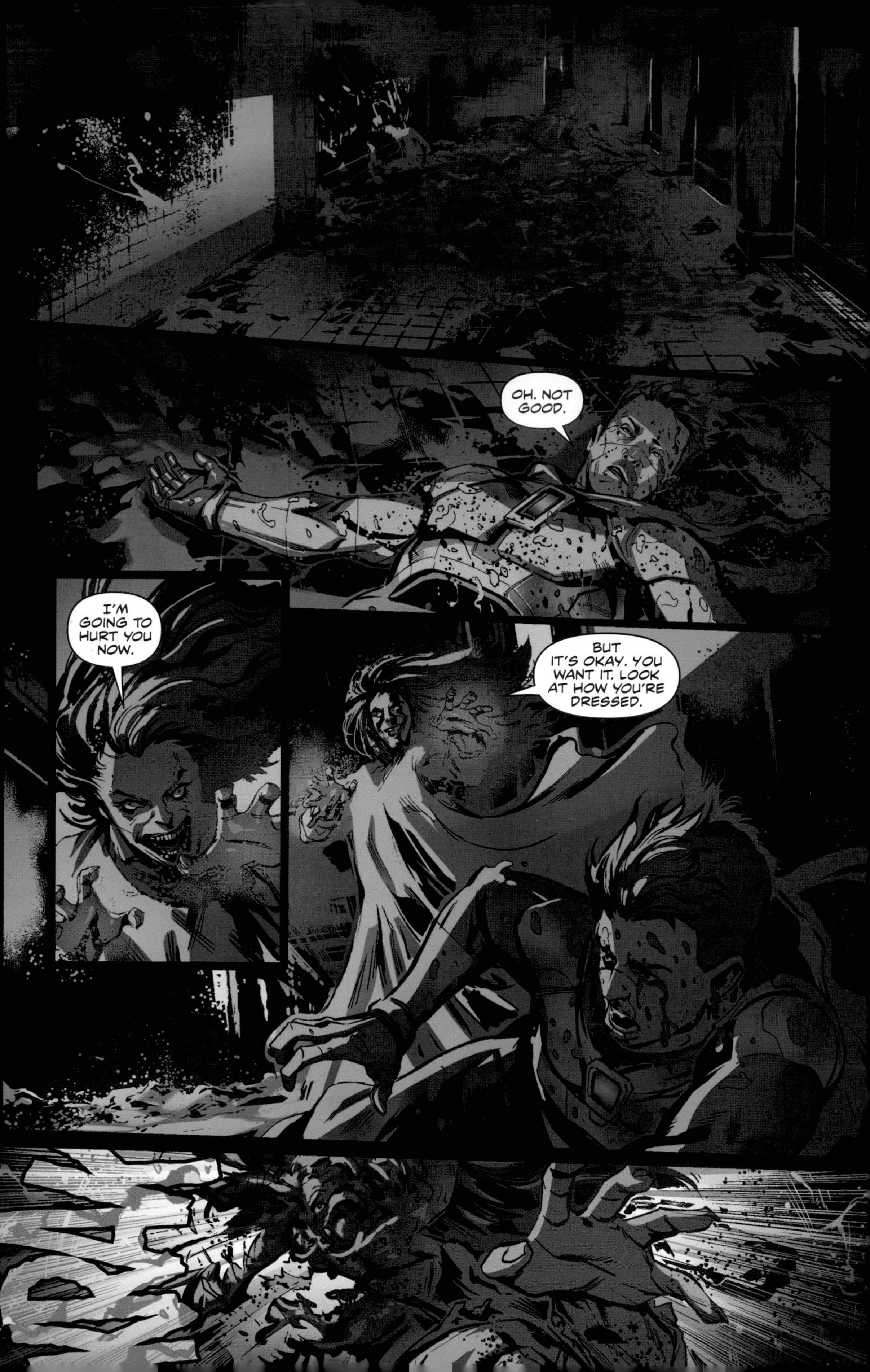
OH. NOT GOOD.
I'M GOING TO HURT YOU NOW.
BUT IT'S OKAY. YOU WANT IT. LOOK AT HOW YOU'RE DRESSED.

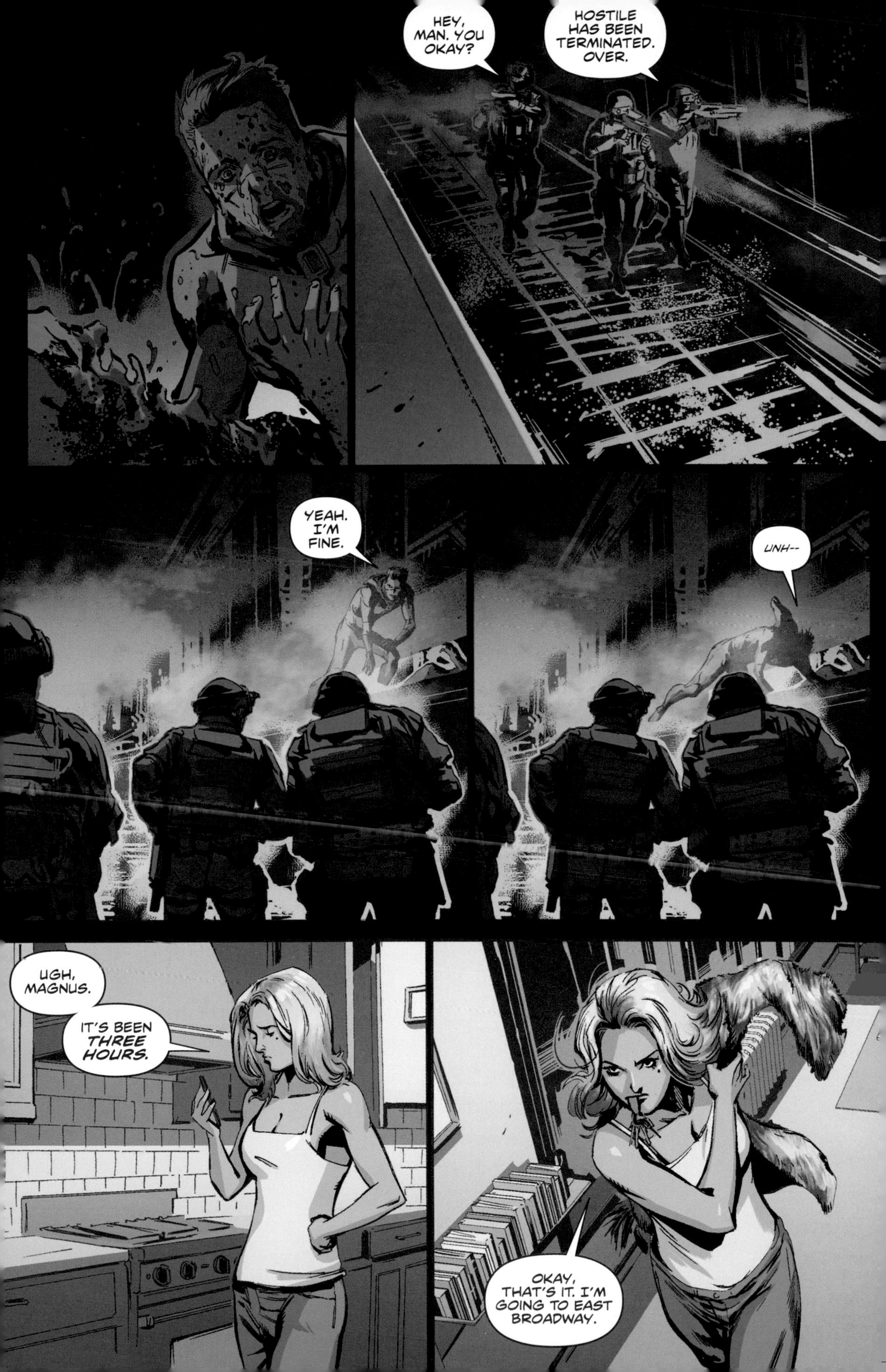
HEY, MAN. YOU OKAY?
HOSTILE HAS BEEN TERMINATED. OVER.
YEAH. I'M FINE.
UNH--
UGH, MAGNUS.
IT'S BEEN *THREE HOURS.*
OKAY, THAT'S IT. I'M GOING TO EAST BROADWAY.

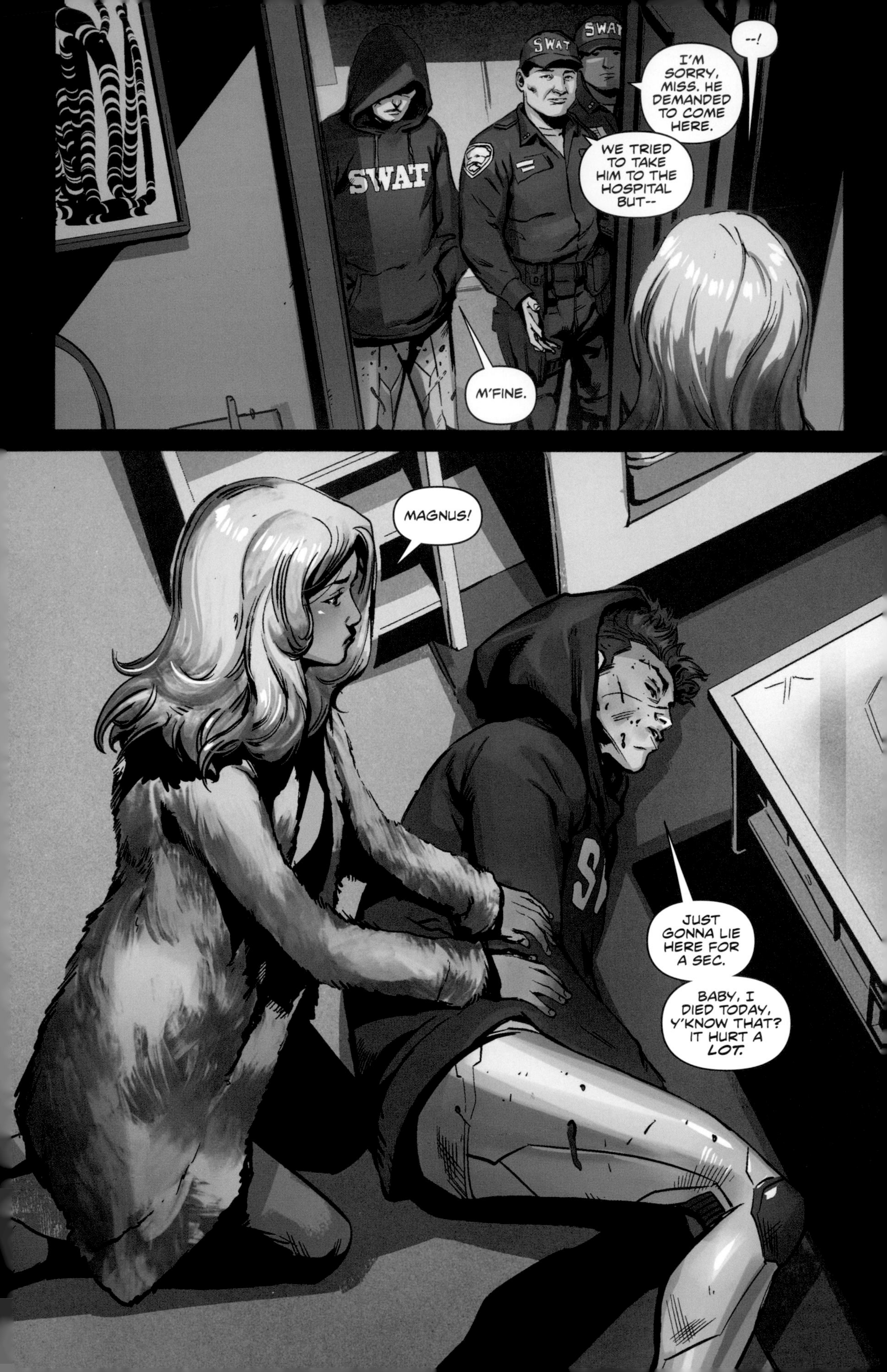
I'M SORRY, MISS. HE DEMANDED TO COME HERE.
WE TRIED TO TAKE HIM TO THE HOSPITAL BUT--
--!
M'FINE.
MAGNUS!
JUST GONNA LIE HERE FOR A SEC.
BABY, I DIED TODAY, Y'KNOW THAT? IT HURT A *LOT.*

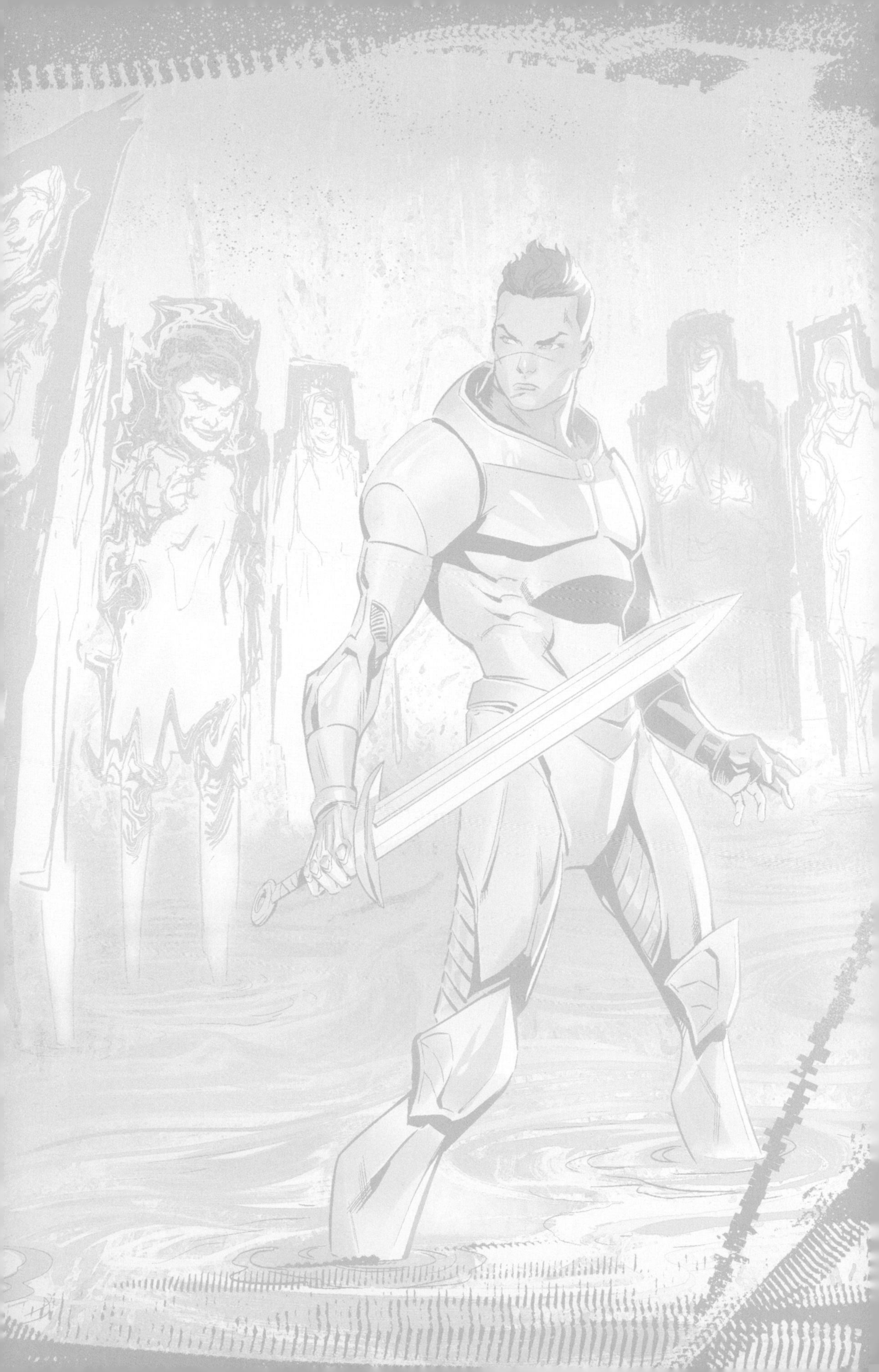

CHAPTER THREE

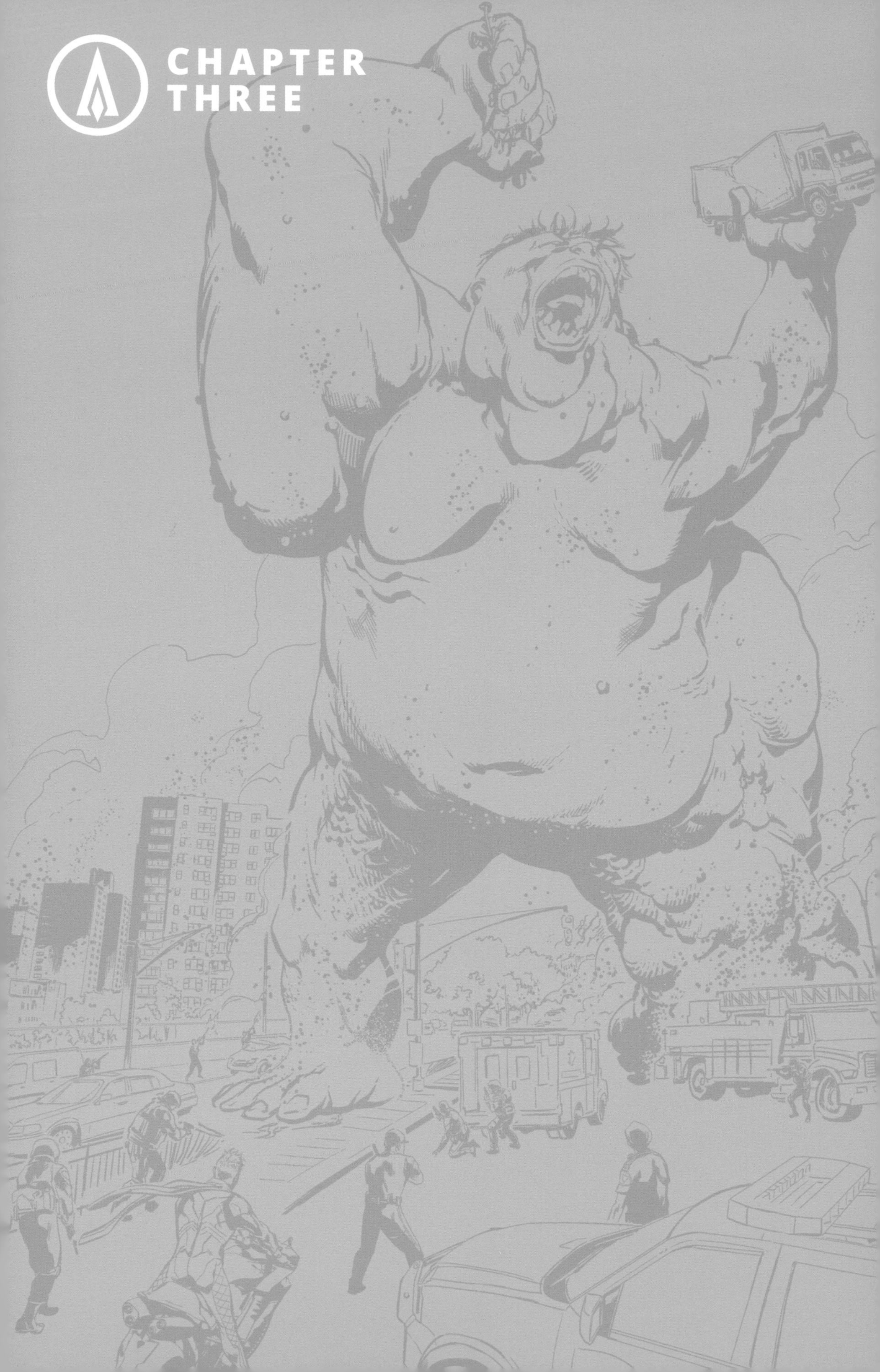

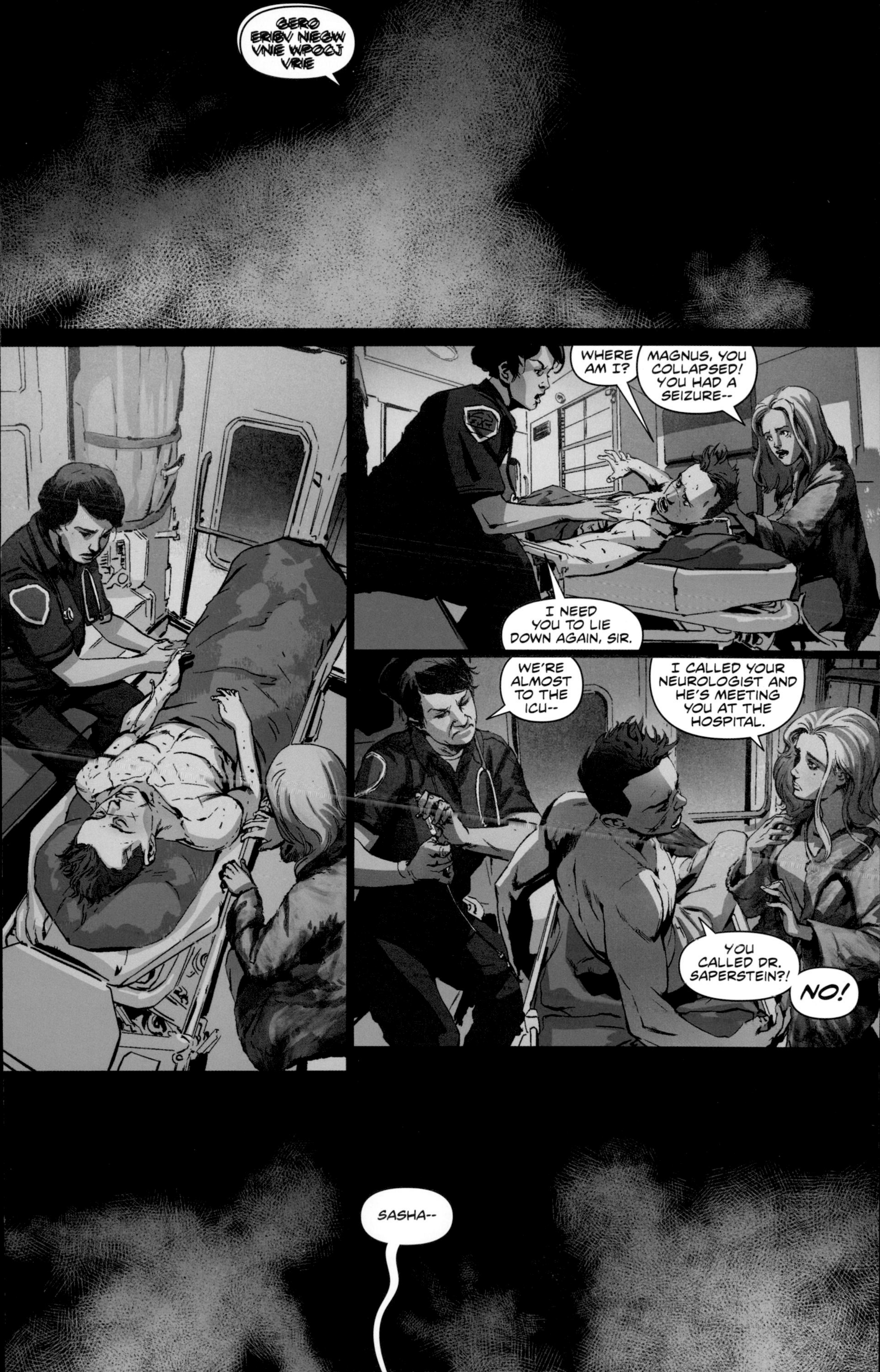
GERO ERIBV NIEGW VNIE WPOCJ VRIE
WHERE AM I?
MAGNUS, YOU COLLAPSED! YOU HAD A SEIZURE--
I NEED YOU TO LIE DOWN AGAIN, SIR.
WE'RE ALMOST TO THE ICU--
I CALLED YOUR NEUROLOGIST AND HE'S MEETING YOU AT THE HOSPITAL.
YOU CALLED DR. SAPERSTEIN?!
NO!
SASHA--

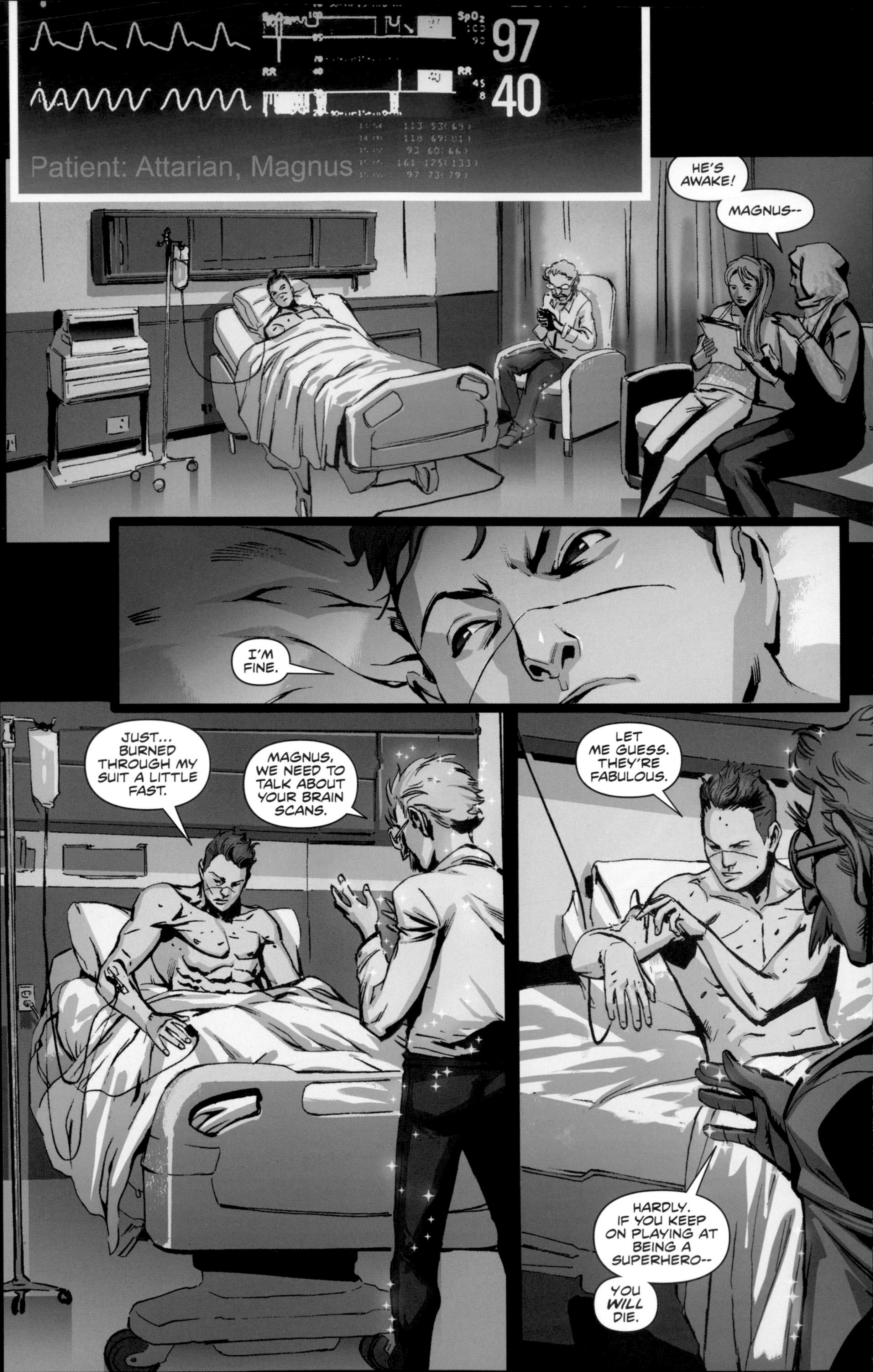

SpO2
97
RR
40
Patient: Attarian, Magnus
HE'S AWAKE!
MAGNUS--
I'M FINE.
JUST... BURNED THROUGH MY SUIT A LITTLE FAST.
MAGNUS, WE NEED TO TALK ABOUT YOUR BRAIN SCANS.
LET ME GUESS. THEY'RE FABULOUS.
HARDLY. IF YOU KEEP ON PLAYING AT BEING A SUPERHERO--
YOU *WILL* DIE.

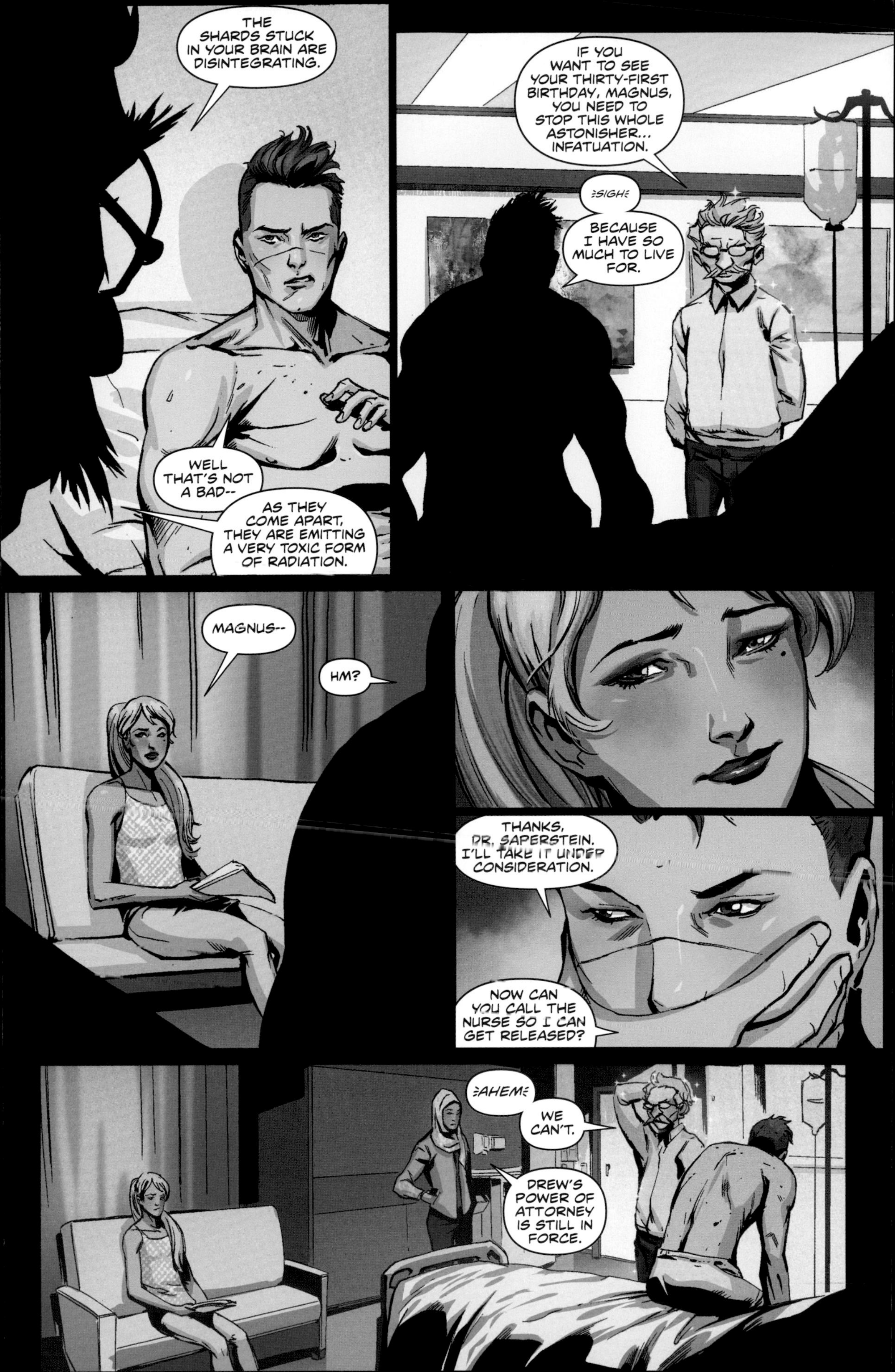
THE SHARDS STUCK IN YOUR BRAIN ARE DISINTEGRATING.
WELL THAT'S NOT A BAD--
AS THEY COME APART, THEY ARE EMITTING A VERY TOXIC FORM OF RADIATION.
IF YOU WANT TO SEE YOUR THIRTY-FIRST BIRTHDAY, MAGNUS, YOU NEED TO STOP THIS WHOLE ASTONISHER... INFATUATION.
SIGH
BECAUSE I HAVE SO MUCH TO LIVE FOR.
MAGNUS--
HM?
THANKS, DR. SAPERSTEIN. I'LL TAKE IT UNDER CONSIDERATION.
NOW CAN YOU CALL THE NURSE SO I CAN GET RELEASED?
AHEM
WE CAN'T.
DREW'S POWER OF ATTORNEY IS STILL IN FORCE.

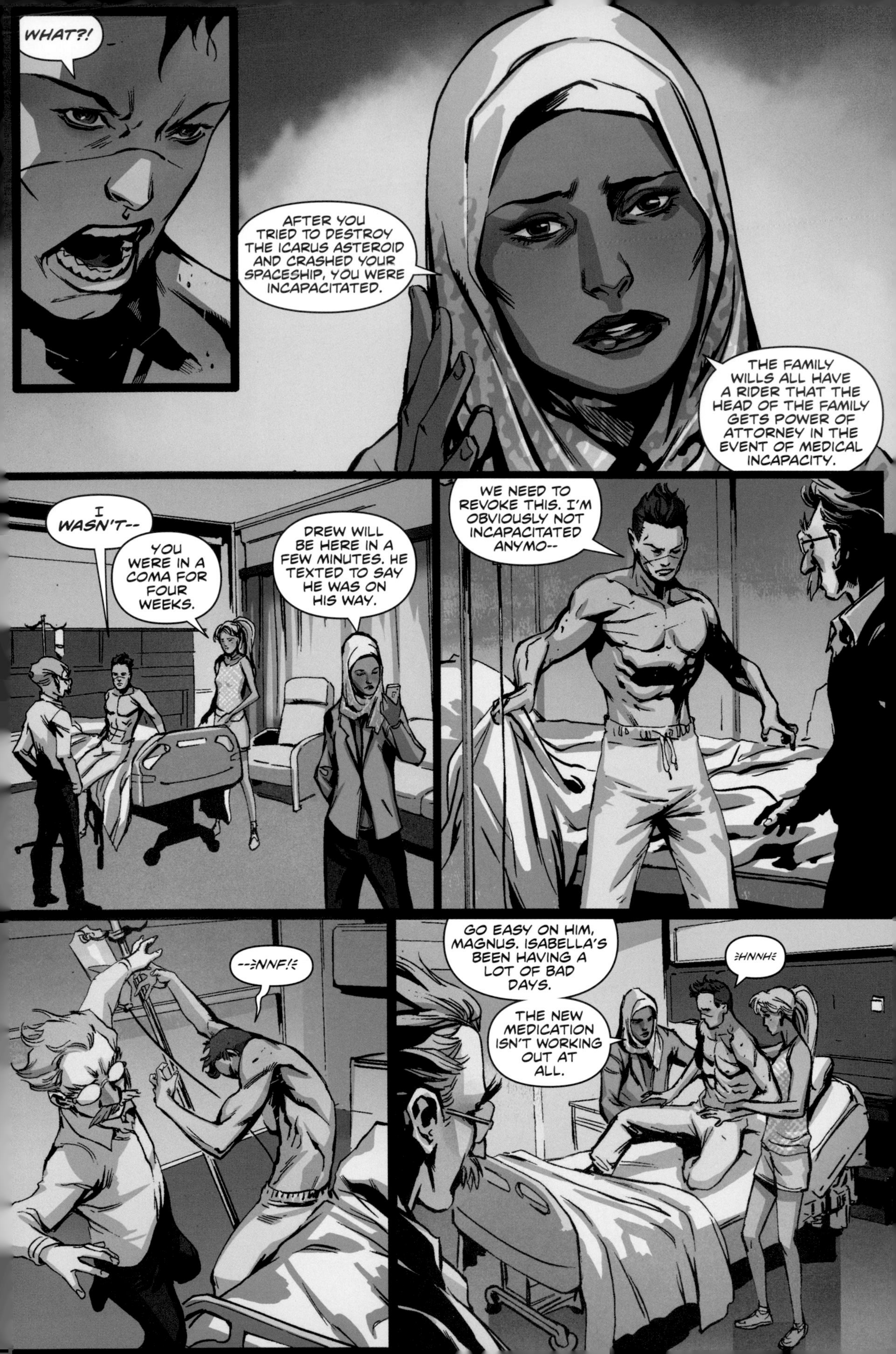
WHAT?!
AFTER YOU TRIED TO DESTROY THE ICARUS ASTEROID AND CRASHED YOUR SPACESHIP, YOU WERE INCAPACITATED.
THE FAMILY WILLS ALL HAVE A RIDER THAT THE HEAD OF THE FAMILY GETS POWER OF ATTORNEY IN THE EVENT OF MEDICAL INCAPACITY.
I WASN'T--
YOU WERE IN A COMA FOR FOUR WEEKS.
DREW WILL BE HERE IN A FEW MINUTES. HE TEXTED TO SAY HE WAS ON HIS WAY.
WE NEED TO REVOKE THIS. I'M OBVIOUSLY NOT INCAPACITATED ANYMO--
--NNF!
GO EASY ON HIM, MAGNUS. ISABELLA'S BEEN HAVING A LOT OF BAD DAYS.
THE NEW MEDICATION ISN'T WORKING OUT AT ALL.
HNNH

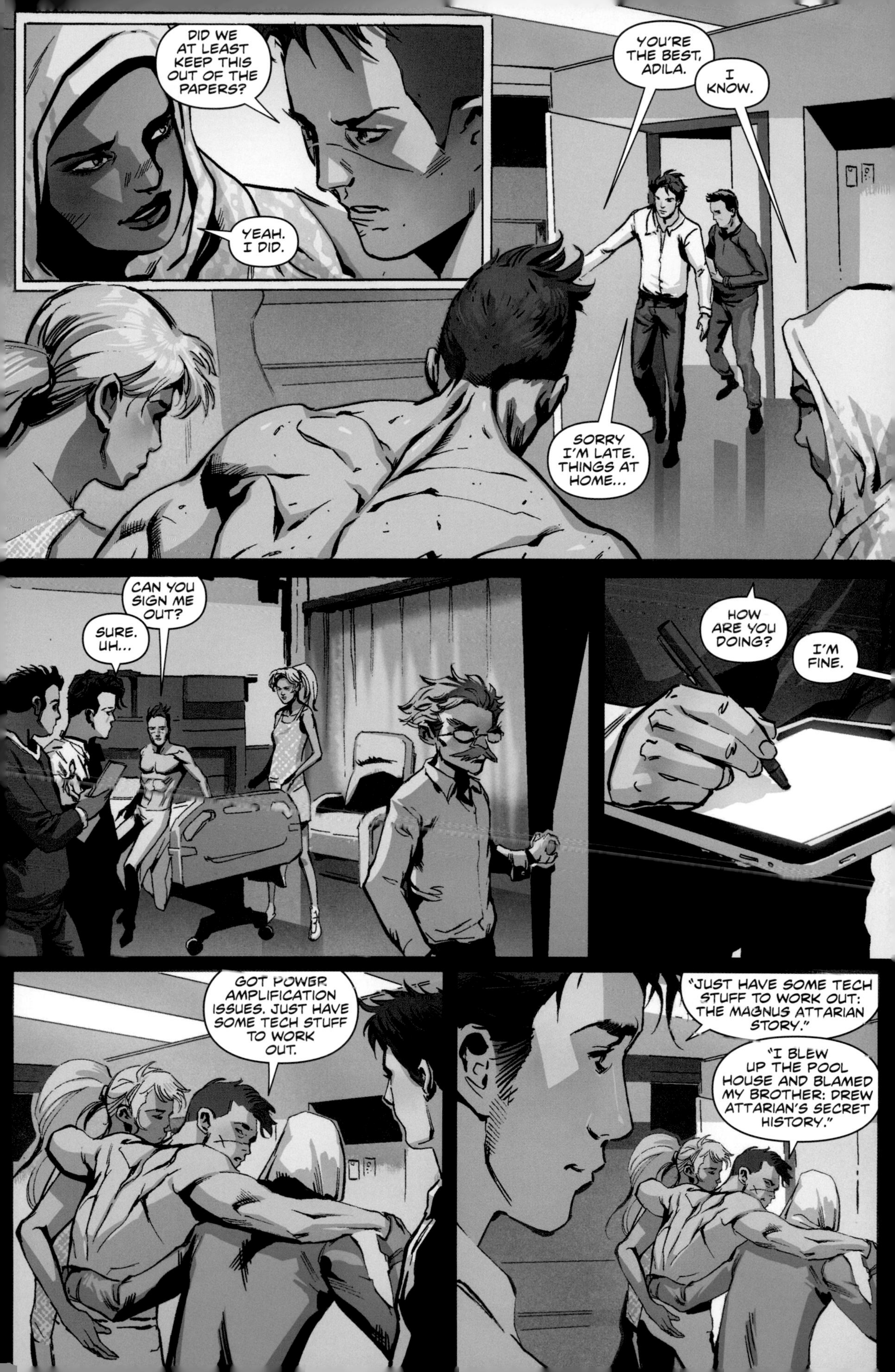

DID WE AT LEAST KEEP THIS OUT OF THE PAPERS?
YEAH. I DID.
YOU'RE THE BEST, ADILA.
I KNOW.
SORRY I'M LATE. THINGS AT HOME...
CAN YOU SIGN ME OUT?
SURE. UH...
HOW ARE YOU DOING?
I'M FINE.
GOT POWER AMPLIFICATION ISSUES. JUST HAVE SOME TECH STUFF TO WORK OUT.
"JUST HAVE SOME TECH STUFF TO WORK OUT: THE MAGNUS ATTARIAN STORY."
"I BLEW UP THE POOL HOUSE AND BLAMED MY BROTHER: DREW ATTARIAN'S SECRET HISTORY."

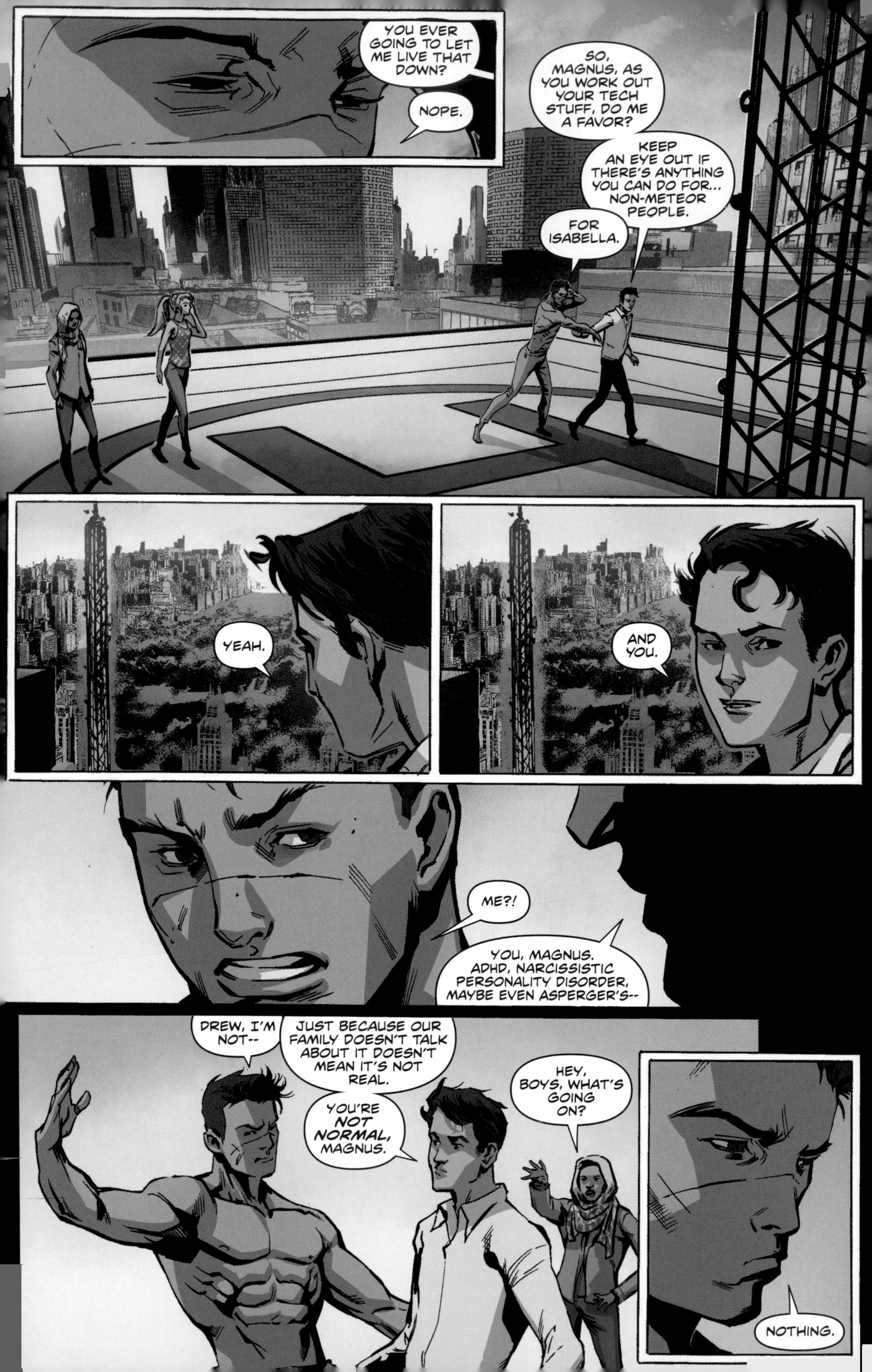
YOU EVER GOING TO LET ME LIVE THAT DOWN?
NOPE.
SO, MAGNUS, AS YOU WORK OUT YOUR TECH STUFF, DO ME A FAVOR?
KEEP AN EYE OUT IF THERE'S ANYTHING YOU CAN DO FOR... NON-METEOR PEOPLE.
FOR ISABELLA.
YEAH.
AND YOU.
ME?!
YOU, MAGNUS. ADHD, NARCISSISTIC PERSONALITY DISORDER, MAYBE EVEN ASPERGER'S--
DREW, I'M NOT--
JUST BECAUSE OUR FAMILY DOESN'T TALK ABOUT IT DOESN'T MEAN IT'S NOT REAL.
YOU'RE NOT NORMAL, MAGNUS.
HEY, BOYS, WHAT'S GOING ON?
NOTHING.

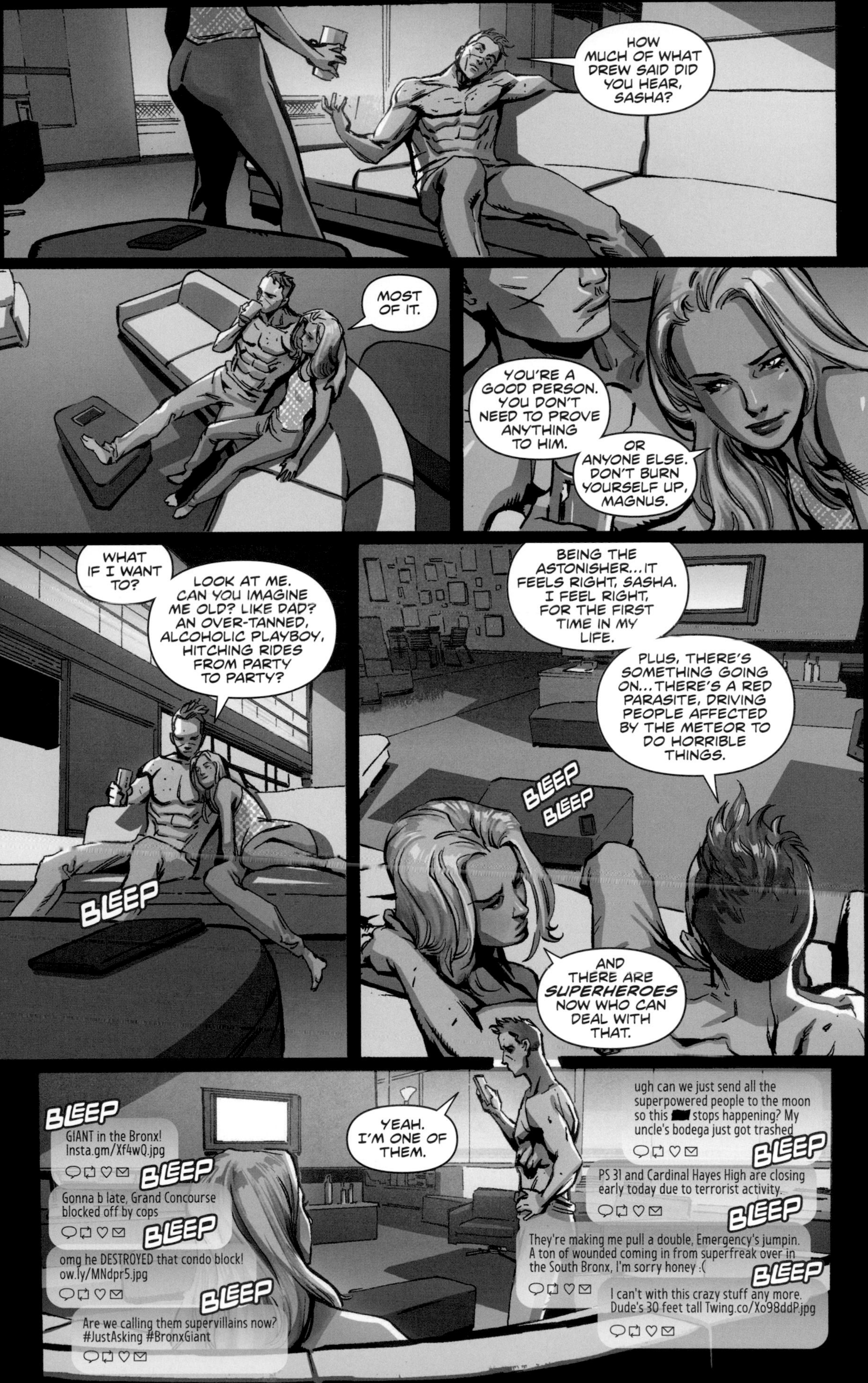
HOW MUCH OF WHAT DREW SAID DID YOU HEAR, SASHA?
MOST OF IT.
YOU'RE A GOOD PERSON. YOU DON'T NEED TO PROVE ANYTHING TO HIM.
OR ANYONE ELSE. DON'T BURN YOURSELF UP, MAGNUS.
WHAT IF I WANT TO?
LOOK AT ME. CAN YOU IMAGINE ME OLD? LIKE DAD? AN OVER-TANNED, ALCOHOLIC PLAYBOY, HITCHING RIDES FROM PARTY TO PARTY?
BLEEP
BEING THE ASTONISHER... IT FEELS RIGHT, SASHA. I FEEL RIGHT, FOR THE FIRST TIME IN MY LIFE.
PLUS, THERE'S SOMETHING GOING ON... THERE'S A RED PARASITE, DRIVING PEOPLE AFFECTED BY THE METEOR TO DO HORRIBLE THINGS.
BLEEP BLEEP
AND THERE ARE SUPERHEROES NOW WHO CAN DEAL WITH THAT.
BLEEP
GIANT in the Bronx! Insta.gm/Xf4wQ.jpg
BLEEP
Gonna b late, Grand Concourse blocked off by cops
BLEEP
omg he DESTROYED that condo block! ow.ly/MNdpr5.jpg
BLEEP
Are we calling them supervillains now? #JustAsking #BronxGiant
YEAH. I'M ONE OF THEM.
ugh can we just send all the superpowered people to the moon so this [redacted] stops happening? My uncle's bodega just got trashed
BLEEP
PS 31 and Cardinal Hayes High are closing early today due to terrorist activity.
BLEEP
They're making me pull a double, Emergency's jumpin. A ton of wounded coming in from superfreak over in the South Bronx, I'm sorry honey :(
BLEEP
I can't with this crazy stuff any more. Dude's 30 feet tall Twing.co/Xo98ddP.jpg

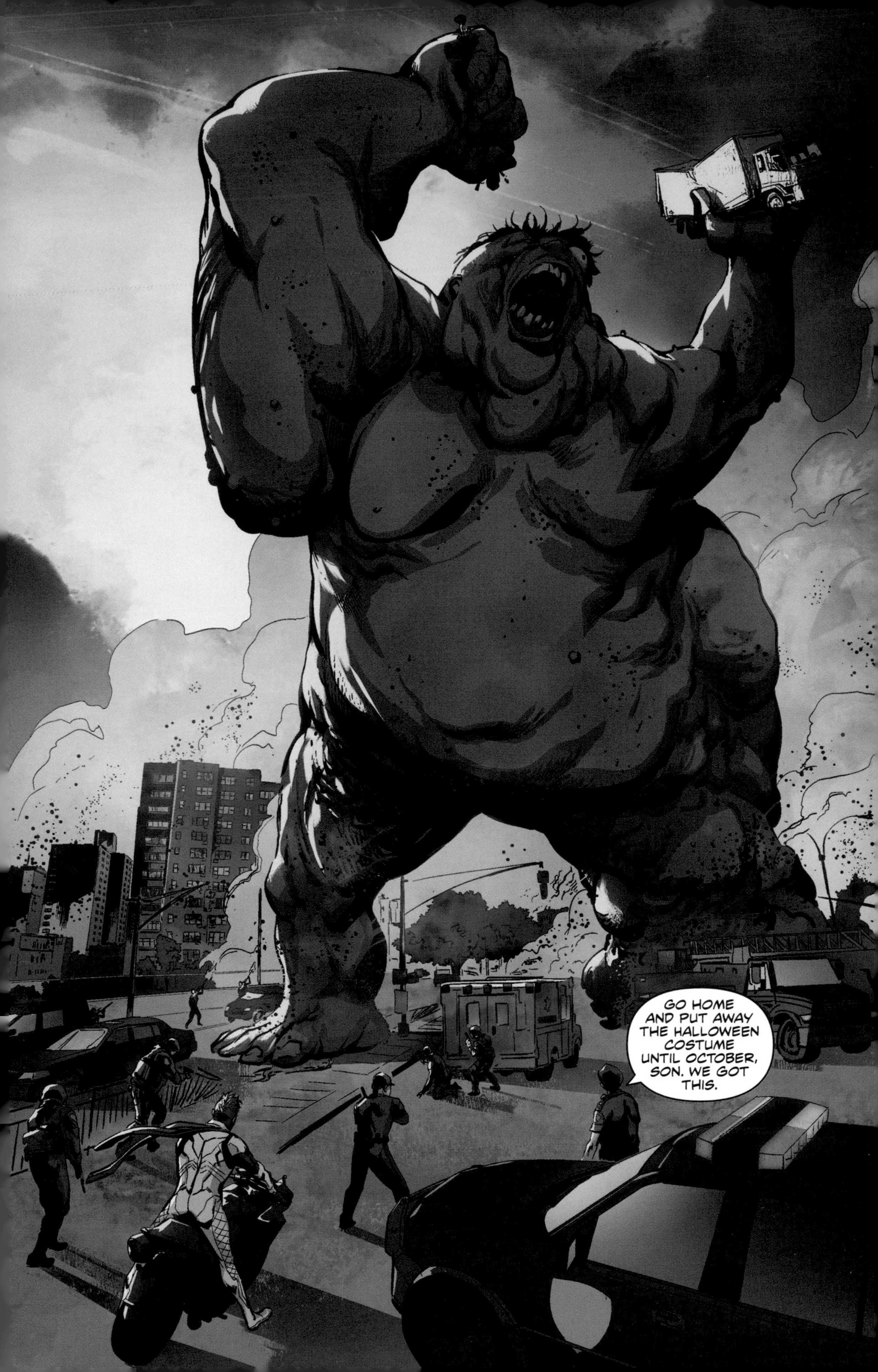
GO HOME AND PUT AWAY THE HALLOWEEN COSTUME UNTIL OCTOBER, SON. WE GOT THIS.

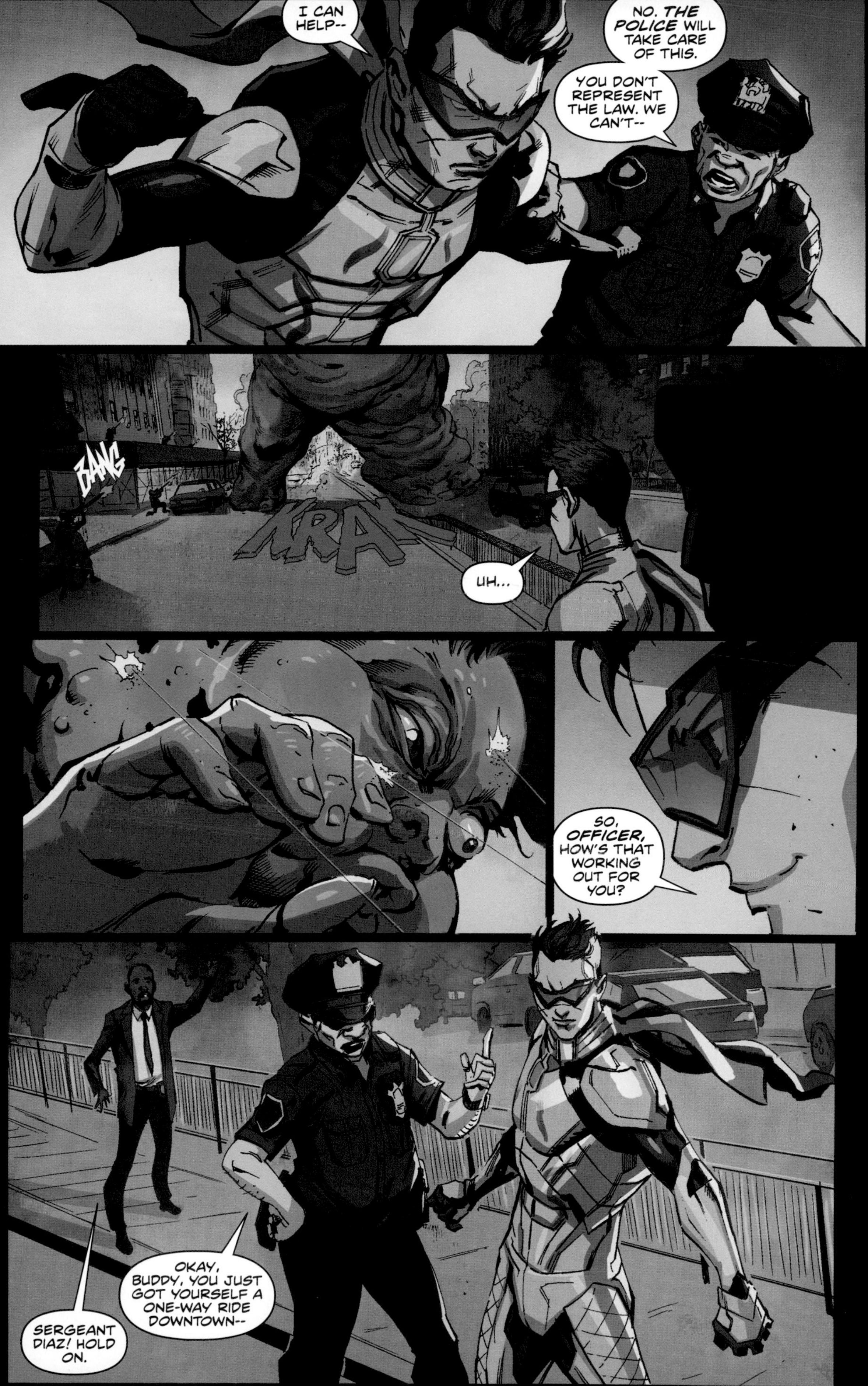
I CAN HELP--
NO. THE POLICE WILL TAKE CARE OF THIS.
YOU DON'T REPRESENT THE LAW. WE CAN'T--
BANG
KRA
UH...
SO, OFFICER, HOW'S THAT WORKING OUT FOR YOU?
OKAY, BUDDY, YOU JUST GOT YOURSELF A ONE-WAY RIDE DOWNTOWN--
SERGEANT DIAZ! HOLD ON.

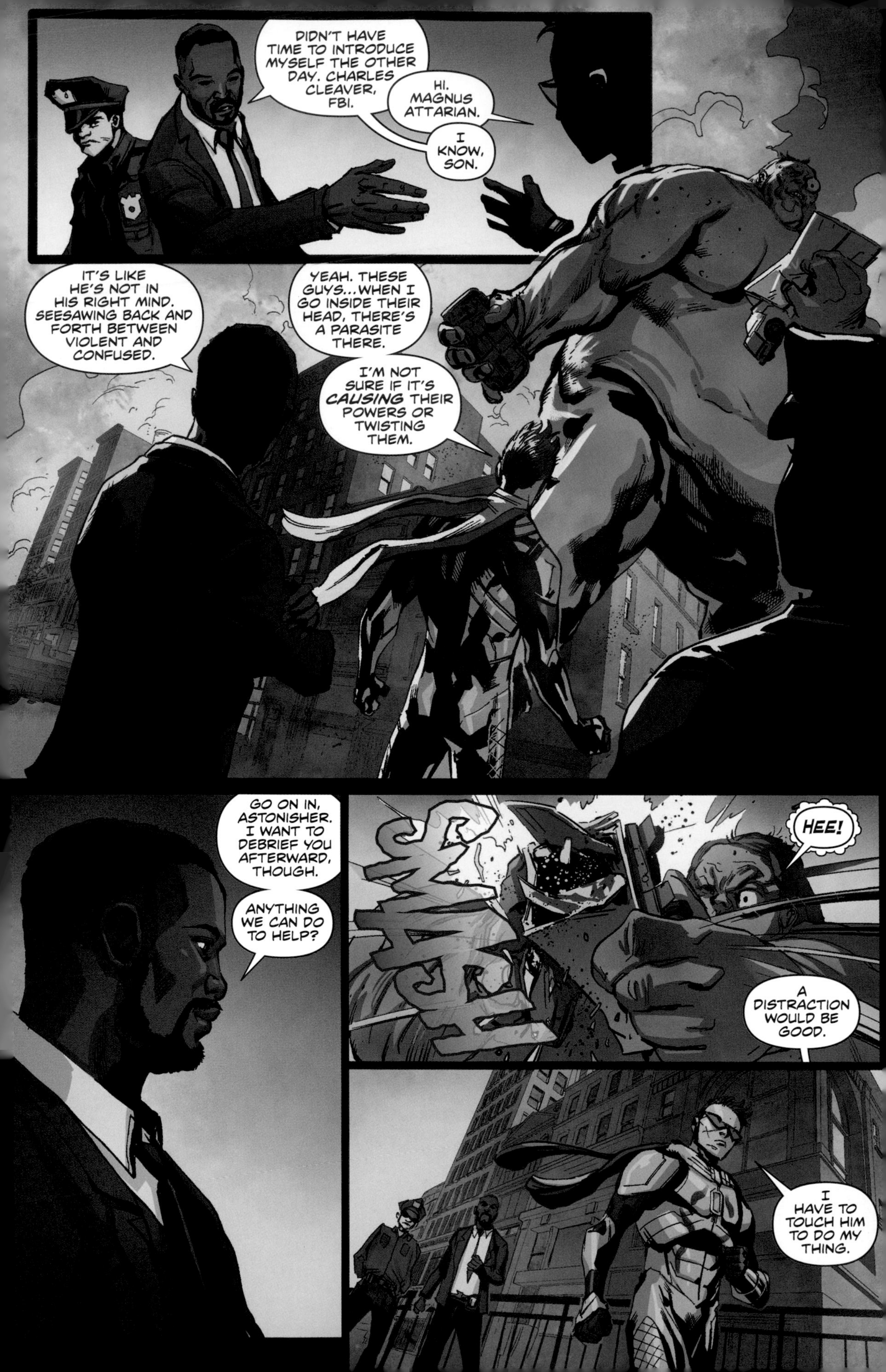
DIDN'T HAVE TIME TO INTRODUCE MYSELF THE OTHER DAY. CHARLES CLEAVER, FBI.
HI. MAGNUS ATTARIAN.
I KNOW, SON.
IT'S LIKE HE'S NOT IN HIS RIGHT MIND. SEESAWING BACK AND FORTH BETWEEN VIOLENT AND CONFUSED.
YEAH. THESE GUYS...WHEN I GO INSIDE THEIR HEAD, THERE'S A PARASITE THERE.
I'M NOT SURE IF IT'S CAUSING THEIR POWERS OR TWISTING THEM.
GO ON IN, ASTONISHER. I WANT TO DEBRIEF YOU AFTERWARD, THOUGH.
ANYTHING WE CAN DO TO HELP?
HEE!
A DISTRACTION WOULD BE GOOD.
I HAVE TO TOUCH HIM TO DO MY THING.

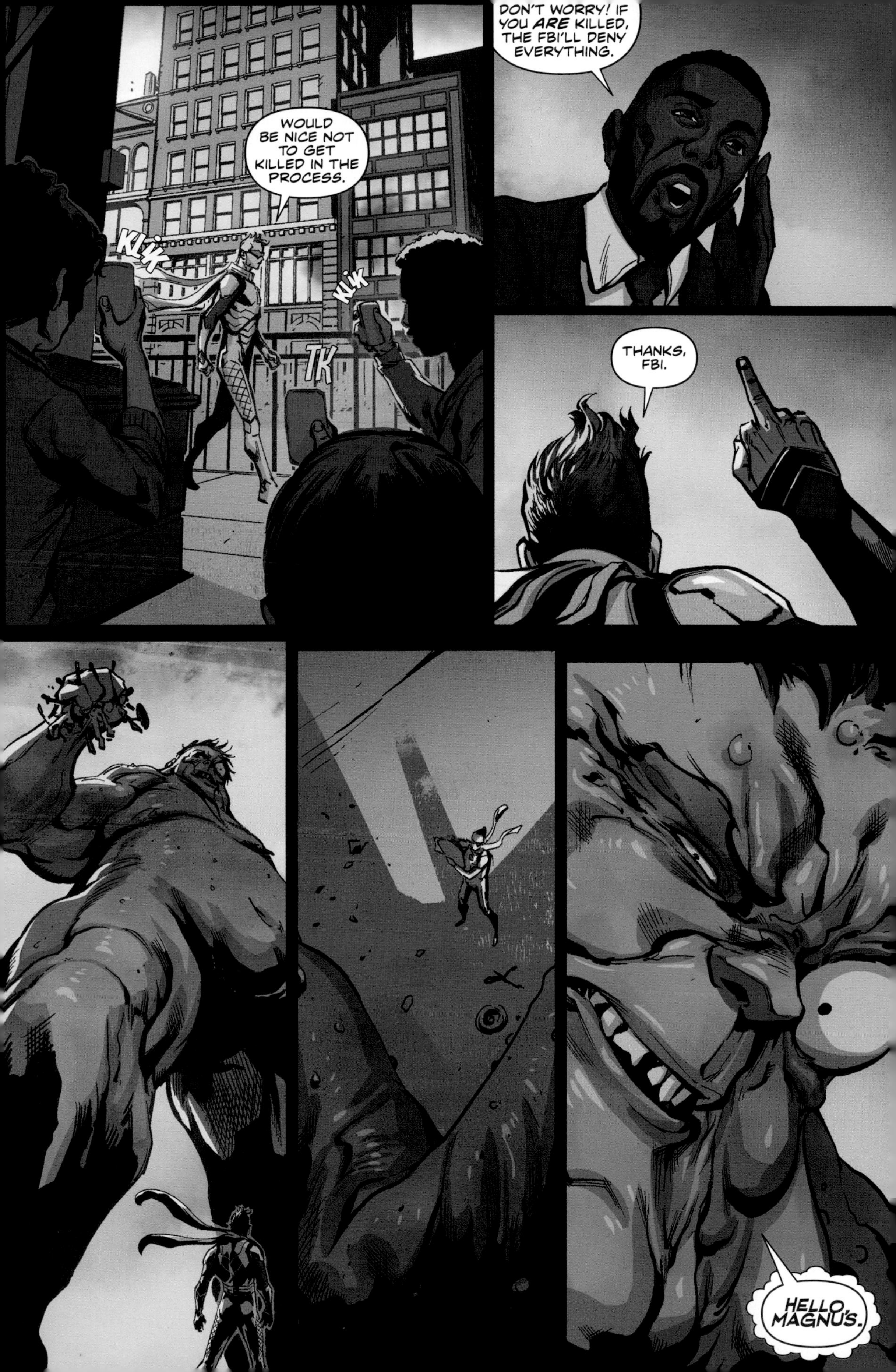

WOULD BE NICE NOT TO GET KILLED IN THE PROCESS.
KLIK
KLIK
TK
DON'T WORRY! IF YOU ARE KILLED, THE FBI'LL DENY EVERYTHING.
THANKS, FBI.
HELLO MAGNUS.

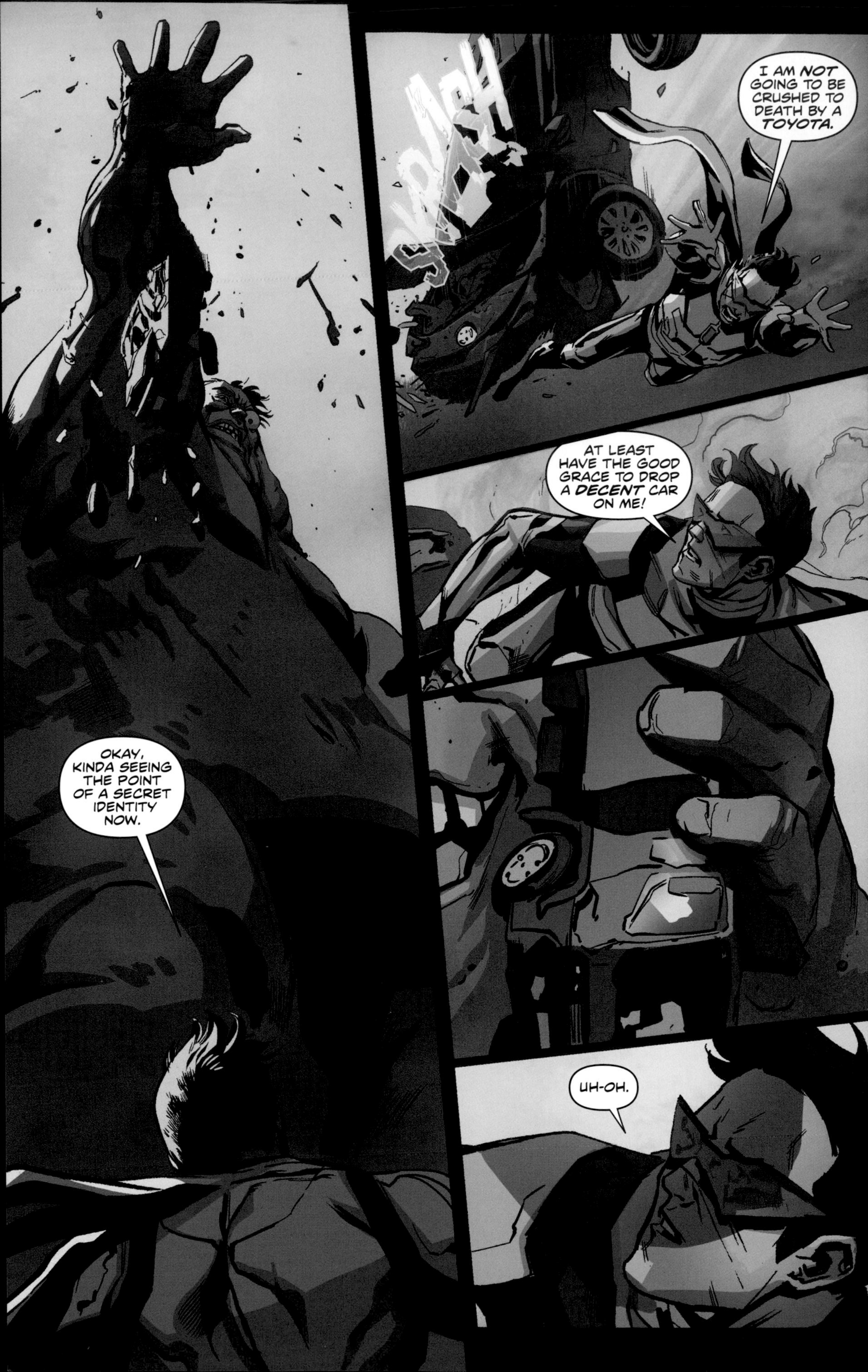
SPLASH
I AM NOT GOING TO BE CRUSHED TO DEATH BY A TOYOTA.
AT LEAST HAVE THE GOOD GRACE TO DROP A DECENT CAR ON ME!
OKAY, KINDA SEEING THE POINT OF A SECRET IDENTITY NOW.
UH-OH.

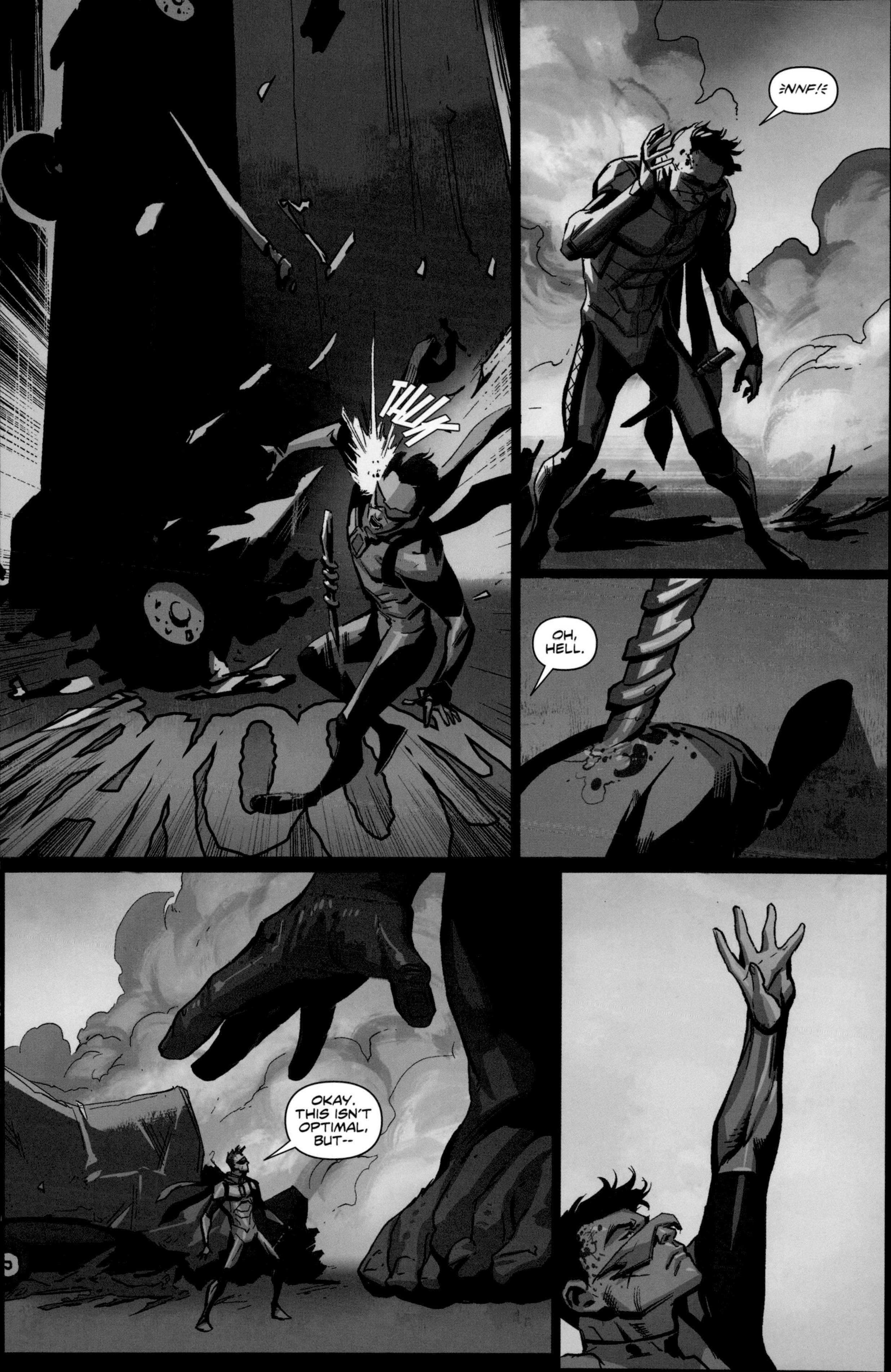
THUK
=NNF!=
OH, HELL.
OKAY. THIS ISN'T OPTIMAL, BUT--

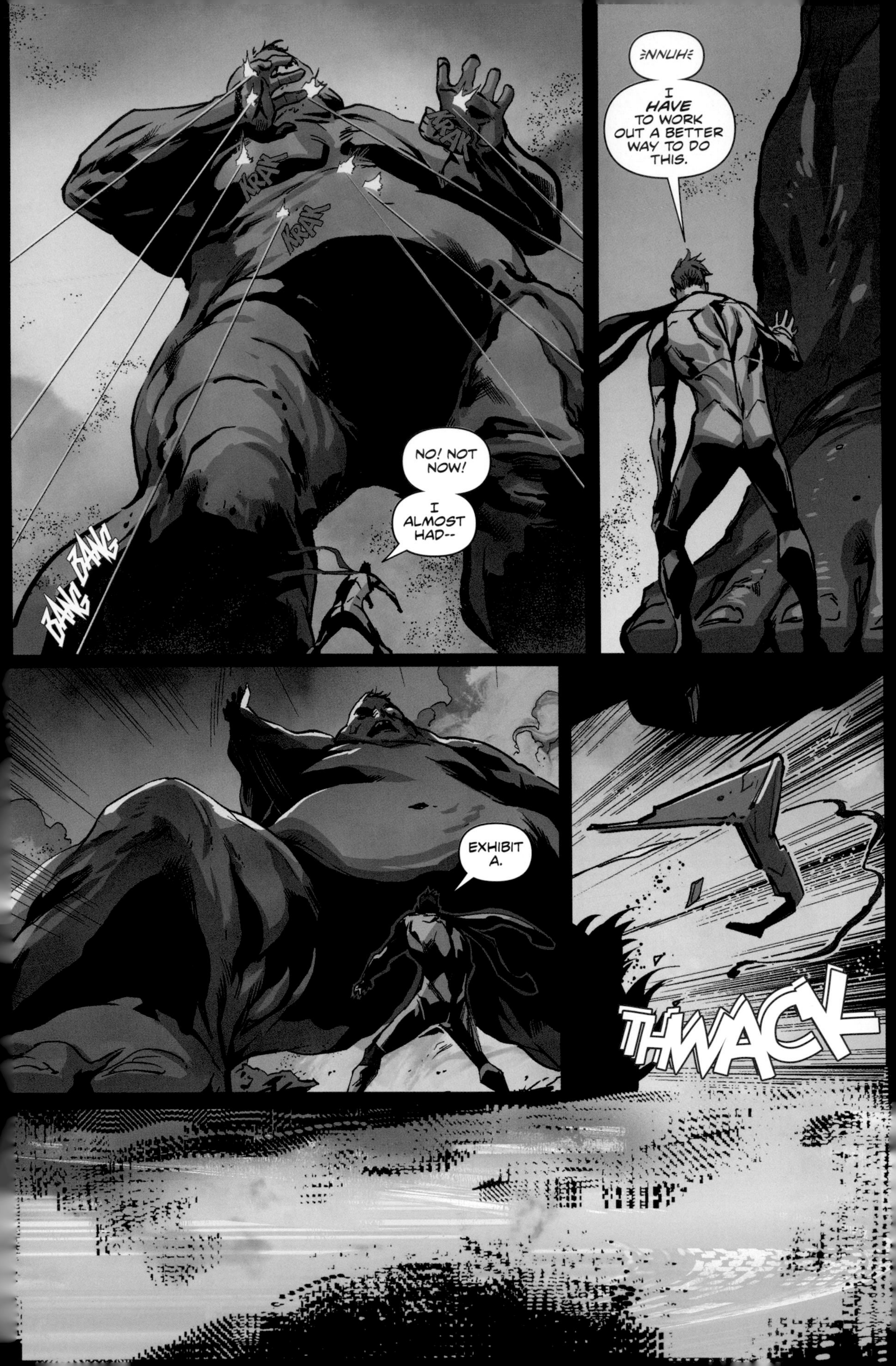
KRAK
KRAK
KRAK
KRAK
NO! NOT NOW!
I ALMOST HAD--
BANG BANG
NNUH
I HAVE TO WORK OUT A BETTER WAY TO DO THIS.
EXHIBIT A.
THWACK

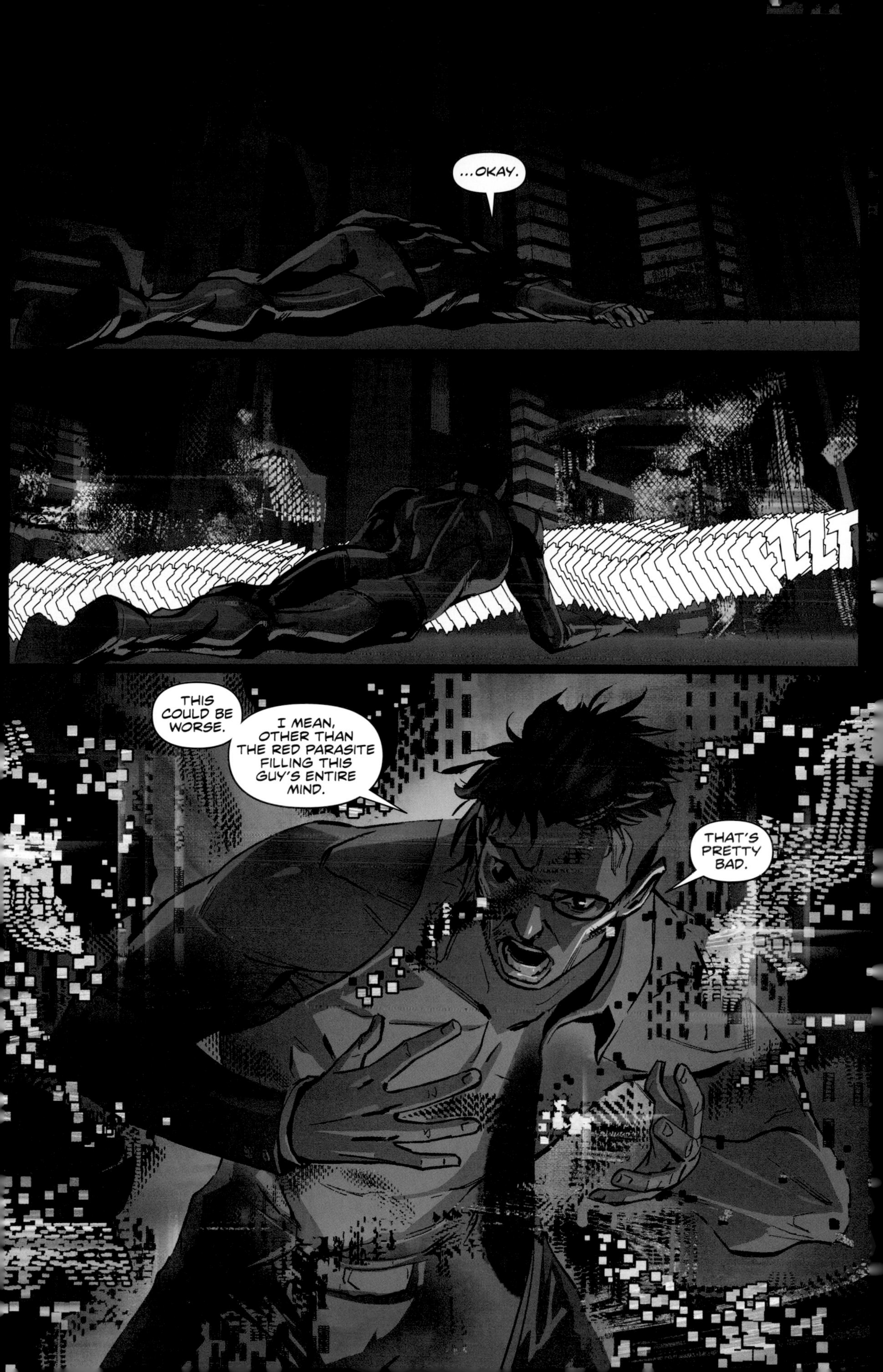
...OKAY.
FZZT
THIS COULD BE WORSE.
I MEAN, OTHER THAN THE RED PARASITE FILLING THIS GUY'S ENTIRE MIND.
THAT'S PRETTY BAD.

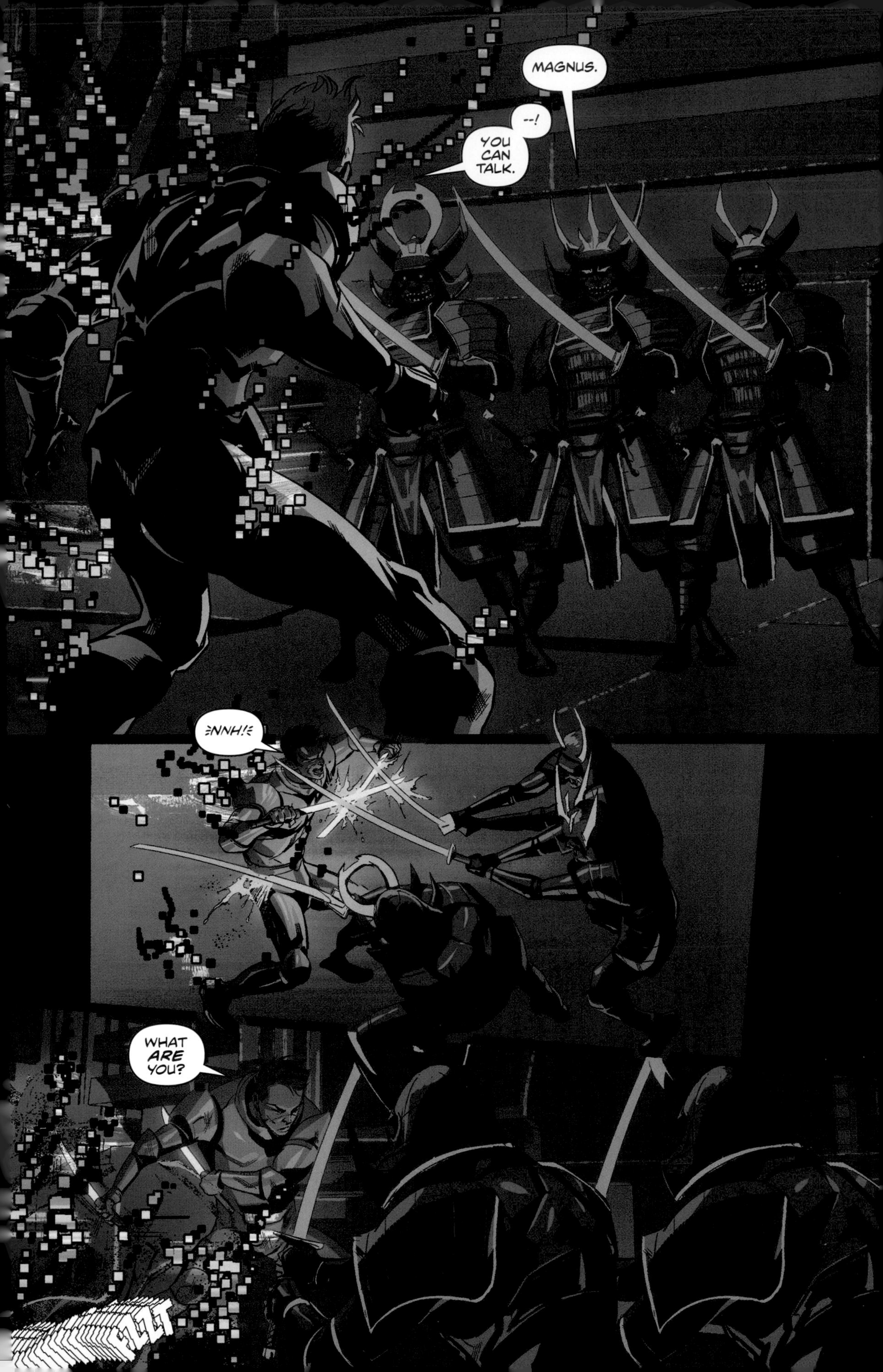
MAGNUS.
--!
YOU CAN TALK.
NNH!
WHAT ARE YOU?
FZZT

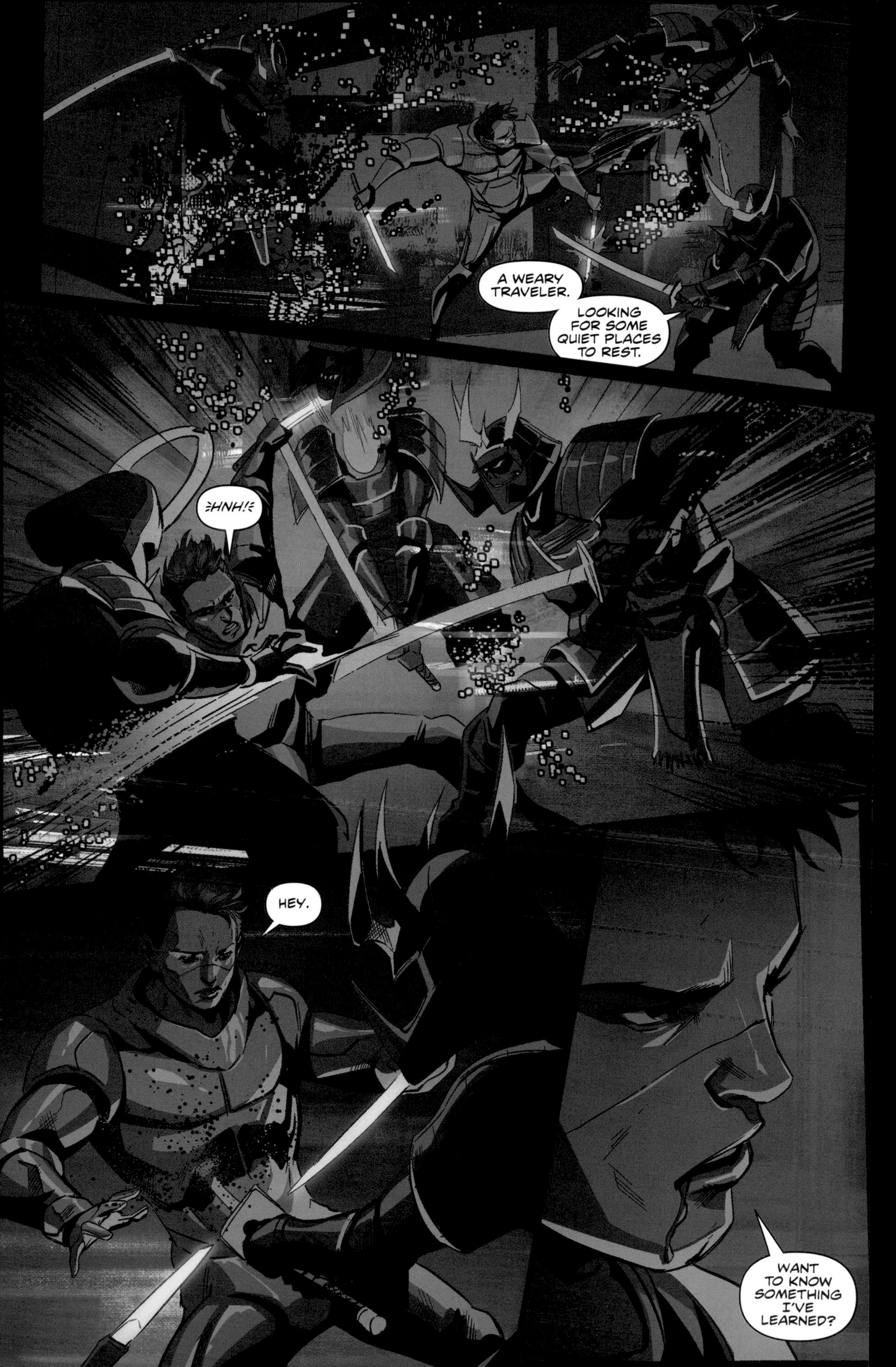
A WEARY TRAVELER.
LOOKING FOR SOME QUIET PLACES TO REST.
HNH!
HEY.
WANT TO KNOW SOMETHING I'VE LEARNED?

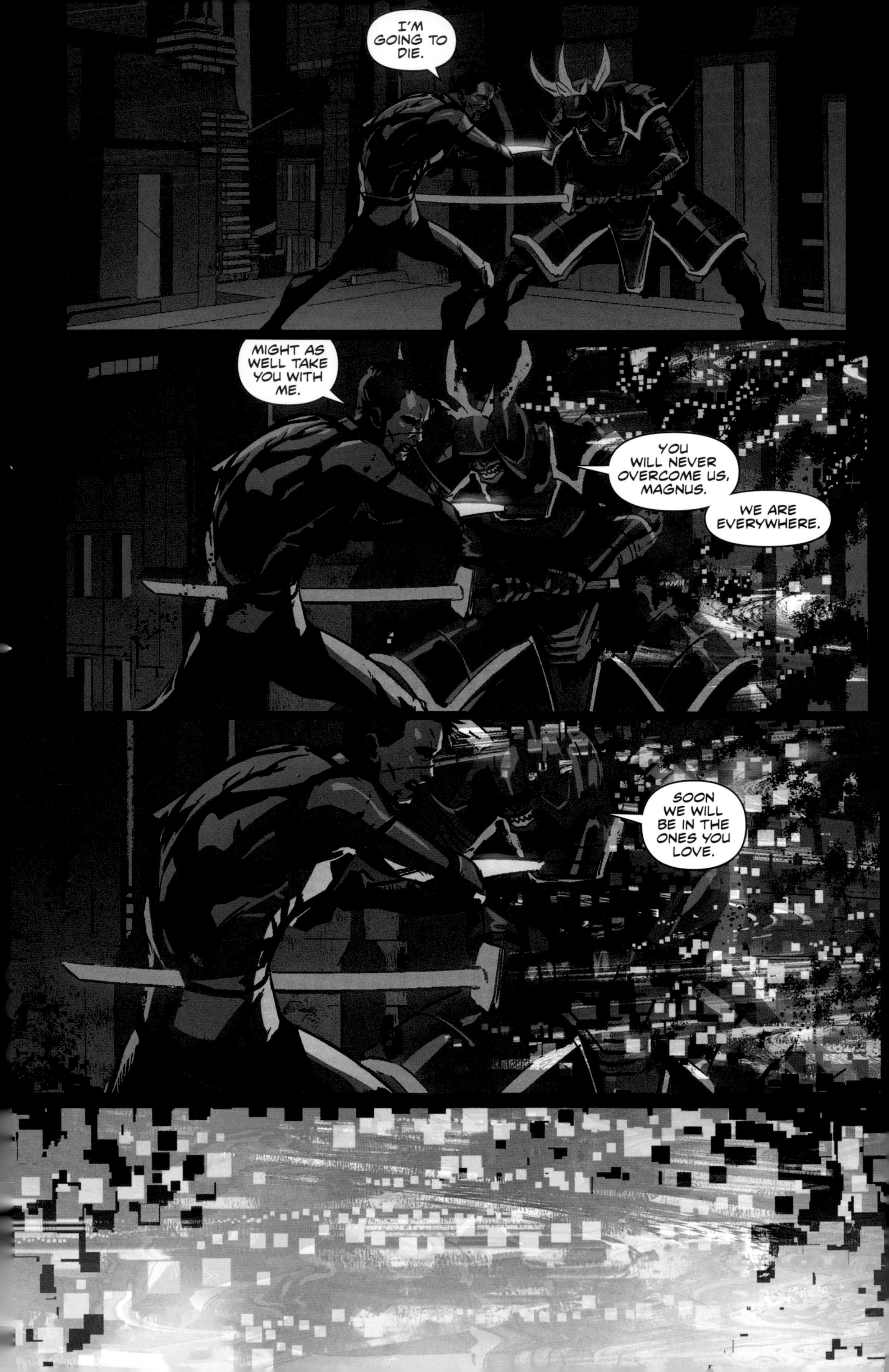
I'M GOING TO DIE.
MIGHT AS WELL TAKE YOU WITH ME.
YOU WILL NEVER OVERCOME US, MAGNUS.
WE ARE EVERYWHERE.
SOON WE WILL BE IN THE ONES YOU LOVE.

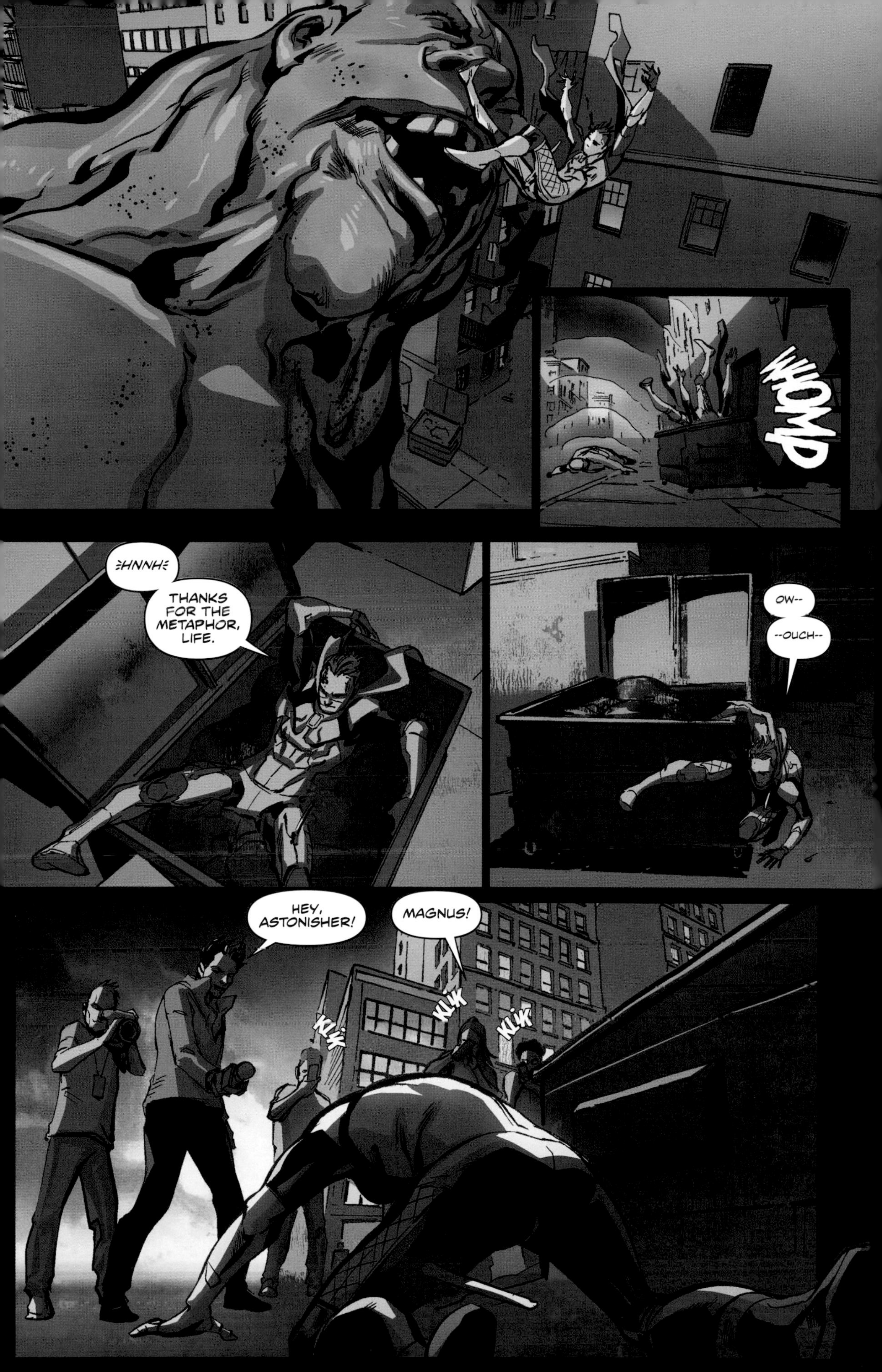
WHOMP
HNNH
THANKS FOR THE METAPHOR, LIFE.
OW--
--OUCH--
HEY, ASTONISHER!
MAGNUS!
KLIK
KLIK
KLIK

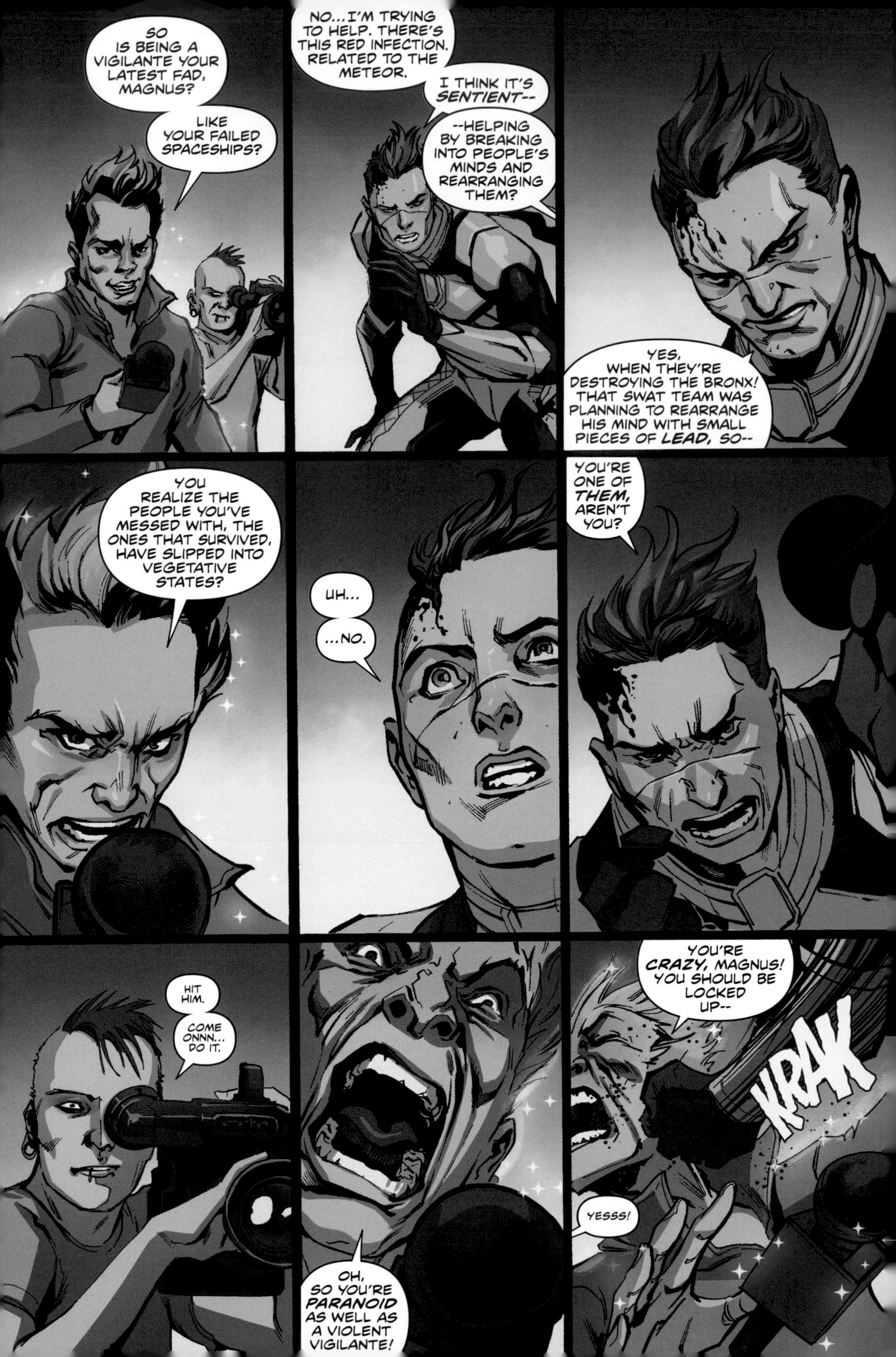
SO IS BEING A VIGILANTE YOUR LATEST FAD, MAGNUS?
LIKE YOUR FAILED SPACESHIPS?
NO... I'M TRYING TO HELP. THERE'S THIS RED INFECTION. RELATED TO THE METEOR.
I THINK IT'S SENTIENT--
--HELPING BY BREAKING INTO PEOPLE'S MINDS AND REARRANGING THEM?
YES, WHEN THEY'RE DESTROYING THE BRONX! THAT SWAT TEAM WAS PLANNING TO REARRANGE HIS MIND WITH SMALL PIECES OF LEAD, SO--
YOU REALIZE THE PEOPLE YOU'VE MESSED WITH, THE ONES THAT SURVIVED, HAVE SLIPPED INTO VEGETATIVE STATES?
UH...
...NO.
YOU'RE ONE OF THEM, AREN'T YOU?
HIT HIM.
COME ONNN... DO IT.
OH, SO YOU'RE PARANOID AS WELL AS A VIOLENT VIGILANTE!
YOU'RE CRAZY, MAGNUS! YOU SHOULD BE LOCKED UP--
KRAK
YESSS!

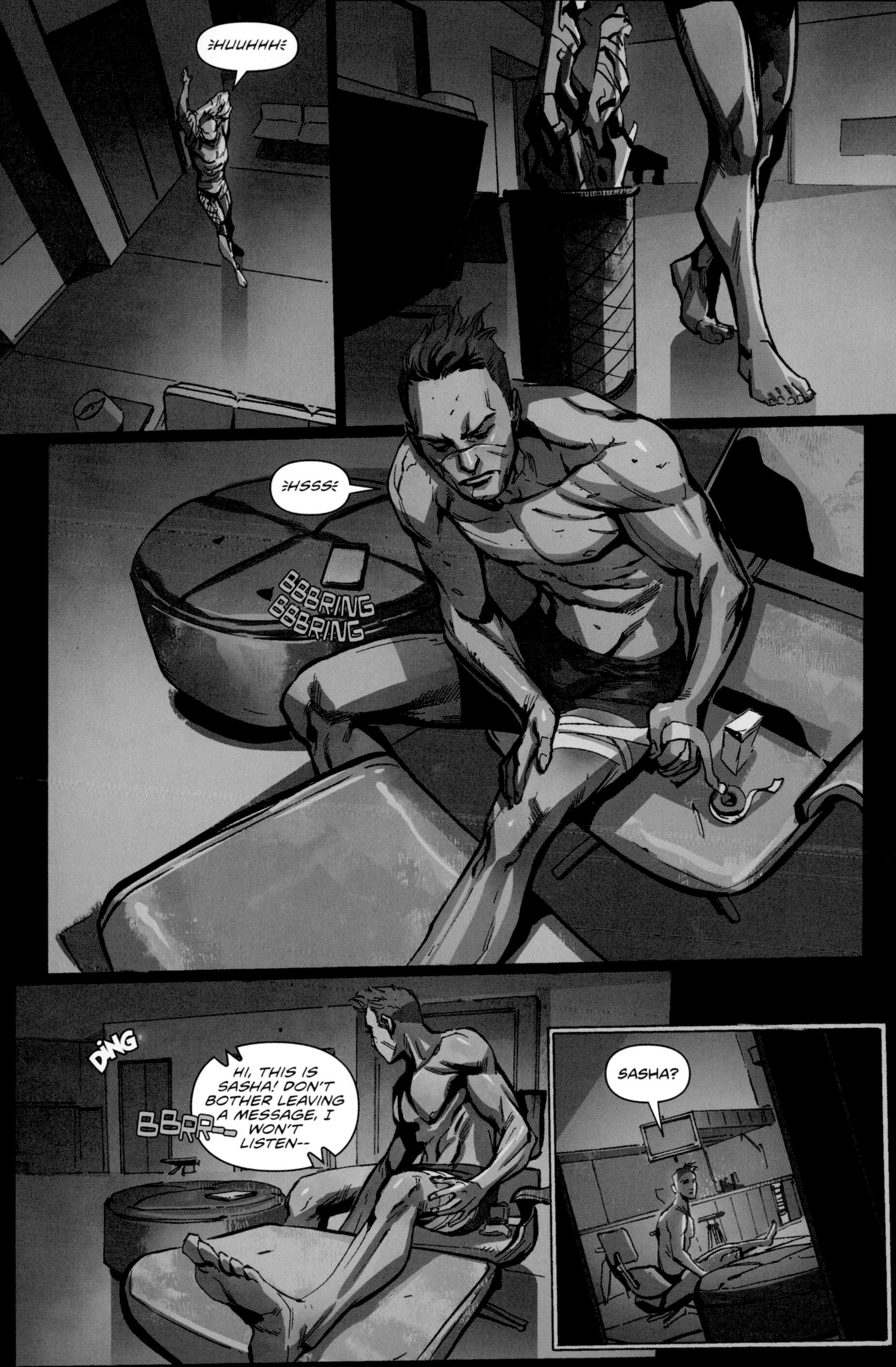

HUUHHH
HSSS
BBBRING
BBBRING
DING
BBRR--
HI, THIS IS SASHA! DON'T BOTHER LEAVING A MESSAGE, I WON'T LISTEN--
SASHA?

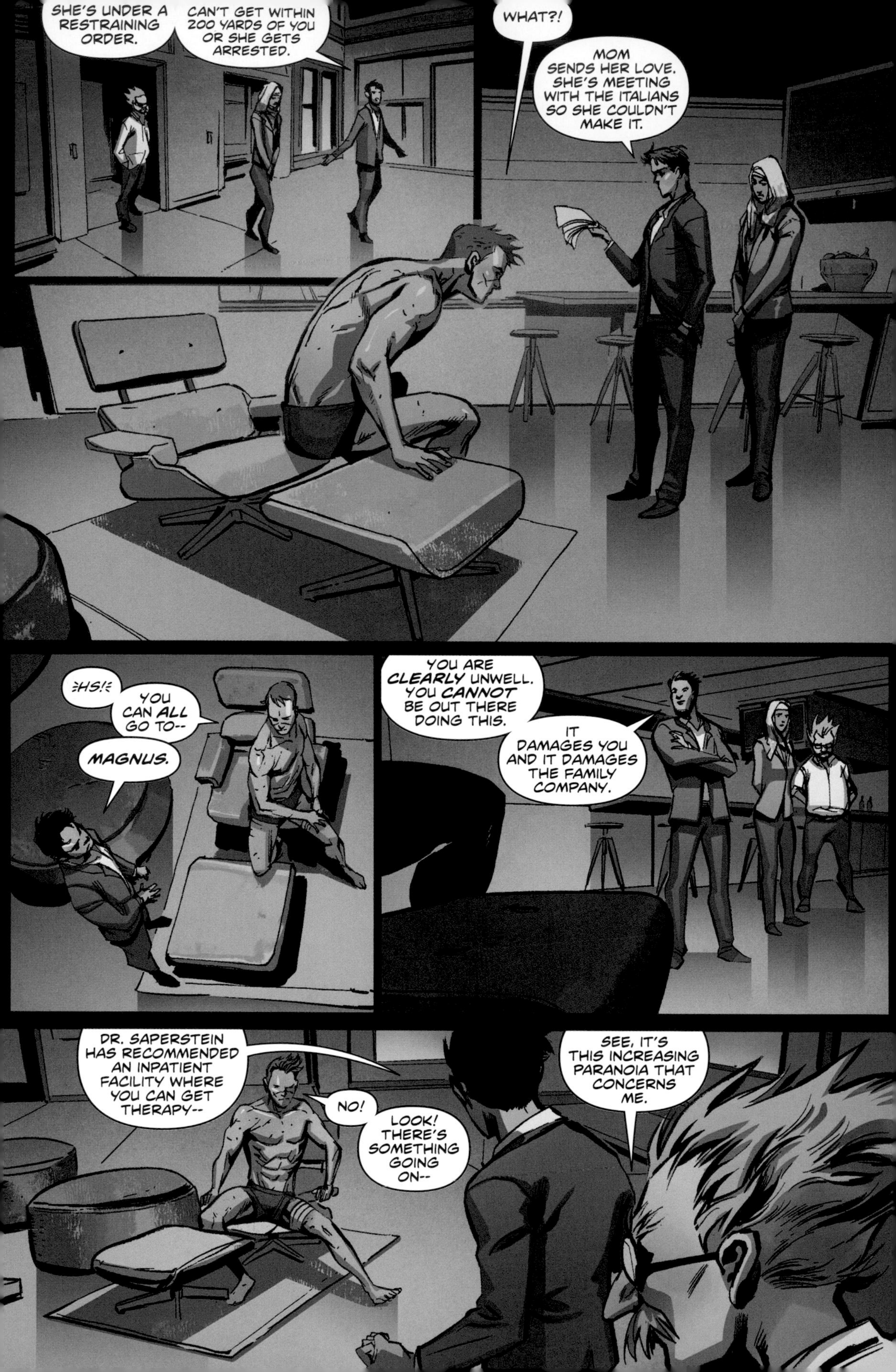
SHE'S UNDER A RESTRAINING ORDER.
CAN'T GET WITHIN 200 YARDS OF YOU OR SHE GETS ARRESTED.
WHAT?!
MOM SENDS HER LOVE. SHE'S MEETING WITH THE ITALIANS SO SHE COULDN'T MAKE IT.
ꟷHS!ꟷ
YOU CAN ALL GO TO--
MAGNUS.
YOU ARE CLEARLY UNWELL. YOU CANNOT BE OUT THERE DOING THIS.
IT DAMAGES YOU AND IT DAMAGES THE FAMILY COMPANY.
DR. SAPERSTEIN HAS RECOMMENDED AN INPATIENT FACILITY WHERE YOU CAN GET THERAPY--
NO!
LOOK! THERE'S SOMETHING GOING ON--
SEE, IT'S THIS INCREASING PARANOIA THAT CONCERNS ME.

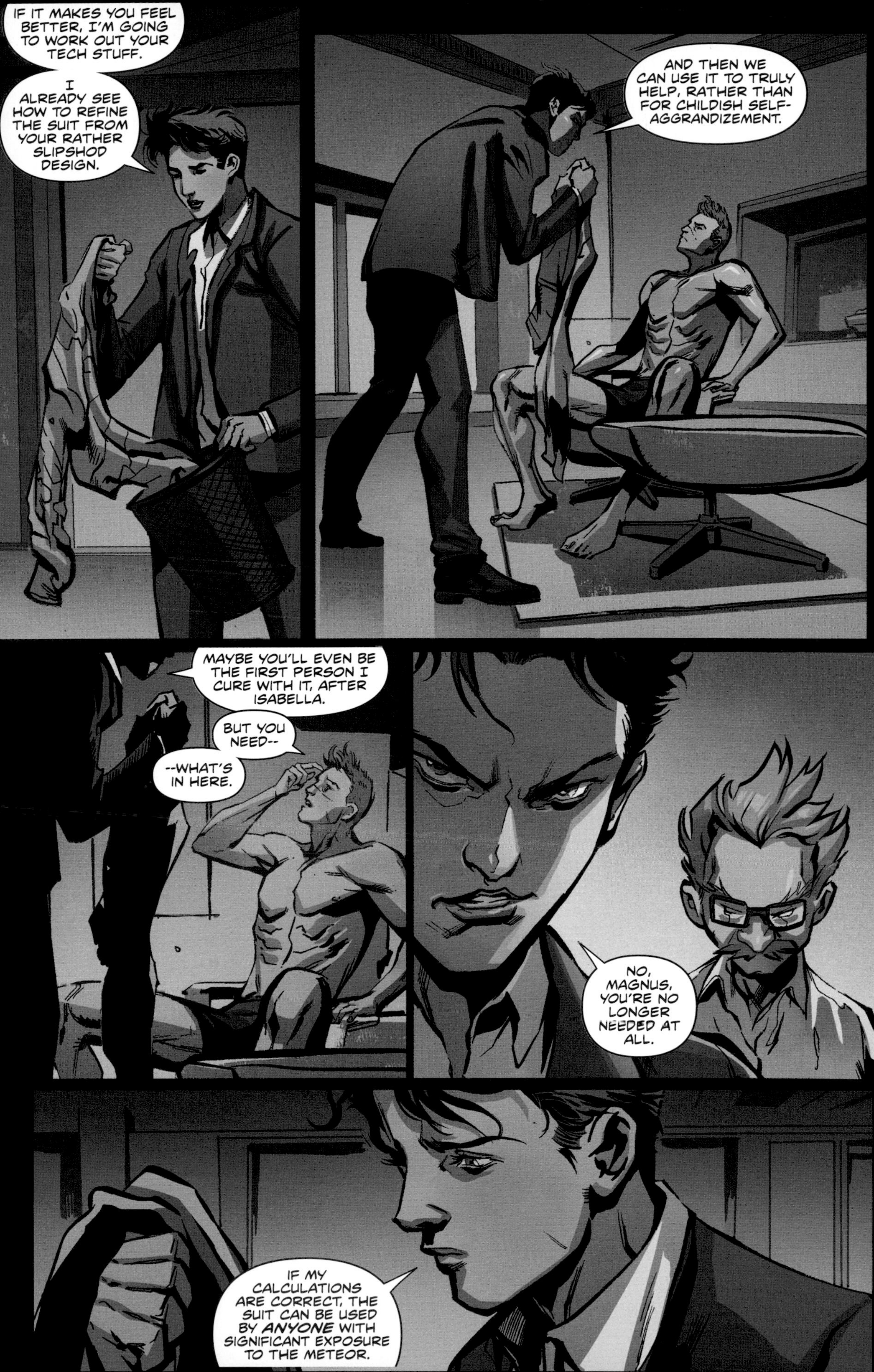
IF IT MAKES YOU FEEL BETTER, I'M GOING TO WORK OUT YOUR TECH STUFF.
I ALREADY SEE HOW TO REFINE THE SUIT FROM YOUR RATHER SLIPSHOD DESIGN.
AND THEN WE CAN USE IT TO TRULY HELP, RATHER THAN FOR CHILDISH SELF-AGGRANDIZEMENT.
MAYBE YOU'LL EVEN BE THE FIRST PERSON I CURE WITH IT, AFTER ISABELLA.
BUT YOU NEED--
--WHAT'S IN HERE.
NO, MAGNUS, YOU'RE NO LONGER NEEDED AT ALL.
IF MY CALCULATIONS ARE CORRECT, THE SUIT CAN BE USED BY *ANYONE* WITH SIGNIFICANT EXPOSURE TO THE METEOR.

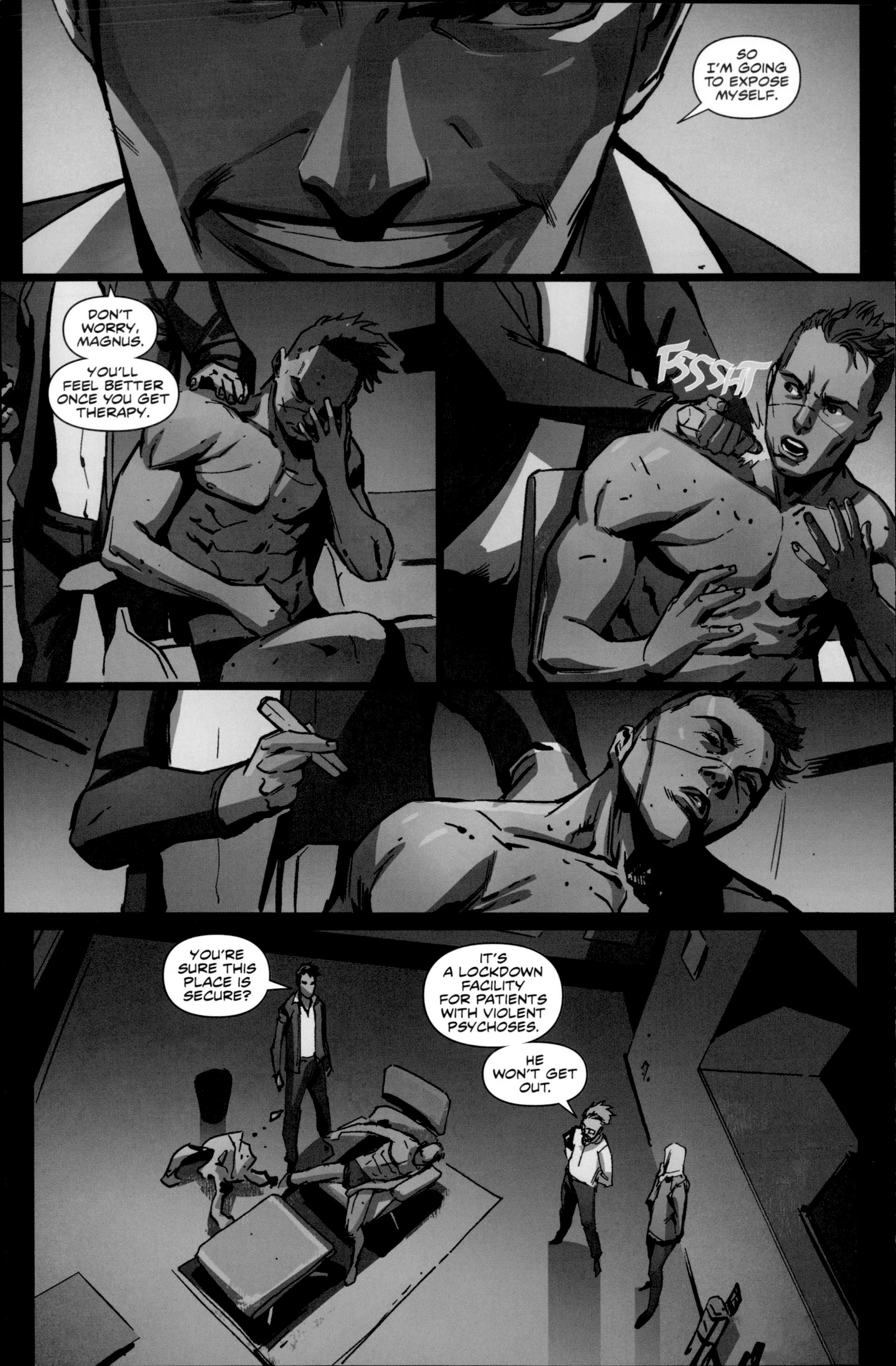
SO I'M GOING TO EXPOSE MYSELF.
DON'T WORRY, MAGNUS.
YOU'LL FEEL BETTER ONCE YOU GET THERAPY.
FSSSHT
YOU'RE SURE THIS PLACE IS SECURE?
IT'S A LOCKDOWN FACILITY FOR PATIENTS WITH VIOLENT PSYCHOSES.
HE WON'T GET OUT.

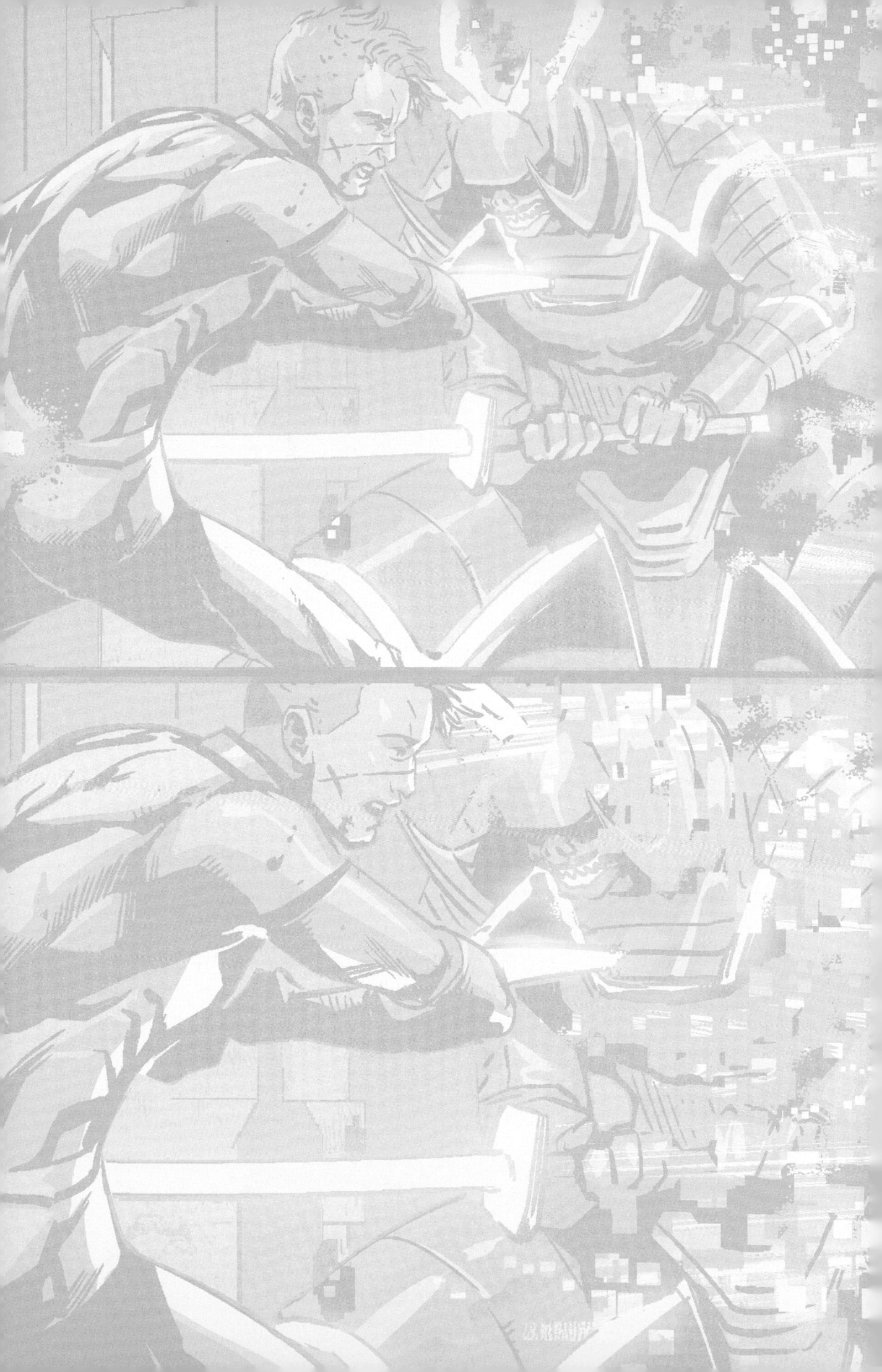

CHAPTER FOUR

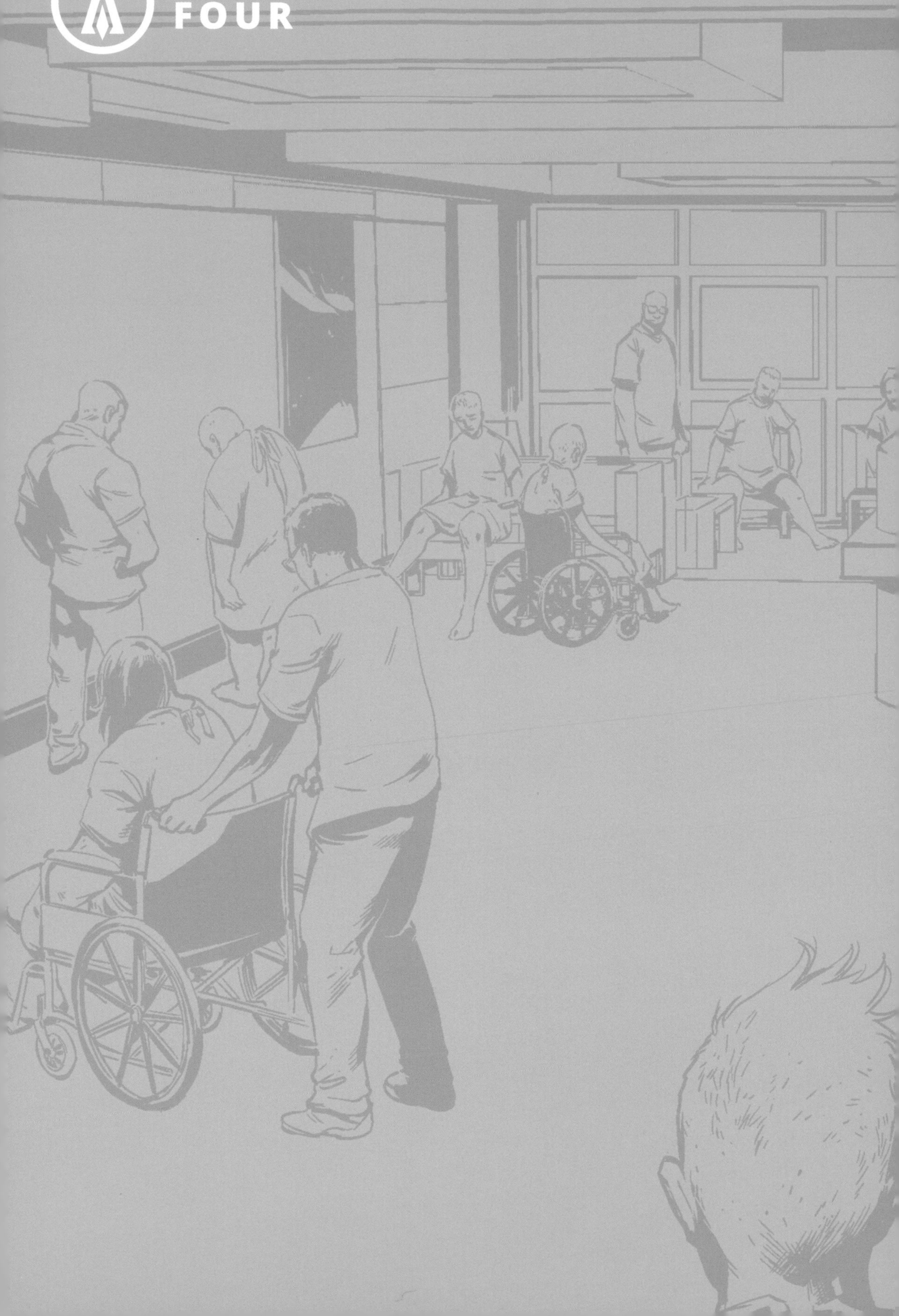

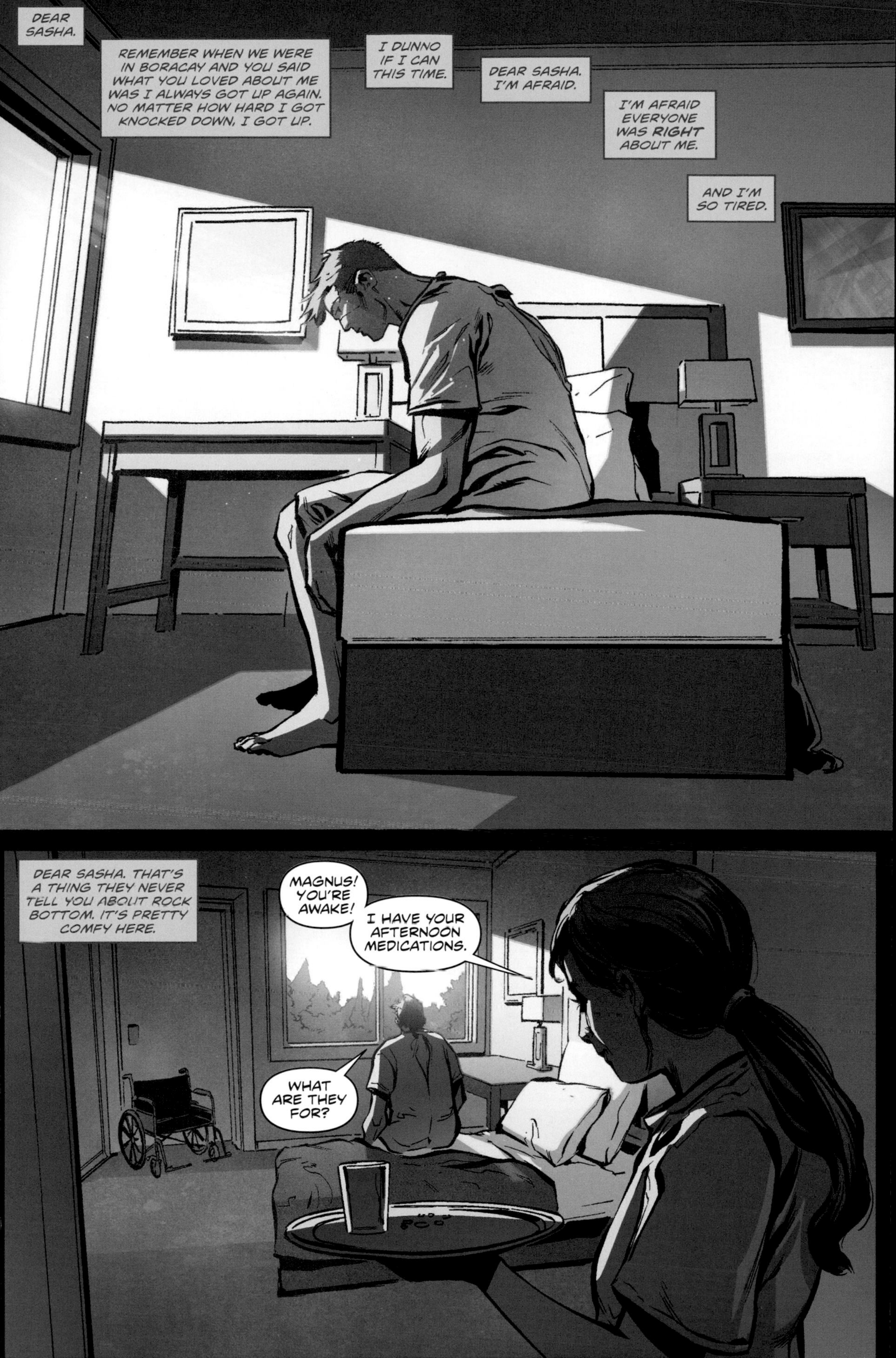
DEAR SASHA.
REMEMBER WHEN WE WERE IN BORACAY AND YOU SAID WHAT YOU LOVED ABOUT ME WAS I ALWAYS GOT UP AGAIN. NO MATTER HOW HARD I GOT KNOCKED DOWN, I GOT UP.
I DUNNO IF I CAN THIS TIME.
DEAR SASHA. I'M AFRAID.
I'M AFRAID EVERYONE WAS RIGHT ABOUT ME.
AND I'M SO TIRED.
DEAR SASHA. THAT'S A THING THEY NEVER TELL YOU ABOUT ROCK BOTTOM. IT'S PRETTY COMFY HERE.
MAGNUS! YOU'RE AWAKE!
I HAVE YOUR AFTERNOON MEDICATIONS.
WHAT ARE THEY FOR?

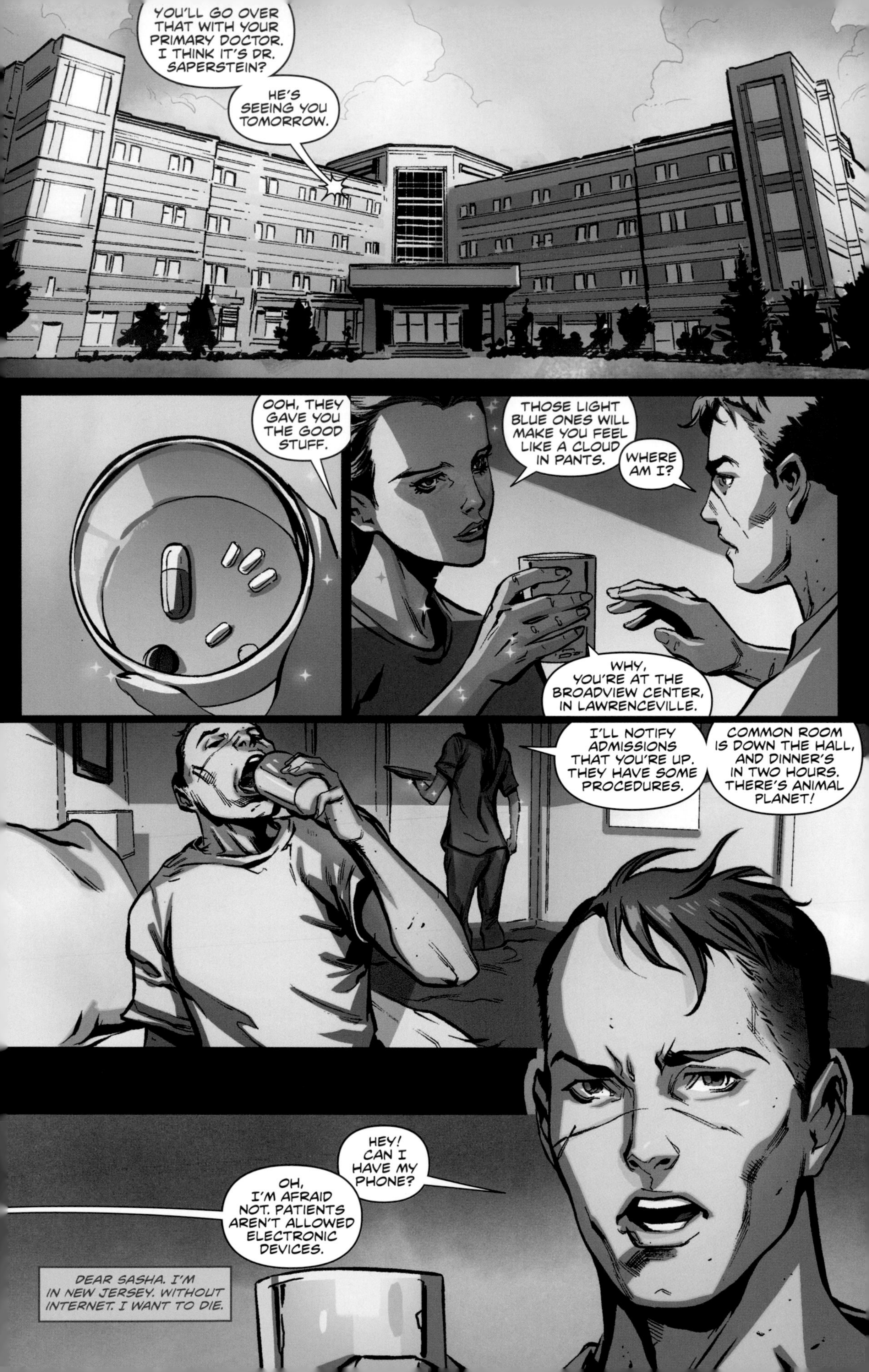
YOU'LL GO OVER THAT WITH YOUR PRIMARY DOCTOR. I THINK IT'S DR. SAPERSTEIN?
HE'S SEEING YOU TOMORROW.
OOH, THEY GAVE YOU THE GOOD STUFF.
THOSE LIGHT BLUE ONES WILL MAKE YOU FEEL LIKE A CLOUD IN PANTS.
WHERE AM I?
WHY, YOU'RE AT THE BROADVIEW CENTER, IN LAWRENCEVILLE.
I'LL NOTIFY ADMISSIONS THAT YOU'RE UP. THEY HAVE SOME PROCEDURES.
COMMON ROOM IS DOWN THE HALL, AND DINNER'S IN TWO HOURS. THERE'S ANIMAL PLANET!
HEY! CAN I HAVE MY PHONE?
OH, I'M AFRAID NOT. PATIENTS AREN'T ALLOWED ELECTRONIC DEVICES.
DEAR SASHA. I'M IN NEW JERSEY. WITHOUT INTERNET. I WANT TO DIE.

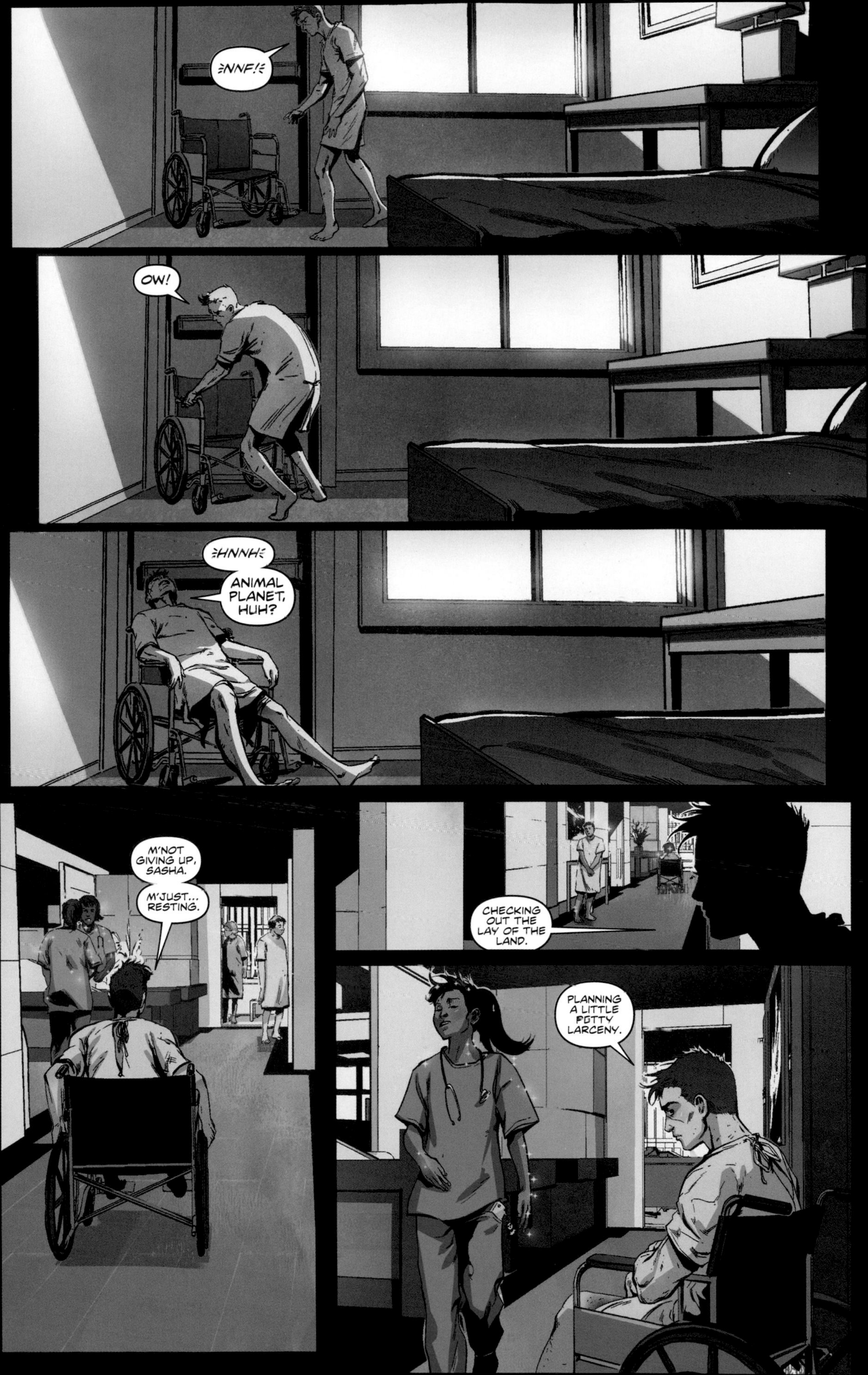
NNF!
OW!
HNNH
ANIMAL PLANET, HUH?
M'NOT GIVING UP, SASHA.
M'JUST... RESTING.
CHECKING OUT THE LAY OF THE LAND.
PLANNING A LITTLE PETTY LARCENY.

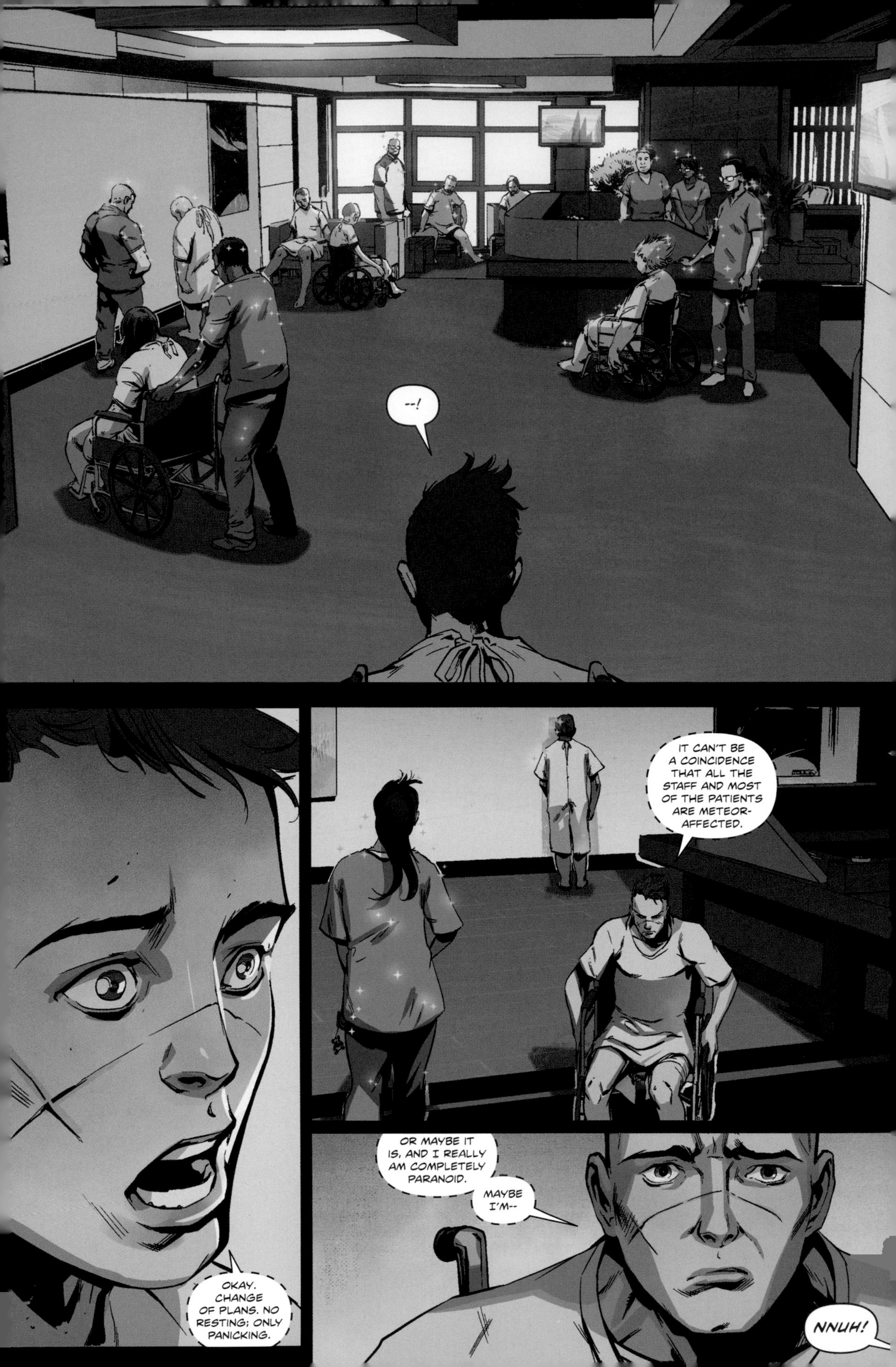
--!
IT CAN'T BE A COINCIDENCE THAT ALL THE STAFF AND MOST OF THE PATIENTS ARE METEOR-AFFECTED.
OR MAYBE IT IS, AND I REALLY AM COMPLETELY PARANOID.
MAYBE I'M--
OKAY. CHANGE OF PLANS. NO RESTING; ONLY PANICKING.
NNUH!

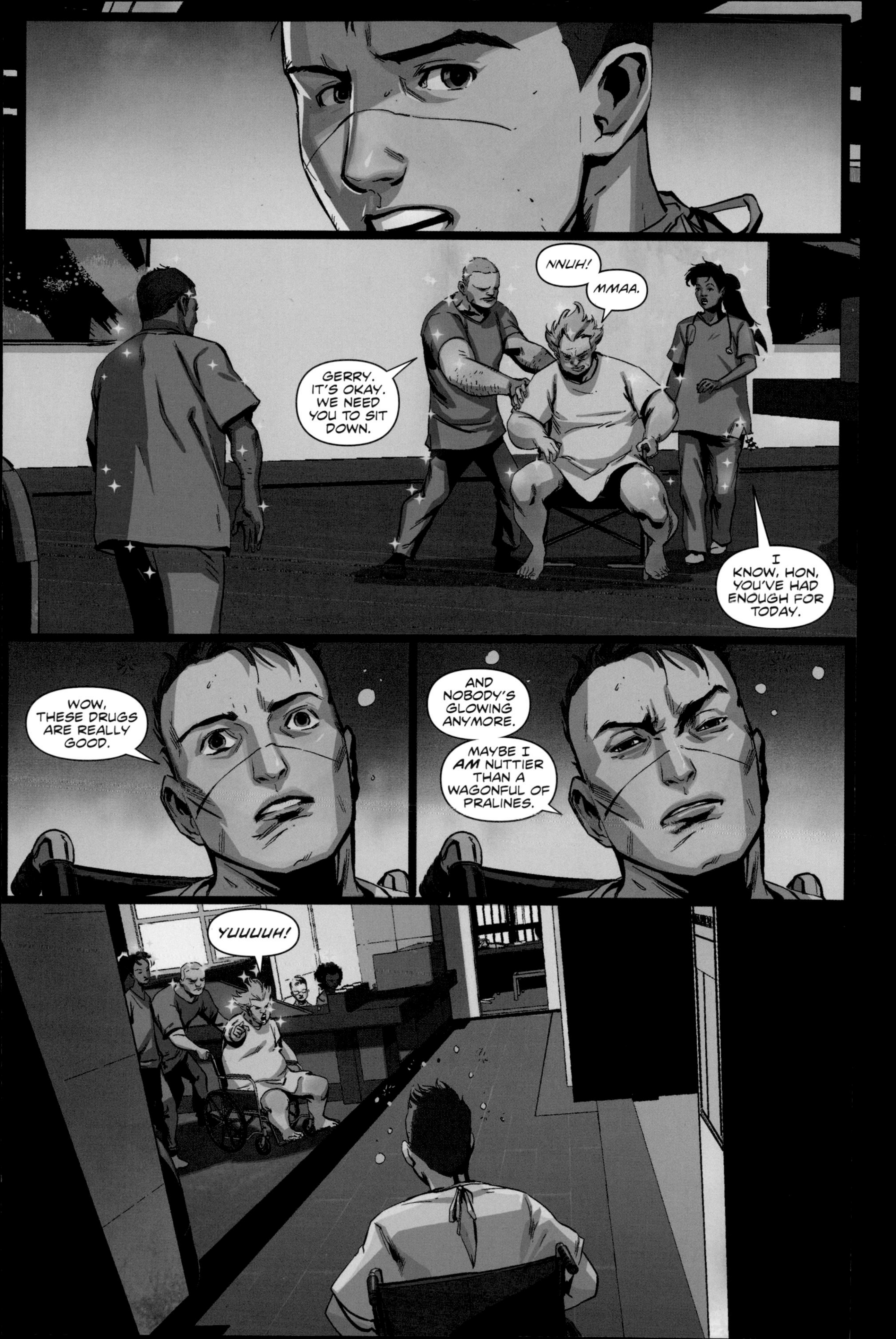
NNUH!
MMAA.
GERRY. IT'S OKAY. WE NEED YOU TO SIT DOWN.
I KNOW, HON, YOU'VE HAD ENOUGH FOR TODAY.
WOW, THESE DRUGS ARE REALLY GOOD.
AND NOBODY'S GLOWING ANYMORE.
MAYBE I AM NUTTIER THAN A WAGONFUL OF PRALINES.
YUUUUH!

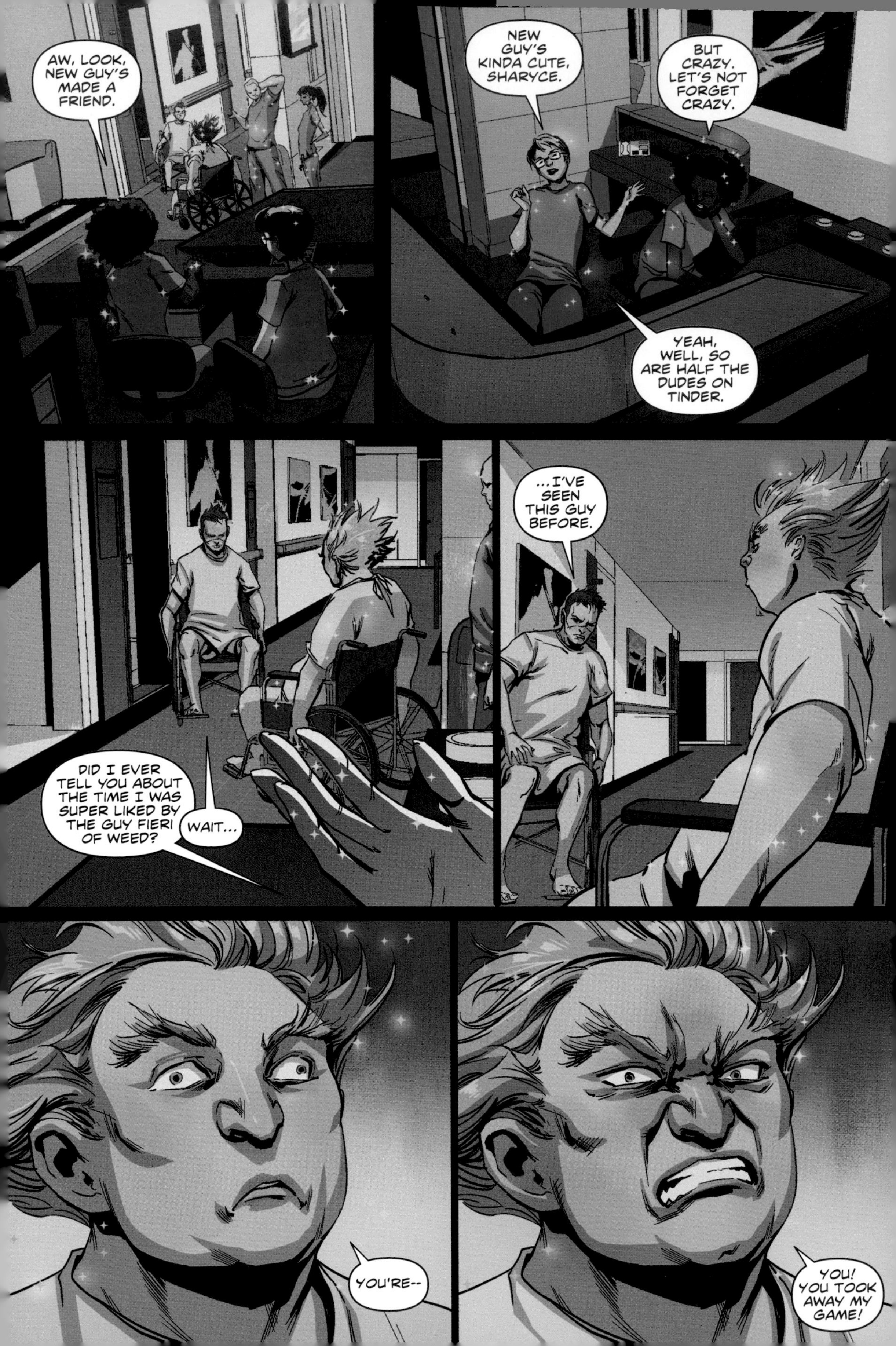
AW, LOOK, NEW GUY'S MADE A FRIEND.
NEW GUY'S KINDA CUTE, SHARYCE.
BUT CRAZY. LET'S NOT FORGET CRAZY.
YEAH, WELL, SO ARE HALF THE DUDES ON TINDER.
DID I EVER TELL YOU ABOUT THE TIME I WAS SUPER LIKED BY THE GUY FIERI OF WEED?
WAIT...
...I'VE SEEN THIS GUY BEFORE.
YOU'RE--
YOU! YOU TOOK AWAY MY GAME!

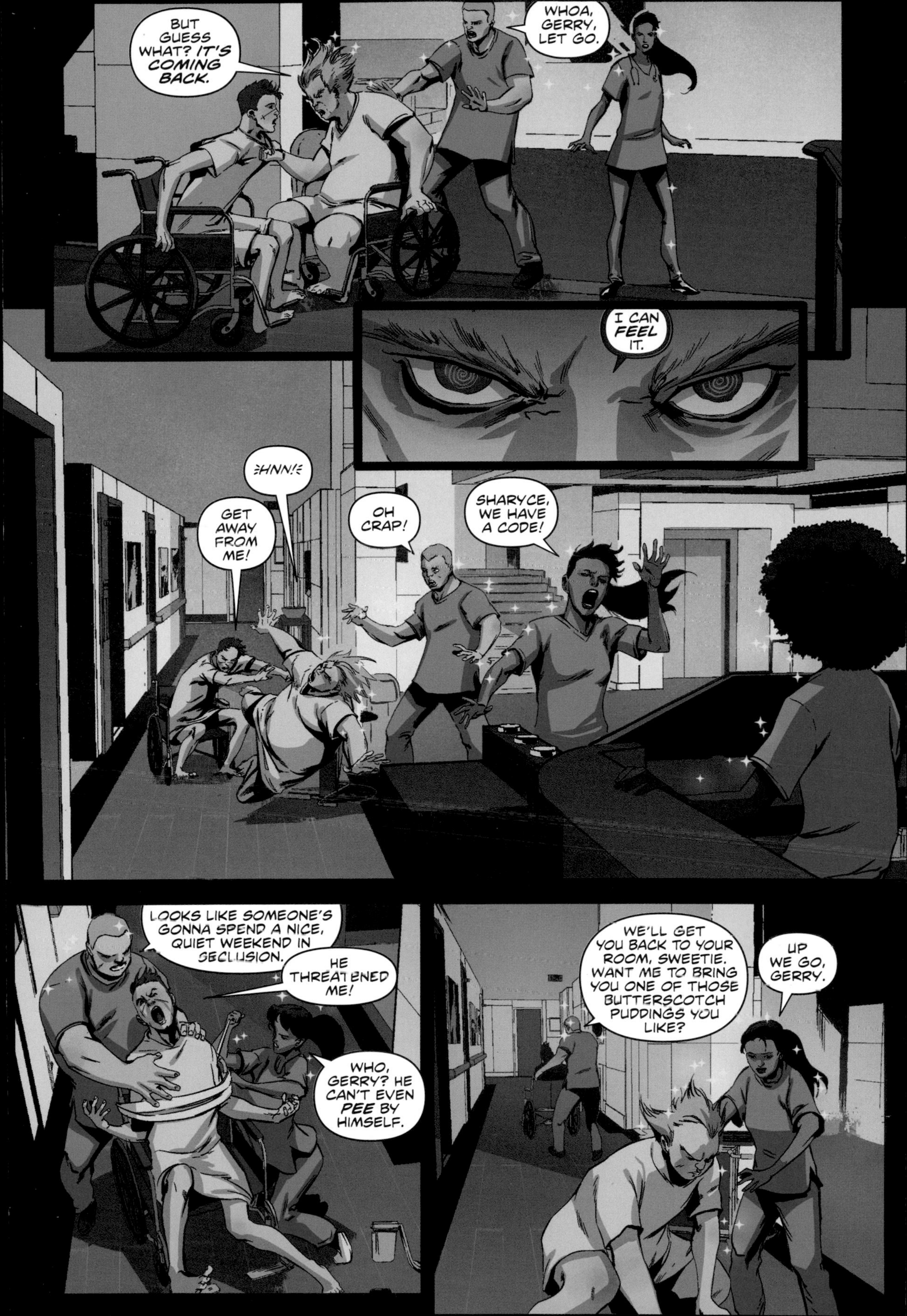
BUT GUESS WHAT? IT'S COMING BACK.
WHOA, GERRY, LET GO.
I CAN FEEL IT.
HNN!
GET AWAY FROM ME!
OH CRAP!
SHARYCE, WE HAVE A CODE!
LOOKS LIKE SOMEONE'S GONNA SPEND A NICE, QUIET WEEKEND IN SECLUSION.
HE THREATENED ME!
WHO, GERRY? HE CAN'T EVEN PEE BY HIMSELF.
WE'LL GET YOU BACK TO YOUR ROOM, SWEETIE. WANT ME TO BRING YOU ONE OF THOSE BUTTERSCOTCH PUDDINGS YOU LIKE?
UP WE GO, GERRY.

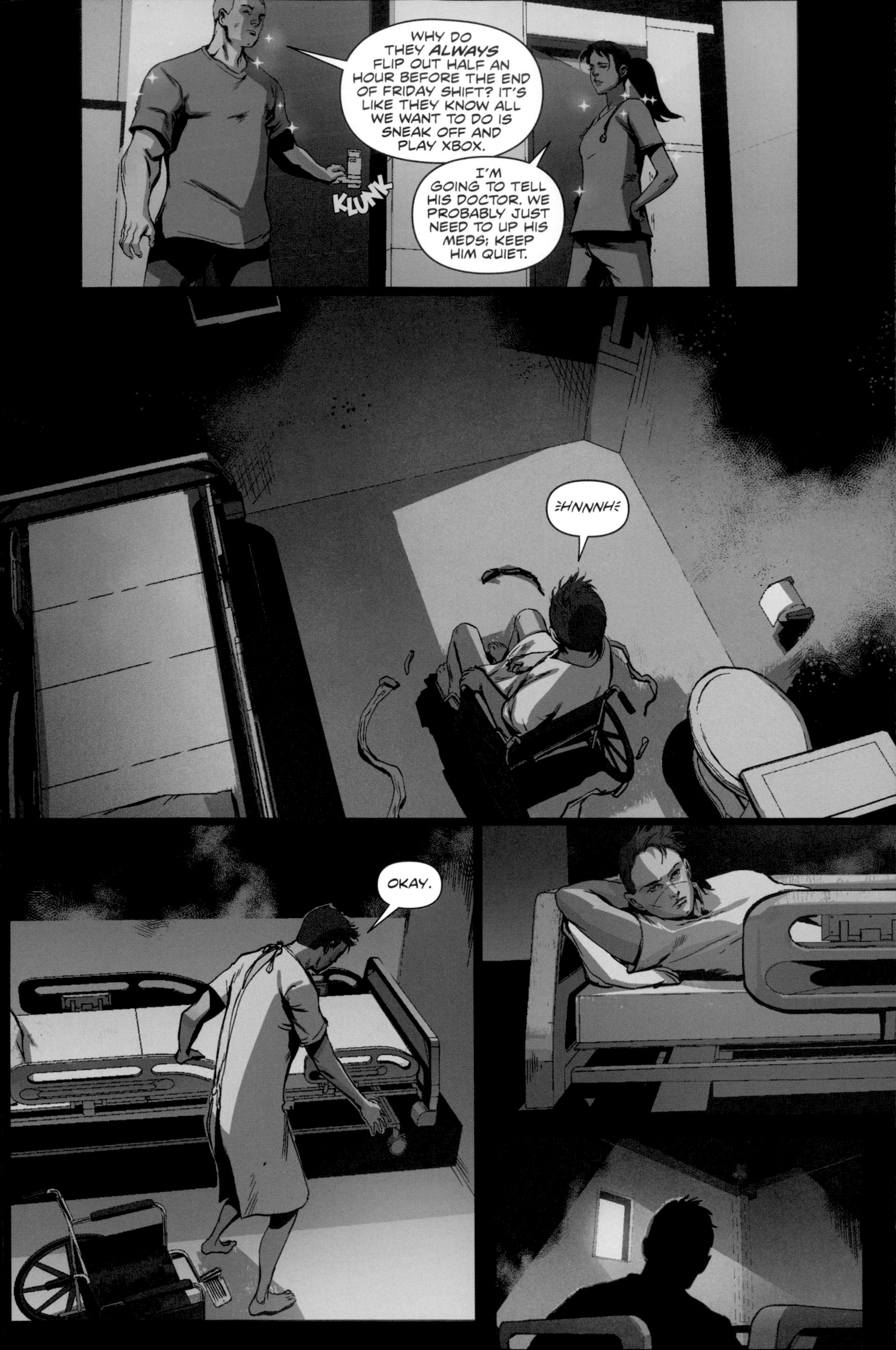
WHY DO THEY ALWAYS FLIP OUT HALF AN HOUR BEFORE THE END OF FRIDAY SHIFT? IT'S LIKE THEY KNOW ALL WE WANT TO DO IS SNEAK OFF AND PLAY XBOX.
KLUNK
I'M GOING TO TELL HIS DOCTOR. WE PROBABLY JUST NEED TO UP HIS MEDS; KEEP HIM QUIET.
HNNNH
OKAY.

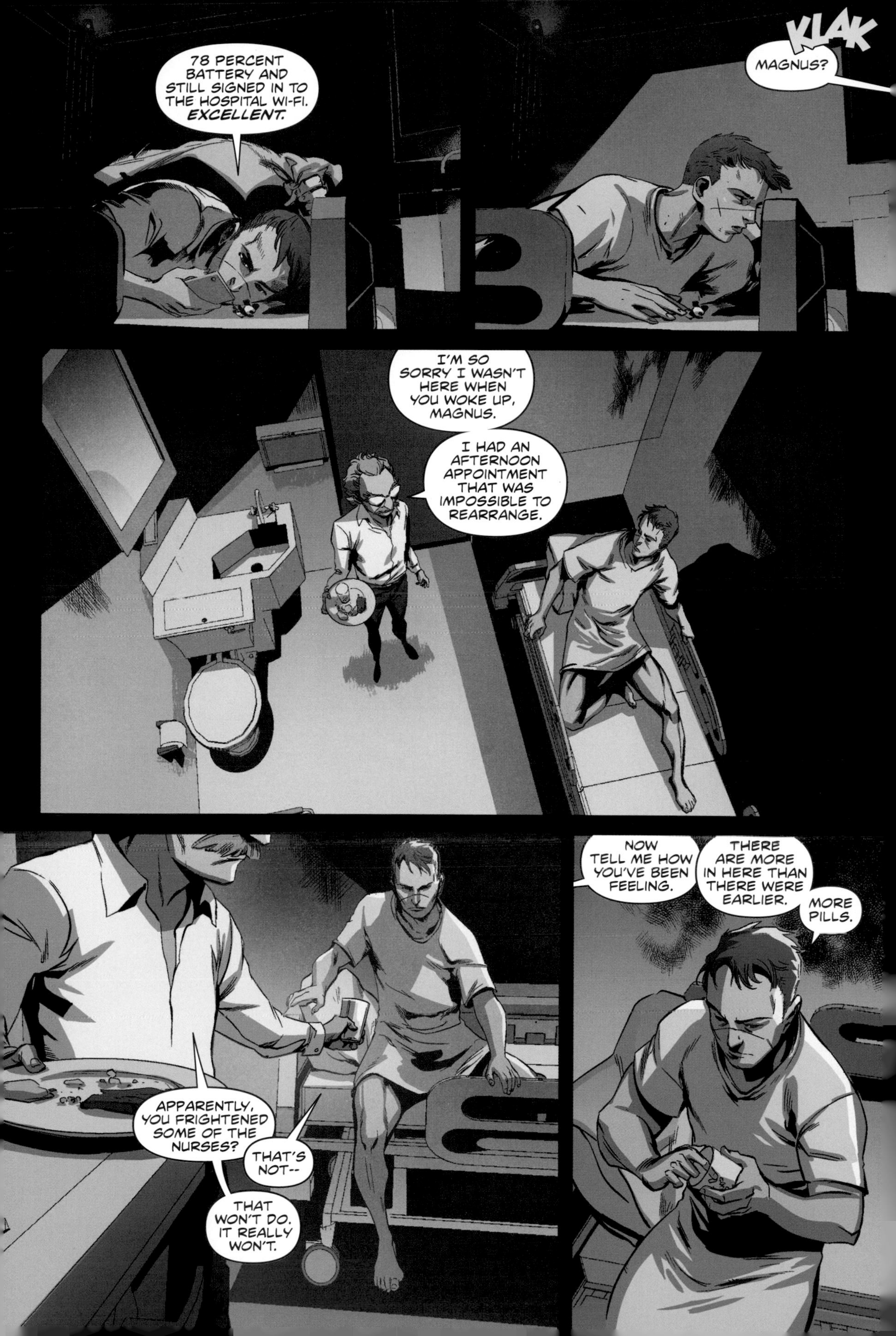
78 PERCENT BATTERY AND STILL SIGNED IN TO THE HOSPITAL WI-FI. *EXCELLENT.*
KLAK
MAGNUS?
I'M SO SORRY I WASN'T HERE WHEN YOU WOKE UP, MAGNUS.
I HAD AN AFTERNOON APPOINTMENT THAT WAS IMPOSSIBLE TO REARRANGE.
APPARENTLY, YOU FRIGHTENED SOME OF THE NURSES?
THAT'S NOT--
THAT WON'T DO. IT REALLY WON'T.
NOW TELL ME HOW YOU'VE BEEN FEELING.
THERE ARE MORE IN HERE THAN THERE WERE EARLIER.
MORE PILLS.

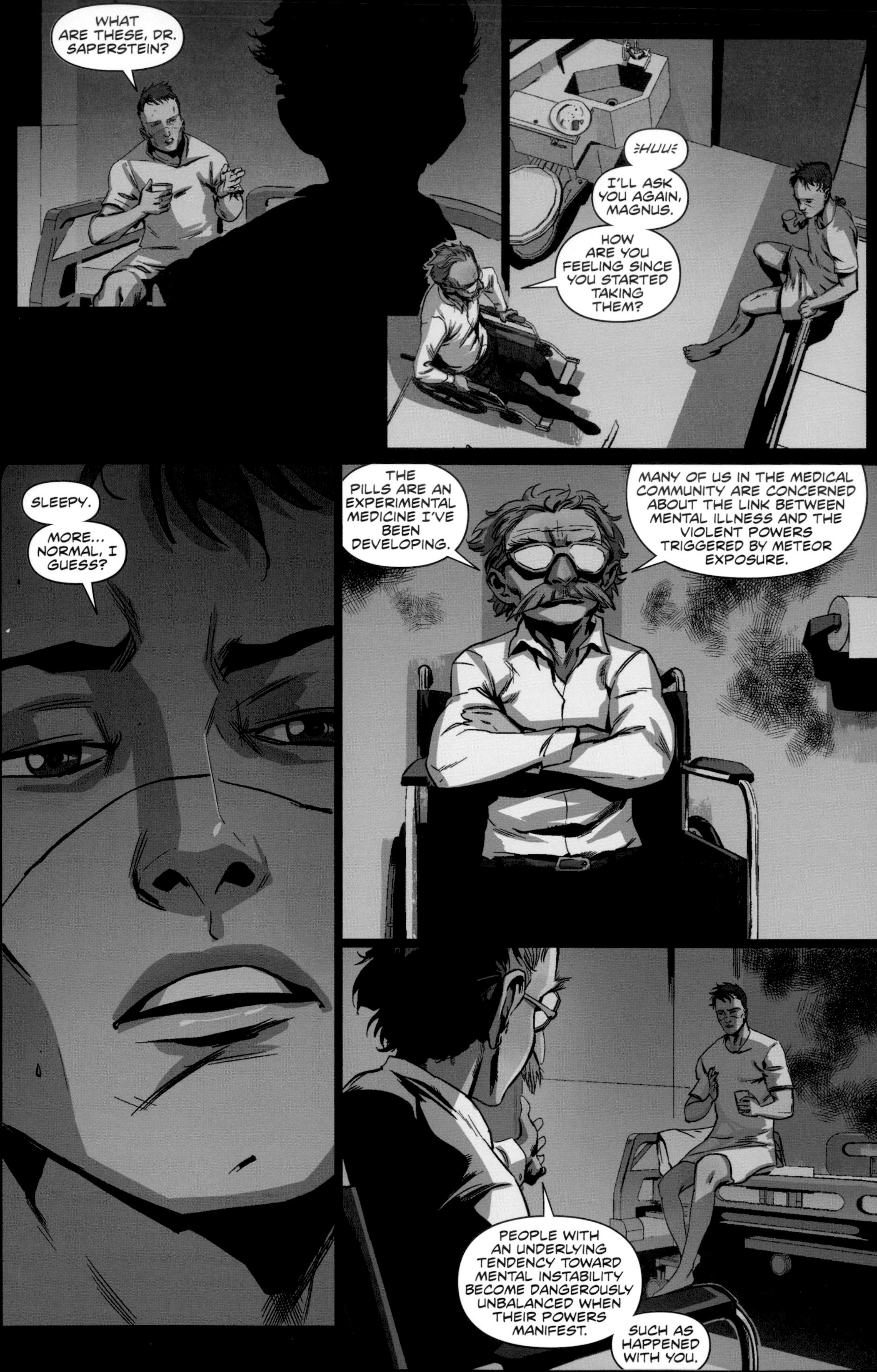
WHAT ARE THESE, DR. SAPERSTEIN?
HUU
I'LL ASK YOU AGAIN, MAGNUS.
HOW ARE YOU FEELING SINCE YOU STARTED TAKING THEM?
SLEEPY.
MORE... NORMAL, I GUESS?
THE PILLS ARE AN EXPERIMENTAL MEDICINE I'VE BEEN DEVELOPING.
MANY OF US IN THE MEDICAL COMMUNITY ARE CONCERNED ABOUT THE LINK BETWEEN MENTAL ILLNESS AND THE VIOLENT POWERS TRIGGERED BY METEOR EXPOSURE.
PEOPLE WITH AN UNDERLYING TENDENCY TOWARD MENTAL INSTABILITY BECOME DANGEROUSLY UNBALANCED WHEN THEIR POWERS MANIFEST.
SUCH AS HAPPENED WITH YOU.

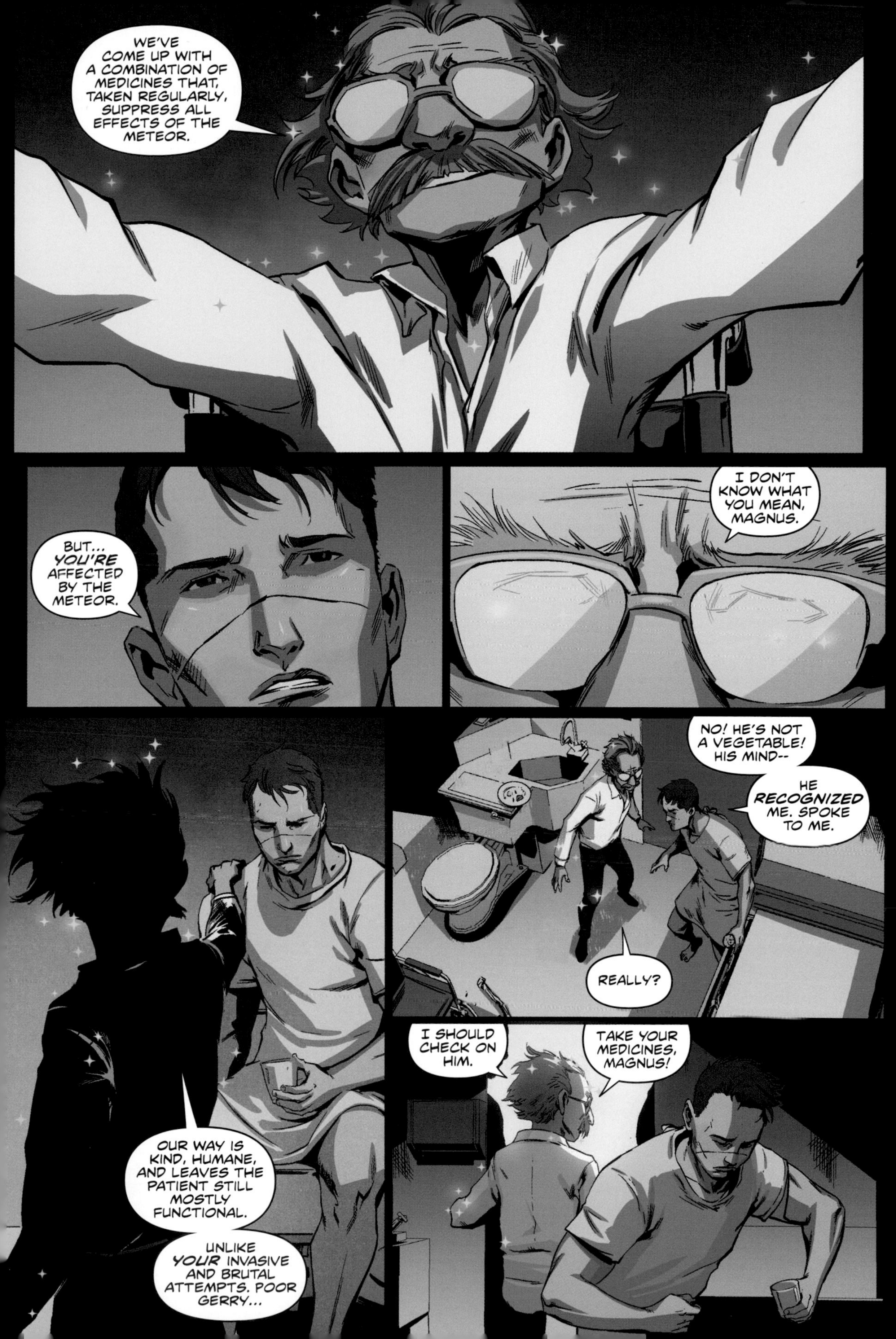
WE'VE COME UP WITH A COMBINATION OF MEDICINES THAT, TAKEN REGULARLY, SUPPRESS ALL EFFECTS OF THE METEOR.
BUT... *YOU'RE* AFFECTED BY THE METEOR.
I DON'T KNOW WHAT YOU MEAN, MAGNUS.
OUR WAY IS KIND, HUMANE, AND LEAVES THE PATIENT STILL MOSTLY FUNCTIONAL.
UNLIKE *YOUR* INVASIVE AND BRUTAL ATTEMPTS. POOR GERRY...
NO! HE'S NOT A VEGETABLE! HIS MIND--
HE *RECOGNIZED* ME. SPOKE TO ME.
REALLY?
I SHOULD CHECK ON HIM.
TAKE YOUR MEDICINES, MAGNUS!

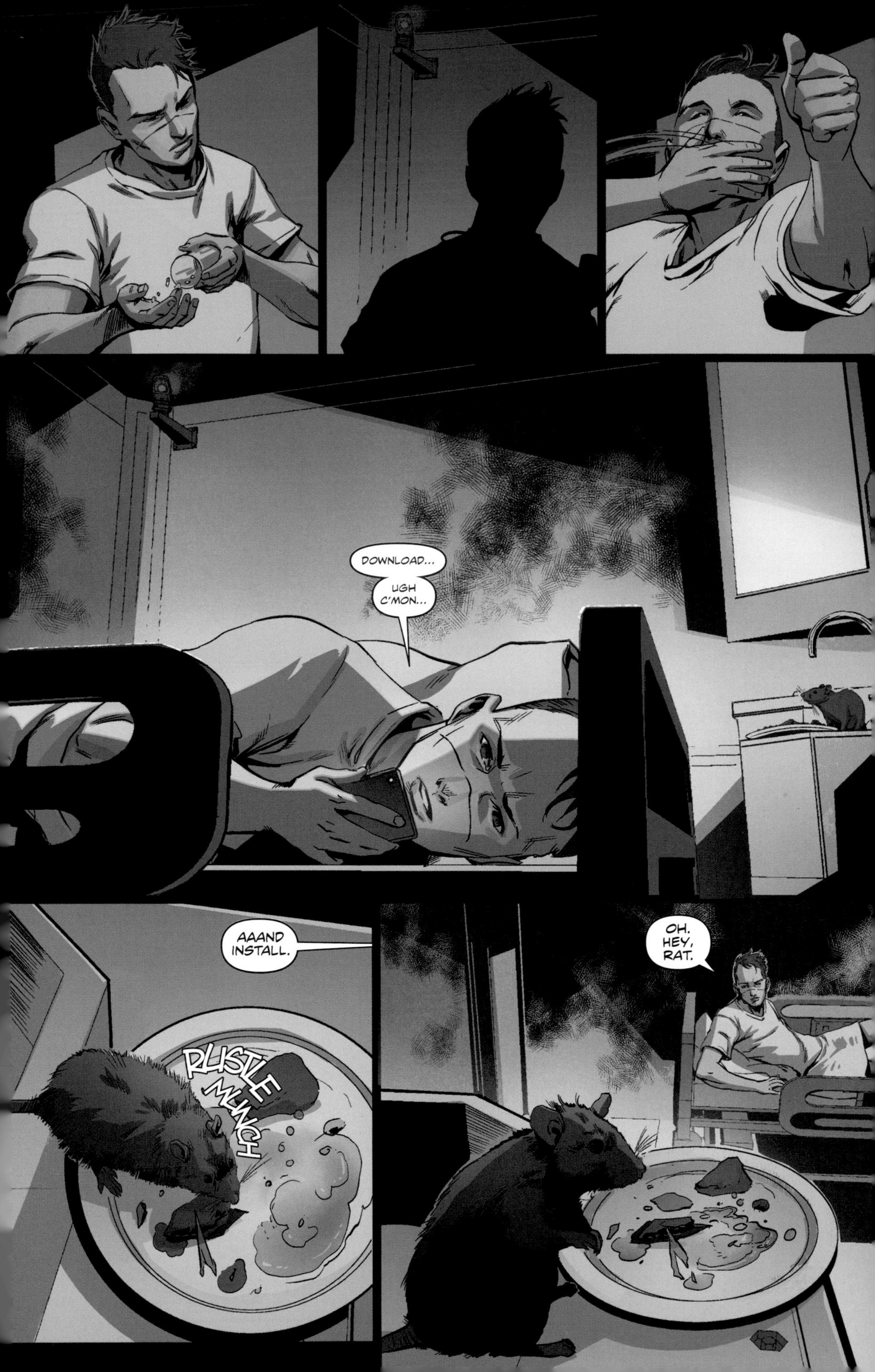
DOWNLOAD...
UGH C'MON...
AAAND INSTALL.
RUSTLE MUNCH
OH. HEY, RAT.

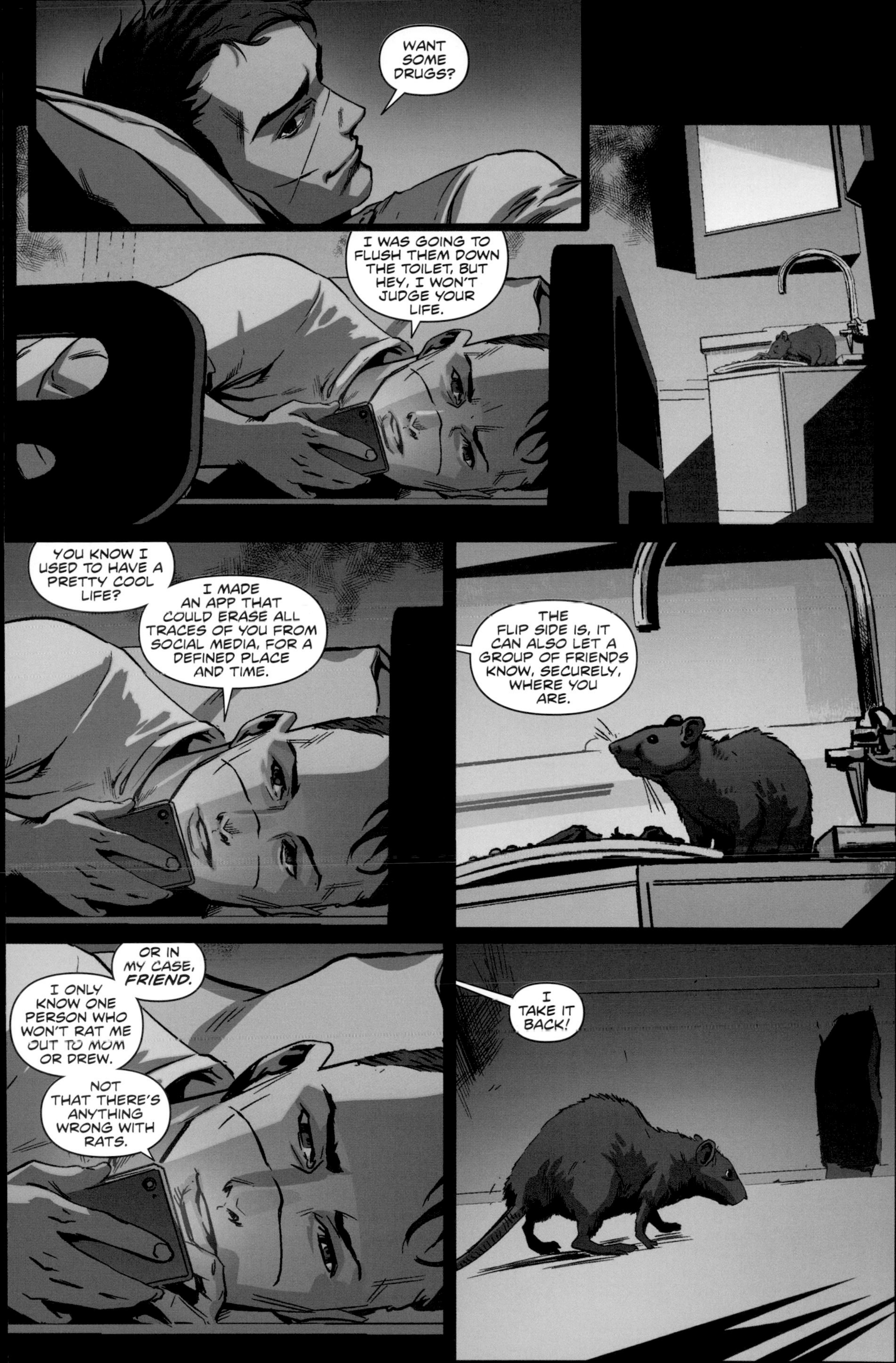
WANT SOME DRUGS?
I WAS GOING TO FLUSH THEM DOWN THE TOILET, BUT HEY, I WON'T JUDGE YOUR LIFE.
YOU KNOW I USED TO HAVE A PRETTY COOL LIFE?
I MADE AN APP THAT COULD ERASE ALL TRACES OF YOU FROM SOCIAL MEDIA, FOR A DEFINED PLACE AND TIME.
THE FLIP SIDE IS, IT CAN ALSO LET A GROUP OF FRIENDS KNOW, SECURELY, WHERE YOU ARE.
OR IN MY CASE, FRIEND.
I ONLY KNOW ONE PERSON WHO WON'T RAT ME OUT TO MOM OR DREW.
NOT THAT THERE'S ANYTHING WRONG WITH RATS.
I TAKE IT BACK!

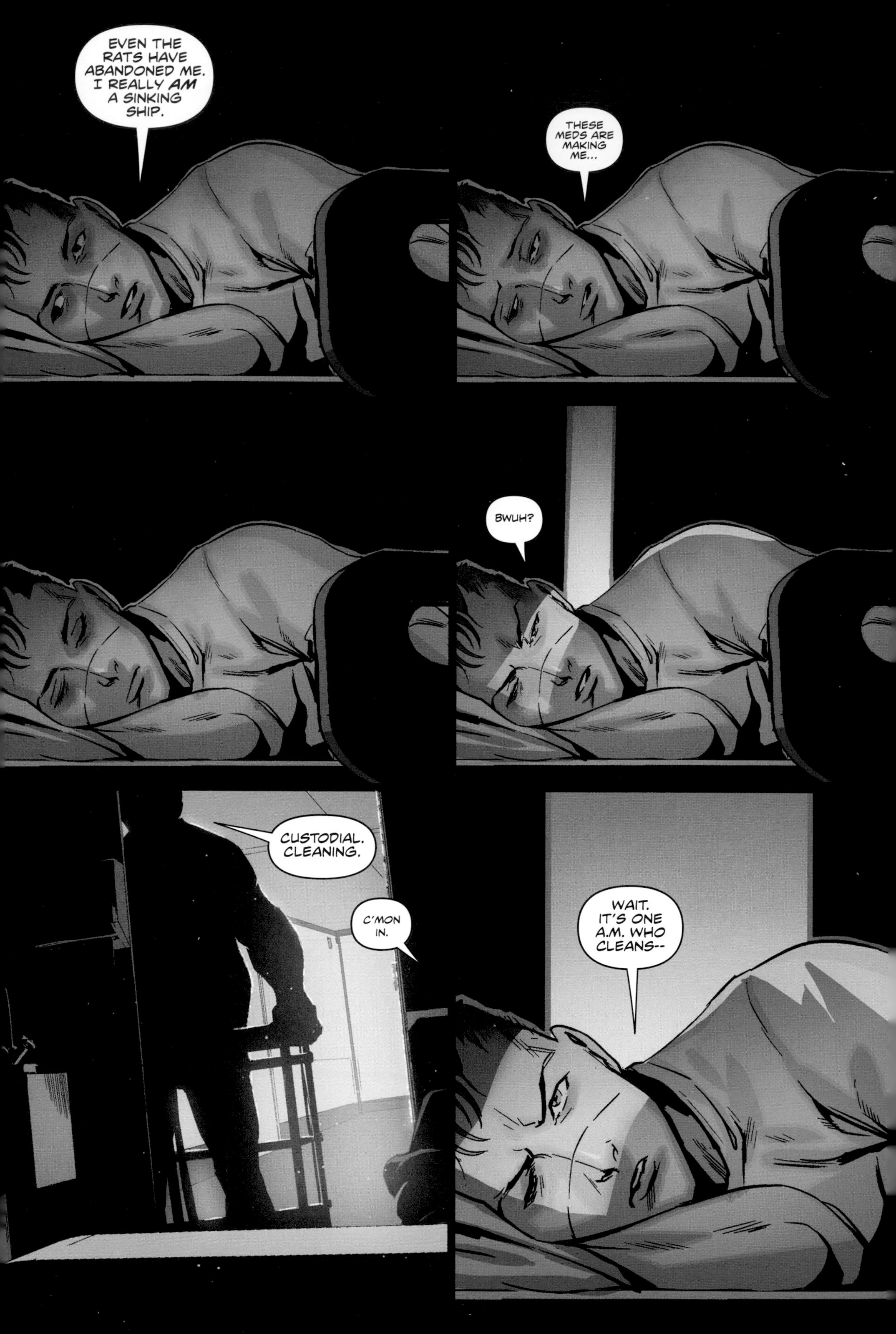
EVEN THE RATS HAVE ABANDONED ME. I REALLY *AM* A SINKING SHIP.
THESE MEDS ARE MAKING ME...
BWUH?
CUSTODIAL. CLEANING.
C'MON IN.
WAIT. IT'S ONE A.M. WHO CLEANS--

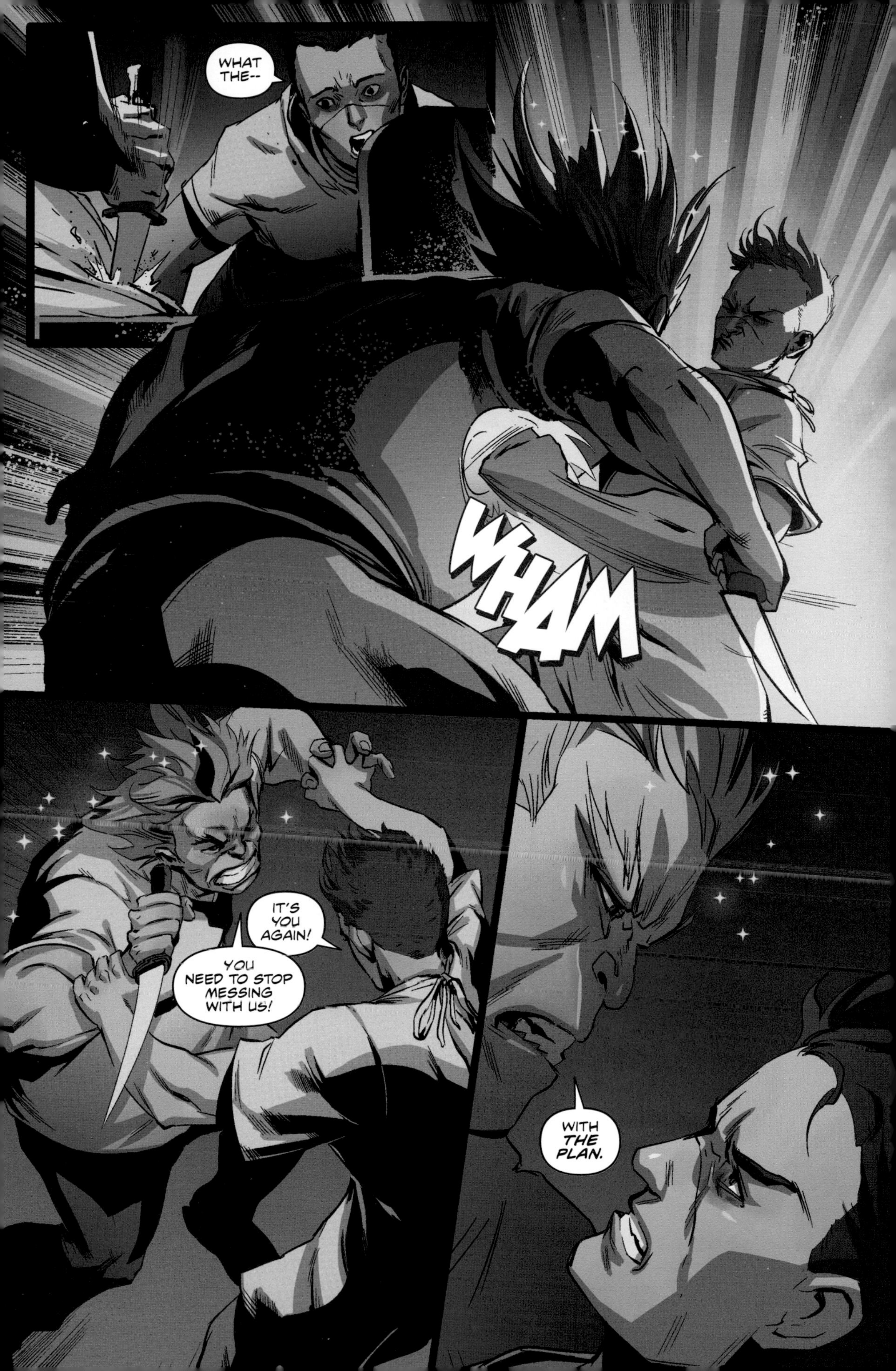
WHAT THE--
WHAM
IT'S YOU AGAIN!
YOU NEED TO STOP MESSING WITH US!
WITH THE PLAN.

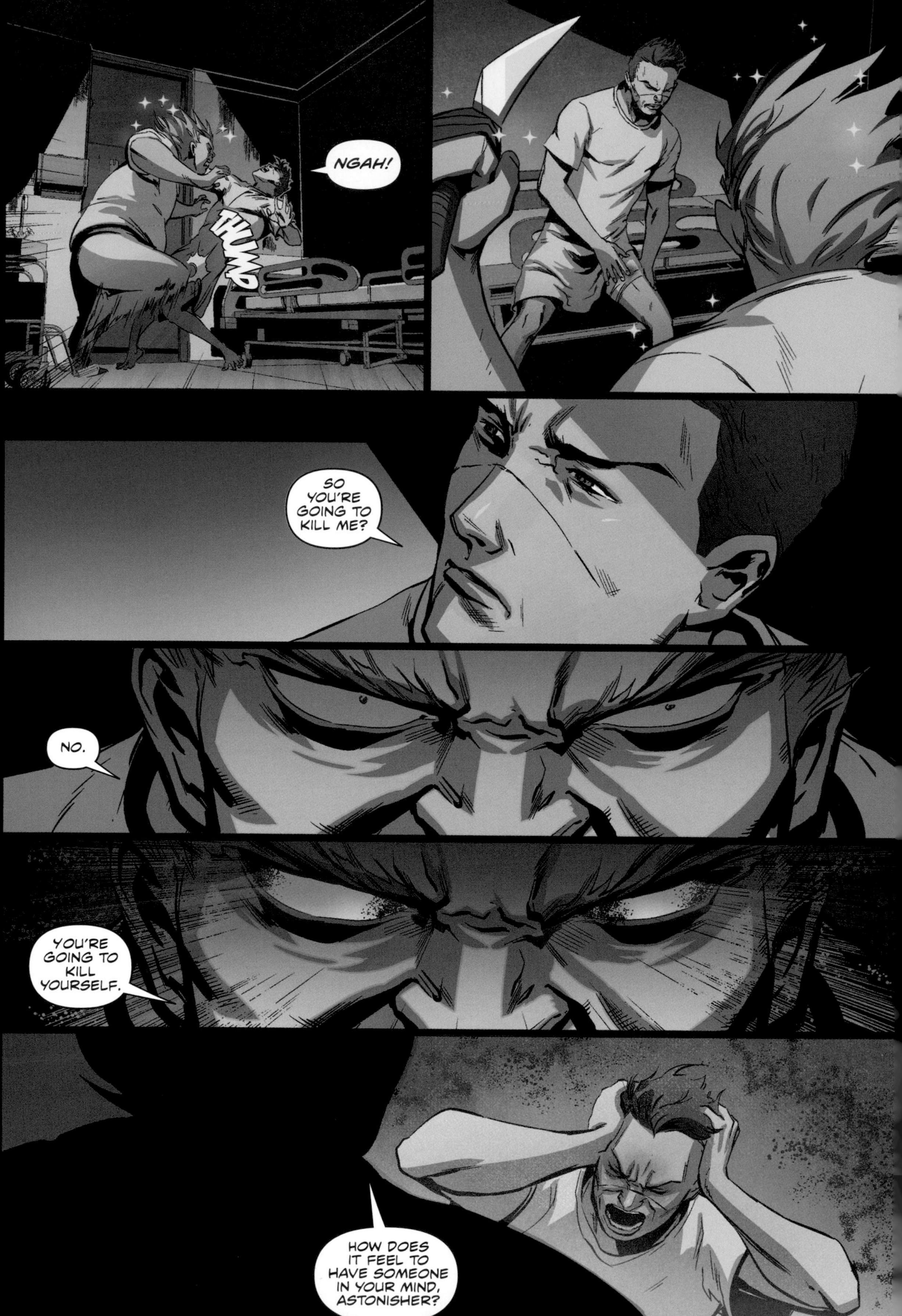
NGAH!
THUMP
SO YOU'RE GOING TO KILL ME?
NO.
YOU'RE GOING TO KILL YOURSELF.
HOW DOES IT FEEL TO HAVE SOMEONE IN YOUR MIND, ASTONISHER?

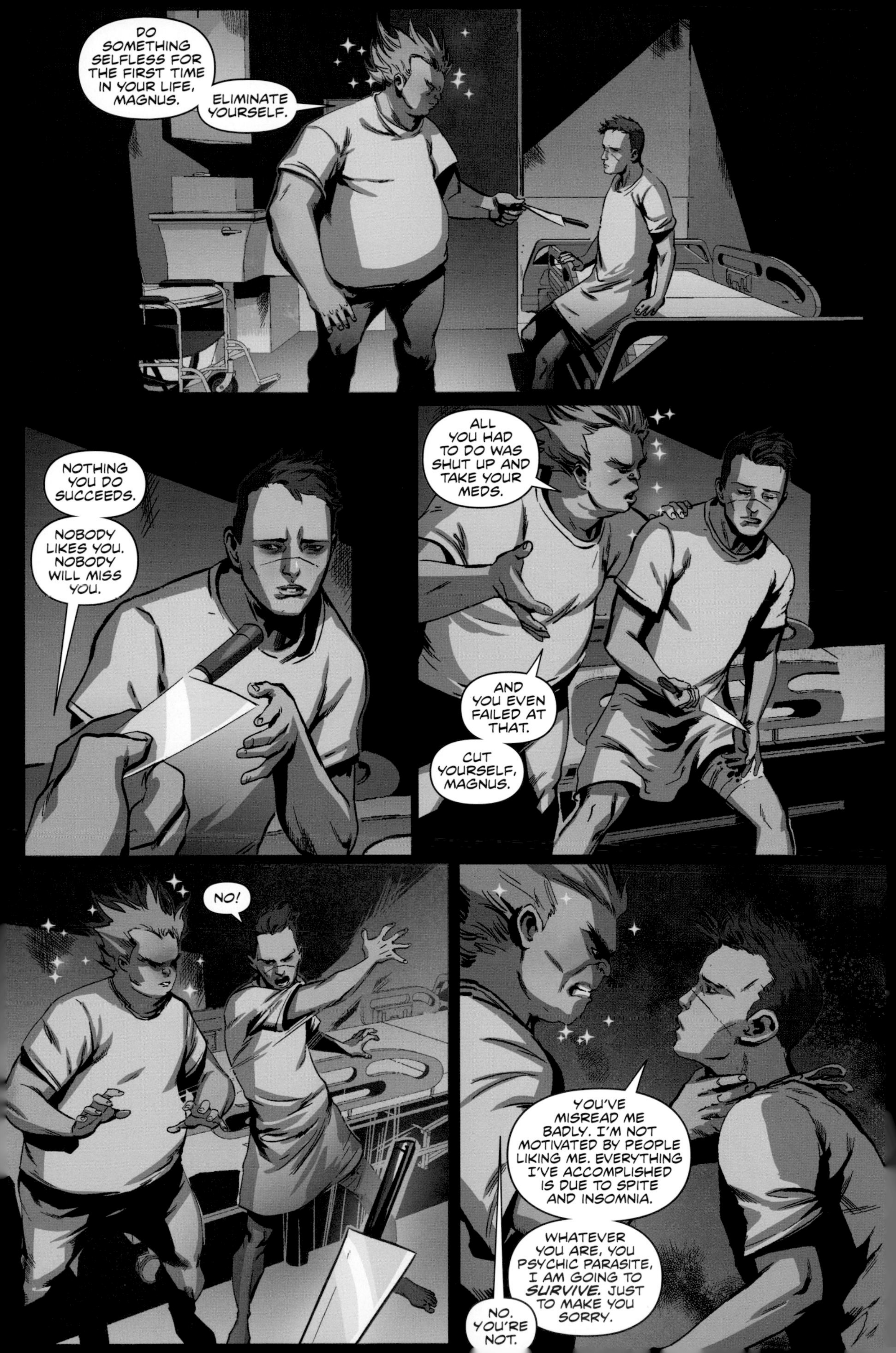

DO SOMETHING SELFLESS FOR THE FIRST TIME IN YOUR LIFE, MAGNUS.
ELIMINATE YOURSELF.
NOTHING YOU DO SUCCEEDS.
NOBODY LIKES YOU. NOBODY WILL MISS YOU.
ALL YOU HAD TO DO WAS SHUT UP AND TAKE YOUR MEDS.
AND YOU EVEN FAILED AT THAT.
CUT YOURSELF, MAGNUS.
NO!
YOU'VE MISREAD ME BADLY. I'M NOT MOTIVATED BY PEOPLE LIKING ME. EVERYTHING I'VE ACCOMPLISHED IS DUE TO SPITE AND INSOMNIA.
WHATEVER YOU ARE, YOU PSYCHIC PARASITE, I AM GOING TO *SURVIVE*. JUST TO MAKE YOU SORRY.
NO. YOU'RE NOT.

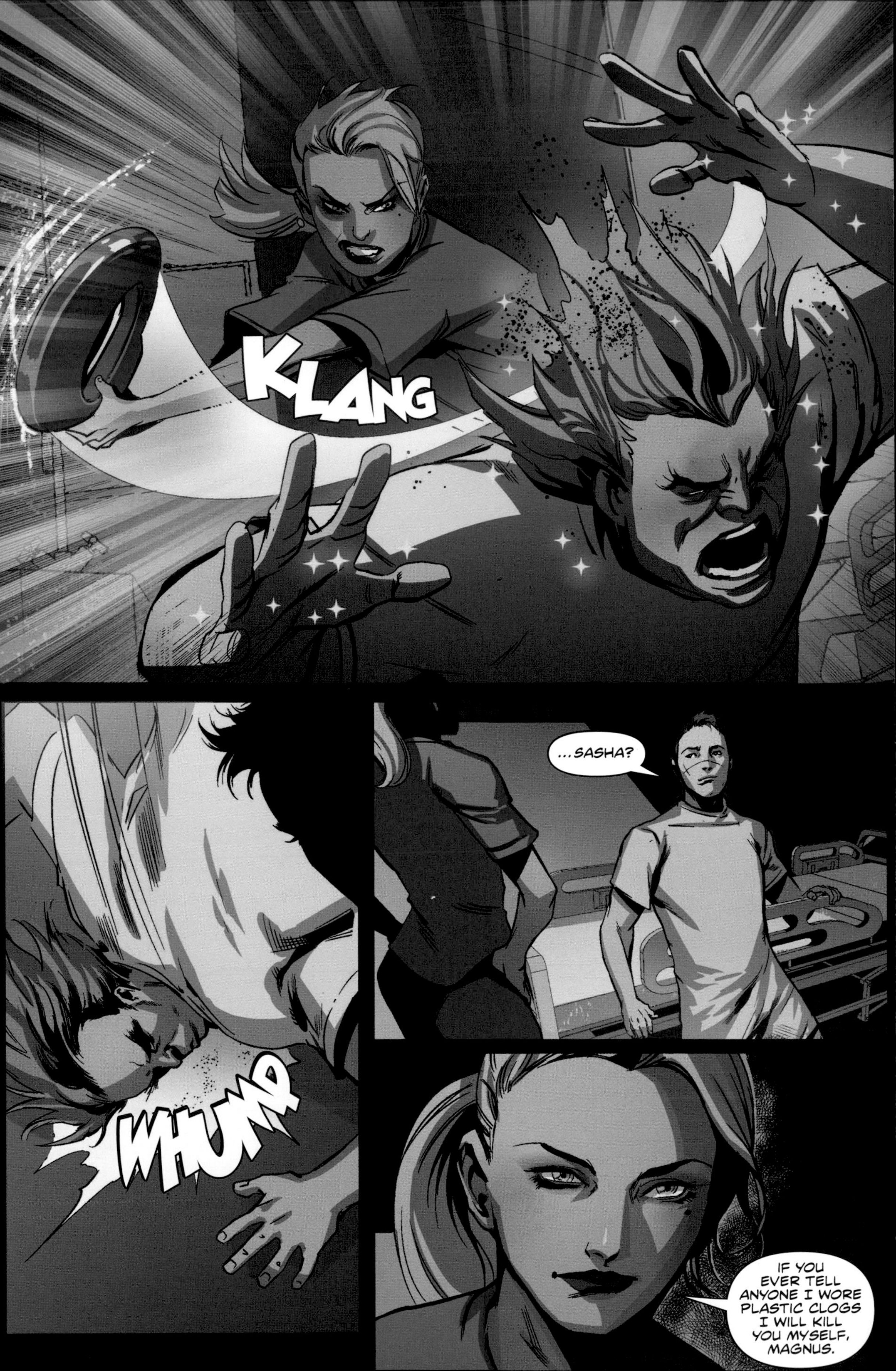
KLANG
WHUMP
...SASHA?
IF YOU EVER TELL ANYONE I WORE PLASTIC CLOGS I WILL KILL YOU MYSELF, MAGNUS.

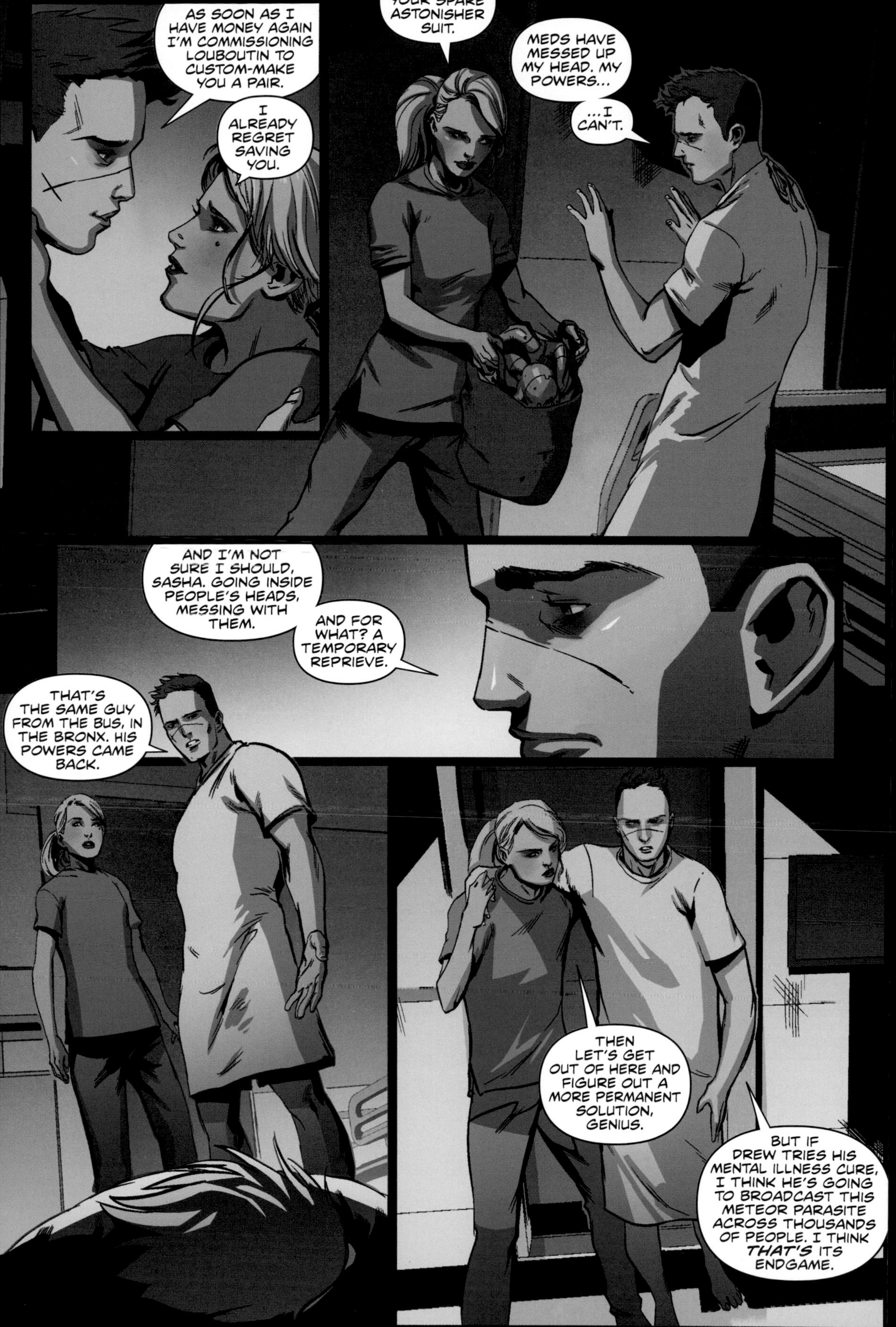
AS SOON AS I HAVE MONEY AGAIN I'M COMMISSIONING LOUBOUTIN TO CUSTOM-MAKE YOU A PAIR.
I ALREADY REGRET SAVING YOU.
I BROUGHT YOUR SPARE ASTONISHER SUIT.
MEDS HAVE MESSED UP MY HEAD. MY POWERS...
...I CAN'T.
AND I'M NOT SURE I SHOULD, SASHA. GOING INSIDE PEOPLE'S HEADS, MESSING WITH THEM.
AND FOR WHAT? A TEMPORARY REPRIEVE.
THAT'S THE SAME GUY FROM THE BUS, IN THE BRONX. HIS POWERS CAME BACK.
THEN LET'S GET OUT OF HERE AND FIGURE OUT A MORE PERMANENT SOLUTION, GENIUS.
BUT IF DREW TRIES HIS MENTAL ILLNESS CURE, I THINK HE'S GOING TO BROADCAST THIS METEOR PARASITE ACROSS THOUSANDS OF PEOPLE. I THINK *THAT'S* ITS ENDGAME.

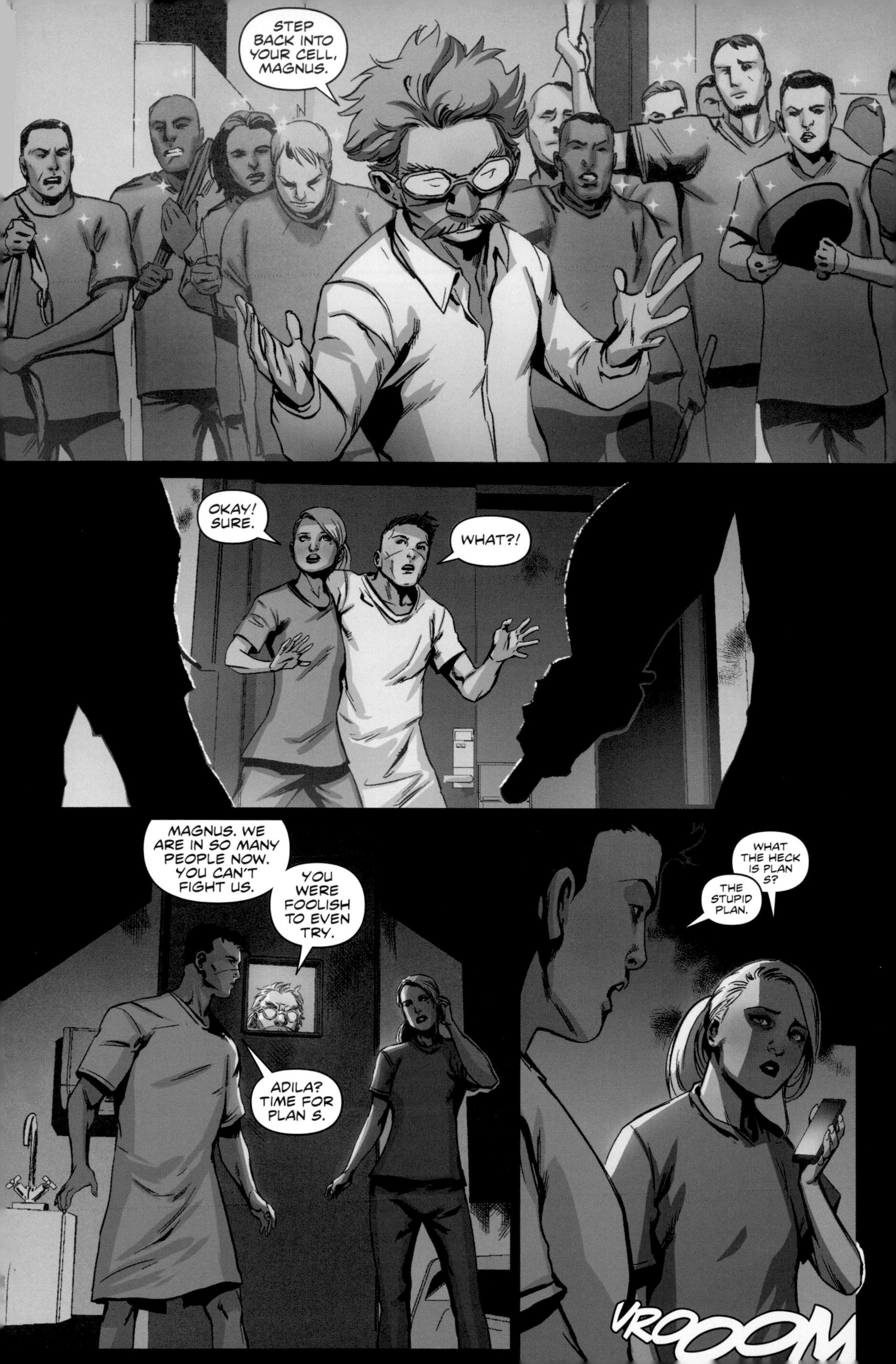
STEP BACK INTO YOUR CELL, MAGNUS.
OKAY! SURE.
WHAT?!
MAGNUS. WE ARE IN SO MANY PEOPLE NOW. YOU CAN'T FIGHT US.
YOU WERE FOOLISH TO EVEN TRY.
ADILA? TIME FOR PLAN S.
WHAT THE HECK IS PLAN S?
THE STUPID PLAN.
VROOOOM

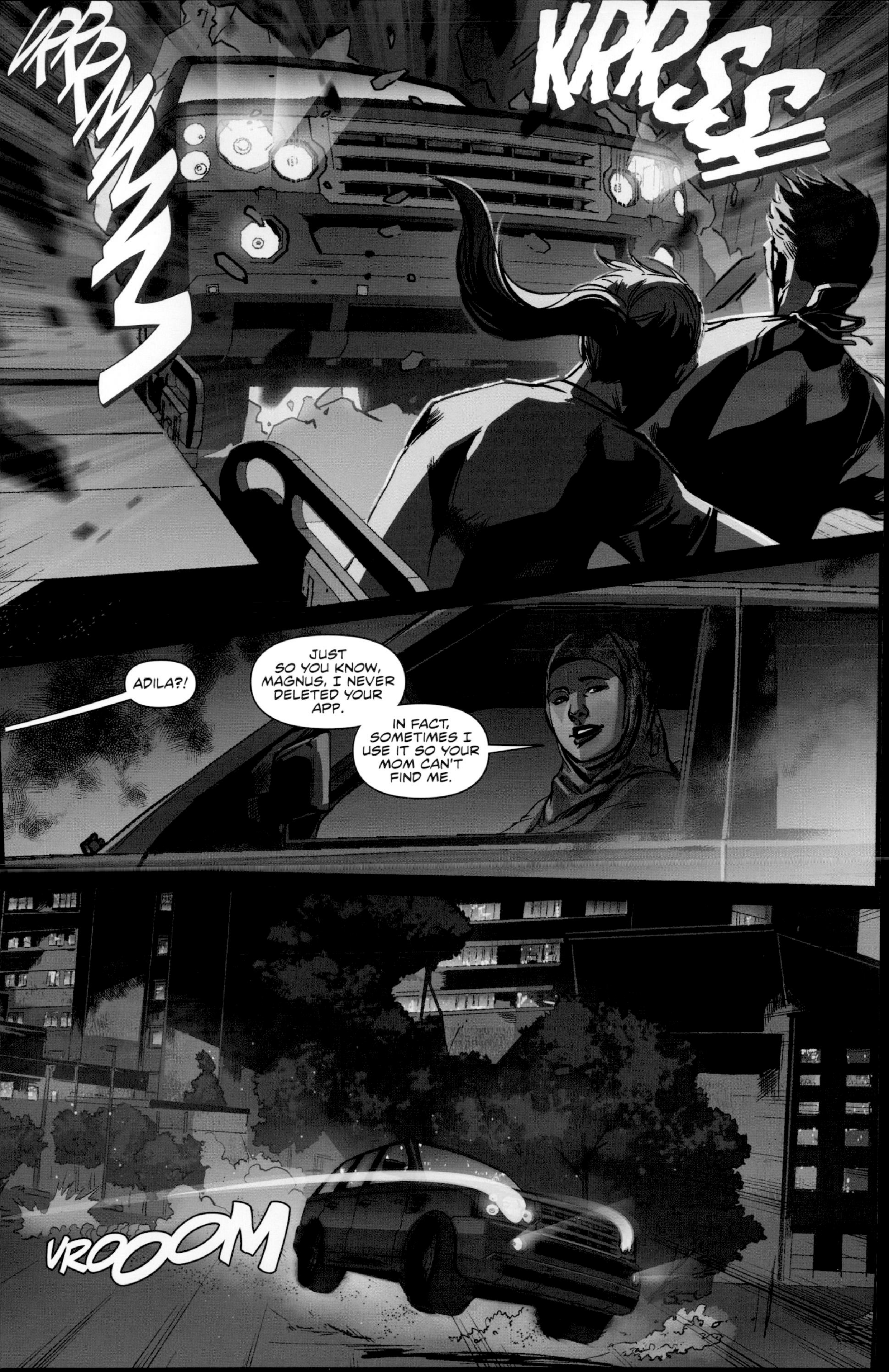
URRRMMMMM
KRRSSH
ADILA?!
JUST SO YOU KNOW, MAGNUS, I NEVER DELETED YOUR APP.
IN FACT, SOMETIMES I USE IT SO YOUR MOM CAN'T FIND ME.
VROOOOM

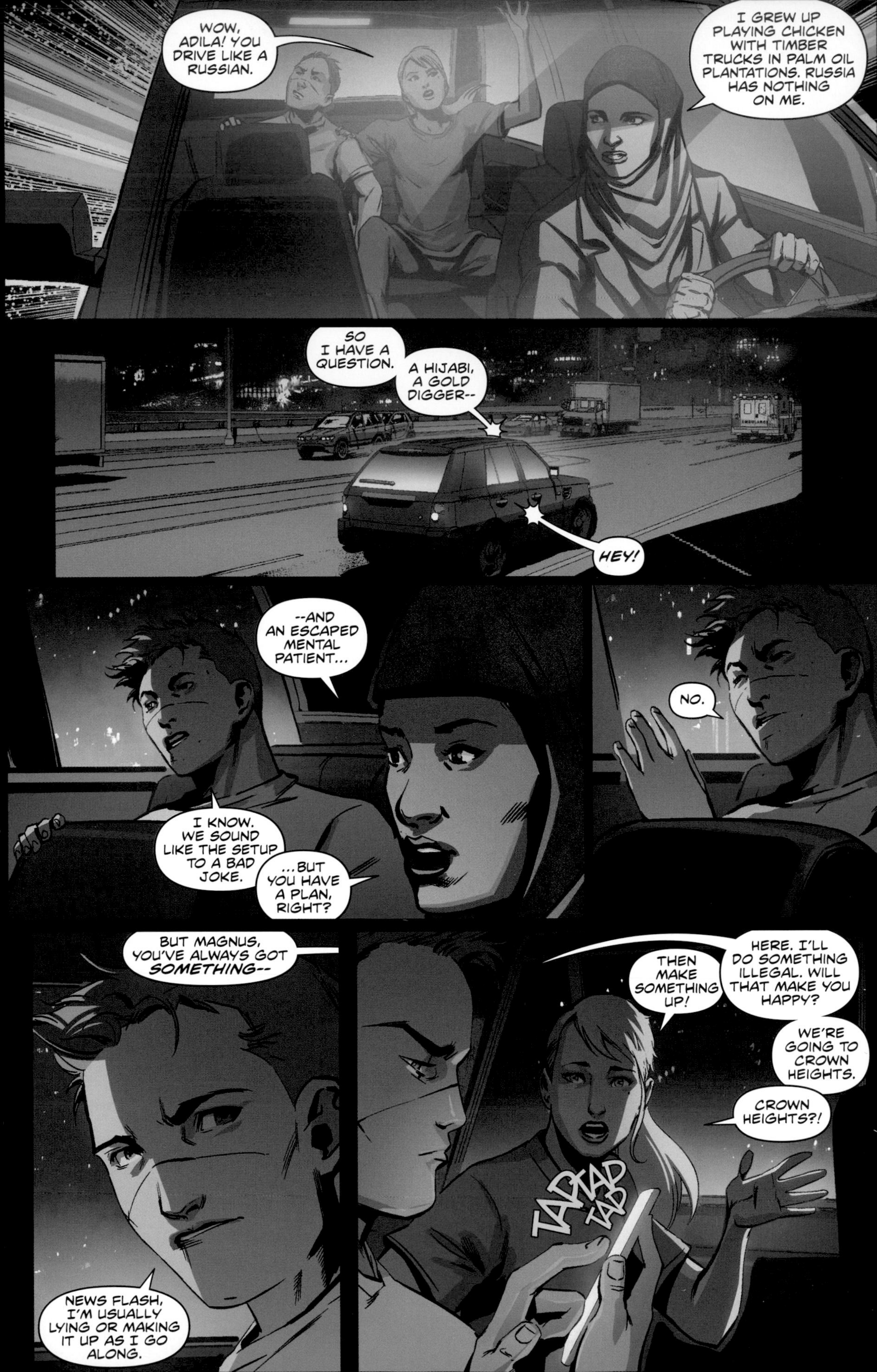
WOW, ADILA! YOU DRIVE LIKE A RUSSIAN.
I GREW UP PLAYING CHICKEN WITH TIMBER TRUCKS IN PALM OIL PLANTATIONS. RUSSIA HAS NOTHING ON ME.
SO I HAVE A QUESTION.
A HIJABI, A GOLD DIGGER--
HEY!
--AND AN ESCAPED MENTAL PATIENT...
I KNOW. WE SOUND LIKE THE SETUP TO A BAD JOKE.
...BUT YOU HAVE A PLAN, RIGHT?
NO.
BUT MAGNUS, YOU'VE ALWAYS GOT SOMETHING--
NEWS FLASH, I'M USUALLY LYING OR MAKING IT UP AS I GO ALONG.
THEN MAKE SOMETHING UP!
HERE. I'LL DO SOMETHING ILLEGAL. WILL THAT MAKE YOU HAPPY?
WE'RE GOING TO CROWN HEIGHTS.
CROWN HEIGHTS?!
TAP TAP TAP

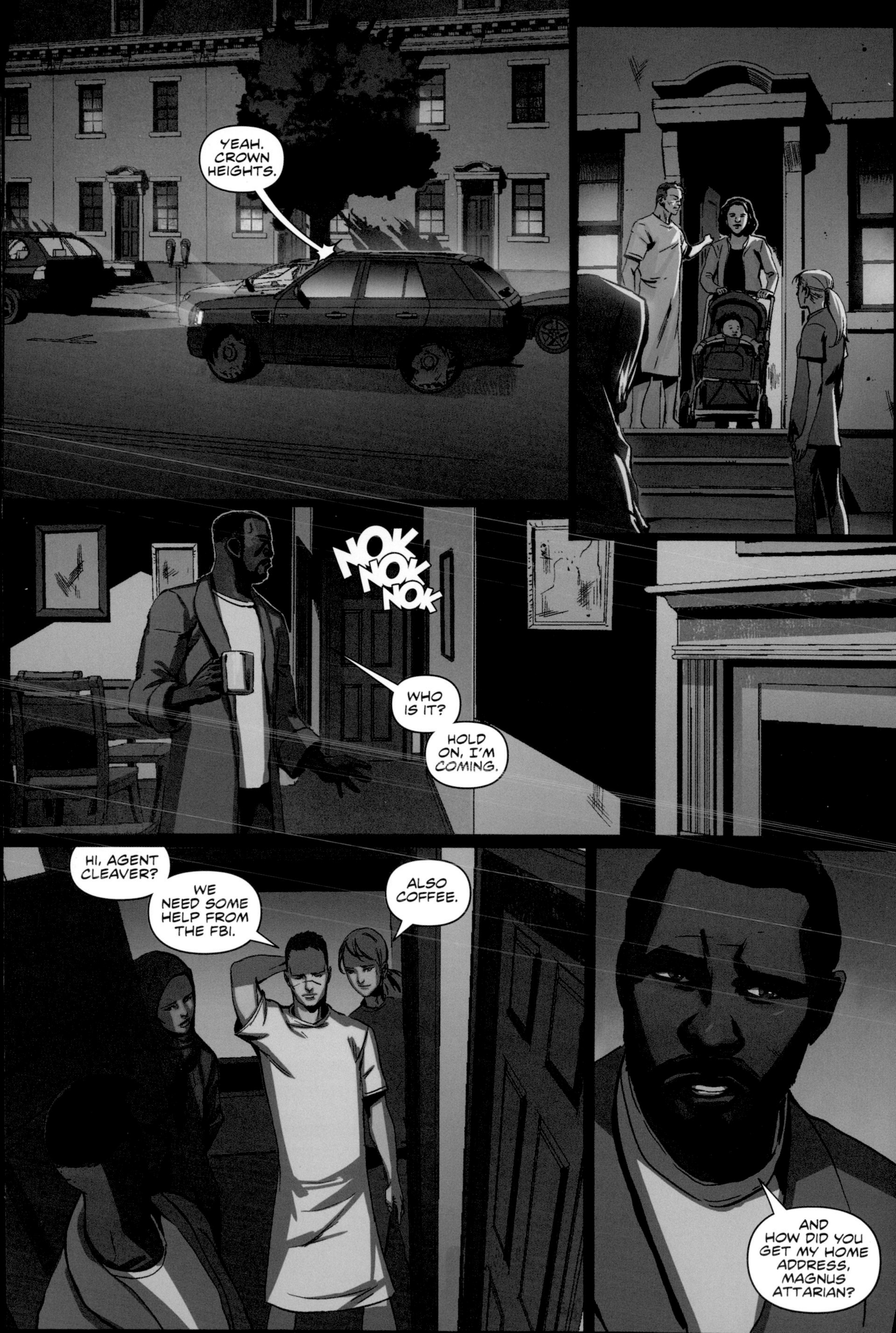
YEAH. CROWN HEIGHTS.
NOK NOK NOK
WHO IS IT?
HOLD ON, I'M COMING.
HI, AGENT CLEAVER?
WE NEED SOME HELP FROM THE FBI.
ALSO COFFEE.
AND HOW DID YOU GET MY HOME ADDRESS, MAGNUS ATTARIAN?

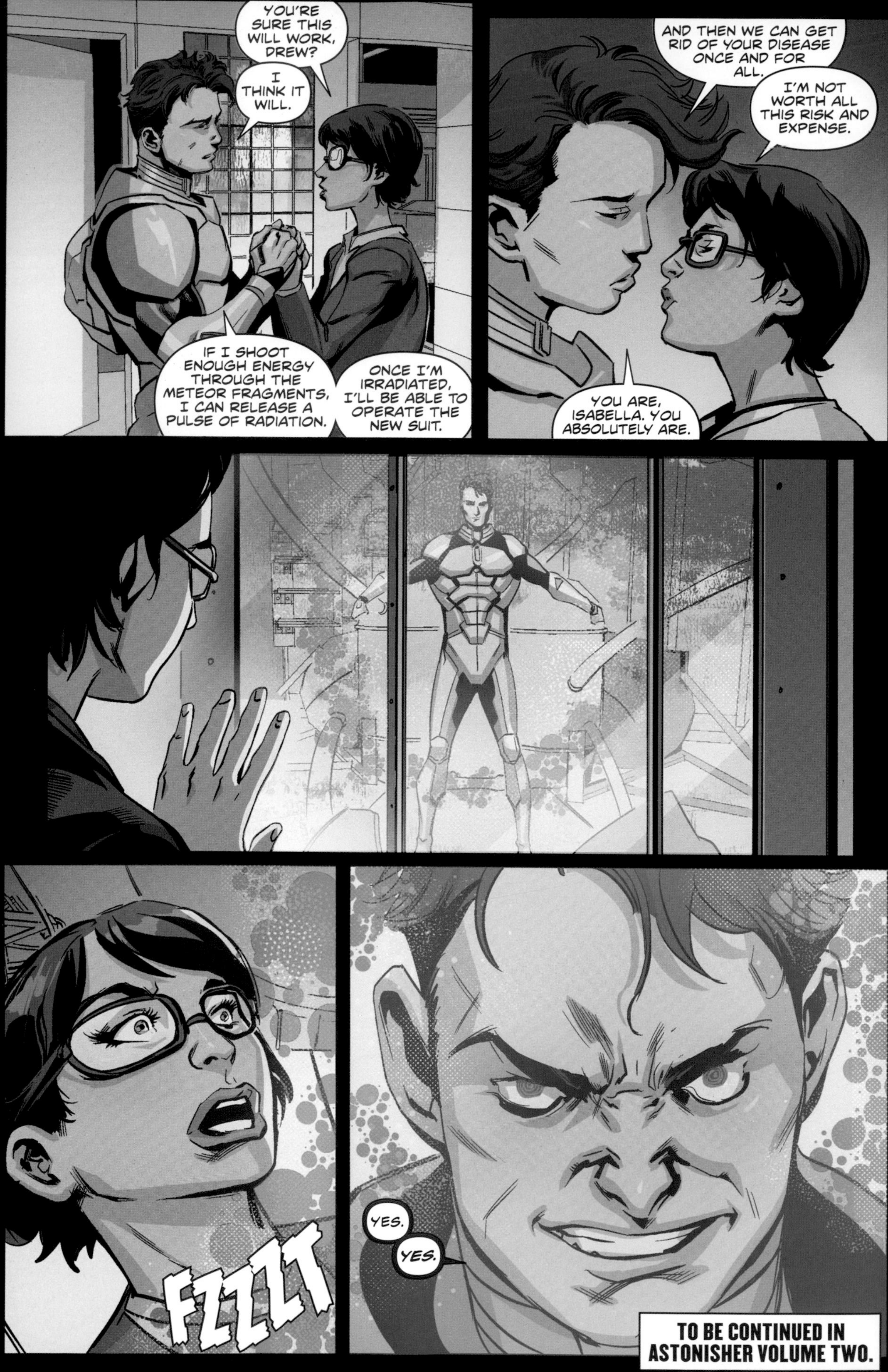
YOU'RE SURE THIS WILL WORK, DREW?
I THINK IT WILL.
IF I SHOOT ENOUGH ENERGY THROUGH THE METEOR FRAGMENTS, I CAN RELEASE A PULSE OF RADIATION.
ONCE I'M IRRADIATED, I'LL BE ABLE TO OPERATE THE NEW SUIT.
AND THEN WE CAN GET RID OF YOUR DISEASE ONCE AND FOR ALL.
I'M NOT WORTH ALL THIS RISK AND EXPENSE.
YOU ARE, ISABELLA. YOU ABSOLUTELY ARE.
FZZZT
YES.
YES.
TO BE CONTINUED IN ASTONISHER VOLUME TWO.

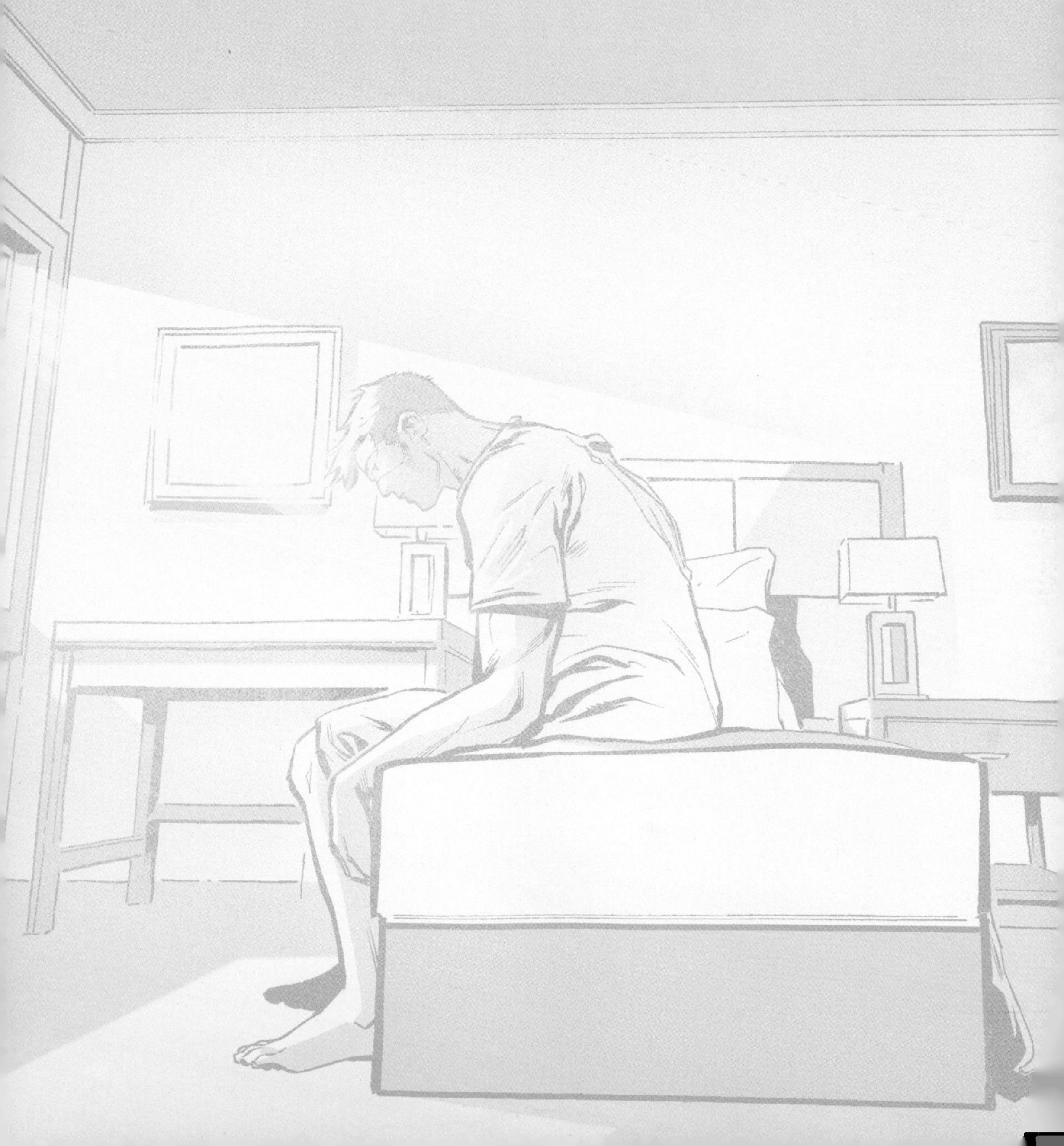

"THE EVENT"

One year before the story of ASTONISHER, humanity was on the verge of extinction. An asteroid detected in space was on a collision course with Earth.

Foresight Corporation, the world's most advanced high-tech humanitarian company led by CEO Lorena Payan, developed the science and ships needed to destroy the asteroid.

A team of astronauts flew into space on a suicide mission to save the world.

This is the story of that heroic mission, and "The Event" from which a new generation of heroes emerged in the world.

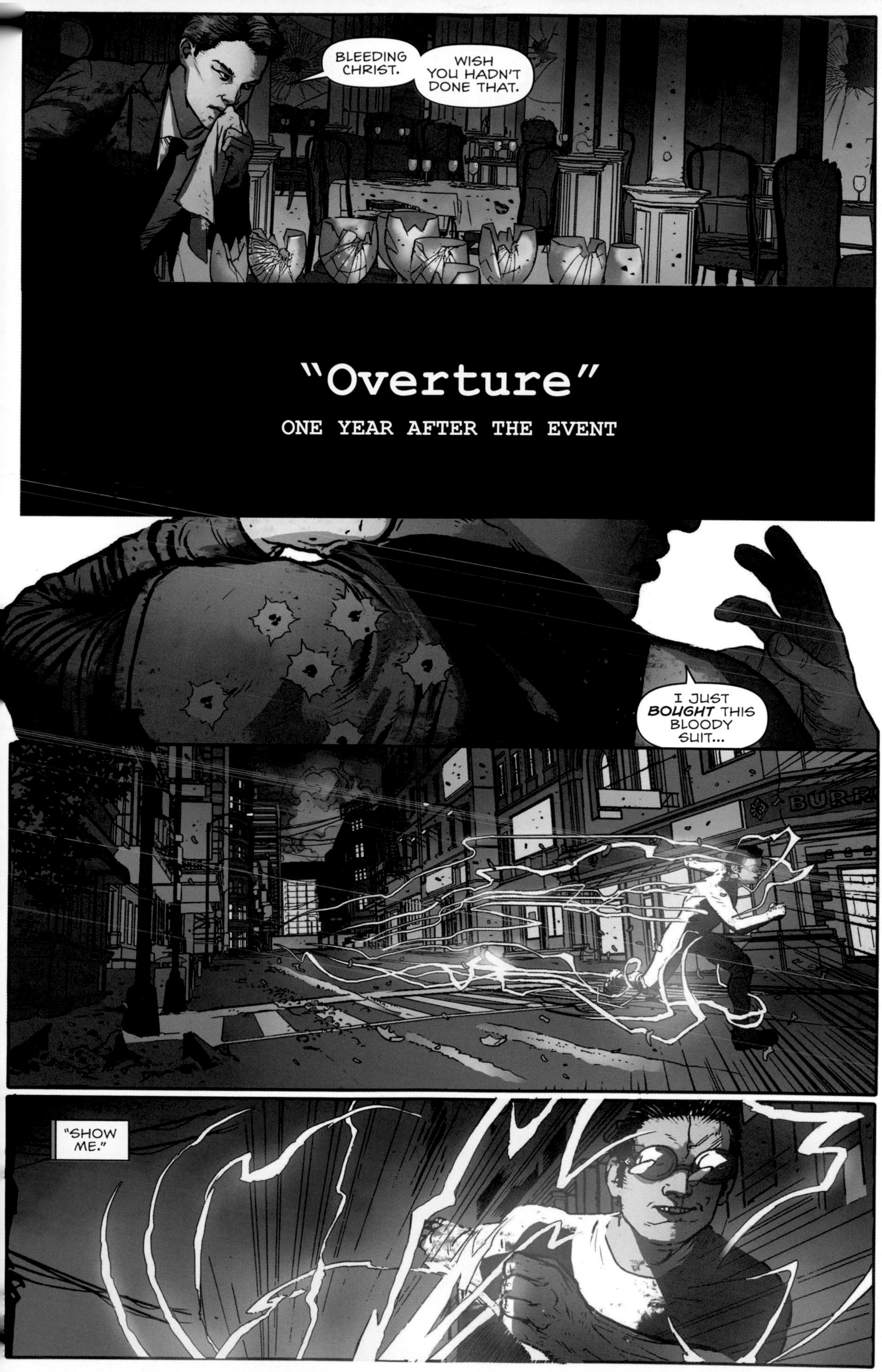
BLEEDING CHRIST.
WISH YOU HADN'T DONE THAT.
"Overture"
ONE YEAR AFTER THE EVENT
I JUST BOUGHT THIS BLOODY SUIT...
"SHOW ME."

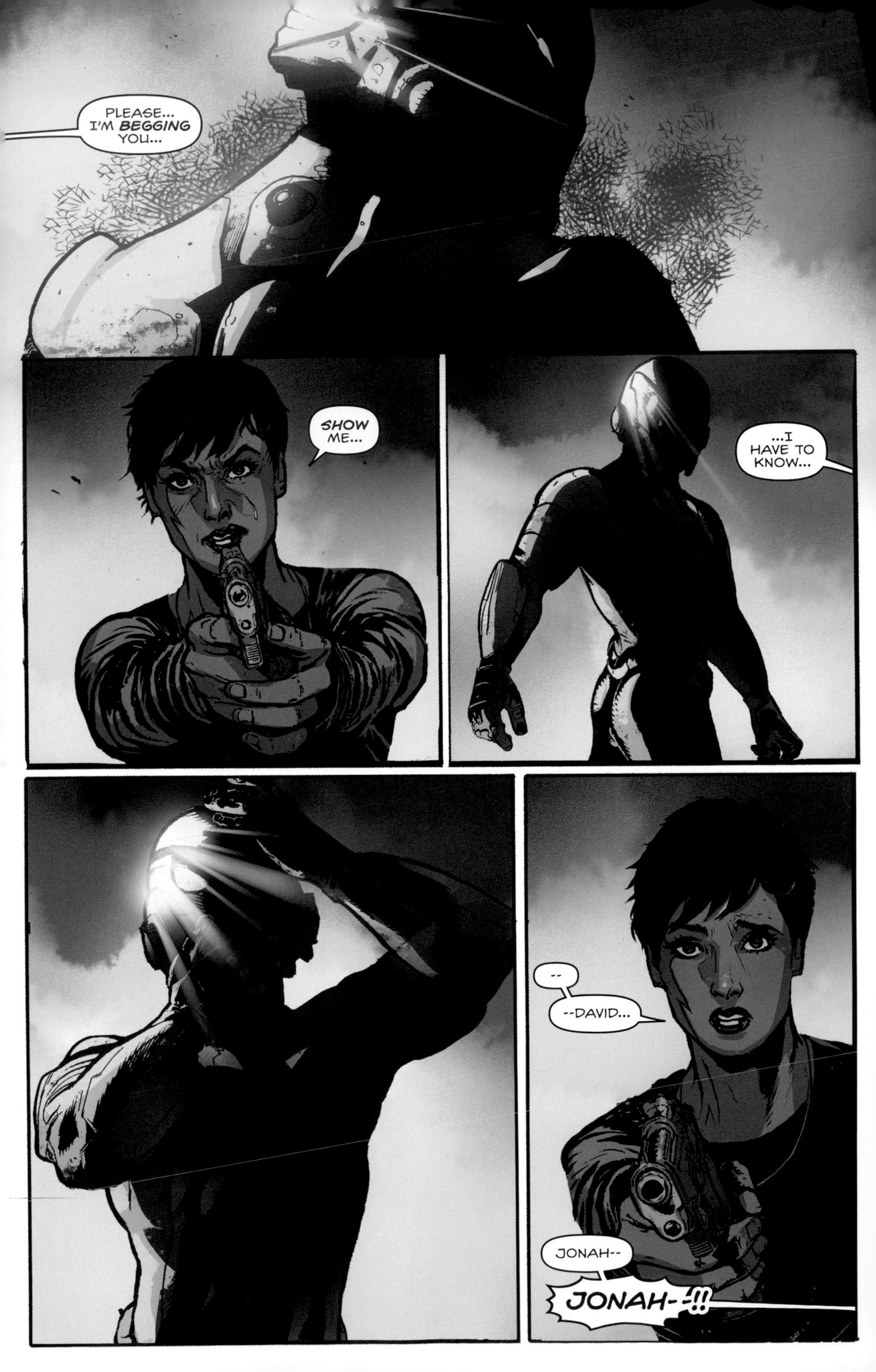
PLEASE... I'M *BEGGING* YOU...
SHOW ME...
...I HAVE TO KNOW...
--
--DAVID...
JONAH--
JONAH--!!

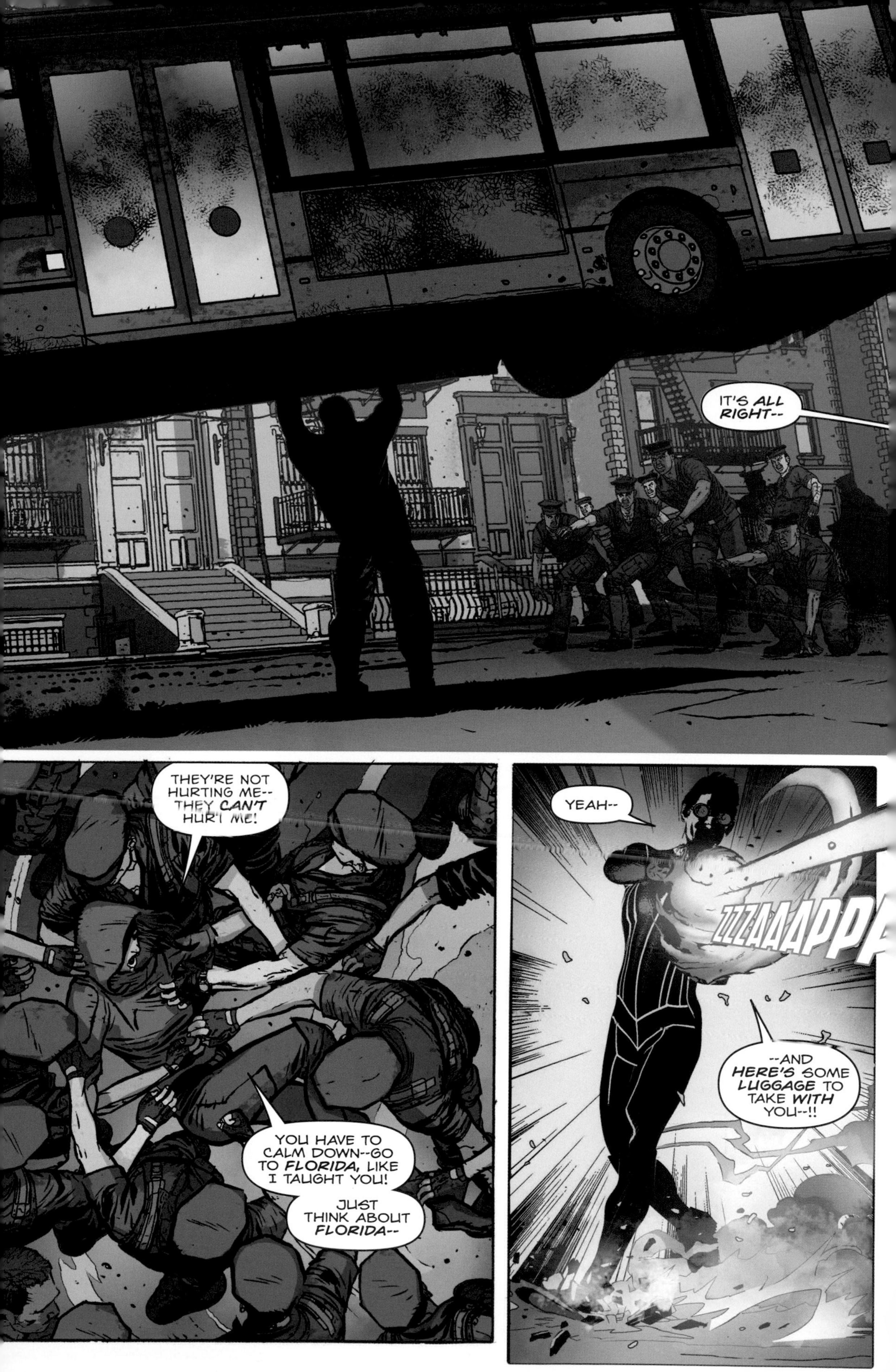
IT'S ALL RIGHT--
THEY'RE NOT HURTING ME--THEY CAN'T HURT ME!
YOU HAVE TO CALM DOWN--GO TO FLORIDA, LIKE I TAUGHT YOU!
JUST THINK ABOUT FLORIDA--
YEAH--
ZZZAAAPPP
--AND HERE'S SOME LUGGAGE TO TAKE WITH YOU--!!

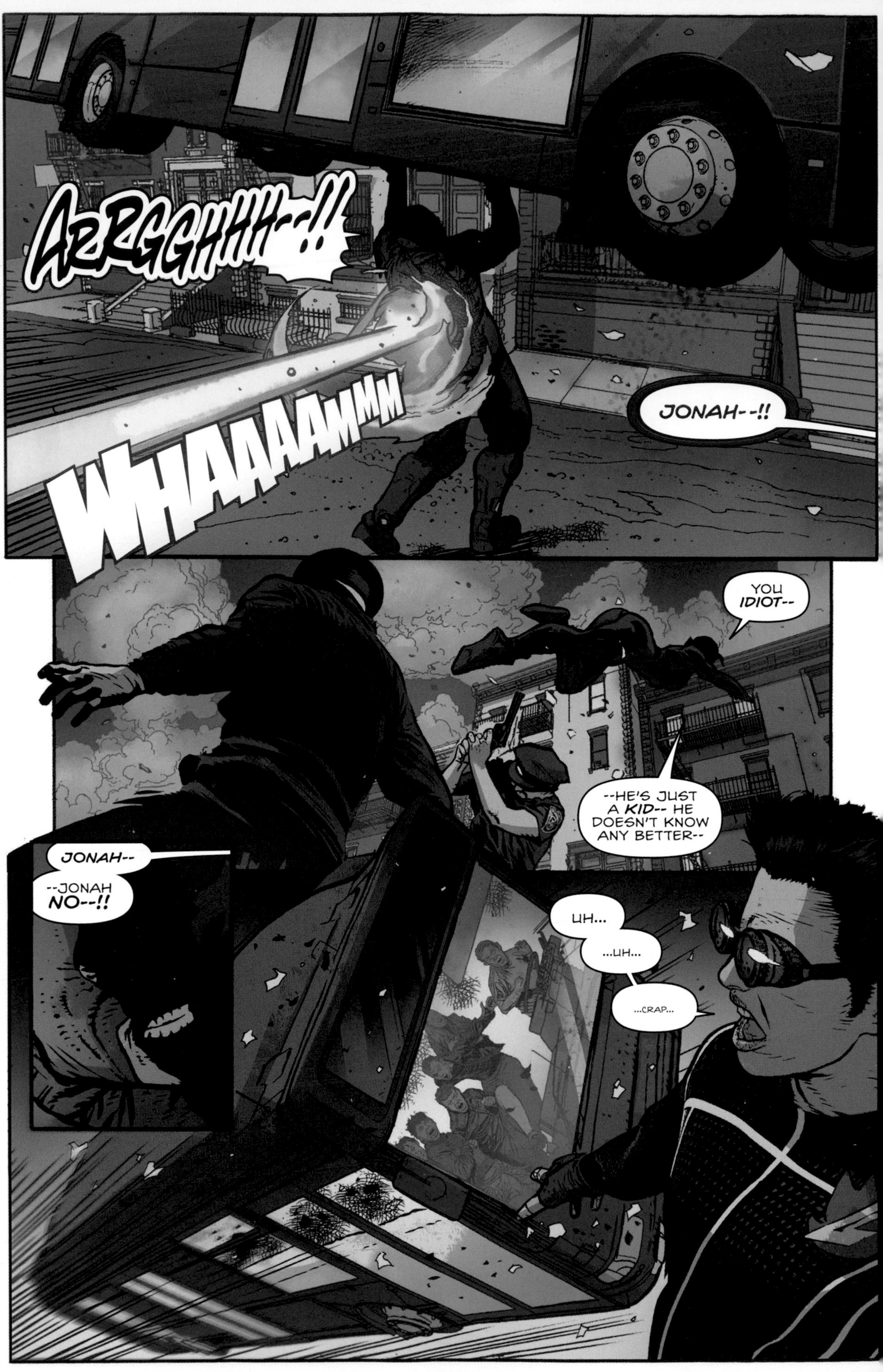

ARRGGHHH--!!
WHAAAAAMMM
JONAH--!!
YOU IDIOT--
--HE'S JUST A KID-- HE DOESN'T KNOW ANY BETTER--
JONAH--
--JONAH NO--!!
UH...
...UH...
...CRAP...

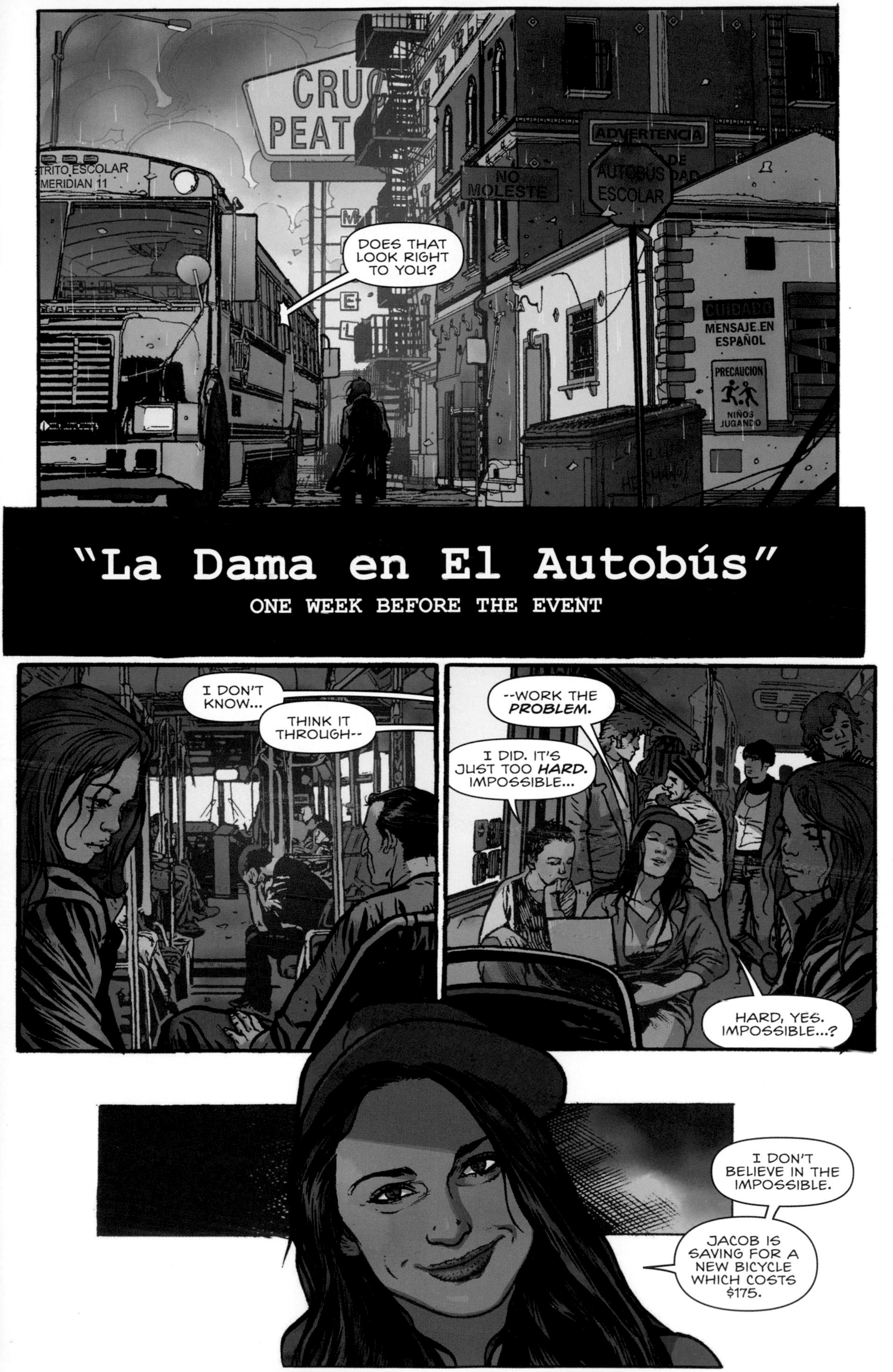

TRITO ESCOLAR
MERIDIAN 11
ADVERTENCIA
NO MOLESTE
AUTOBUS ESCOLAR
CUIDADO
MENSAJE EN ESPAÑOL
PRECAUCION
NIÑOS JUGANDO
DOES THAT LOOK RIGHT TO YOU?
"La Dama en El Autobús"
ONE WEEK BEFORE THE EVENT
I DON'T KNOW...
THINK IT THROUGH--
--WORK THE *PROBLEM.*
I DID. IT'S JUST TOO *HARD.* IMPOSSIBLE...
HARD, YES. IMPOSSIBLE...?
I DON'T BELIEVE IN THE IMPOSSIBLE.
JACOB IS SAVING FOR A NEW BICYCLE WHICH COSTS $175.

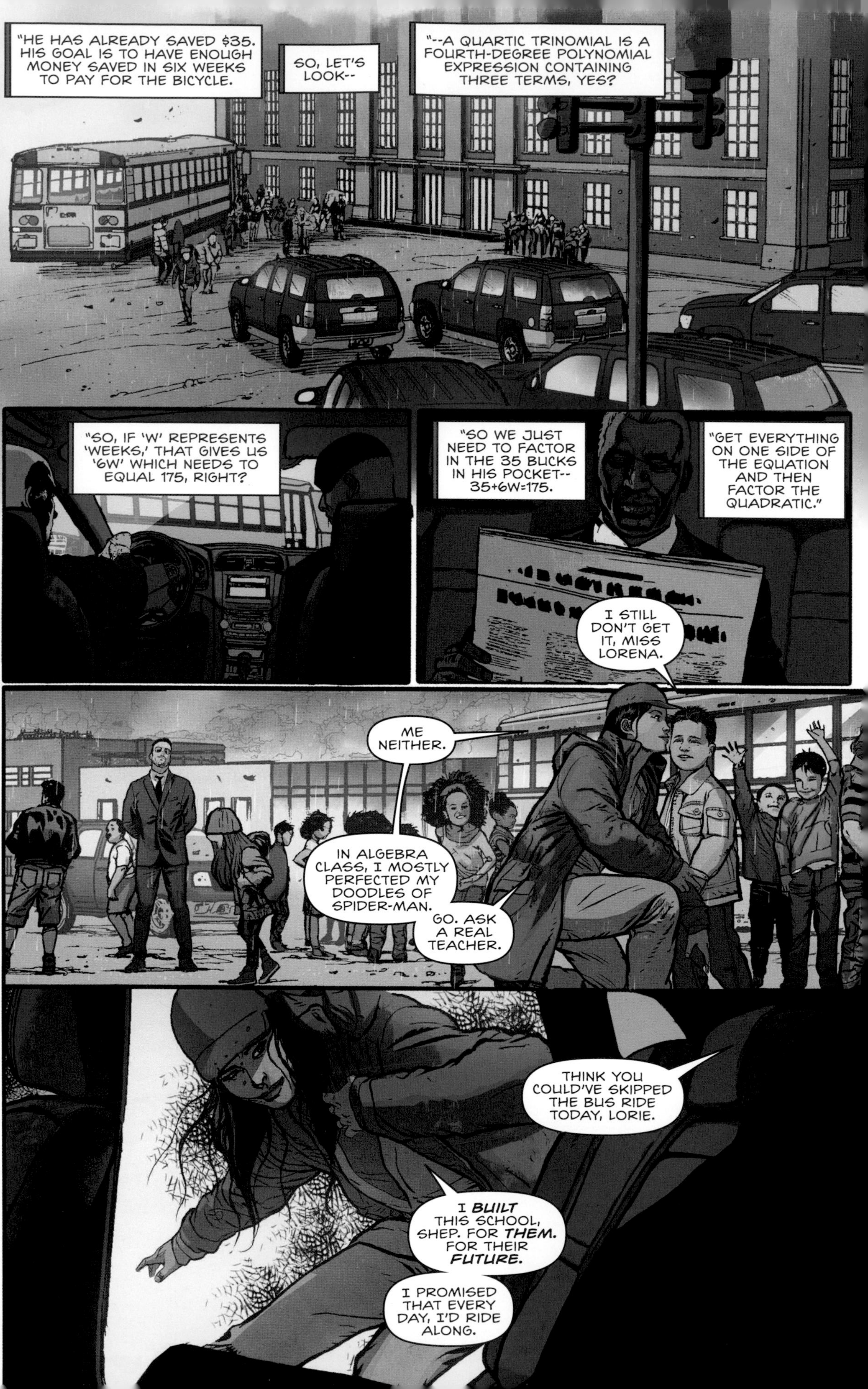
"HE HAS ALREADY SAVED $35. HIS GOAL IS TO HAVE ENOUGH MONEY SAVED IN SIX WEEKS TO PAY FOR THE BICYCLE.
SO, LET'S LOOK--
"--A QUARTIC TRINOMIAL IS A FOURTH-DEGREE POLYNOMIAL EXPRESSION CONTAINING THREE TERMS, YES?
"SO, IF 'W' REPRESENTS 'WEEKS,' THAT GIVES US '6W' WHICH NEEDS TO EQUAL 175, RIGHT?
"SO WE JUST NEED TO FACTOR IN THE 35 BUCKS IN HIS POCKET-- 35+6W=175.
"GET EVERYTHING ON ONE SIDE OF THE EQUATION AND THEN FACTOR THE QUADRATIC."
I STILL DON'T GET IT, MISS LORENA.
ME NEITHER.
IN ALGEBRA CLASS, I MOSTLY PERFECTED MY DOODLES OF SPIDER-MAN.
GO. ASK A REAL TEACHER.
THINK YOU COULD'VE SKIPPED THE BUS RIDE TODAY, LORIE.
I BUILT THIS SCHOOL, SHEP. FOR THEM. FOR THEIR FUTURE.
I PROMISED THAT EVERY DAY, I'D RIDE ALONG.

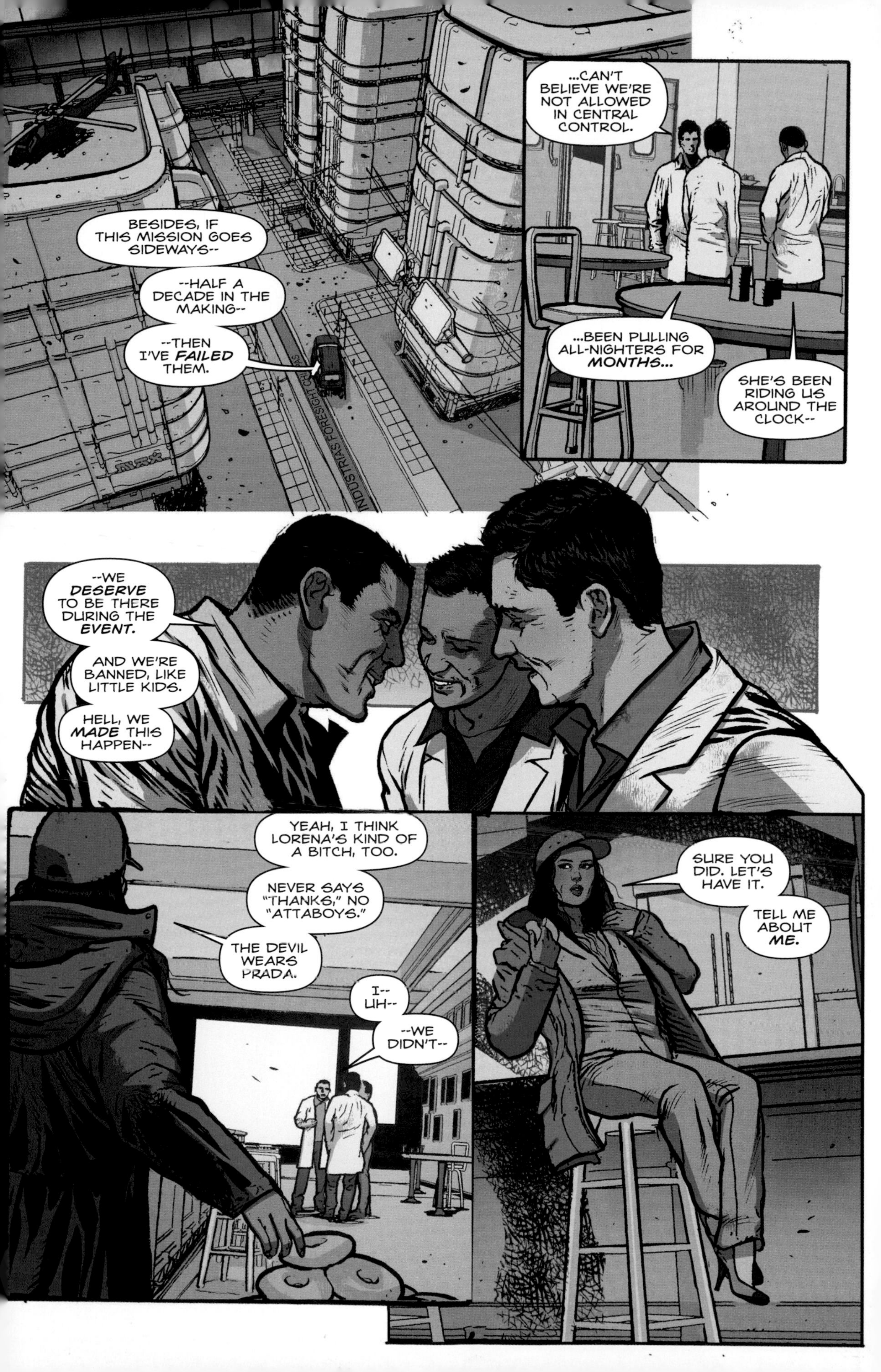
BESIDES, IF THIS MISSION GOES SIDEWAYS--
--HALF A DECADE IN THE MAKING--
--THEN I'VE FAILED THEM.
INDUSTRIAS FORESIGHT
...CAN'T BELIEVE WE'RE NOT ALLOWED IN CENTRAL CONTROL.
...BEEN PULLING ALL-NIGHTERS FOR MONTHS...
SHE'S BEEN RIDING US AROUND THE CLOCK--
--WE DESERVE TO BE THERE DURING THE EVENT.
AND WE'RE BANNED, LIKE LITTLE KIDS.
HELL, WE MADE THIS HAPPEN--
YEAH, I THINK LORENA'S KIND OF A BITCH, TOO.
NEVER SAYS "THANKS," NO "ATTABOYS."
THE DEVIL WEARS PRADA.
I-- UH--
--WE DIDN'T--
SURE YOU DID. LET'S HAVE IT.
TELL ME ABOUT ME.

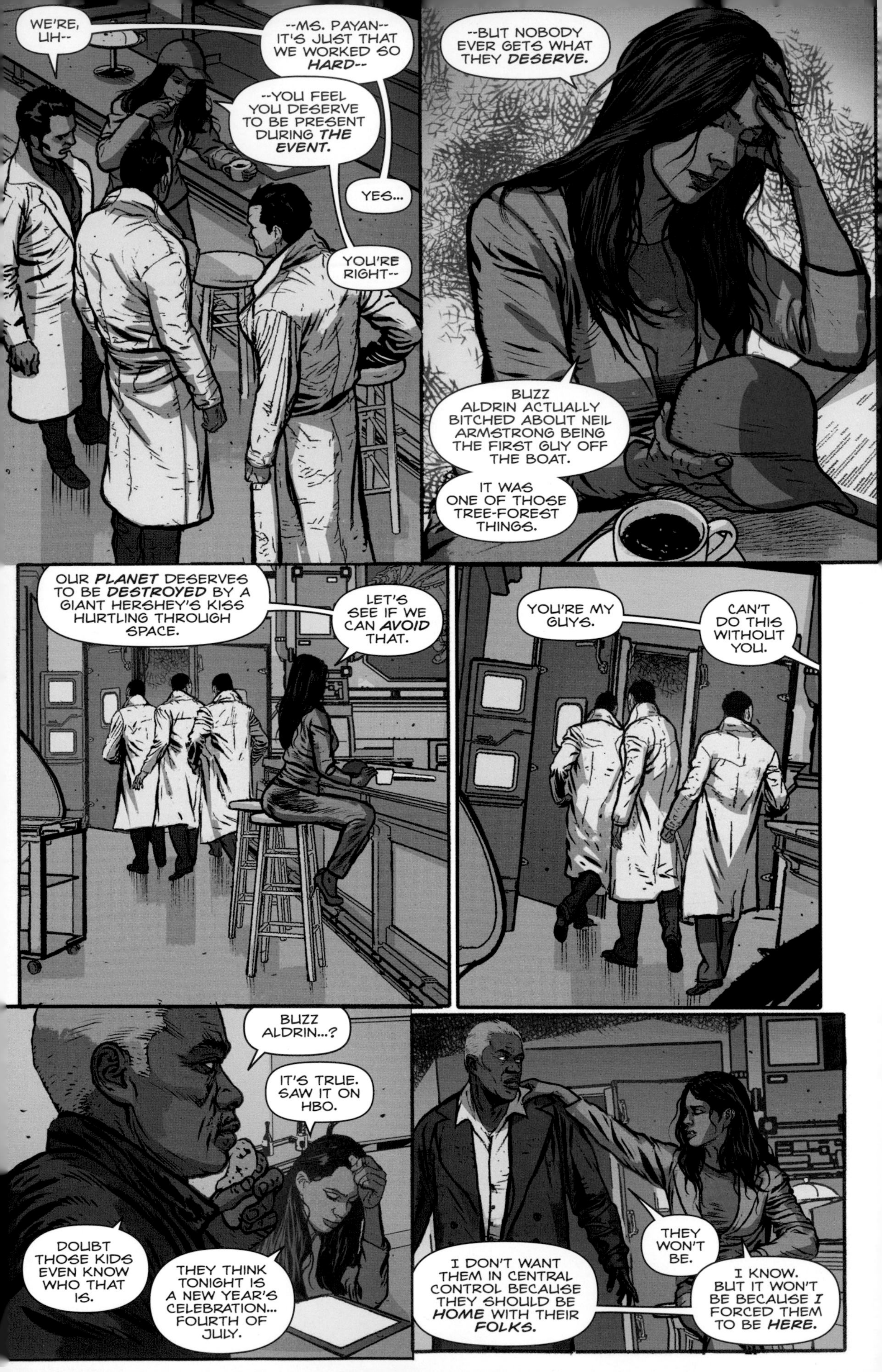
WE'RE, UH--
--MS. PAYAN-- IT'S JUST THAT WE WORKED SO HARD--
--YOU FEEL YOU DESERVE TO BE PRESENT DURING THE EVENT.
YES...
YOU'RE RIGHT--
--BUT NOBODY EVER GETS WHAT THEY DESERVE.
BUZZ ALDRIN ACTUALLY BITCHED ABOUT NEIL ARMSTRONG BEING THE FIRST GUY OFF THE BOAT.
IT WAS ONE OF THOSE TREE-FOREST THINGS.
OUR PLANET DESERVES TO BE DESTROYED BY A GIANT HERSHEY'S KISS HURTLING THROUGH SPACE.
LET'S SEE IF WE CAN AVOID THAT.
YOU'RE MY GUYS.
CAN'T DO THIS WITHOUT YOU.
BUZZ ALDRIN...?
IT'S TRUE. SAW IT ON HBO.
DOUBT THOSE KIDS EVEN KNOW WHO THAT IS.
THEY THINK TONIGHT IS A NEW YEAR'S CELEBRATION... FOURTH OF JULY.
THEY WON'T BE.
I DON'T WANT THEM IN CENTRAL CONTROL BECAUSE THEY SHOULD BE HOME WITH THEIR FOLKS.
I KNOW. BUT IT WON'T BE BECAUSE I FORCED THEM TO BE HERE.

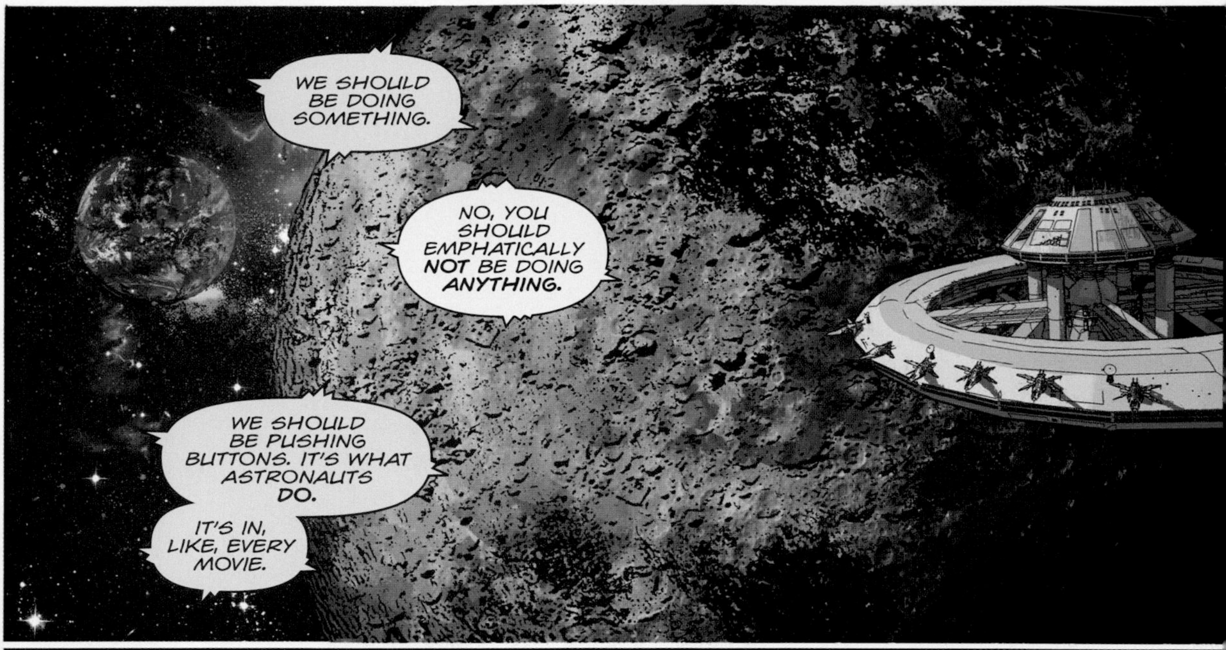
WE SHOULD BE DOING SOMETHING.
NO, YOU SHOULD EMPHATICALLY NOT BE DOING ANYTHING.
WE SHOULD BE PUSHING BUTTONS. IT'S WHAT ASTRONAUTS DO.
IT'S IN, LIKE, EVERY MOVIE.

"Monkeys"

FORESIGHT AMERICO LUNAR PLATFORM
ONE WEEK BEFORE THE EVENT

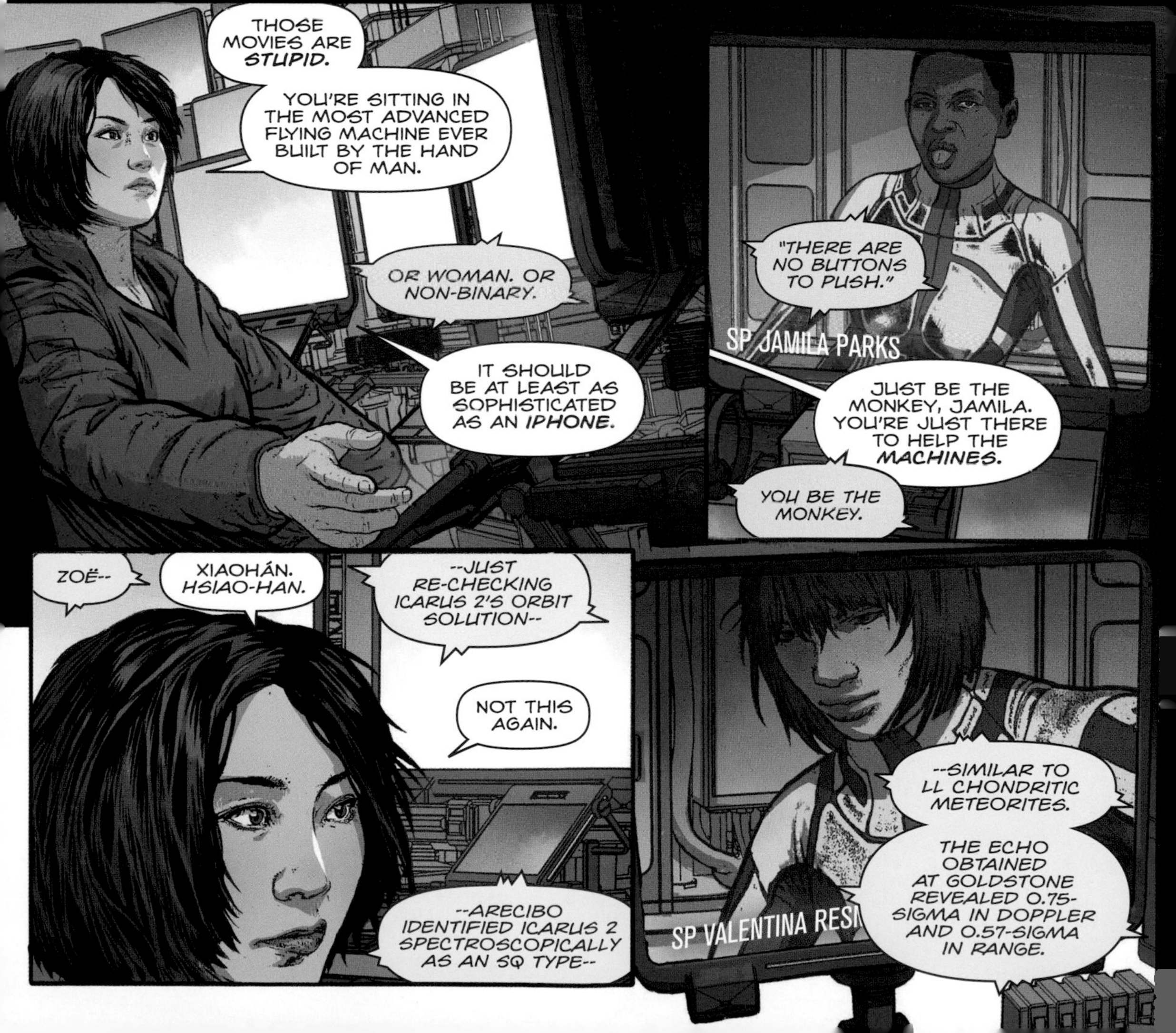
THOSE MOVIES ARE STUPID.
YOU'RE SITTING IN THE MOST ADVANCED FLYING MACHINE EVER BUILT BY THE HAND OF MAN.
OR WOMAN. OR NON-BINARY.
IT SHOULD BE AT LEAST AS SOPHISTICATED AS AN IPHONE.
"THERE ARE NO BUTTONS TO PUSH."
SP JAMILA PARKS
JUST BE THE MONKEY, JAMILA. YOU'RE JUST THERE TO HELP THE MACHINES.
YOU BE THE MONKEY.
ZOË--
XIAOHÁN. HSIAO-HAN.
--JUST RE-CHECKING ICARUS 2'S ORBIT SOLUTION--
NOT THIS AGAIN.
--ARECIBO IDENTIFIED ICARUS 2 SPECTROSCOPICALLY AS AN SQ TYPE--
SP VALENTINA RESM
--SIMILAR TO LL CHONDRITIC METEORITES.
THE ECHO OBTAINED AT GOLDSTONE REVEALED 0.75-SIGMA IN DOPPLER AND 0.57-SIGMA IN RANGE.

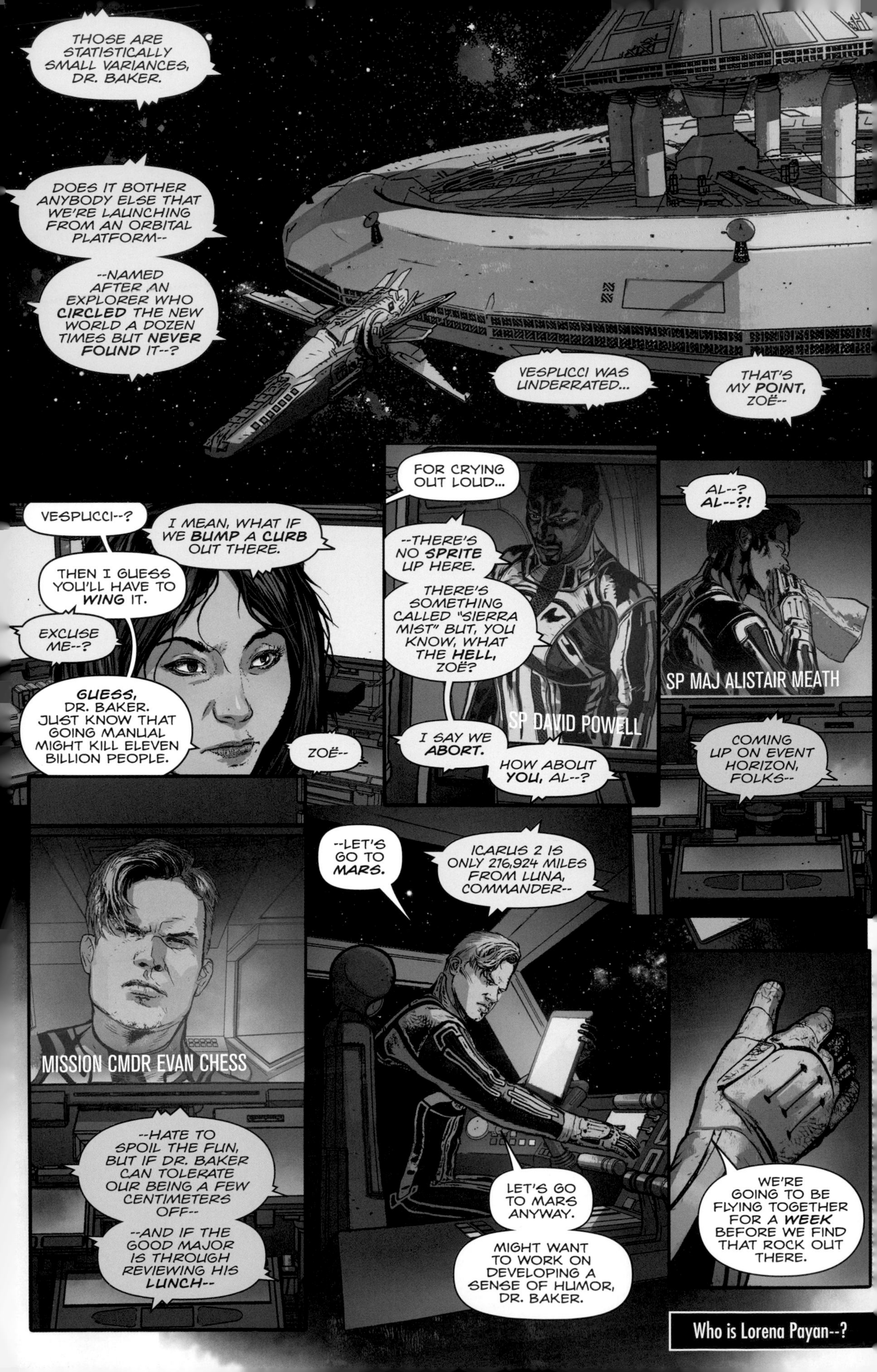
THOSE ARE STATISTICALLY SMALL VARIANCES, DR. BAKER.
DOES IT BOTHER ANYBODY ELSE THAT WE'RE LAUNCHING FROM AN ORBITAL PLATFORM--
--NAMED AFTER AN EXPLORER WHO CIRCLED THE NEW WORLD A DOZEN TIMES BUT NEVER FOUND IT--?
VESPUCCI WAS UNDERRATED...
THAT'S MY POINT, ZOË--
VESPUCCI--?
I MEAN, WHAT IF WE BUMP A CURB OUT THERE.
THEN I GUESS YOU'LL HAVE TO WING IT.
EXCUSE ME--?
GUESS, DR. BAKER. JUST KNOW THAT GOING MANUAL MIGHT KILL ELEVEN BILLION PEOPLE.
ZOË--
FOR CRYING OUT LOUD...
--THERE'S NO SPRITE UP HERE.
THERE'S SOMETHING CALLED "SIERRA MIST" BUT, YOU KNOW, WHAT THE HELL, ZOË?
SP DAVID POWELL
I SAY WE ABORT.
HOW ABOUT YOU, AL--?
AL--? AL--?!
SP MAJ ALISTAIR MEATH
COMING UP ON EVENT HORIZON, FOLKS--
MISSION CMDR EVAN CHESS
--HATE TO SPOIL THE FUN, BUT IF DR. BAKER CAN TOLERATE OUR BEING A FEW CENTIMETERS OFF--
--AND IF THE GOOD MAJOR IS THROUGH REVIEWING HIS LUNCH--
--LET'S GO TO MARS.
ICARUS 2 IS ONLY 216,924 MILES FROM LUNA, COMMANDER--
LET'S GO TO MARS ANYWAY.
MIGHT WANT TO WORK ON DEVELOPING A SENSE OF HUMOR, DR. BAKER.
WE'RE GOING TO BE FLYING TOGETHER FOR A WEEK BEFORE WE FIND THAT ROCK OUT THERE.
Who is Lorena Payan--?

GLOBAL **NOW**

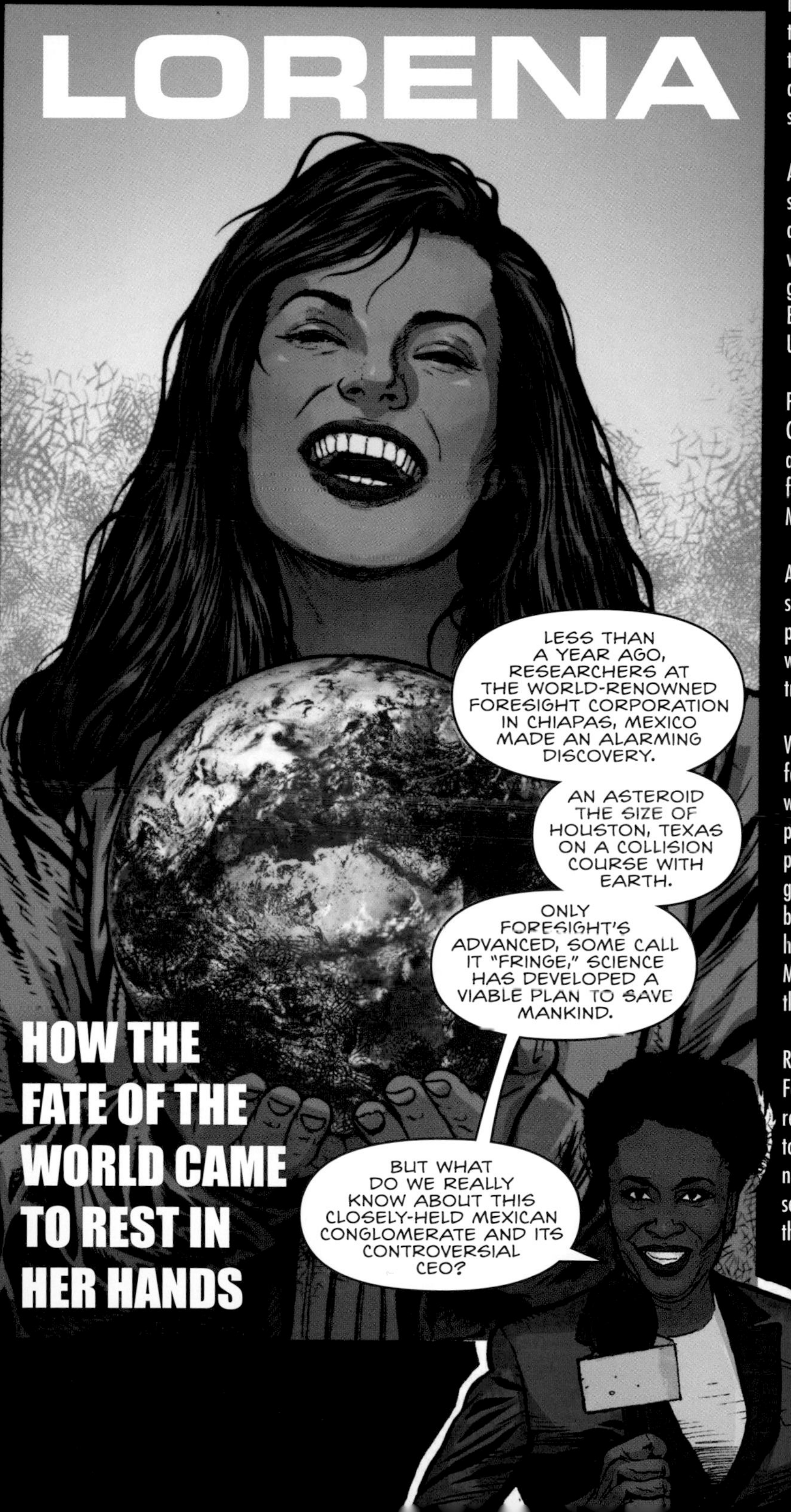
LORENA
LESS THAN A YEAR AGO, RESEARCHERS AT THE WORLD-RENOWNED FORESIGHT CORPORATION IN CHIAPAS, MEXICO MADE AN ALARMING DISCOVERY.
AN ASTEROID THE SIZE OF HOUSTON, TEXAS ON A COLLISION COURSE WITH EARTH.
ONLY FORESIGHT'S ADVANCED, SOME CALL IT "FRINGE," SCIENCE HAS DEVELOPED A VIABLE PLAN TO SAVE MANKIND.
BUT WHAT DO WE REALLY KNOW ABOUT THIS CLOSELY-HELD MEXICAN CONGLOMERATE AND ITS CONTROVERSIAL CEO?
HOW THE FATE OF THE WORLD CAME TO REST IN HER HANDS

In less than ten years, Lorena Payan built the Foresight Corporation into a global titan through innovations in aerospace development, space exploration, and so-called "fringe" science.

A native of the impoverished Mexican state of Chiapas, Payan lost her mother at age twelve. She and her brother Ramon were raised by their paternal grandmother Isabel, while their father Enrique Payan attended M.I.T. in the United States.

Payan's father founded the Foresight Corporation in Silicon Valley when she was a teenager, using wealth accumulated from his various business ventures in Mexico.

After immigrating to America, Payan studied under the tutelage of the eminent physicist, Dr. Parker "Shep" Bingham, who has served as her mentor and most trusted advisor.

While Payan lived in America with her father, her brother returned to Mexico, where Ramon Payan rose within the political structure. While Enrique Payan planted himself and his daughter in the ground of the American Dream, Lorena's brother chose to fight for his people back home, to work within the system to pull Mexico out of corruption and save it from the drug cartels.

Ramon Payan inherited the leadership of Foresight upon their father's death and relocated the corporation's central office to Chiapas. The Payan siblings hired a near 100% Mexican labor force in every section of the company and revolutionized the local economy while bringing global attention to the plight of Chiapas's indigenous tribes and social conflicts. Lorena Payan assumed control of Foresight after her brother was killed in a car bombing.

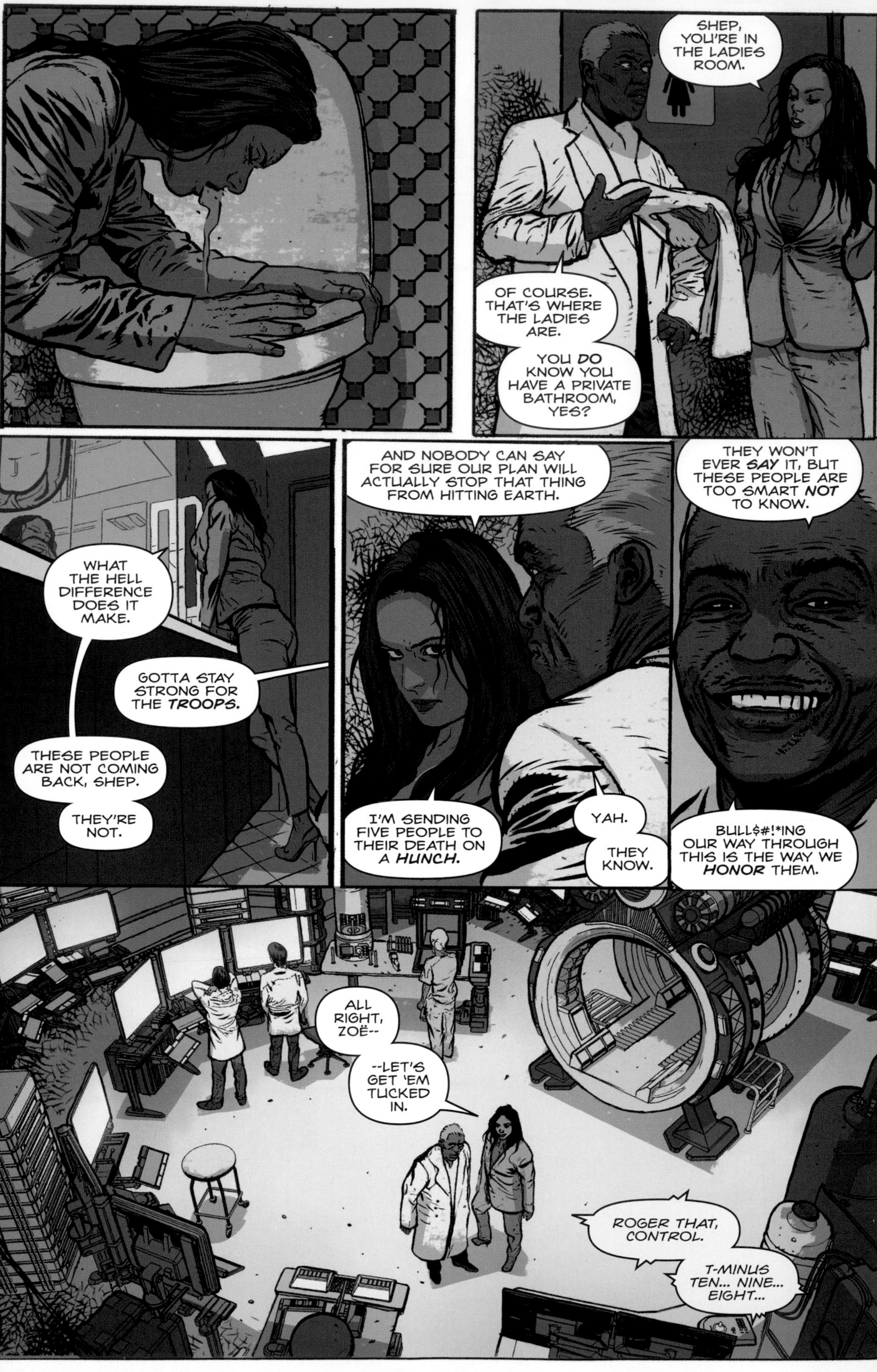
SHEP, YOU'RE IN THE LADIES ROOM.
OF COURSE. THAT'S WHERE THE LADIES ARE.
YOU DO KNOW YOU HAVE A PRIVATE BATHROOM, YES?
WHAT THE HELL DIFFERENCE DOES IT MAKE.
GOTTA STAY STRONG FOR THE TROOPS.
THESE PEOPLE ARE NOT COMING BACK, SHEP.
THEY'RE NOT.
AND NOBODY CAN SAY FOR SURE OUR PLAN WILL ACTUALLY STOP THAT THING FROM HITTING EARTH.
I'M SENDING FIVE PEOPLE TO THEIR DEATH ON A HUNCH.
YAH.
THEY KNOW.
THEY WON'T EVER SAY IT, BUT THESE PEOPLE ARE TOO SMART NOT TO KNOW.
BULL$#!*ING OUR WAY THROUGH THIS IS THE WAY WE HONOR THEM.
ALL RIGHT, ZOË--
--LET'S GET 'EM TUCKED IN.
ROGER THAT, CONTROL.
T-MINUS TEN... NINE... EIGHT...

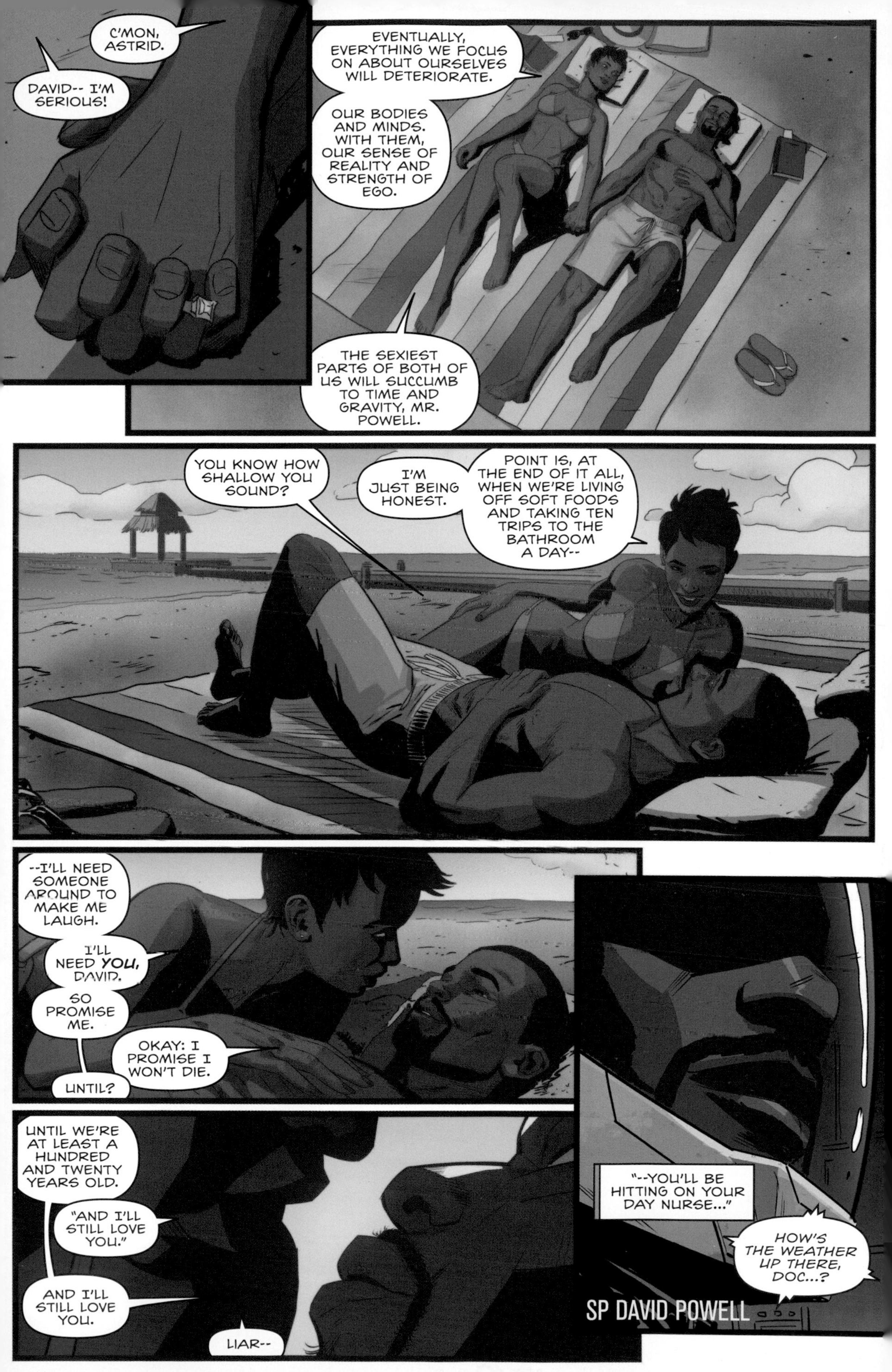
C'MON, ASTRID.
DAVID-- I'M SERIOUS!
EVENTUALLY, EVERYTHING WE FOCUS ON ABOUT OURSELVES WILL DETERIORATE.
OUR BODIES AND MINDS. WITH THEM, OUR SENSE OF REALITY AND STRENGTH OF EGO.
THE SEXIEST PARTS OF BOTH OF US WILL SUCCUMB TO TIME AND GRAVITY, MR. POWELL.
YOU KNOW HOW SHALLOW YOU SOUND?
I'M JUST BEING HONEST.
POINT IS, AT THE END OF IT ALL, WHEN WE'RE LIVING OFF SOFT FOODS AND TAKING TEN TRIPS TO THE BATHROOM A DAY--
--I'LL NEED SOMEONE AROUND TO MAKE ME LAUGH.
I'LL NEED YOU, DAVID.
SO PROMISE ME.
OKAY: I PROMISE I WON'T DIE.
UNTIL?
UNTIL WE'RE AT LEAST A HUNDRED AND TWENTY YEARS OLD.
"AND I'LL STILL LOVE YOU."
AND I'LL STILL LOVE YOU.
LIAR--
"--YOU'LL BE HITTING ON YOUR DAY NURSE..."
HOW'S THE WEATHER UP THERE, DOC...?
SP DAVID POWELL

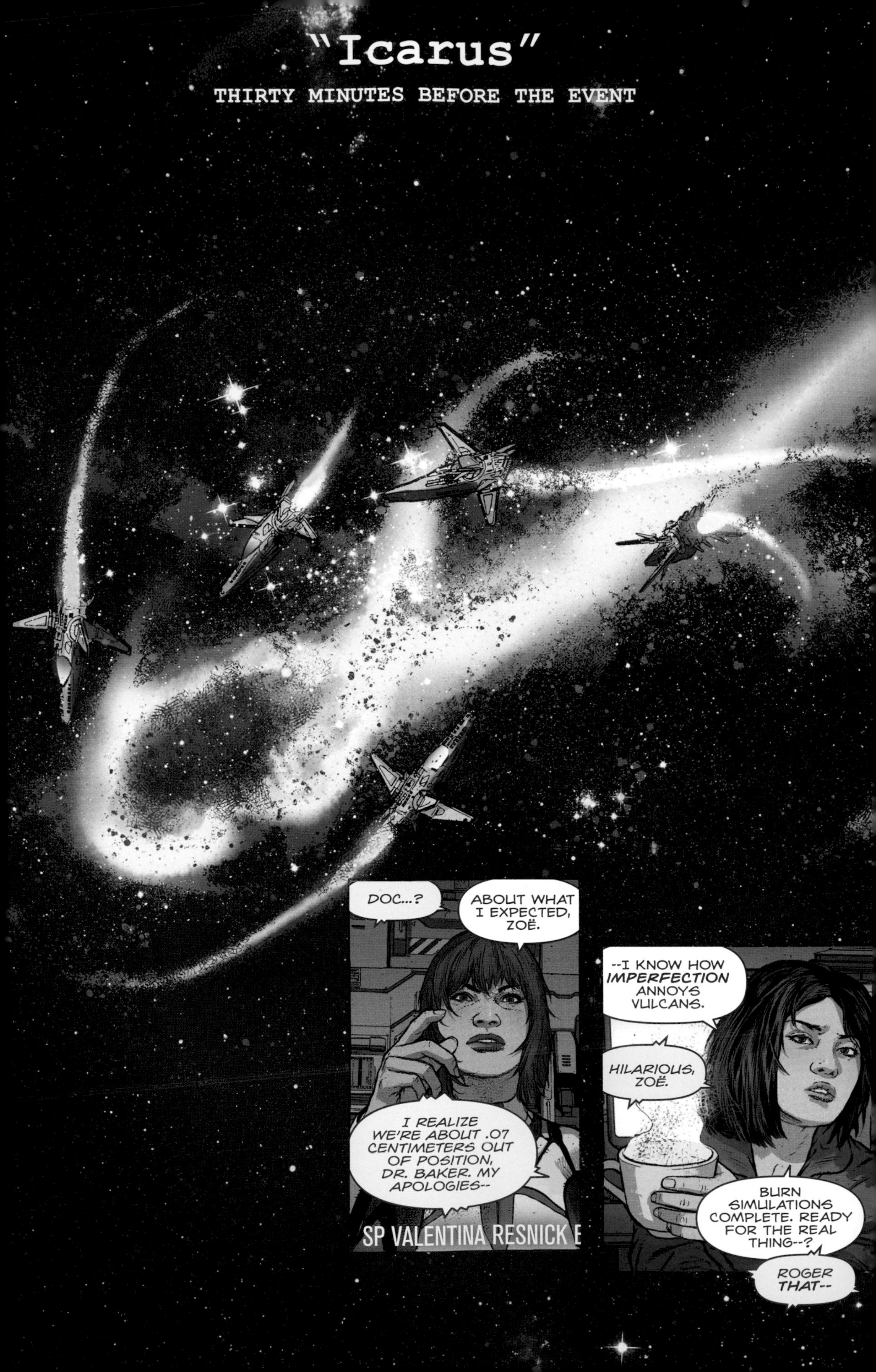
"Icarus"
THIRTY MINUTES BEFORE THE EVENT
DOC...?
ABOUT WHAT I EXPECTED, ZOË.
I REALIZE WE'RE ABOUT .07 CENTIMETERS OUT OF POSITION, DR. BAKER. MY APOLOGIES--
SP VALENTINA RESNICK E
--I KNOW HOW IMPERFECTION ANNOYS VULCANS.
HILARIOUS, ZOË.
BURN SIMULATIONS COMPLETE. READY FOR THE REAL THING--?
ROGER THAT--

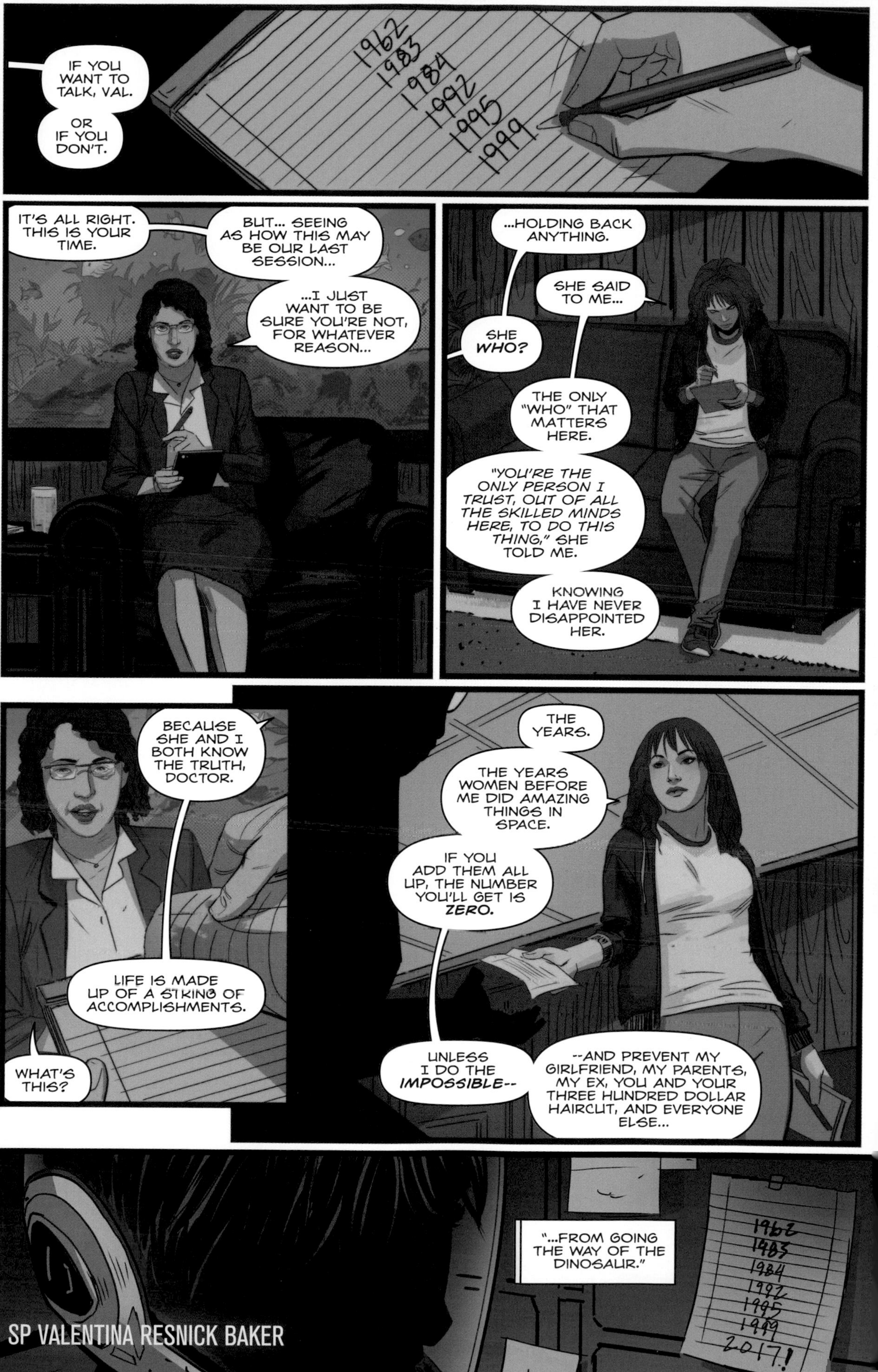
1962
1983
1984
1992
1995
1999
IF YOU WANT TO TALK, VAL.
OR IF YOU DON'T.
IT'S ALL RIGHT. THIS IS YOUR TIME.
BUT... SEEING AS HOW THIS MAY BE OUR LAST SESSION...
...I JUST WANT TO BE SURE YOU'RE NOT, FOR WHATEVER REASON...
...HOLDING BACK ANYTHING.
SHE SAID TO ME...
SHE *WHO?*
THE ONLY "WHO" THAT MATTERS HERE.
"YOU'RE THE ONLY PERSON I TRUST, OUT OF ALL THE SKILLED MINDS HERE, TO DO THIS THING," SHE TOLD ME.
KNOWING I HAVE NEVER DISAPPOINTED HER.
BECAUSE SHE AND I BOTH KNOW THE TRUTH, DOCTOR.
LIFE IS MADE UP OF A STRING OF ACCOMPLISHMENTS.
WHAT'S THIS?
THE YEARS.
THE YEARS WOMEN BEFORE ME DID AMAZING THINGS IN SPACE.
IF YOU ADD THEM ALL UP, THE NUMBER YOU'LL GET IS **ZERO.**
UNLESS I DO THE ***IMPOSSIBLE--***
--AND PREVENT MY GIRLFRIEND, MY PARENTS, MY EX, YOU AND YOUR THREE HUNDRED DOLLAR HAIRCUT, AND EVERYONE ELSE...
"...FROM GOING THE WAY OF THE DINOSAUR."
1962
1983
1984
1992
1995
1999
2017!
SP VALENTINA RESNICK BAKER

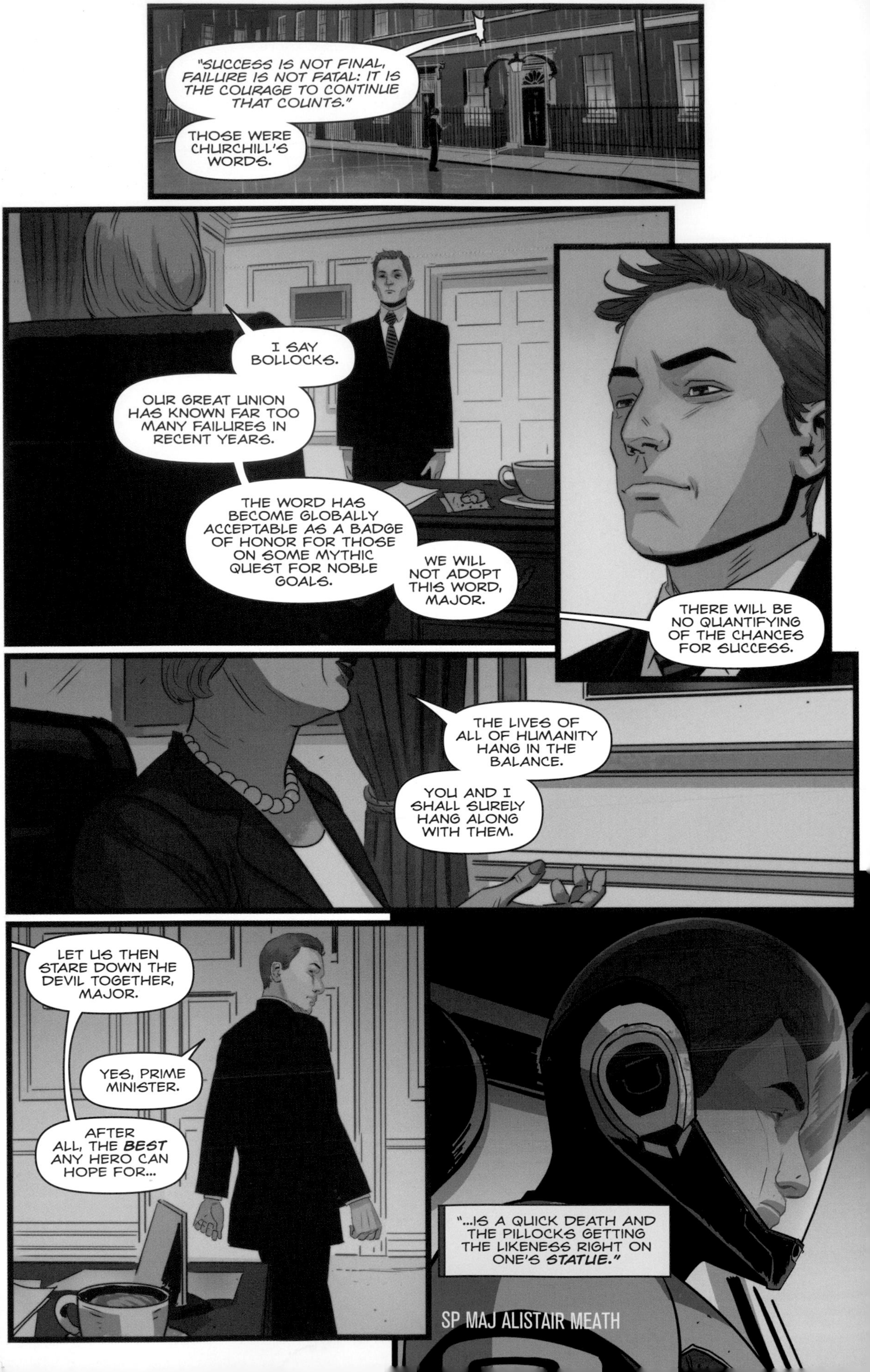
"SUCCESS IS NOT FINAL, FAILURE IS NOT FATAL: IT IS THE COURAGE TO CONTINUE THAT COUNTS."
THOSE WERE CHURCHILL'S WORDS.
I SAY BOLLOCKS.
OUR GREAT UNION HAS KNOWN FAR TOO MANY FAILURES IN RECENT YEARS.
THE WORD HAS BECOME GLOBALLY ACCEPTABLE AS A BADGE OF HONOR FOR THOSE ON SOME MYTHIC QUEST FOR NOBLE GOALS.
WE WILL NOT ADOPT THIS WORD, MAJOR.
THERE WILL BE NO QUANTIFYING OF THE CHANCES FOR SUCCESS.
THE LIVES OF ALL OF HUMANITY HANG IN THE BALANCE.
YOU AND I SHALL SURELY HANG ALONG WITH THEM.
LET US THEN STARE DOWN THE DEVIL TOGETHER, MAJOR.
YES, PRIME MINISTER.
AFTER ALL, THE *BEST* ANY HERO CAN HOPE FOR...
"...IS A QUICK DEATH AND THE PILLOCKS GETTING THE LIKENESS RIGHT ON ONE'S *STATUE*."
SP MAJ ALISTAIR MEATH

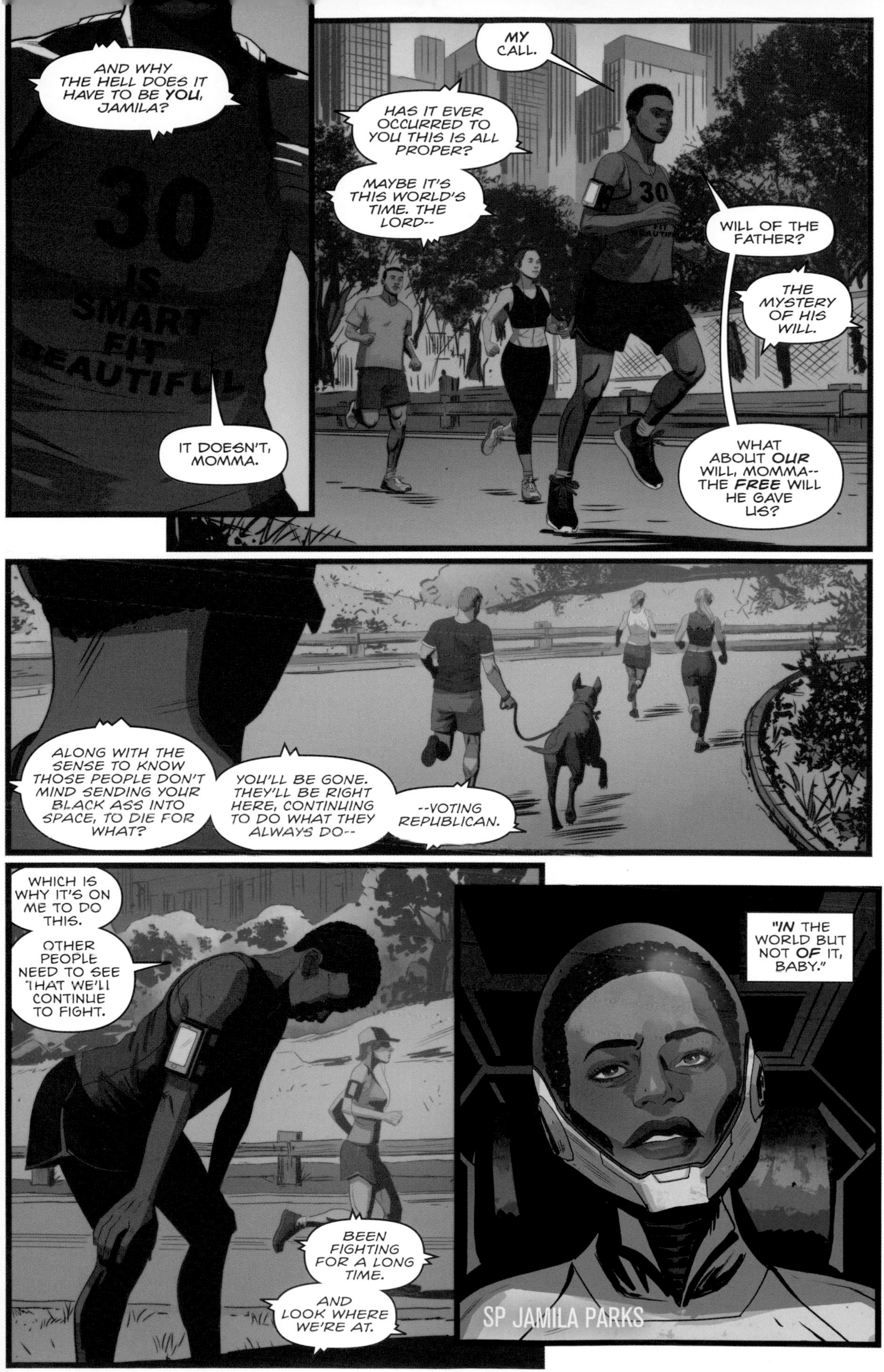
AND WHY THE HELL DOES IT HAVE TO BE YOU, JAMILA?
30 IS SMART FIT BEAUTIFUL
IT DOESN'T, MOMMA.
MY CALL.
HAS IT EVER OCCURRED TO YOU THIS IS ALL PROPER?
MAYBE IT'S THIS WORLD'S TIME. THE LORD--
WILL OF THE FATHER?
THE MYSTERY OF HIS WILL.
WHAT ABOUT OUR WILL, MOMMA-- THE FREE WILL HE GAVE US?
ALONG WITH THE SENSE TO KNOW THOSE PEOPLE DON'T MIND SENDING YOUR BLACK ASS INTO SPACE, TO DIE FOR WHAT?
YOU'LL BE GONE. THEY'LL BE RIGHT HERE, CONTINUING TO DO WHAT THEY ALWAYS DO--
--VOTING REPUBLICAN.
WHICH IS WHY IT'S ON ME TO DO THIS.
OTHER PEOPLE NEED TO SEE THAT WE'LL CONTINUE TO FIGHT.
BEEN FIGHTING FOR A LONG TIME.
AND LOOK WHERE WE'RE AT.
"IN THE WORLD BUT NOT OF IT, BABY."
SP JAMILA PARKS

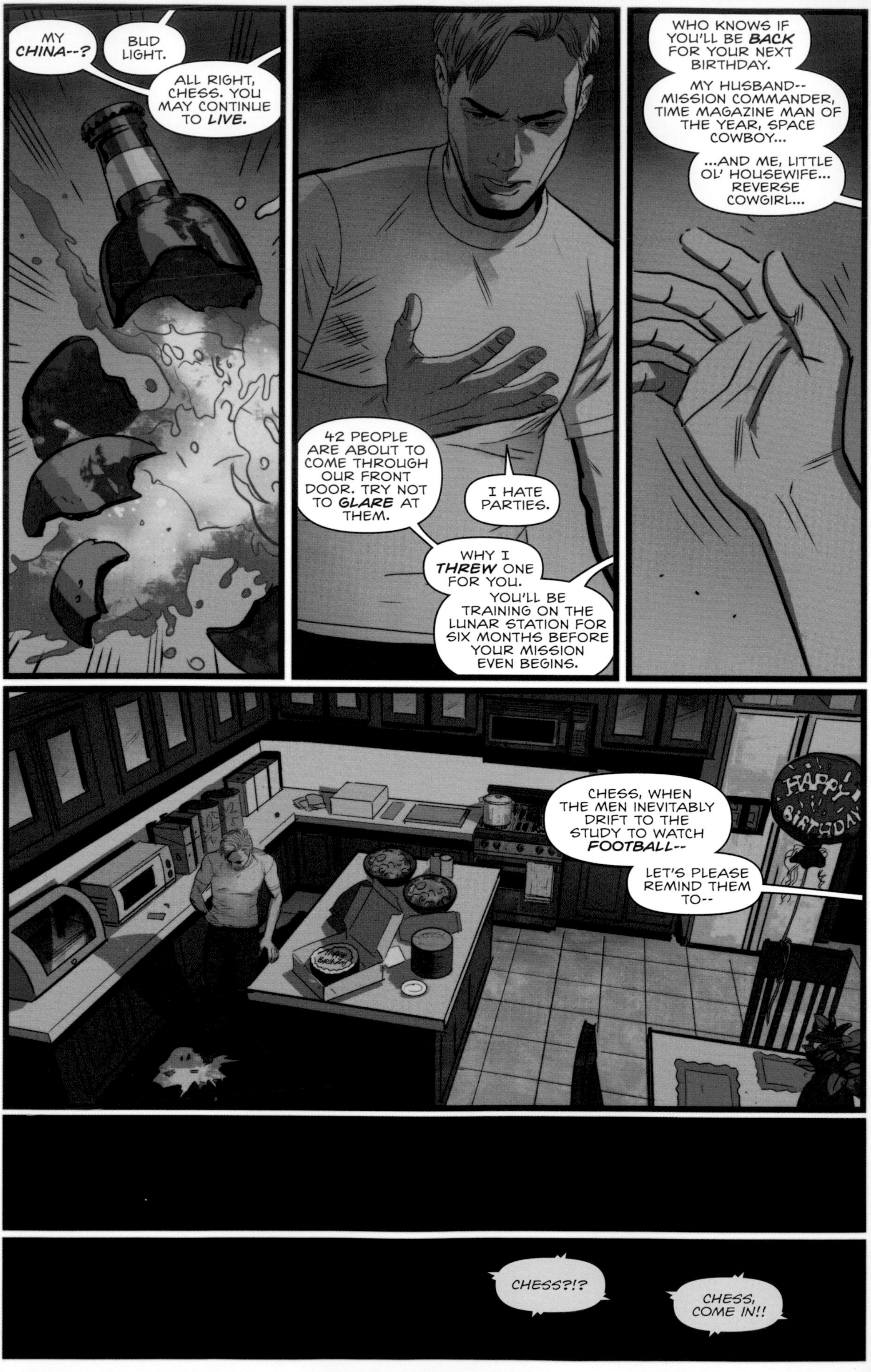
MY CHINA--?
BUD LIGHT.
ALL RIGHT, CHESS. YOU MAY CONTINUE TO LIVE.
42 PEOPLE ARE ABOUT TO COME THROUGH OUR FRONT DOOR. TRY NOT TO GLARE AT THEM.
I HATE PARTIES.
WHY I THREW ONE FOR YOU.
YOU'LL BE TRAINING ON THE LUNAR STATION FOR SIX MONTHS BEFORE YOUR MISSION EVEN BEGINS.
WHO KNOWS IF YOU'LL BE BACK FOR YOUR NEXT BIRTHDAY.
MY HUSBAND-- MISSION COMMANDER, TIME MAGAZINE MAN OF THE YEAR, SPACE COWBOY...
...AND ME, LITTLE OL' HOUSEWIFE... REVERSE COWGIRL...
HAPPY BIRTHDAY
CHESS, WHEN THE MEN INEVITABLY DRIFT TO THE STUDY TO WATCH FOOTBALL--
LET'S PLEASE REMIND THEM TO--
CHESS?!?
CHESS, COME IN!!

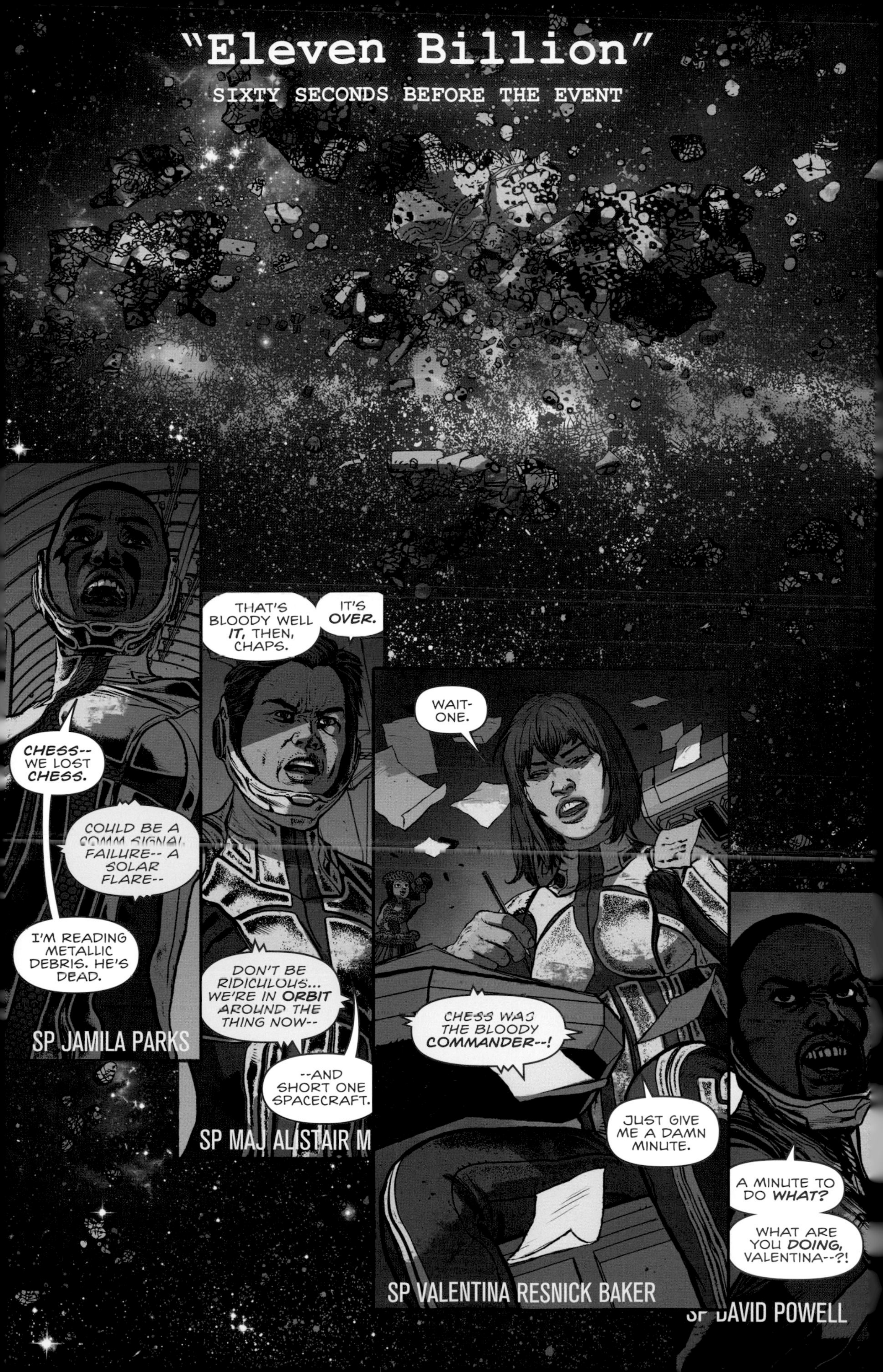
"Eleven Billion"
SIXTY SECONDS BEFORE THE EVENT
CHESS-- WE LOST CHESS.
COULD BE A COMM SIGNAL FAILURE-- A SOLAR FLARE--
I'M READING METALLIC DEBRIS. HE'S DEAD.
SP JAMILA PARKS
THAT'S BLOODY WELL IT, THEN, CHAPS.
IT'S OVER.
DON'T BE RIDICULOUS... WE'RE IN ORBIT AROUND THE THING NOW--
--AND SHORT ONE SPACECRAFT.
SP MAJ ALISTAIR M
WAIT-ONE.
CHESS WAS THE BLOODY COMMANDER--!
JUST GIVE ME A DAMN MINUTE.
SP VALENTINA RESNICK BAKER
A MINUTE TO DO WHAT?
WHAT ARE YOU DOING, VALENTINA--?!
SP DAVID POWELL

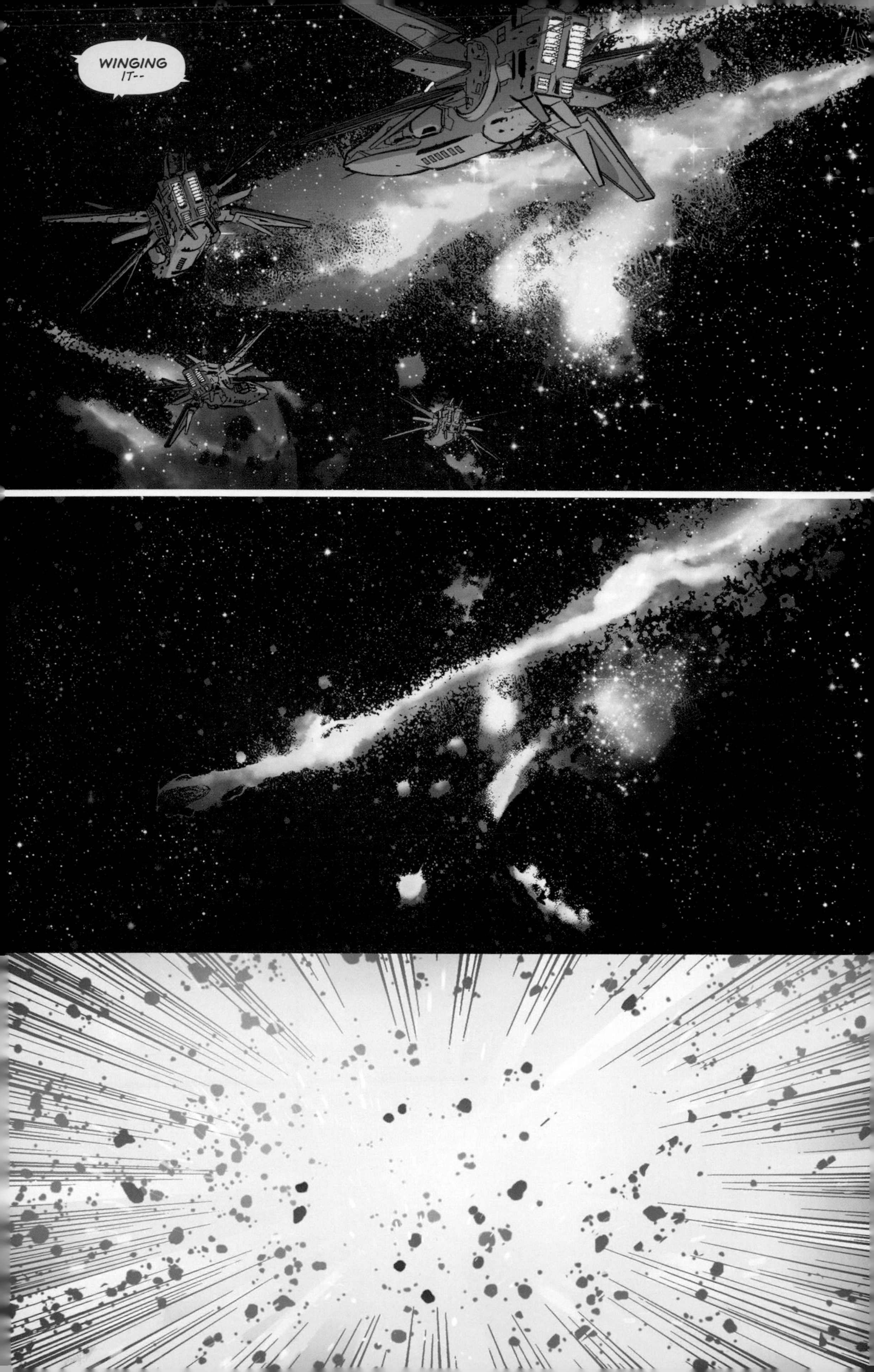
WINGING IT--

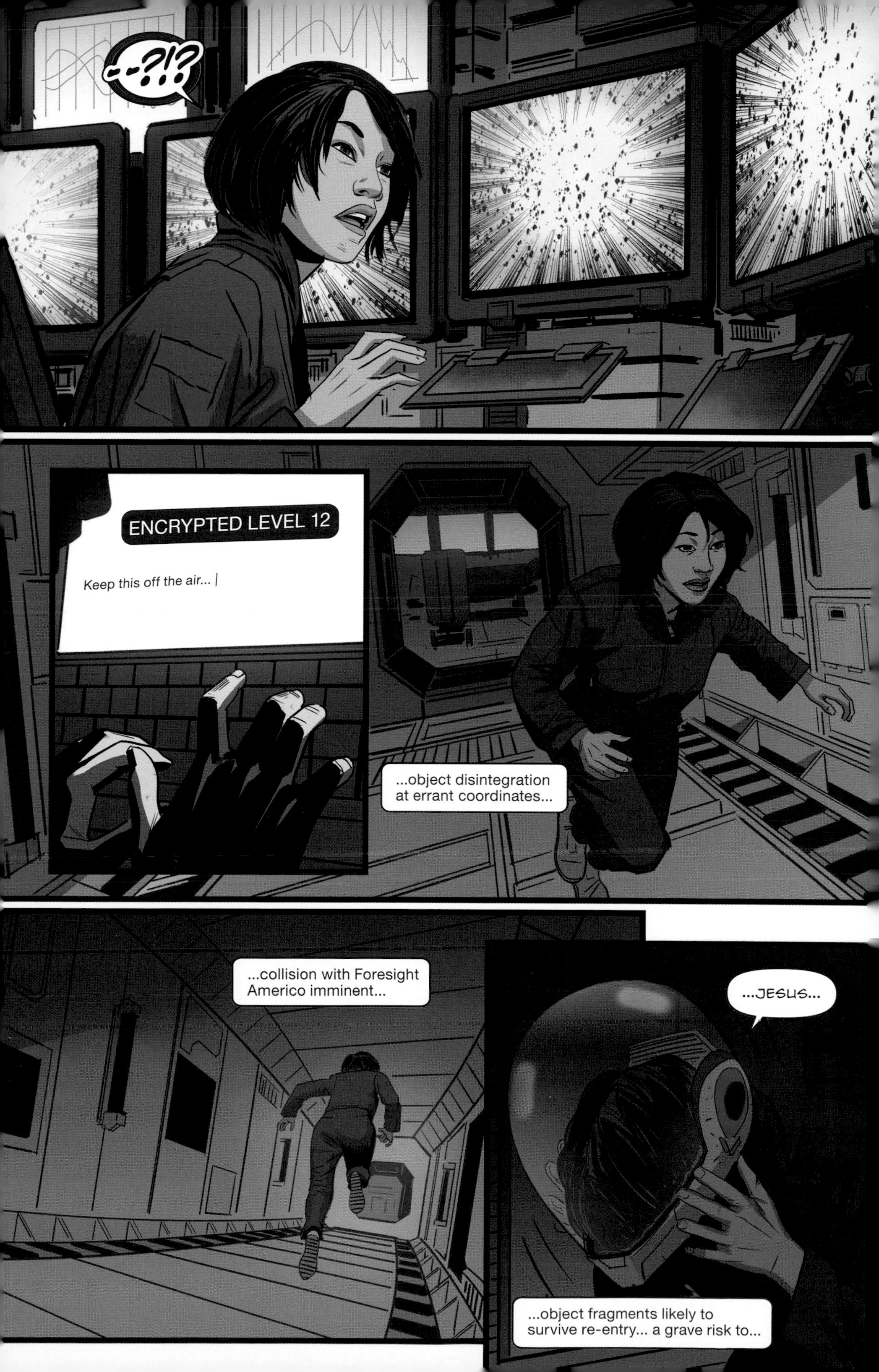
--?!?
ENCRYPTED LEVEL 12
Keep this off the air... |
...object disintegration at errant coordinates...
...collision with Foresight Americo imminent...
...JESUS...
...object fragments likely to survive re-entry... a grave risk to...

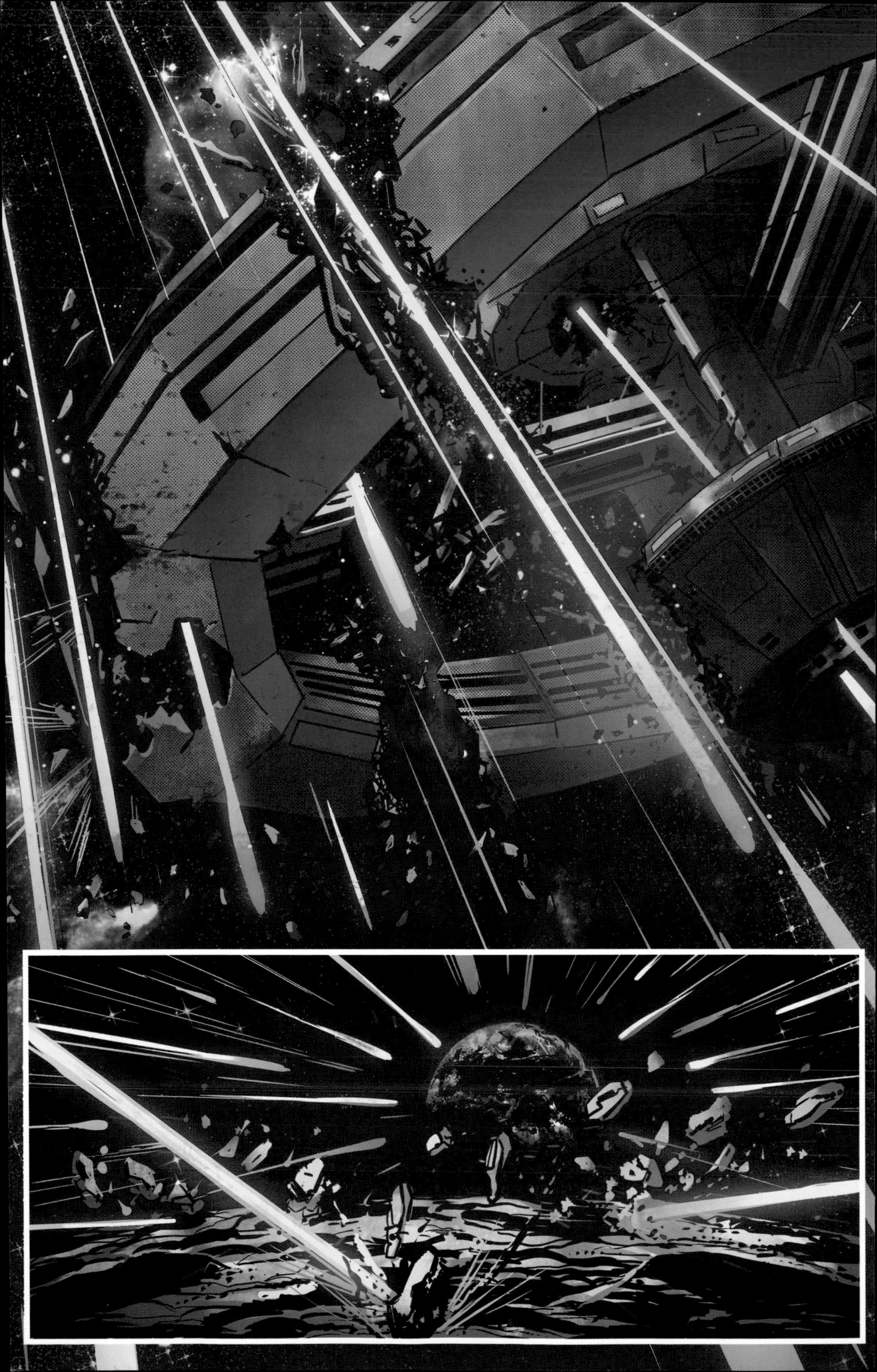

"The Beginning"

THE EVENT

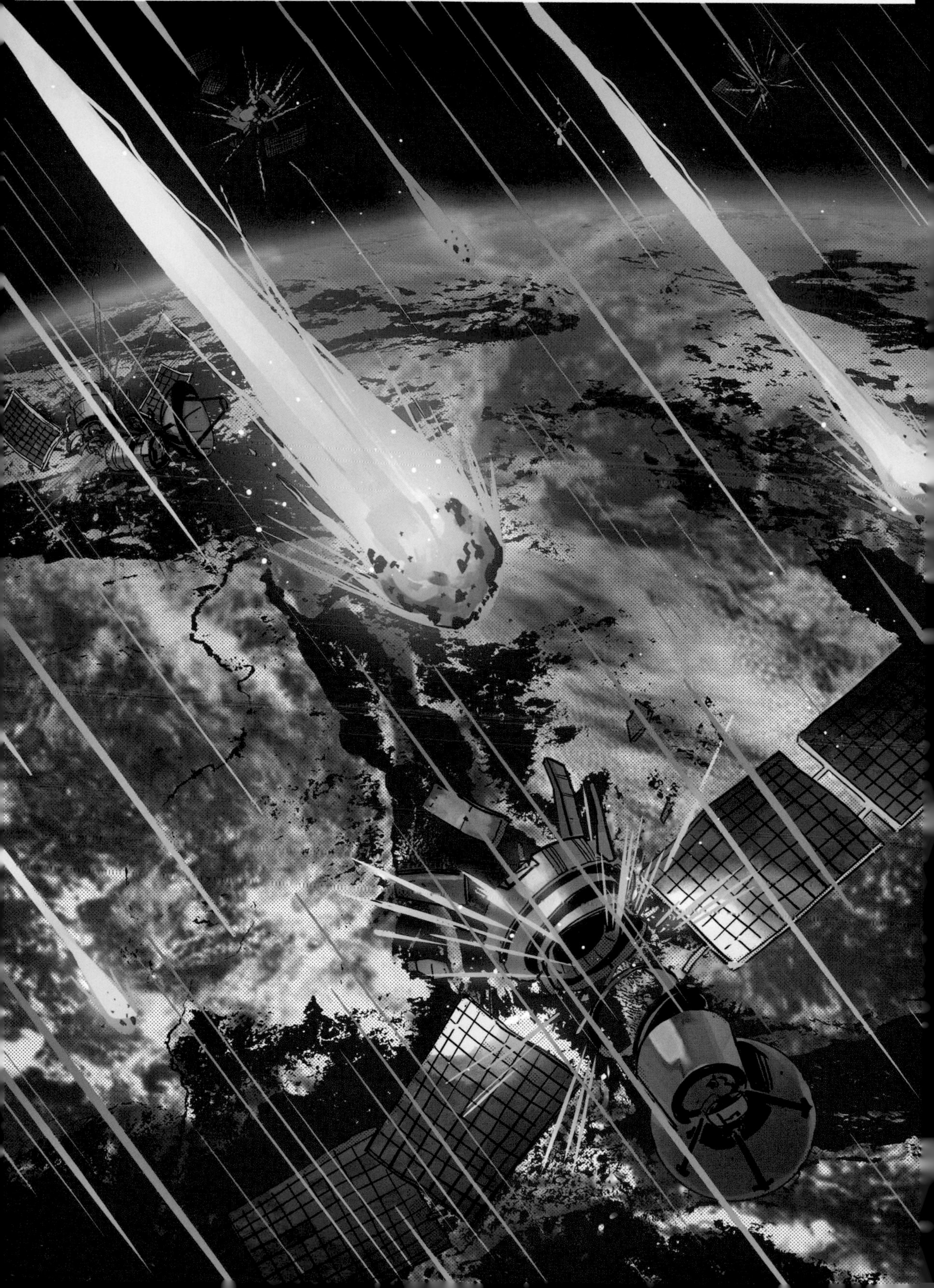

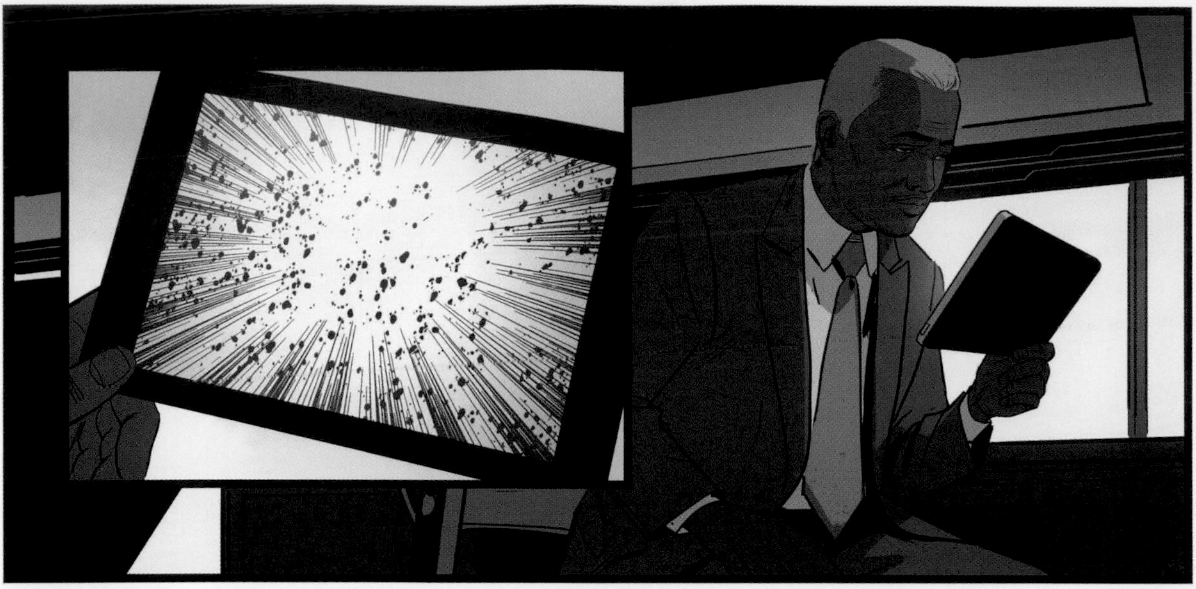

"Clouds"

TWO WEEKS AFTER THE EVENT

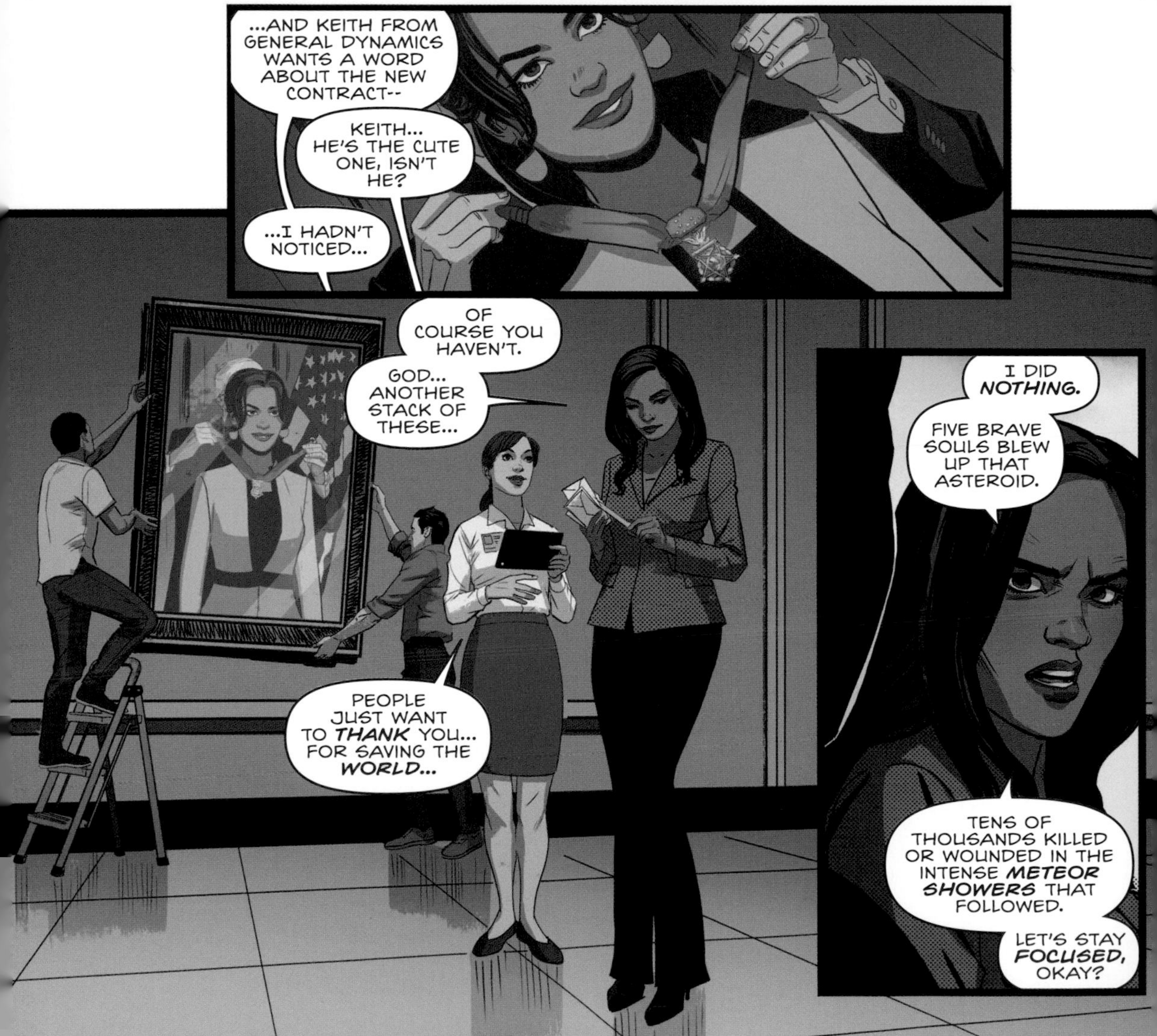

...AND KEITH FROM GENERAL DYNAMICS WANTS A WORD ABOUT THE NEW CONTRACT--
KEITH... HE'S THE CUTE ONE, ISN'T HE?
...I HADN'T NOTICED...
OF COURSE YOU HAVEN'T.
GOD... ANOTHER STACK OF THESE...
PEOPLE JUST WANT TO ***THANK*** YOU... FOR SAVING THE ***WORLD...***
I DID ***NOTHING.***
FIVE BRAVE SOULS BLEW UP THAT ASTEROID.
TENS OF THOUSANDS KILLED OR WOUNDED IN THE INTENSE ***METEOR SHOWERS*** THAT FOLLOWED.
LET'S STAY ***FOCUSED,*** OKAY?

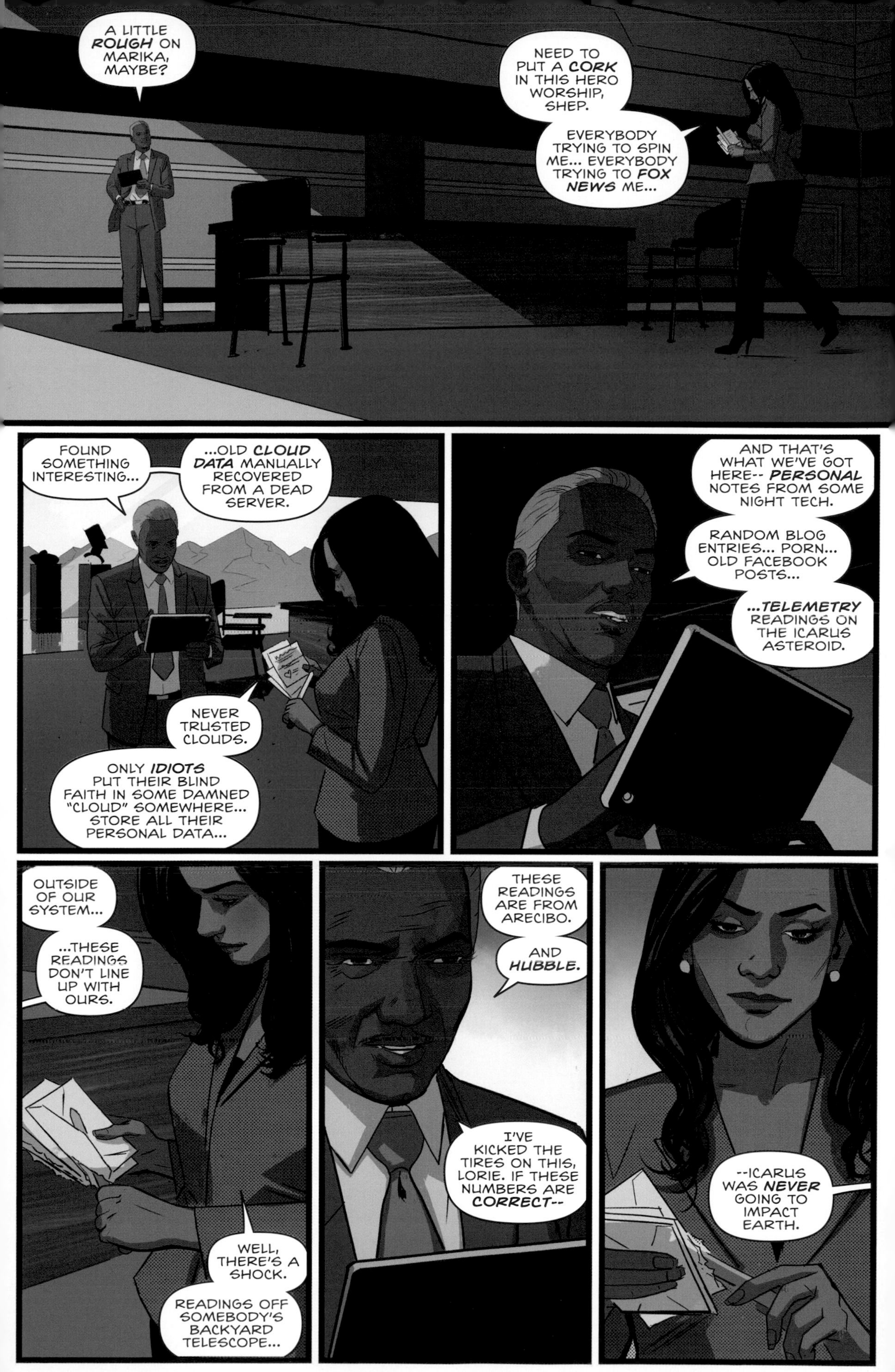
A LITTLE ROUGH ON MARIKA, MAYBE?
NEED TO PUT A CORK IN THIS HERO WORSHIP, SHEP.
EVERYBODY TRYING TO SPIN ME... EVERYBODY TRYING TO FOX NEWS ME...
FOUND SOMETHING INTERESTING...
...OLD CLOUD DATA MANUALLY RECOVERED FROM A DEAD SERVER.
NEVER TRUSTED CLOUDS.
ONLY IDIOTS PUT THEIR BLIND FAITH IN SOME DAMNED "CLOUD" SOMEWHERE... STORE ALL THEIR PERSONAL DATA...
AND THAT'S WHAT WE'VE GOT HERE-- PERSONAL NOTES FROM SOME NIGHT TECH.
RANDOM BLOG ENTRIES... PORN... OLD FACEBOOK POSTS...
...TELEMETRY READINGS ON THE ICARUS ASTEROID.
OUTSIDE OF OUR SYSTEM...
...THESE READINGS DON'T LINE UP WITH OURS.
WELL, THERE'S A SHOCK.
READINGS OFF SOMEBODY'S BACKYARD TELESCOPE...
THESE READINGS ARE FROM ARECIBO.
AND HUBBLE.
I'VE KICKED THE TIRES ON THIS, LORIE. IF THESE NUMBERS ARE CORRECT--
--ICARUS WAS NEVER GOING TO IMPACT EARTH.

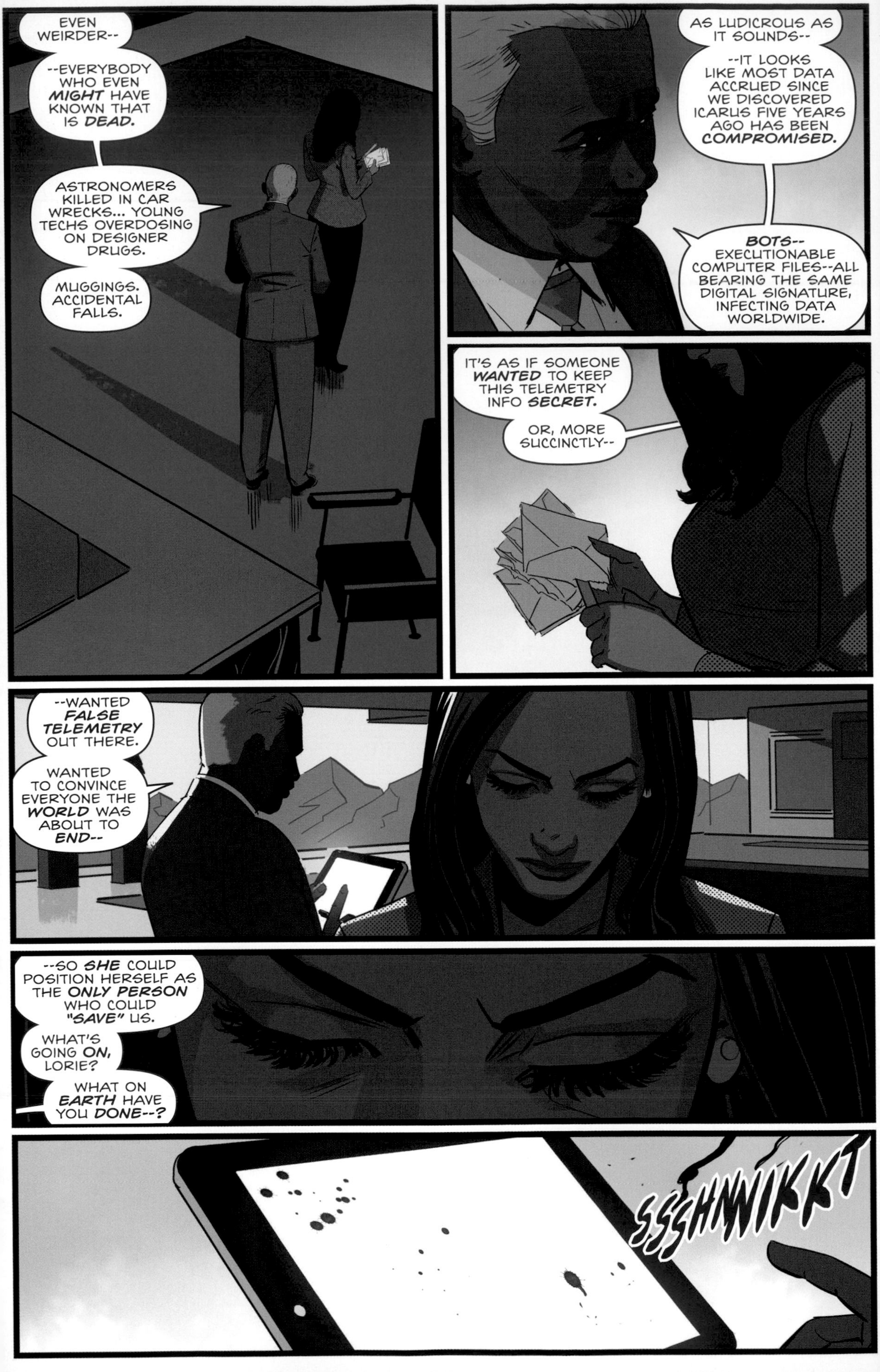
EVEN WEIRDER--
--EVERYBODY WHO EVEN MIGHT HAVE KNOWN THAT IS DEAD.
ASTRONOMERS KILLED IN CAR WRECKS... YOUNG TECHS OVERDOSING ON DESIGNER DRUGS.
MUGGINGS. ACCIDENTAL FALLS.
AS LUDICROUS AS IT SOUNDS--
--IT LOOKS LIKE MOST DATA ACCRUED SINCE WE DISCOVERED ICARUS FIVE YEARS AGO HAS BEEN COMPROMISED.
BOTS-- EXECUTIONABLE COMPUTER FILES--ALL BEARING THE SAME DIGITAL SIGNATURE, INFECTING DATA WORLDWIDE.
IT'S AS IF SOMEONE WANTED TO KEEP THIS TELEMETRY INFO SECRET.
OR, MORE SUCCINCTLY--
--WANTED FALSE TELEMETRY OUT THERE.
WANTED TO CONVINCE EVERYONE THE WORLD WAS ABOUT TO END--
--SO SHE COULD POSITION HERSELF AS THE ONLY PERSON WHO COULD "SAVE" US.
WHAT'S GOING ON, LORIE?
WHAT ON EARTH HAVE YOU DONE--?
SSSHNIKKT

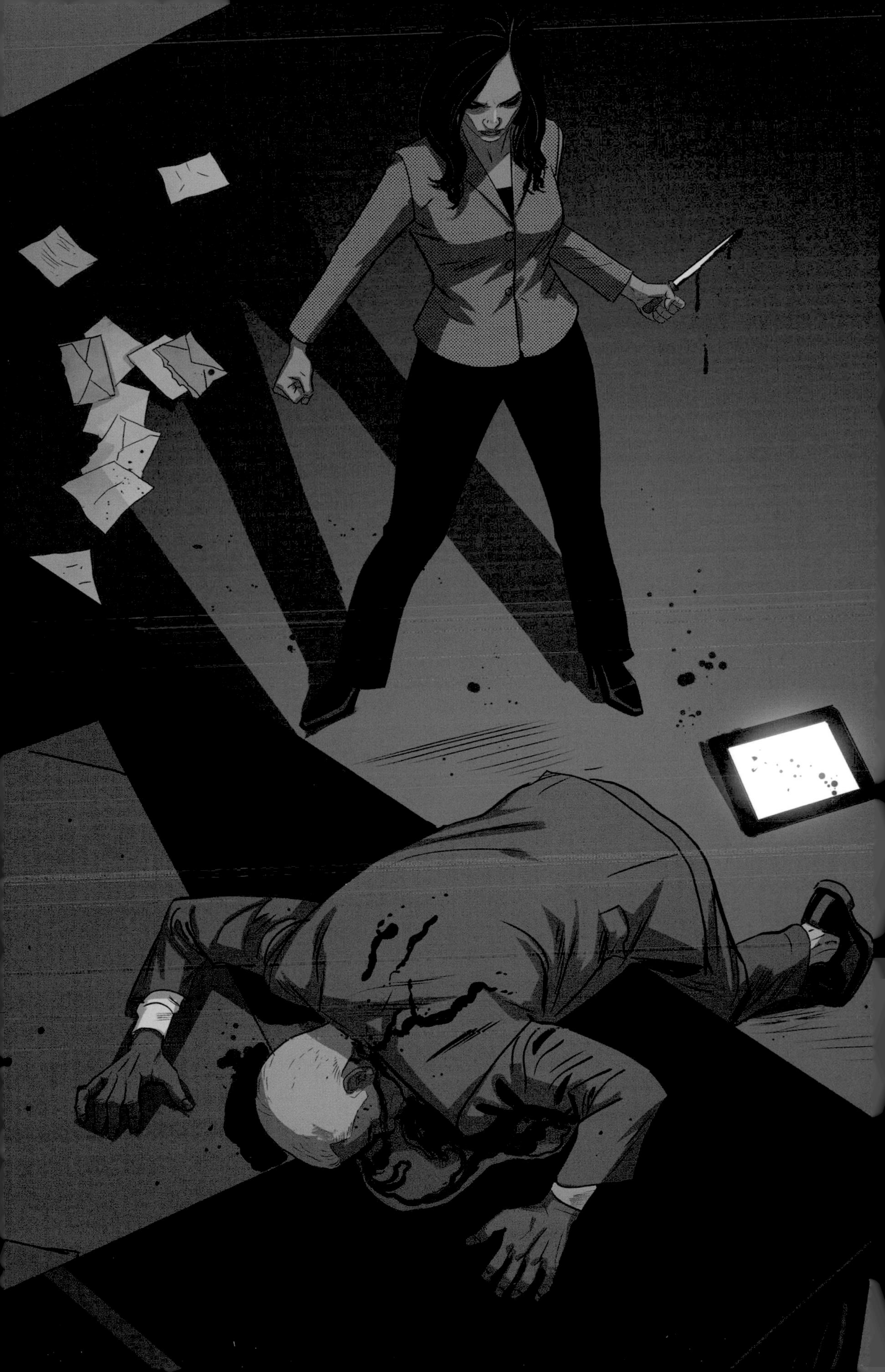

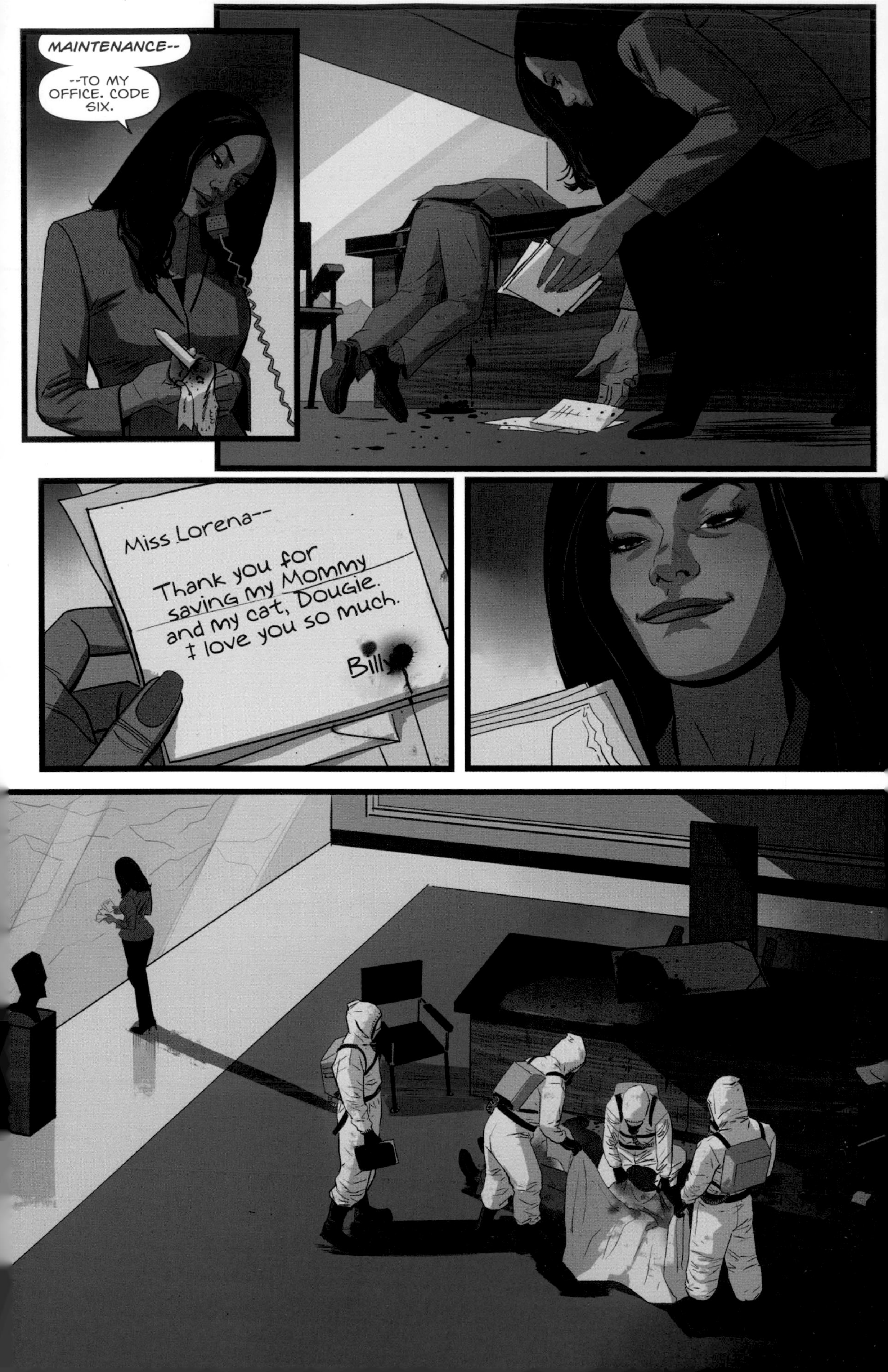
MAINTENANCE--
--TO MY OFFICE. CODE SIX.
Miss Lorena--
Thank you for saving my Mommy and my cat, Dougie. I love you so much.
Billy

COVER GALLERY

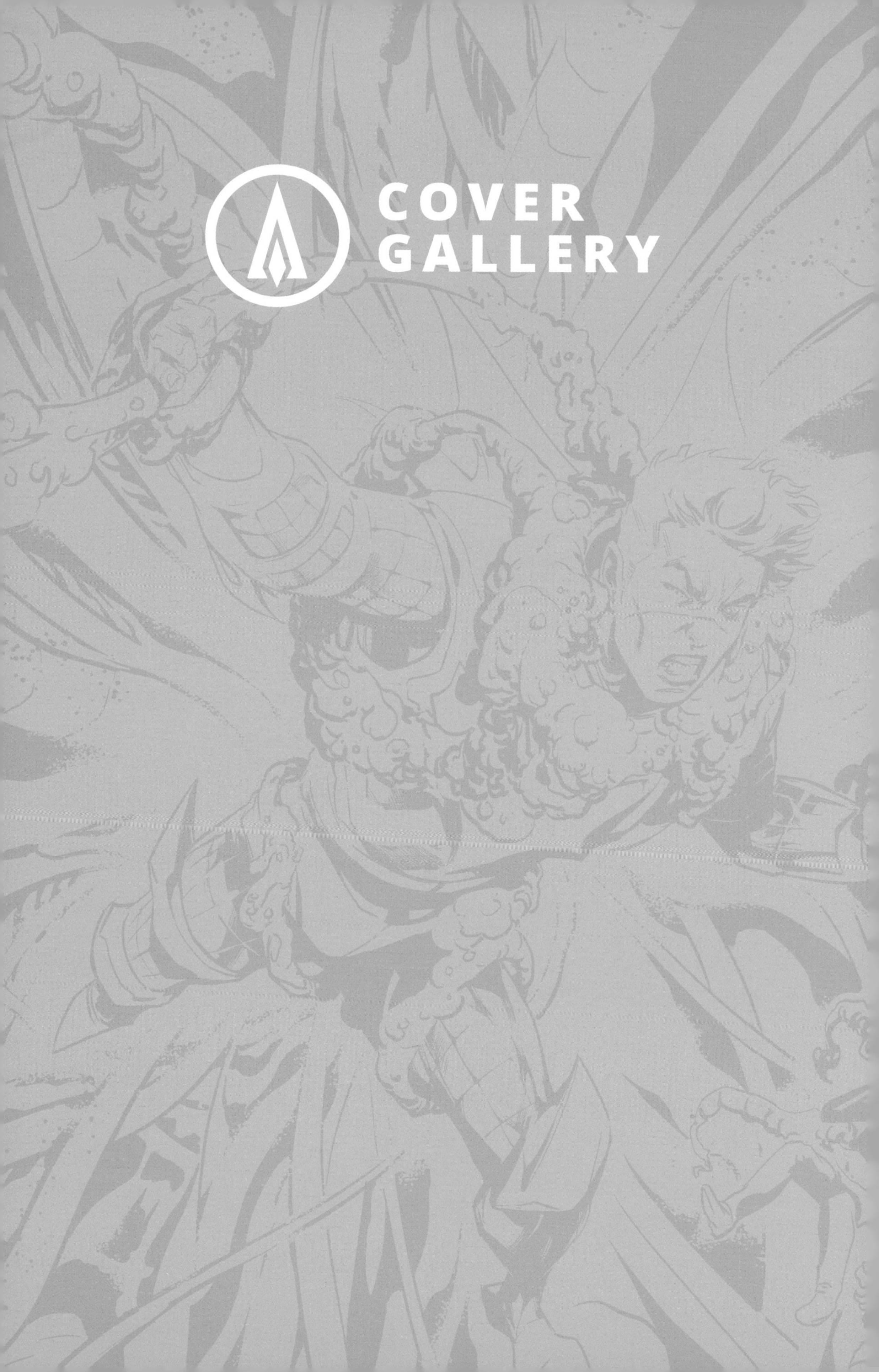

Art by **POP MHAN**
and **JESSICA KHOLINNE**

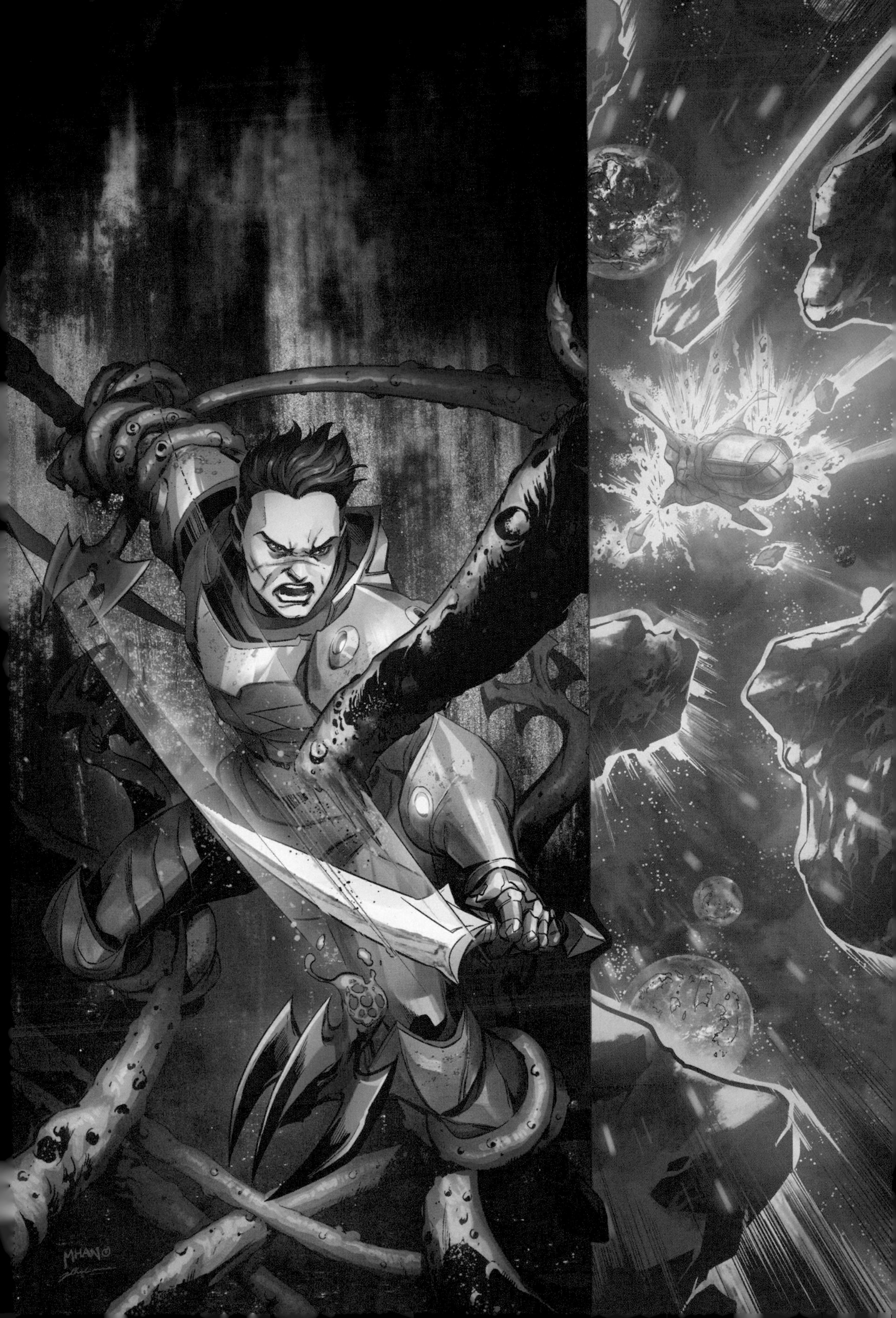
MHAN

Art by **JOHN CASSADAY**
and **LAURA MARTIN**

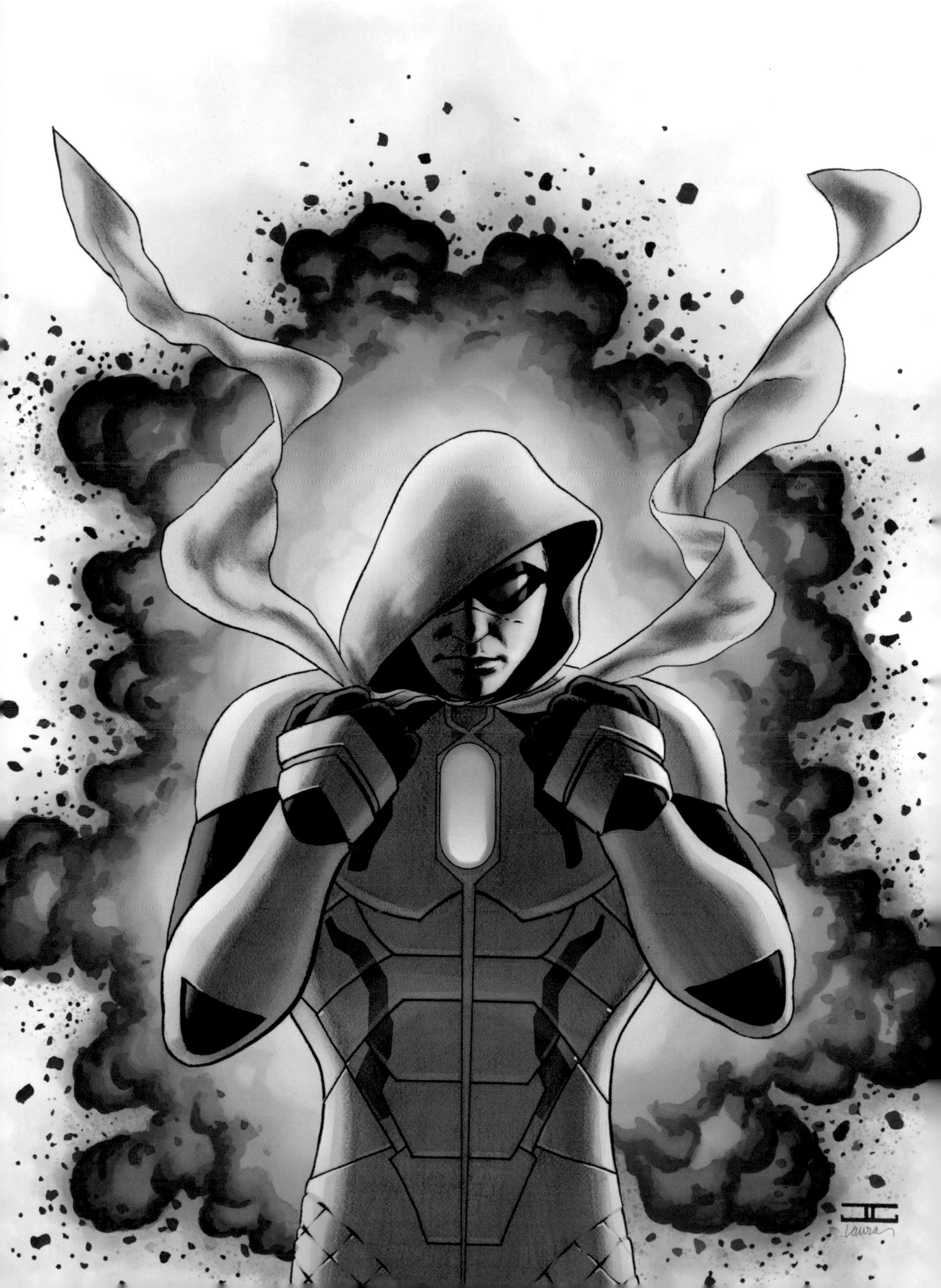

Art by **KHARY RANDOLPH**
and **EMILIO LOPEZ**

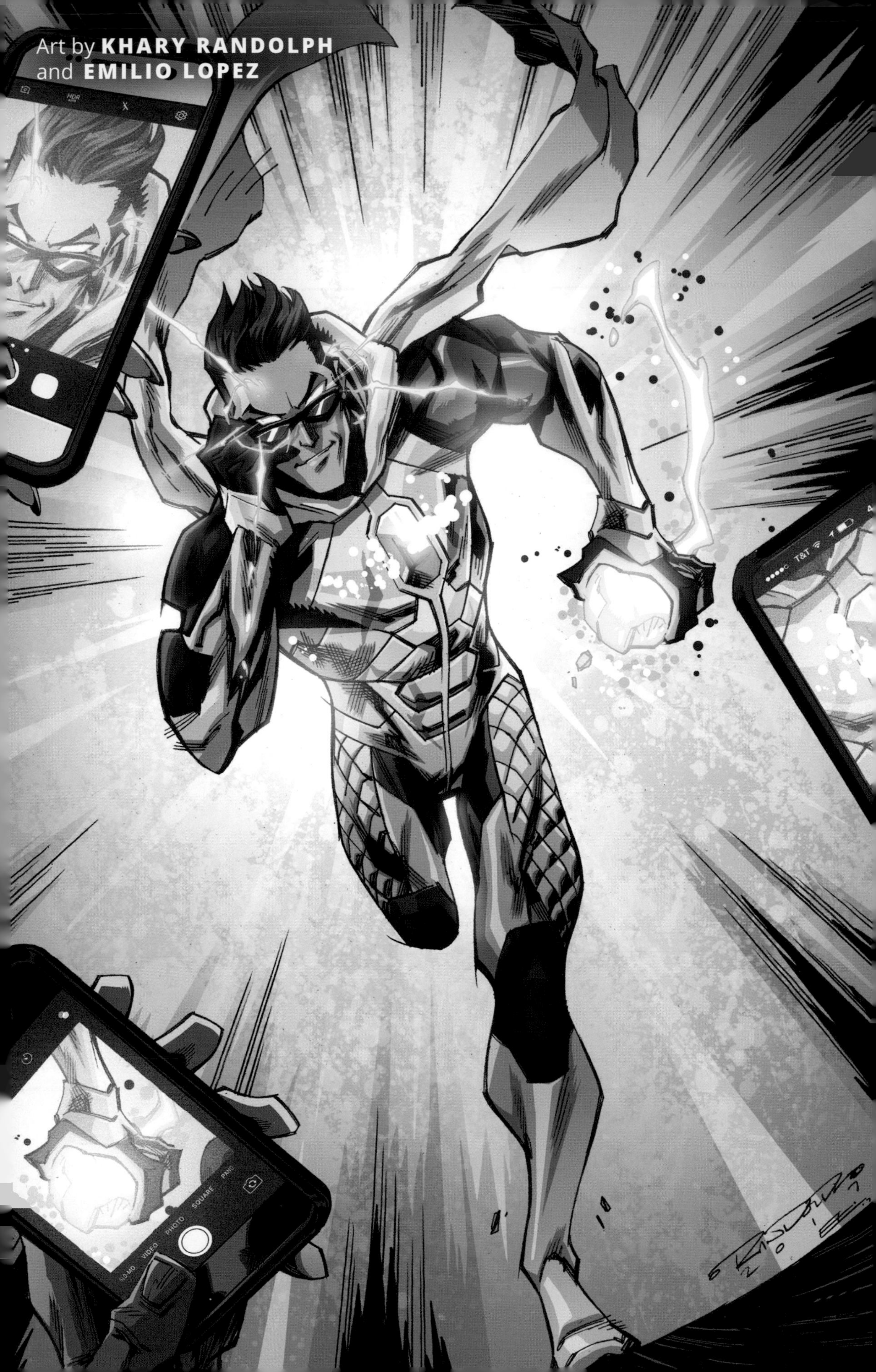
HDR
T&T
SLO-MO
VIDEO
PHOTO
SQUARE
PANO

Art by **PHIL JIMENEZ** and **ROMULO FAJARDO, JR.**

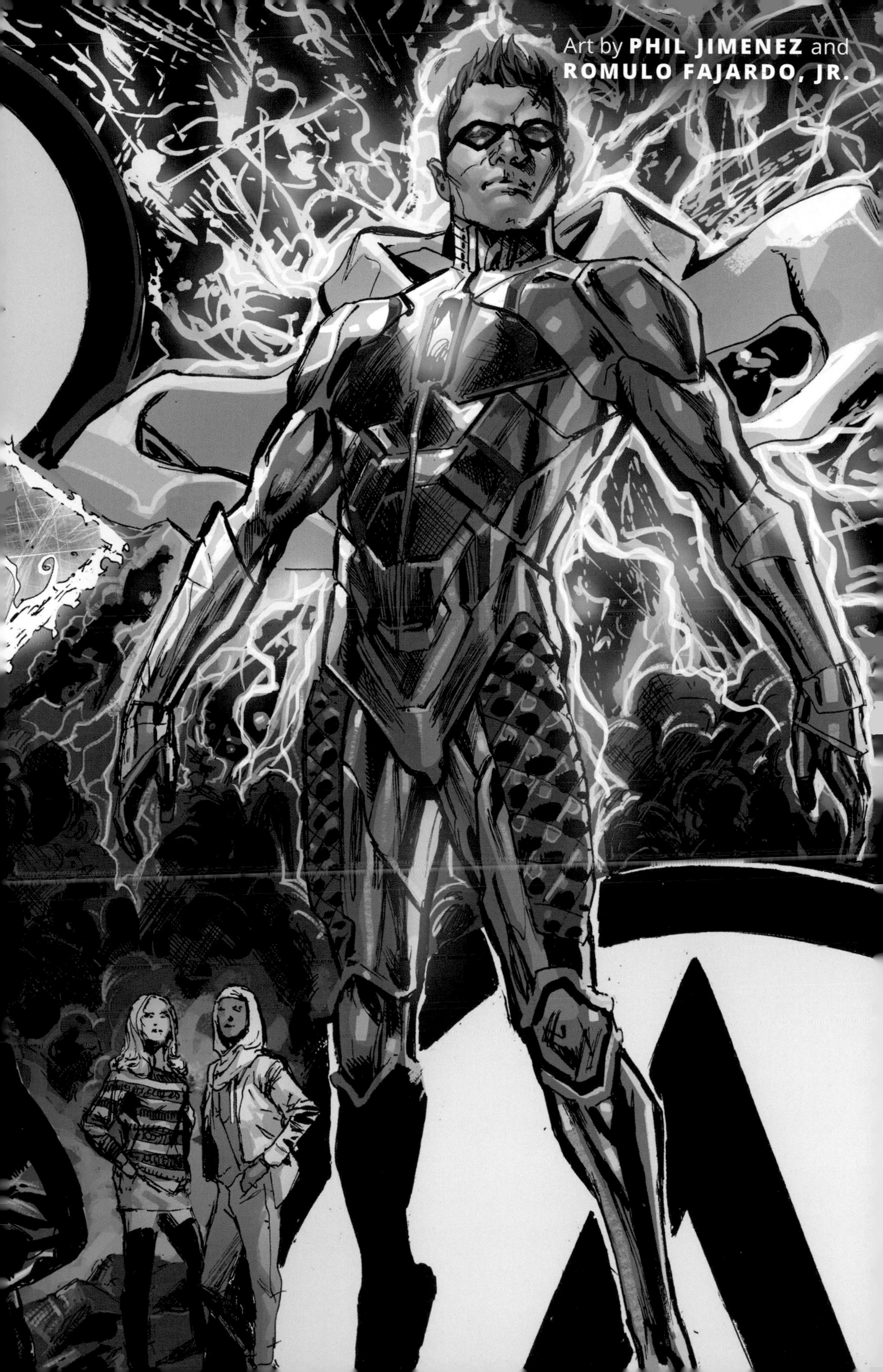

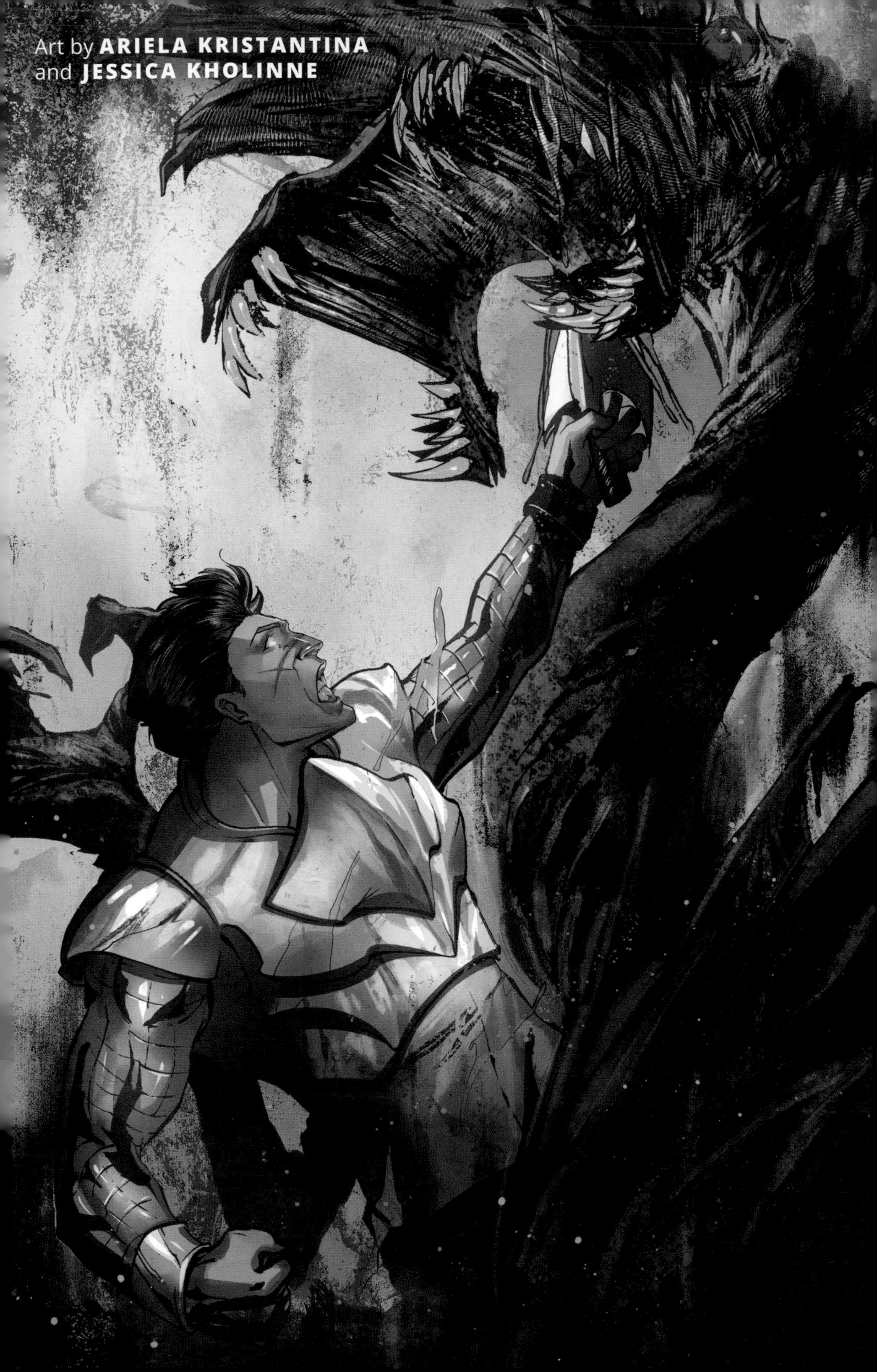

Art by **ARIELA KRISTANTINA**
and **JESSICA KHOLINNE**

Art by **POP MHAN**
and **JESSICA KHOLINNE**

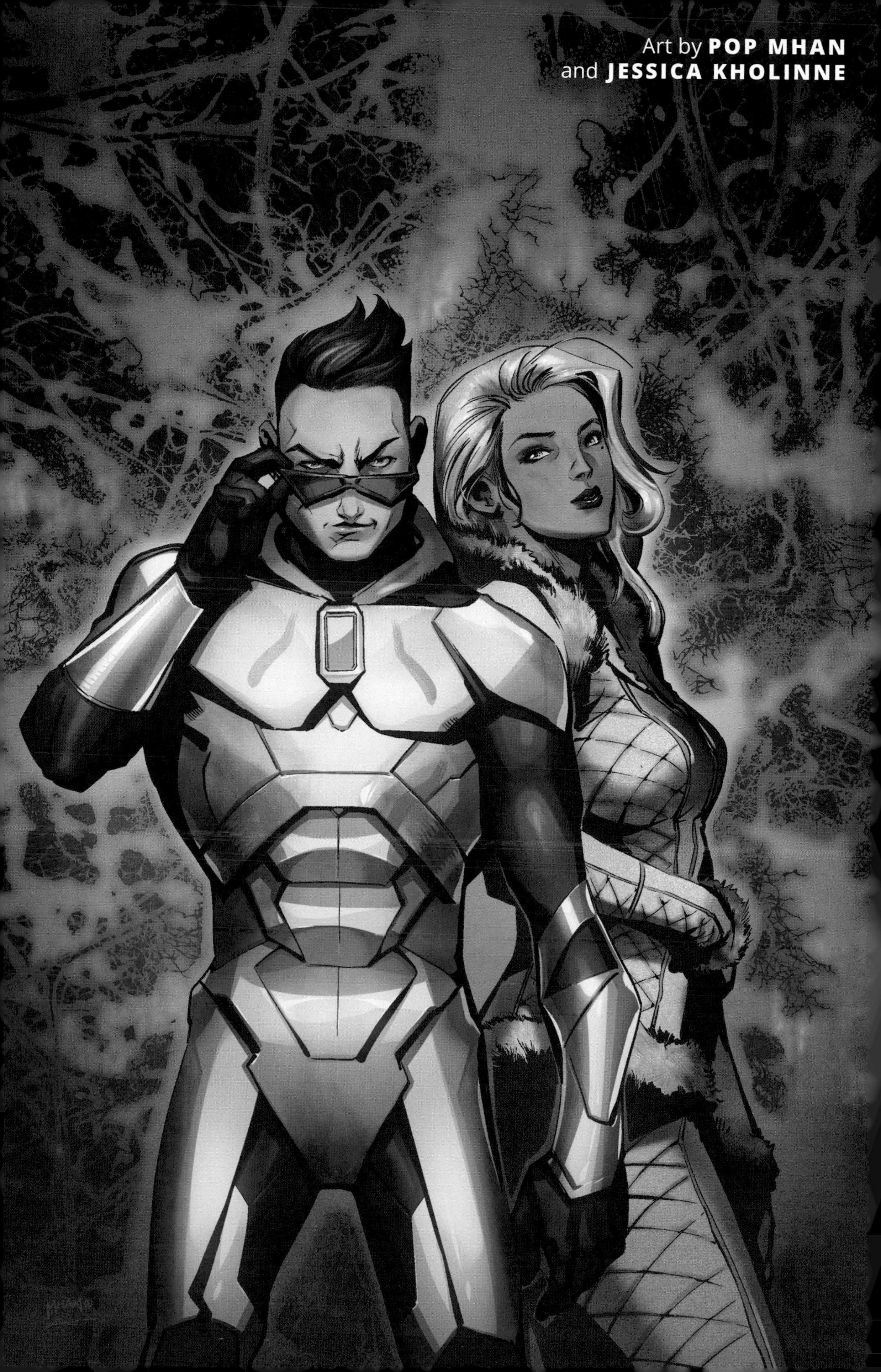

Art by **KERON GRANT**

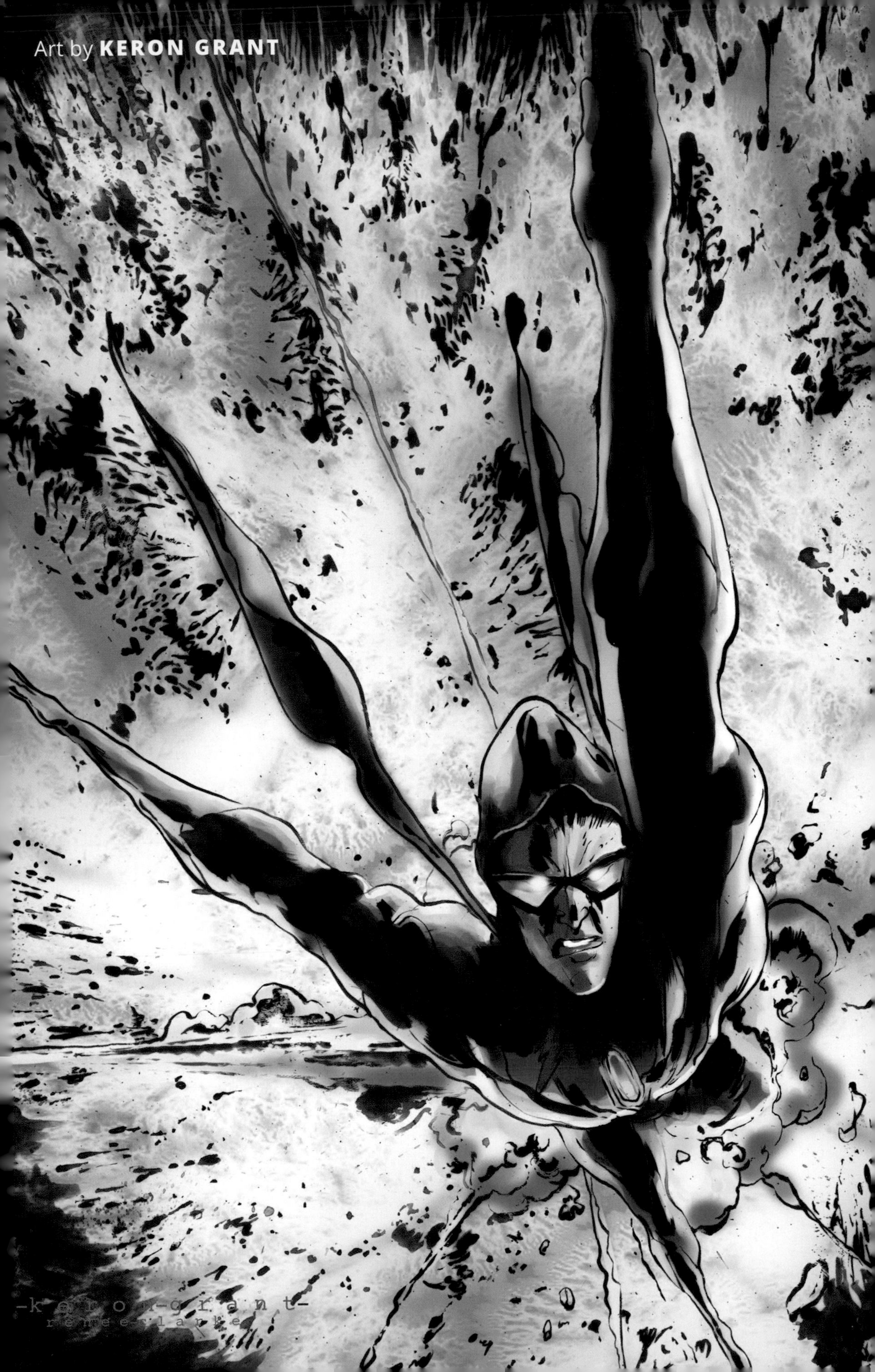
-keron-grant-
renee-clarke

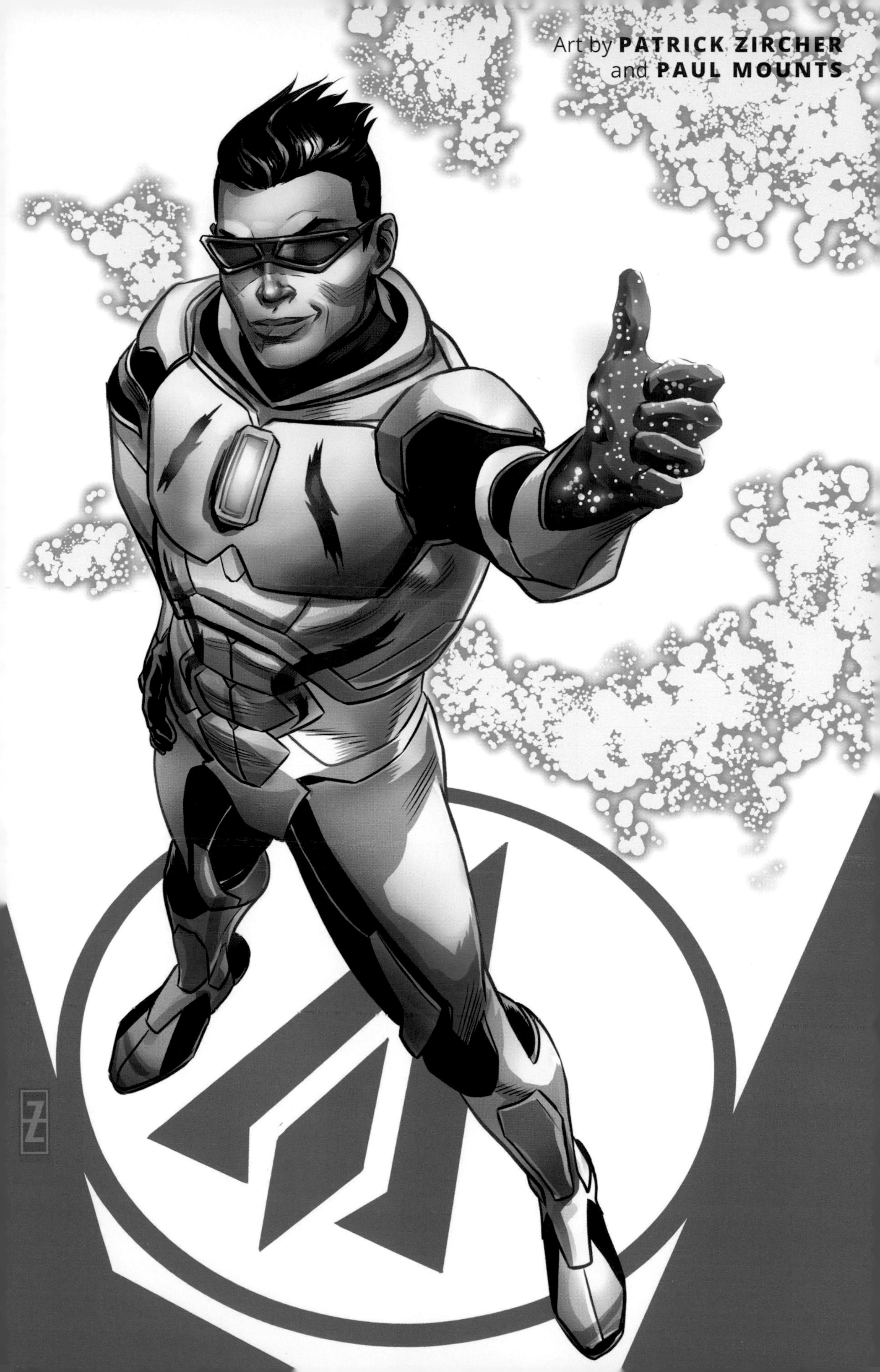

Art by **PATRICK ZIRCHER**
and **PAUL MOUNTS**

Art by **POP MHAN**
and **JESSICA KHOLINNE**

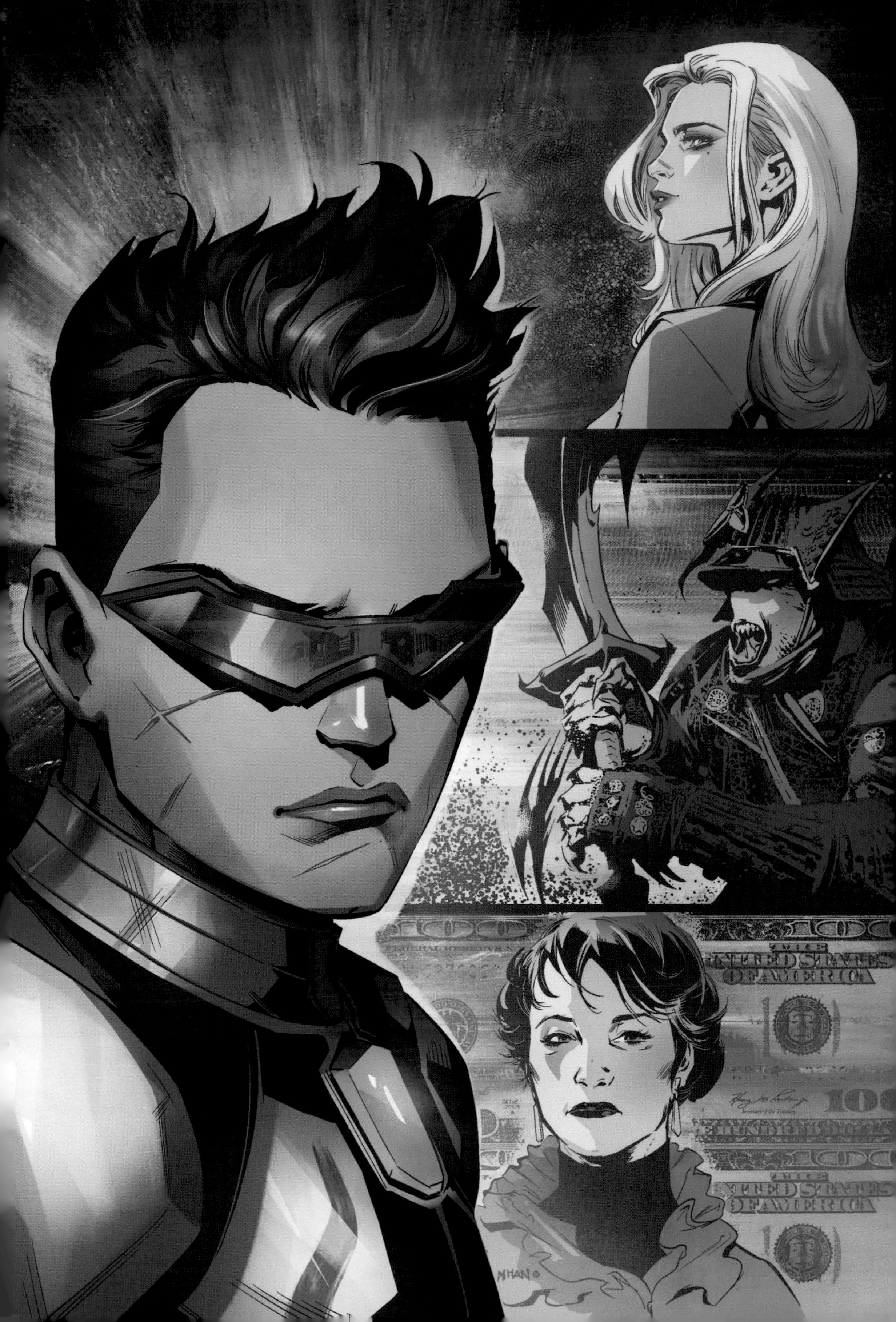

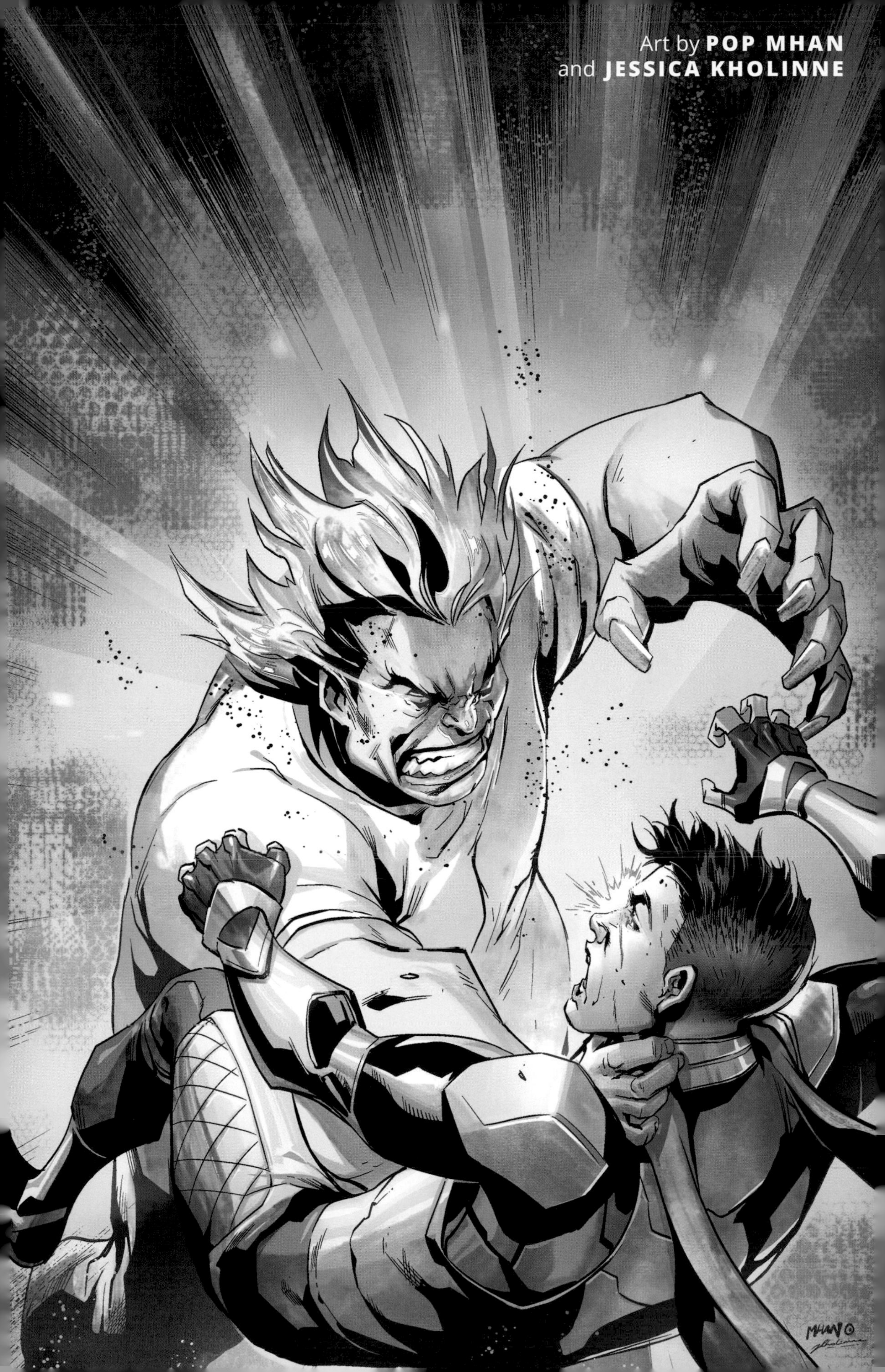

Art by **POP MHAN**
and **JESSICA KHOLINNE**

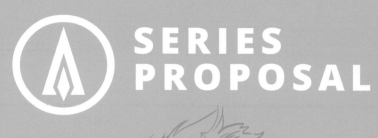

SERIES PROPOSAL

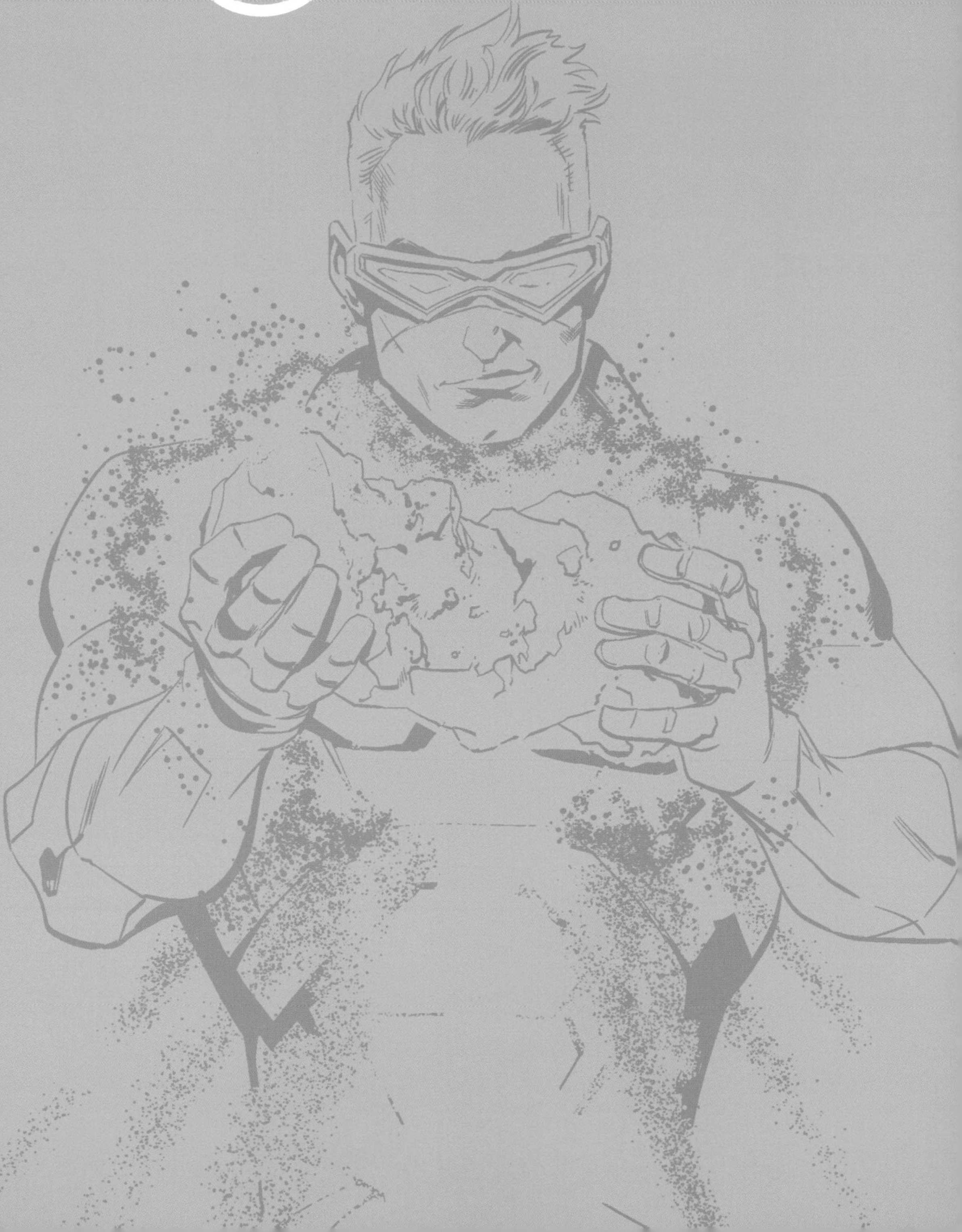

by Alex de Campi

Magnus Attarian is the smart, handsome heir to the Attarian satellite telecoms empire.

Or at least, he was.

Here's what the world knows about Magnus: He's rich. He's a dilettante who frittered away his college education with an art history degree, then sold his privacy app Gone to a CIA front company for several billion dollars at age twenty-five. Gone is an app he designed so he and his jet-set friends could "disappear" from social media in a location or pretend to be elsewhere than they actually were. He dates Sasha Sokolova, a Russian "model" and presumed gold digger.

The day the meteor hit would have been his thirtieth birthday.

He had been in steady decline since the sale of Gone, enamored with a plan to modify his family's aerospace knowledge into near-light speed travel ... so he can offer cruises of the galaxy to the super-rich; clubbing and gambling in space. While his little brother Drew, with his aerospace engineering degree and lovely, blue-blooded wife Isabella, climbs through the ranks at Atisat (the family company), Magnus has been testing (and mostly blowing up) experimental spaceships at the family spaceport in Guiana. But remote-controlled rocket drones to launch and repair satellites in high Earth orbit are a far cry from space yachts carrying real human beings to Saturn and back. The billions he earned from Gone are now down to mere hundreds of million. His investors (a.k.a. his friends) are backing away slowly from his increasingly insane-seeming pipe dream. The tech doesn't work and doesn't seem like it will ever work.

The meteor seemed like the perfect opportunity to prove them all wrong. Magnus took The Astonisher, his latest test space yacht, and launched himself in it to stop the meteor and save the Earth.

The meteor blew up first.

And The Astonisher's tech failed, locking Magnus on a collision course with the detritus.

His ship crashed back to Earth, extremely damaged, and Magnus near death. The photos of Magnus's bloody, broken body being carried out of the failed ship had the most hits of any photo of Magnus ever taken.

Happy birthday, Magnus. You're the most famous failure of your age.

* * *

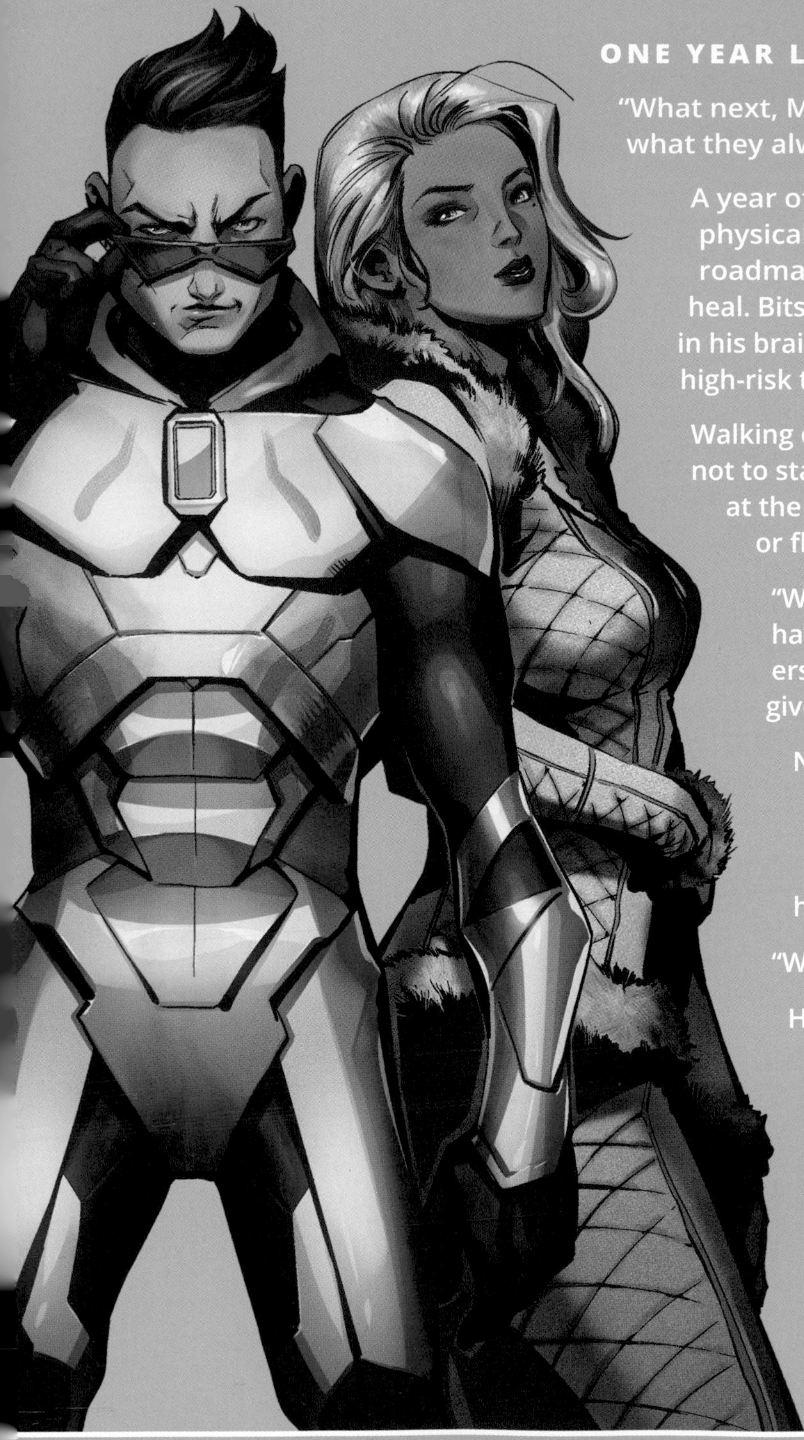

ONE YEAR LATER:

"What next, Magnus? What now?" It's what they always ask, the reporters.

A year of intensive surgeries and physical rehab. A body that is a roadmap of scars that will never heal. Bits of meteor still embedded in his brain that are considered too high-risk to remove.

Walking out of the hospital. Trying not to stagger. Trying not to jump at the crash of a dropped light or flinch in the flashbulbs.

"What about the people who have developed strange powers, Magnus? Did the meteor give anything to you?"

Nightmares, both waking and sleeping. Headaches. Looking at certain people causes ... sparks, behind his eyes.

"What next, Magnus?"

He has no clue. His family wants him to settle down and take a nice, quiet job in management at Atisat. To grow up.

And he almost does.

Until he goes home and is sitting with Sasha, and he pulls out a meteor shard from the collection he kept of the ones taken out of his ship and his body. He squeezes it in frustration and it lights up, begins to sparkle. And he sees into Sasha's head, very briefly. He sees a memory of hers, goes into a memory of hers.

He dresses quickly and goes to talk to his family, who are at a gala for the meteor-affected emergency service workers (firefighters, EMTs, etc.) in NYC. He pushes through the crowd to his mother and brother, who are standing near a memorial statue carved from a chunk of meteor. His mother is chiding Drew for Isabella (who has severe depression) not showing up at the gala, not accepting her mental illness as an actual thing.

Magnus is about to interrupt them with his big news when he gets a weird sense about someone else. The sparks happen again. He realizes it's someone else who has been affected by the meteor.

Someone with powers.

Someone who can't control his powers.

Magnus pushes his family out of the way as the man transforms into a J-horror style creature, his head opening into a quatrefoil mouth, full of teeth and a long tongue.

On instinct, Magnus hits the statue carved from meteor rock. It begins to spark and glow, as do Magnus's eyes. Magnus rushes forward and grabs the mutated human horror-creature—and finds himself in the guy's head. He fights through a surreal atmosphere until he finds a red shard (or a small red parasite) wormed into what seems like a favorite memory. He destroys the parasitical red worm and falls out of the guy's head.

Magnus comes to with his hands around the head of a former volunteer fireman, human again after his transformation. And half of New York's finest pointing a gun at him.

Adila, his Atisat-employed PR woman, intervenes. The meteor statue is now a duller color, "used up." It won't glow anymore. We keep this subtle, for now.

But Magnus has a revelation. He has powers. And If he can harness the neural-network technology inherent in the meteor ... well, Magnus can found a new company! He can become famous again; adored again!

Magnus smiles up at Adila. He's going to market his new company by becoming a superhero. He needs a suit that can harness and amplify his powers via more meteor rock. And some of the hyper-conductive tech he developed for The Astonisher would work just fine.

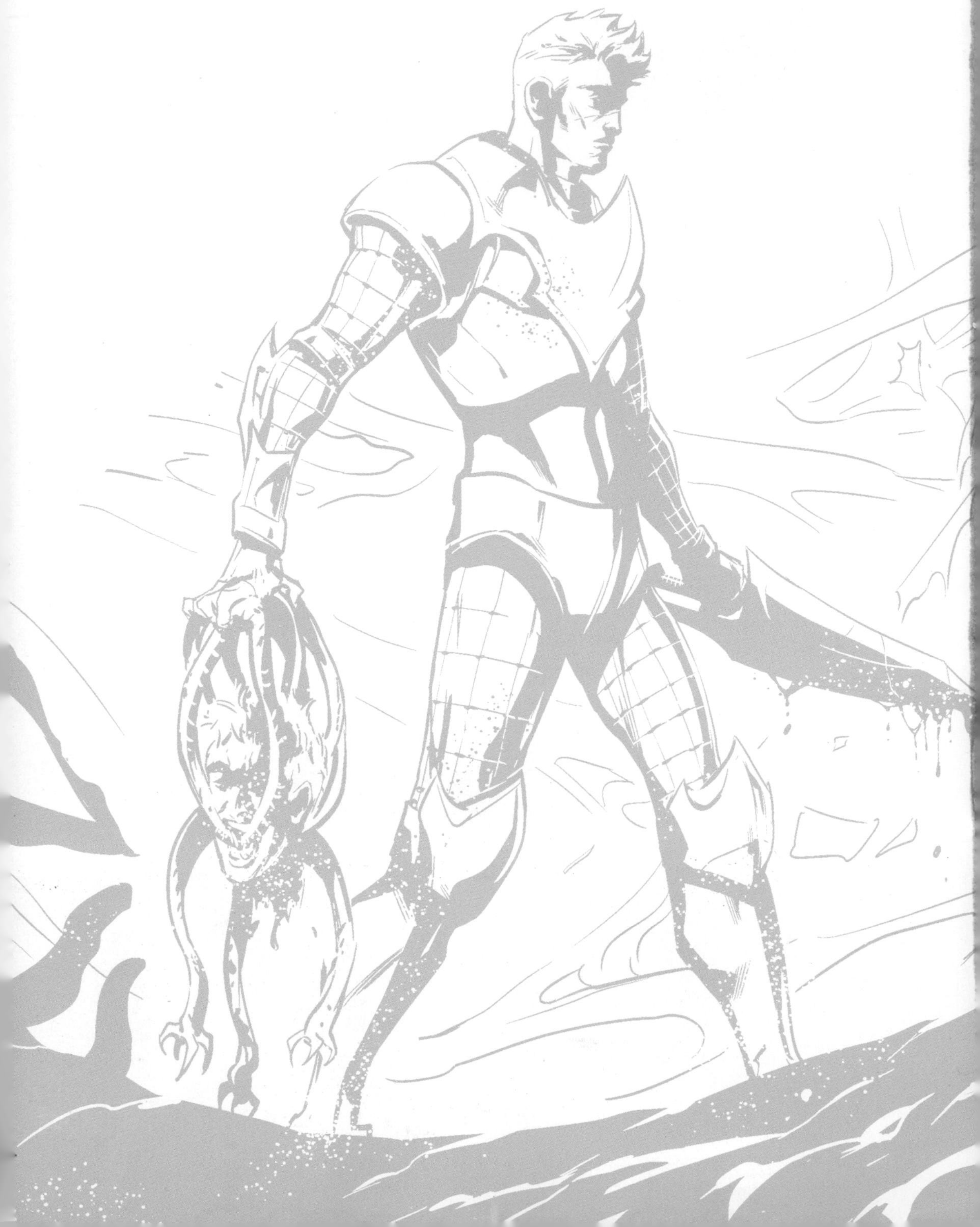